MW01037349

GOD'S INVISIBLE HAND

GOD'S INVISIBLE HAND

*The Life and Work of
Francis Cardinal Arinze*

An Interview with
GERARD O'CONNELL

IGNATIUS PRESS   SAN FRANCISCO

Cover photograph:
Francis Cardinal Arinze
© Pizzoli Alberto / CORBIS SYGMA

Cover design by Roxanne Mei Lum

Contents

Introduction

The man who inspired the young Francis Arinze to become a priest was also, at least indirectly, the inspiration for this book. That man was Blessed Cyprian Michael Iwene Tansi, the first native-born Nigerian to be beatified by the Roman Catholic Church. It was the interview I did with Cardinal Arinze, immediately following Father Tansi's beatification by Pope John Paul II, in Nigeria, March 1998, that gave me the idea of putting together this book of interviews.

That interview, which forms chapters 6, 7, and 12 of this book, is for me the most significant of a number of interviews I have had with Cardinal Arinze. Speaking in the days following the beatification, a moment of immense joy for the Nigerian cardinal, he recalled how he had begun to discern Divine Providence—or "the Invisible Hand of God", as he sometimes refers to it—in his own life. He spoke about his vocation as a priest, about being nominated bishop and cardinal, and about his life as the leading Catholic bishop in the area then known as Biafra during the Nigerian civil war.

In that interview, probably without fully realizing it, the cardinal revealed a great deal about what motivates him. He talked about matters at the heart of his life. With simplicity and without a trace of arrogance or self-promotion, he spoke about faith and prayer and about his abandonment to the will of God. He also revealed his profound veneration and admiration for Saint Francis of Assisi, who, along with the Blessed Tansi, occupies a special place in his own spirituality and outlook on the world.

I had originally planned to publish that three-and-a-half-hour interview as an article. However, it was far too long to present to most magazines or journals, so I put it aside while I pondered what to do with it. Two and a half years later, as the Jubilee Year 2000 was drawing to a close, I showed the cardinal the text. I proposed that he grant me a further, extended interview with the aim of allowing me to publish a collection of interviews as a small book. I already had, in fact, some unpublished interviews with Cardinal Arinze from earlier periods,

including one recorded in May 1994, immediately after the Synod of
Bishops for Africa. In that interview, the cardinal shared his own reflections in the immediate aftermath of that historic event in the life of the
Church in the African continent. I decided to include those interviews
in my text, as well. He agreed, but laid down a condition: "Yes, as long
as I am not the main focus of the book."

In preparation for the new interview, I drew up seven pages of
questions and, toward the end of the Jubilee Year, I interviewed the
cardinal on two separate occasions in December 2000. Two months later,
in February 2001, I requested and was given a supplementary interview
to fill in missing information.

These many interviews could not simply be placed in chronological
order. The book would have lacked any internal logic or coherence. The
only structure that seemed to work well was a semi-biographical one,
built around key moments in the cardinal's life. I therefore reorganized all
the material on that basis and, in June 2001, presented the cardinal with
the draft text.[1] He was somewhat taken aback with the result. "But the
book is now focused on me", he said. I acknowledged that this was not
what we had agreed, but explained why I had done it.

I have noticed, in the course of what are now many interviews and
meetings, that Cardinal Arinze is not given to hasty decisions or pro-
nouncements. He normally listens carefully and thinks about the matter
raised (sometimes suggesting a second meeting to give time for due
consideration), and then expresses his opinion. In this case too he thought
carefully about my explanation before graciously accepting the text as I
had reorganized it.

At the same time, he acceded to my request for a brief interview and
shared his reflections on the visit of Pope John Paul II to Greece, Syria,
and Malta in May 2001, a visit on which he had accompanied the Pope.
He granted another in February 2002, to help me update the work.
While I was putting the finishing touches to this text, Pope John Paul II
sprung one of his many surprises. On October 1, 2002, the Holy Father
appointed the cardinal to head one of the major Vatican departments, the
Congregation for Divine Worship and the Discipline of the Sacraments.
Naturally, I could not fail to record this important event in this book, and
so I requested one final interview from the cardinal, which he graciously
granted on December 11, 2002.

---

[1] I later revised the whole text, added three new chapters, rewrote the introductions to
some of the chapters, and inserted the footnotes.

As the reader will understand, this is something of an accidental book. It did not set out to be, and does not pretend to be, a full biography. Nevertheless, in ways beyond my original intention, and certainly beyond the intention of the cardinal, it tells much of the story of Francis Arinze's life. Its value, I believe, is that it tells the story in the cardinal's own words. It also offers a precious insight into the important work of dialogue between the Roman Catholic Church and major world religions. For eighteen years, together with his dedicated staff, Cardinal Arinze had been entrusted by the Pope to lead the Church in that dialogue.

By the end of 2002, the cardinal was fully engaged in another very important kind of dialogue, this time with those inside the Church regarding important questions linked to the celebration and worship of God in the liturgy. He is the only African cardinal ever to head this congregation and, indeed, is the only African heading a Vatican department today.

I have known Francis Cardinal Arinze since 1986, when I first interviewed him on the eve of the Synod on the Laity.[2] A friend of mine in the Vatican suggested he would be "a good man" to interview. "He's open", said my friend. "He is a man of deep faith, but he is also very approachable, down to earth, a man with a lot of common sense and a good communicator. He also has long and wide experience, including experience as a pastor of his people during one of Africa's bloodiest civil wars." I phoned the cardinal's office and, much to my surprise, he himself answered the phone. He accepted my request for an interview and proposed I come to his apartment in a building owned by the Vatican in the heart of Rome's Trastevere.

I turned up at his apartment on a hot and humid afternoon and rang the doorbell. A man dressed in a cotton sweatshirt and dark trousers opened the door and warmly welcomed me. It was the cardinal. He was truly charming, humorous and relaxed, and he answered my every question.

Since that first meeting, I have interviewed him many times and spoken with him on numerous occasions. He has always been gracious and kind and never once refused to respond to my questions, letters, or requests for a meeting.

On a personal level, I have come to appreciate not only his deep

---

[2] The synod took place in October 1987.

spirituality but also his great humanity and kindness, especially when my mother was seriously ill. I had planned to go to Nigeria for the beatification of Father Tansi, but, three weeks before my departure date, my mother suffered a cerebral hemorrhage (a stroke). For a time it looked as though she would die. I flew to Ireland to be with her. Thankfully, she began to show signs of recovery. Knowing that I had planned to travel to Nigeria to report on the beatification, she told me, "You go; I want you to go to Nigeria and be with the Holy Father. God will look after me; I will not die while you are away." I returned to Rome and told the cardinal about this situation. "Do as your mother told you", he said. "Go to Nigeria; God will take care of her, and I will pray to Father Tansi to intercede for her."

I flew into Nigeria ahead of the Pope and was there, with other journalists, on the tarmac at Abuja airport when he stepped off the plane. The head of state, General Sanni Abacha, greeted the Pope and then led him and his entourage, including Cardinal Arinze, to a podium for the formal state welcome.

As the Pope, the head of state, government ministers, and cardinals processed along the red carpet to the podium under the eyes of the world's TV cameras, Cardinal Arinze spotted me among the journalists. He broke away from the group and came over to me.

"How is your mother?" he asked. I told him she had improved. "Thanks be to God! Don't worry. She will be all right. I will continue praying for her." The cardinal then moved back quickly to rejoin the papal group for the official welcome ceremony.

My mother recovered as the cardinal had predicted and lived almost two years more. I shall never forget that unexpected gesture at Abuja airport, Nigeria. It was thoughtful and thoroughly human. It is typical of the man I have come to know over these past seventeen years. I am honored to have interviewed him for this book.

GERARD O'CONNELL

Rome, May 1, 2003

Chapter 1

The Early Years

(1932–1955)

The future Francis Cardinal Arinze was born in 1932 into a farming family, in the little rural village of Eziowelle, not far from the town of Onitsha, in the present Anambra State of Nigeria. He was the third of the seven children of Joseph Arinze Nwankwu and Bernadette Arinze (née Ekwoanya, of Abagana). He had three brothers: Christopher, Linus, and Justin; and three sisters: Cecilia, Victoria, and Catherine.

Nigeria was then under British colonial rule and remained so until it gained independence in 1960. In the area where he lived, and indeed throughout the whole of Eastern Nigeria, the Spiritans, or the Irish Holy Ghost Fathers as they were then called, were preaching the Gospel, opening schools, and bringing many young people to believe in Christ.

I began the interview by asking him about his family and early life.[1]

---

[1] This interview was recorded on February 16, 2001.

Q. *Your Eminence, you were born on November 1, 1932, in the village of Eziowelle, into a family that was religious and followed the Traditional Religion. What are your early childhood memories of this religious background?*

A. It is what we call the African Traditional Religion, which is the religion that most people had in Nigeria and in many other countries in Africa, before they became Christians or Muslims. In some parts of Africa it is stronger than in others, but essentially it is this: the people believe in God—one God, the Creator, who is always good and who never does harm.

Then they believe in spirits: good spirits and bad spirits. Some of the bad spirits were regarded as idiosyncratic; they could sometimes do harm to an innocent person; and some of them were regarded as hard—as the people would say, "wicked spirits"—who would cause thunder to kill somebody.

Also they believe in ancestors, not the same as spirits. Ancestors would be the spirits of the fathers and mothers who lived in the past. They lived good lives and are believed to have reached the happy spirit land, and they look lovingly on their children and their children's children who continue in this world. So the people see their family as not just in this world but also in the ancestors who have reached home—the happy spirit land.

Their religion is that.

Q. *Would this ancestor link be like the Christian "communion of saints", in an earlier version, as it were?*

A. Yes, it is a shadow, where the reality is the Christian communion of saints. But that shadow is the providential preparation of the people for the novelty of Christianity.

Some of the most visible signs of that religion in my youth would be that the father of the family would pray in the morning, when he got up.

There's a little shrine in his house where he would have statues representing the ancestors, and there he would call on God, the Creator, and thank him for the night.

Then he would call on the spirits—the good ones—and tell the bad spirits, "We don't want to have anything to do with you." Then he would call on the ancestors, asking them to protect him and his wife and his children and to guide them and preserve them from all harm. Then he would offer them some cola nut. It's a bitter fruit—it tastes a bit like coffee; it is a sign of welcome. He would offer them just a little bit, and a little drop of wine. It's a symbol; it's a libation to the ancestors and the spirits. And he would say, "Take a bit of cola; take a bit of wine. Look after us; we are in your hands. Let no harm come on us." That's the sort of prayer he would say in the morning.

Q. *Would the family stand around as he prayed?*
A. Not really. Maybe one of the sons would be around and be listening, but not a case of all the children gathering around. Not that.

Another visible sign of that religion is when there would be a sacrifice. Every year, one month is dedicated to the ancestors, and there is a big feast in the whole village or clan in honor of the ancestors. It is a very happy feast.

Q. *In what month is that?*
A. Oh, I cannot tell the month anymore. But I only know that it used to be one month in the year when the harvest of yams—the local favorite tuber—was done. So it would be generally in the rainy season of Nigeria, which means August or September.

Q. *And they offered sacrifice in this month?*
A. Sacrifice would be one of the items of that feast. They would sacrifice a chicken to the ancestors, and then the people would also eat. It doesn't mean they burned the whole chicken. They sprinkled the blood on the statues, and then they cooked the rest of the chicken; and the whole family would partake of it.

Q. *So there's almost a parallel with the history of Israel here, and its sacrifice.*
A. You can see the reason why, when I did my thesis in theology, I took sacrifice for my subject: sacrifice in the Traditional Religion of our

people as an introduction to the catechesis of Holy Mass. I studied this because sacrifice is very prominent in this religion.

Then, in this religion, in the whole area that we call a town—that is, a collection of villages—they would have one celebration in the year for the major spirit, the good spirit who is regarded as the protector of the whole town. There would be a big shrine in the town, and there would be masquerades, as exercise. Then there would be sacrifice, done by the priest dedicated to that spirit. That would be another visible sign in the Traditional Religion.

This religion also appeared in ordinary conversation, for example, in the names. The parents would give names to their children, and the names always had a particular significance. So my father's name, "Arinze", was given him by his father; and it meant, "If it had not been for God, this would not have happened." The full name is Arinze Chukwu—"Thanks be to God that this happened."

There are other names, very many of them, that correspond exactly to Christian names, such as Ngozi: "Benedict" or "blessing"; and Chinyere or Chwukwunyelu, Deusdedit: "God gave". One of our priests, a professor who later became archbishop—Archbishop Stephen Ezeanya, who died in 1996—made a whole booklet of Igbo names that correspond exactly to Christian ones.

Q. *Ngozi, as in the South African national hymn?*

A. In central Africa there is also that name, but it need not mean the same as in my language. I don't even know what it means in central Africa. There are very many names that show what the people think of God, of the spirits, and the ancestors. A lot can be understood about this religion from the very names parents give their children and from the proverbs that are usual in this language. There are very many ways in which this religion shows itself in daily life.

Q. *Today you are called Francis, but when you were born you had another name.*

A. Yes, when I was born my father gave me the name "Anizoba". In the African Traditional Religion there is a spirit who cares for the earth and the traditions and customs of the people. That spirit, the earth spirit, was called "Ani". So *Anizoba* meant, "May the land save, may the spirit save, may the earth spirit save you." When he gave me that name he was saying, "May the guardian spirit of the earth, of the traditions, save you.

May Ani, the earth spirit, save and protect you." He was praying that the spirit of the earth would protect this child of his.

Q. *Did you ever ask him why he gave you this name?*
A. I did not. I was not so curious. Maybe if I were working on a thesis today, I might ask. But at that time, I was not so curious.

Q. *But you remember your father praying, and you remember the celebrations in the town as part of this Traditional Religion. So, in a way, you had a sense of God being present in life.*
A. Very much so, very much so. There wasn't anything like that secular spirit of a society going on as if God were not there. In this religion, and in the culture it inspired, "the other world", as they called it—"the higher world", "the invisible world"—was very present in a way that wasn't forced. It was just regarded as normal. If a person hit his foot against a stone while walking, he would say a short prayer immediately, a short ejaculation, "May the spirits protect me" or "May my fathers look after me." It was just spontaneous.

Q. *So in that spirit world there was a kind of heaven and hell, as it were.*
A. Obviously the ideas were not so clear, but the idea of "the happy spirit land" was very clear. Those who did well, or were good in this world, and died, and for whom the funeral services were properly performed, would reach that place and be happy. Whereas if they were wicked people in this world, or if they died but the funeral ceremonies were not performed, it was believed that they would be wandering in the spirit world without rest; and if they got angry, they would come back to harass their relatives who didn't perform the ceremonies for them.

That was the belief, but there was no clear idea of one place where they would go and suffer forever. That's clearly Christian.

Q. *Your father prayed. Did your mother pray, too?*
A. There wasn't, in this religion, formal prayer conducted by the mother in a family. There would be one feast in the year when women—and it really was the women's feast—would honor their own protector spirits. That feast was for women. Then they would pray. But the women were not the ones to offer sacrifices; it would always be the men.

Q. *And when you were a boy, did someone tell you all about this religion?*

A. There was no formal teaching in this religion. The child picked it up in the ordinary events of everyday life. If, however, a student, a university professor, or a priest really wanted to do some research then he would consult the elders in this religion and pose questions, and these would give him answers. But otherwise in the Traditional Religion there was no formal teaching, nothing to correspond to the Christian catechism class. The child picked it up in the very events of every day. When a child was born, for instance, the older children saw how the parents prayed, how they offered him to the spirits and the ancestors, and how they prayed that God would look after them.

Q. *This, then, was the religious atmosphere in which you and your brothers and sisters grew up.*

A. Yes, it was normal. We can say that the African Traditional Religion was the religious context, the religious background, from which most Africans come, except those who live in areas that have been heavily Muslim for centuries. Of course, in some parts of Africa, the Traditional Religion would not be as strong—in some parts of eastern Africa, for example. In other parts it is very strong, as in Ghana, Benin Republic, and parts of Nigeria. There must be no generalization. But one thing is clear, it permeated the atmosphere, and it was a major influence in African culture, and still is.

Q. *So you felt very strongly this presence of God in early life.*

A. Oh, yes. It was not a life in which the individual forgot God, in which man was regarded as supreme. It was a life in which man obviously recognized beings who were invisible and superior, and to whom he referred, and whom he did not ignore.

Q. *Given this background, how was it that you went to a Catholic school?*

A. Simple. My father sent me there.[2] There was a church school in the town, and by town I mean a group of villages, not a town in the European sense of city.

What happened is that, in those days, the British were the colonizing power. They were interested in law and order, and in trade. The mission-

---

[2] He received his primary education in St. Edward's Catholic School, Eziowelle (1939–1942), and in St. Anthony's Catholic School, Dunukofia. He completed standard 6 in 1946.

aries, the Catholic missionaries especially, but also the Anglicans, were nearer the people, and they promoted the school.

I understand that in the earlier days, when the Irish missionaries came, they met the elderly people and were speaking to them about Christ. At that time, one old man said, "Father, don't you see we are old? Why don't you start with the young ones? Don't you see that we are old, and we're not going to learn new ways so easily?" So the Irish missionaries got the idea to start the schools, and both they and the parents realized that the British administration needed clerks and teachers for their civil bureaucracy. Therefore the Irish began the schools.

The school served in many ways. It made the children literate, and literacy opened many doors—political, cultural, economic, and religious. The young people learned about Christ, but they also acquired a literary education, which made it possible for them to become teachers, to become clerks, to become engineers.

Gradually the school system was reinforced. There was the secondary school; there was the technical school; and, at one time, the missionaries were about to start a university, but the government had begun to do this, and so it was thought best to leave it to the government.

The school was a major means, not just of evangelization—in the sense of being baptized—but also of what we now call development, integral development. We can say that the school, at least in Nigeria but also in many other parts of Africa, is one of the most powerful instruments of integral human development.

The Irish missionaries began the schools, and the British government saw it was a good thing. The Anglicans also had schools, and the Baptists too. As the government approved the schools from the point of view of standards, deciding which functioned and which did not, it also gave some grants to the schools. The children paid fees too, but what was paid in fees was minimal, and the Irish missionaries got money elsewhere. It was from the schools then that we became Christians. It was not by force. Every child in school was free to become a Catholic or not, so that a child could finish the entire primary school and not be baptized. There was no force.

Q. *Did some children actually go through the school and not become Catholics?*

A. Oh, yes, but not very many. Most of the children would ask for baptism. However, in those days the whole mentality was not what one would see in Europe today, where people are always suspecting that somebody is being forced to be a Christian. For us, in those days, it was a prestige to be a Christian—to get a new name and to join the religion of the missionaries. It was a prestige for the children. Not only were we not forced, but we were actually in a hurry to become Christians.

Q. *Were you the first of the children in your family to become Christian?*
A. I was not. I was really number three. We were seven in the family: four boys and three girls. Two of my brothers became Christians before I did, just the same way, through the school.

Q. *Didn't your parents, who followed the Traditional Religion, object at all?*
A. No. My parents didn't object. The only point my father objected to was one: he used to ask us to go with him to farm on Sunday, and we said, "No, our Christian law is that we don't work on Sunday." He smiled, and said to me, "Do you eat on Sunday?" I said, "Yes, we eat on Sunday." Then he said, "Well, you should work on Sunday, too." I said, "No, we don't farm on Sunday, but everything else is okay."

When the parents saw that the Christian schools taught their children to work with them (except on Sunday), to behave well, and to be honest, then they had nothing against it. Not only had they nothing against it, but they were in favor. It was often the parents, who were non-Christian themselves, who begged the Irish missionaries to start a school in their village. It was beautiful. They often gave the land for the school, and sometimes they even helped with the manual labor themselves. And when their children went to school, they were happy.

My father once told me one of the reasons he sent all his children to school, at least the boys first—because in those days the boys were regarded as the ones to go to school first, and the girls afterward. My father said they were going to a court, a local court for a land case, and the British administration's district officer was there. They had an interpreter, because they didn't know English. Their group had won the case, but the interpreter was deceiving them; each time telling them to come back again, saying, "It is postponed again", and they would give him some little money to make him happy. This continued until one day the British officer saw them and asked: "What the hell are these people doing here? The case was finished long ago." And that's how they got to know what happened.

So my father said, "Ah, that's because I don't know English; that's why the interpreter has been cheating us." Then, he said, he decided that all his boys would go to school, every one of them.

Q. *This is a very interesting story, for something similar happened in Ireland in the early 1800s. The Irish people started learning English then for a reason similar to the one your father gave: they wanted to be able to defend themselves in the courts, and they could not do so in Gaelic, so they had to learn English.*

A. It's interesting. Divine Providence uses many ways. And looking back now at evangelization and development, and political emancipation in Africa, I think we can say that the missionaries, especially the Catholic missionaries, can easily be called the number one agent of development in Africa: development in the political, economic, cultural, and religious fields; because, if the people asked for political independence, it is because they had gone to school, and they could formulate their own stand.

If our people have been led to love our culture and not to regard it as pagan; to love our dances and not to condemn them all as pagan; to love our way of dressing and so on; it is because we have gone to school, and not just primary school, but we have also studied in Britain and the United States. And when you study you begin to appreciate much more what God has given your people, and then you begin to see that human nature is basically the same, all around the world. And what we call a colonial mentality becomes a thing of the past.

But if people don't go to school, we will have all the problems, also medical ones. When people are sick, they will attribute it to bad spirits or some other hidden power; whereas, if they studied medicine or . . . even without being a doctor, they would know the simplest hygienic standards.

So there is no alternative to the school. We must thank the missionaries for that. Whether the missionaries worked out the whole thing before they began the school is not necessary. It's the fact that the school has been the major key to open up development.

Q. *How old were you when you began to desire or want to be a Christian?*

A. I was baptized at about the age of nine, by Father Tansi; now Blessed Tansi. He was the first priest I ever knew. And to be baptized, at that time, you would have to go through a catechumenate lasting two years, at least; which means that I must have begun to study catechism for

baptism at the age of six or seven. That means that I began practically at
the beginning of primary school. It was just normal in those days. It was
normal in the year 1940. That's already sixty years ago.

Q. *Do you remember what started you on the road to baptism?*

A. It was nothing dramatic. It was simply when we went to school,
religion was one of the subjects taught, and in those religion classes we
gradually learned what we would call catechism. And then we saw some
of the older children asking for baptism, and we desired it. It was just
normal. In those days, the teachers also—they were local teachers—were
practically like evangelizers, they were like catechists.

Q. *Were all the teachers Catholic?*

A. Oh, yes, since the whole school was Catholic, although Protestant children could attend and nobody discriminated against them. If
there was a Protestant school in that village, then the parents who sympa-
thized with Protestantism were likely to send their child to that school.
But all the teachers in a Catholic school were Catholic, and they were
very missionary-minded. They taught catechism also in the evening, and
they were not thinking of extra money.

Q. *So you told your father and mother that you wanted to get baptized?*

A. Yes, but there was nothing dramatic because they knew that
once they sent their child to that school, the child would become a
Christian. It was normal in those days.

Q. *What do you remember of the day you were baptized?*

A. My memory is that we were quite a number, and Father Tansi
arranged it for All Saints' Day, November 1, 1941.

Q. *It was your ninth birthday.*

A. Yes. But it was his usual day every year for baptisms. We had to
wear white. The boys wore white shorts and white shirts, and the girls
white skirts. And each of us found a sponsor. My sponsor was Anthony
Aguocha, a man who has since died; a very poor man from my town who
did little bits of trade, but who was a very convinced Christian.

In those days it was usual that in the catechizing—what we call the
catechumenate—the child would go through three examinations; the
first was conducted by the local catechist in his little village, the second

would be by the catechist for the whole parish, and then the third would be by the parish priest himself. Only if a child passed all three—and that would be over a period of about two years—would the child be approved for baptism.

Q. *You took the name Francis at baptism. Why?*

A. I must have heard that name from Christians, and I wanted that name without knowing about Assisi or Xavier or Borgia. At that time, I didn't even know who Francis of Assisi was, or Francis Xavier, or any other Francis. Only later did I become informed about Francis Xavier and Francis of Assisi.

Q. *And to which of the two—Francis Xavier or Francis of Assisi—do you feel closer today?*

A. To both of them, really. Francis Xavier attracted me by his missionary zeal.

Q. *So you had this big celebration for the baptism.*

A. Oh, yes. We had the baptism then, and it was a very big ceremony. But do not imagine that we would have had a big feast in the family afterward. No, not exactly. But we were so full of joy we didn't bother about food.

Q. *Did you receive Communion at the same celebration?*

A. No. It was a separate affair. For First Communion, we had to undergo examinations all over again.

Q. *When did you receive Communion, then?*

A. It must have been a year after, because I remember confirmation was two years later, in 1943. So my First Communion must have been in 1942, a year after baptism, which was in 1941.

Q. *Father Tansi baptized you; did he also give you First Communion?*

A. Yes, my first confession was to him. My First Communion was at his hands, and he prepared me for confirmation.

Q. *So from the moment of baptism you were a Christian, but, in a sense, you were already inserted into the Christian community with your brothers who had already become Christian.*

A. Yes, and many people of the village and town went to Mass. We were in the parish run by Father Tansi, the parish of Dunukofia, which is now fifteen parishes. He used to go around on a push bicycle or an old motorcycle. We went especially to Mass on Sunday, but sometimes, when the Mass would be about seven miles away, we would not go. If it was within five miles we would go, although we were told we were not bound to go if it was beyond three miles away. And it was just normal for us to walk there and back. Then we had other celebrations. For instance, the first Friday of the month, that was frequented not only by grown-ups, but also by very many children.

Q. *How did you meet Father Tansi?*
A. He opened our parish in 1939. He had been an assistant curate at Nnewi, about twelve miles from my home, from 1937 to 1939. At that time, I was a catechumen, going to catechism class, and he signed my catechumen card. I must have been about seven years old then.

Then, in 1939, he opened what is now Dunukofia parish and remained there as parish priest until 1945, when he was transferred to Akpu, another parish. Later, in 1949, he was transferred from there to Aguleri, his hometown, again as parish priest. From there he went to the Mount Saint Bernard Monastery in England in 1950, where he remained for the rest of his life, until his death in 1964.

Father Tansi was known for asceticism. He ate very little, and the person who used to cook for him in Dunukofia didn't have much work to do because of this. But he always looked after other people very well indeed. His homilies were full of fire, and nobody could be indifferent. You either liked him or you didn't like him, but there was no question of not taking notice of Father Tansi.

He paid great attention to the sacrament of marriage. All the girls had to be prepared for marriage, and he would not allow them to live with their prospective husbands before marriage. He got the religious sisters of the Holy Rosary to help. They prepared a beautiful place for these girls to learn home cleaning, domestic science, catechism, and so on. They prepared them for two, three, four, or even five months before marriage. Father Tansi was very rigid about that.

Then he was also very careful about the children studying in the school. Primary school in those days lasted seven or eight years. He gave special attention to children in the last two classes of primary school; they would be between ten and twelve years old. He got a boarding school built, near the parish center, for the two last classes in primary school. The boys lived there from Sunday evening till Friday, when they went home. There were a small number of girls in those classes; they lived at home and attended school from their homes.

Q. *Did you go to this boarding school?*

A. Oh, yes, for two years. That's where we learned to serve Mass; all of us. We took turns in serving Mass. He read spiritual reading to us every day—for fifteen minutes!

Father Tansi looked after those boys so well that many wanted to become priests. Indeed, in 1944 the entire final class took the entrance exam to the seminary, to become seminarians, and passed it. The whole class! We heard that the seminary authorities said, "How can a whole class have a vocation to the priesthood?" They couldn't believe it, so they told them that they all failed. We heard later that they decided if any came back after one year they would know that he was serious, but the following year only one came back.

One of my brothers[3] was in that class, and he passed the exam, but he didn't repeat it. It's that brother of mine who died on October 10, this year, the one whose funeral I just attended. He was just three years older than I.

Q. *But what happened to your brother? What did he feel when they told him he had failed?*

A. We didn't know what to think. We were too small to know. We were not the type to question the priests at that age. We just accepted.

But it's very interesting that the parish in Dunukofia that Father Tansi ran is now many parishes, maybe as many as fifteen. What he did on a push bicycle and later on an old motorbike was phenomenal. The number of priests and religious sisters from that area is the highest in the whole region, which means the spiritual touch of this man really moved people. The Christian families who were part of that process have endured to this day. Last month, I saw one of those women whom he had prepared for marriage in the 1940s, and she does not forget Father Tansi. So for these reasons people thought that Father Tansi could be proposed as a model Christian.

---

[3] His brother Linus.

Q. *Do you attribute your own vocation to him?*

A. After God, yes; under God, yes! Finally, only God can really tell how a priestly vocation works. But seeing that he is the first priest I ever knew, he was the first person who gave me an image of what a priest is, and I liked to be like him.

God's grace can work through such means. Of course, there were others who inspired me. There was Father Mark Unegbu, now the bishop emeritus of Owerri; he actually got me into seminary in 1946–1947, and he followed my progress all the way through. He is over eighty now, but he is still alive.

And then there were some teachers, lay people. One of them, Patrick Okeke, died two years ago. He was my headmaster for five years in the primary school. He was a very dedicated teacher, and he also influenced me. And there were many others.

But I would say that, without doubt, under Divine Providence, Father Tansi would be the number one among those who inspired me.

Q. *Did you keep in touch with him through seminary?*

A. I wrote, but not too often. You see, he went to the monastery (in England) in 1950. I went to the junior seminary in 1947, and I visited him in the parish at Akpu, where he was in 1948, and in Aguleri in 1949. Then he went to the monastery of Mount Saint Bernard in 1950.

I wrote to him from time to time. I was not wise enough to keep his letters, so I don't have any now, unfortunately. Some religious sisters kept his letters; they were more careful. Then, as I said, I kept him informed when he was in the monastery, and he followed my progress up to ordination. I visited him then when I could, on two occasions in the monastery before he died.

Q. *So he would have prayed for you all through the time you were in seminary?*

A. I hope so. I think so.

Q. *You have many memories of Father Tansi from this period. Which ones stand out today?*

A. Well, several. I remember once when we were in primary school, we were doing manual labor; we were building a school. We had to fetch water and then make mud; with that mud we made blocks. We didn't have enough cement to use for the blocks. He himself actually joined us in making the mud. And when I was fetching water, he saw me and said the vessel I was using was too small; that meant I should have used a bigger vessel. You see, the stream would be about half a kilometer away. That was a sign of his generosity. He was really telling me to use a bigger vessel. Of course, a bigger vessel would be heavier for me to carry at that age. But it showed the man! I still remember that.

Then I also remember that he was very tidy and clean, even in the surroundings. I remember his home—mud blocks, but when finished and painted it looked good. A bungalow. In front of his home there was a beautiful tree that had nice flowers at Easter time, April or so. And then there was the football [soccer] field, the school and the church—the same building for school and church.

On the right-hand side of that complex there were the homes for the boys of standards 5 and 6, those in the last two years of primary school. There were four footpaths, and they were kept clean and straight. Now, he would not allow any boy to walk outside the footpaths to make a journey shorter. So if he saw you cutting it short through the soccer field or plots of grass, he would say "Stop! Go back, and then take the footpath." So that seemed meticulous and minor, but it taught us order, discipline. When I see, in some parts of the world, beautiful and cared-for lawns with signs that say "Keep off the grass", I often remember Father Tansi. It seemed minor, but it was something too.

Then he was also very humorous, without spending too much time on jokes. He used to stammer a bit when he was doing catechism exam. This would be difficult to say in English because the whole humor would be lost, but it was funny in our language. He asked a boy, "What did Saint Paul say about those who received the Holy Eucharist unworthily?" And the boy said, "He who drinks the cup, the cup, the cup." And Father Tansi stammered, and said: "Is it the cup, the cup, the cup that they wrote in the book?"

Of course, we had just to reproduce the answer that was written in the catechism book. Some people may smile at it now and say, "We don't want this memory work." Well, they should be informed that they are mistaken because those formulae in the *Penny Catechism* were carefully thought out, and they encapsulated the theology, our faith for centuries, and some of the best formulations of great theologians and Churchmen. And individuals who now think to formulate it in their own way, if they will succeed in coming anywhere near those exact formulations—very well. But often what we hear is rather poor.

In any case, a boy who is twelve years old is not meant to be
Thomas Aquinas. But if he gets the formulations first, then, later in life,
he understands better, each one according to his formation. I remember
when I used to preach as bishop and archbishop, I took the formulae in
the catechism with which people were familiar and then analyzed
them, and they took on new life for the people. So there is room for
memory.

I am very happy today that in the new *Catechism of the Catholic
Church*—with its seven hundred pages, and with an abundance of Scripture, Vatican II and papal documents, and the lives of the saints—there is
after each major section what they call "in brief", and they have it in
short form. We need it, because most people will not be Saint Bona-
venture or Dun Scotus or, let us say, modern professors who would be
able to give you an exact articulation of our faith. You actually need these
giants in the faith. If you take the hymn "*Adoro Te devote, latens Deitas . . .*"
(We adore you, hidden God . . .) and if a person recites all that and
analyzes it, you have there the doctrine of the Real Presence. So Father
Tansi was very good at this, and I still remember him for that. There are
other points, but we can't go into everything.

Q. *So order, discipline, and sound doctrine?*

A. Very sound doctrine, discipline, and order. And the doctrine, he
would explain and teach; he would explain the catechism and preach in
church. You couldn't come out of the church and say, "I don't remember
what he said"; it was clear, it was sound, and it was delivered in a lively
way. That's very good for every preacher to know because sometimes we
can hear a homily, and generally the longer it is, the more we suspect that
it was not well prepared. And at the end, what do the people take away
with them? If every priest would engage in a type of feedback, without
looking for self-glory, but looking for some minimum feedback to see
how the Gospel message he transmits is actually received, it would make
our homilies, perhaps, more to the point.

Q. *You served his Mass at this time.*

A. I was his altar boy in 1945—one of his altar boys, because he
had all the boys in the last two classes of primary school serve his Mass.
All the boys were obliged to serve Mass; we took turns. Everyone had
to do it; there was no question of choosing. In any case we liked it,
though there would be a few boys who couldn't care less. Then that's

why in 1944, as I mentioned earlier, almost the whole class took the entrance exam to the seminary, saying they wanted to be priests. Our group was in 1946.

It was therefore not extraordinary that a person who would be seeing Father Tansi day in and day out, and hearing him, would think of becoming a priest. He used to read spiritual reading to us every day; that is, to those of us living in the boarding house. I remember hearing him reading about Saint Dominic Savio, the young fourteen-year-old student of Saint Don Bosco. It was not surprising that in that area where Father Tansi worked there were priestly and religious vocations in large numbers.

Q. *And your own vocation? Can you trace how it started?*

A. I cannot tell when I first desired to be a priest. But I know that when I was in the primary school, even before I went to boarding school for the last two years of primary school, I used to watch him. And you know what children do when they are at home: they get a little biscuit and a small cloth and say they are "saying Mass". Little brothers and sisters were told to stay there, and we'd be mumbling something and saying that it was Latin.

Q. *That was when you were nine years old?*

A. Yes, maybe nine or ten. That I remember. But obviously I came nearer the altar when we were serving Mass in 1945.

Q. *But when the idea began to crystallize in your mind, with whom did you talk first?*

A. The parish priest. It was no longer Father Tansi then, because he had been transferred to another parish—Akpu, in 1945. But the following year, in 1946, in my final year in primary school, I wanted to be a priest.

Q. *By then, the idea of becoming a priest was very clear in your mind?*

A. Yes. It was very clear in my mind, and I told the parish priest, who was then Father Mark Unegbu—he later became a bishop. In fact, I ordained him bishop of Owerri in 1970. He's still alive, though he's getting on—he must be about eighty-four now, and a retired bishop.

Q. *So you went to Father Mark and told him you wanted to be a priest.*

A. Yes, I told him. He was my parish priest, and I served Mass for him. I told him that I wanted to go to the seminary. He supported and helped me, and he even began to teach me Latin before I went to seminary.

Q. *You would have been then about thirteen or fourteen.*

A. Yes, this was in 1946, and I would have been about thirteen or fourteen years. I took the entrance exam then. The junior seminary[4] was attached to the secondary school for boys, called Christ the King College. It was the best Catholic school in the area. They had a section for boys who wanted to be priests, but you took the examination to the school as such. Then those who passed went on for an interview, and after that they decided whom they would select for the seminary.

I went through that process, and when I passed both, I told my parents. I did not tell them before that.

Q. *Nobody else in your family knew at that stage?*

A. No, I didn't tell them, but maybe one or two of my elder brothers guessed, but we didn't tell our parents until I had passed. When I finally told my parents that I wanted to be a priest, and that I had passed the exam, as you would guess, my father's reaction was negative.

Q. *What did your father say? What did he want you to do?*

A. He said, "You will not be a priest, because if you become a priest you are not going to marry—number one—and you won't have children. And number two, you will be hearing all the bad things people do in your two ears, and that's not good." So he knew something about confession.

And then he said, "Then you will be eating eggs and bananas from town to town. No. No. No, my son!" Because that was the image the missionaries gave to the people. When a missionary, the priest, came on trek to visit a town, the people collected eggs and bananas. They also gave other items. But for older people like my father, it was just funny that a grown-up man would ask people to bring eggs and bananas. And my father had a sense of humor too.

So he said, "No, you will not be a priest for these three reasons." I

---

[4] All Hallows Junior Seminary at Nnewi.

said, "No, I want to be a priest." He said, "You will not be a priest." I told him that I had passed the examination. He said, "No problem. I will give you money and with that money you will buy a pencil, and you will send them that pencil, and with that pencil they will cancel your name from the list" [*laughs*].

Q. *So he wanted you to withdraw.*
A. He was ready to give the money to buy the pencil. I wasn't harsh, but I was clear. So we didn't agree, but we stopped there.

Q. *But his real reason was that you couldn't marry.*
A. Yes. You can see it. But the other reason he gave—"You'll be hearing all the bad things people do in your two ears"—that's not to be set aside. But obviously that a person would not marry would figure very much in the eyes of the people of the Traditional Religion, where the family line is regarded as very important. And also my father loved me very much, and I knew that; there was no need to compare me with my other brothers, but I knew that. And he often wanted me to be with him, sit with him, and go places with him. I knew it would pain him. I knew that.

Q. *So you were very close to your father.*
A. Yes, yes. I knew that, and he knew that. So I knew it would pain him. I understood. I held out, but I said no more at that time.
Then I told my mother also, and she opposed it too.

Q. *Why?*
A. I don't remember whether she gave me reasons, but she said, "No, no, no." So I kept on saying, "That's what I want to do." Finally she said, "Okay, my son. If that's what you want to do, you go ahead." She no longer opposed it.

Q. *Your parents were not Christian at that time.*
A. No, they were not yet Christians then. But it was not too difficult to get my mother's blessing, but my father said no.

Q. *And what was your grandparents' reaction?*
A. Only my grandmother was alive, my mother's mother. On her side, she was a follower of the African Traditional Religion also, but later on her children became Anglicans, and later still she became an Anglican

too. She was not yet a Christian at that time. But there was no need to get her approval. I'm not even sure whether she heard of it at that time, but later on she was not enthusiastic. Also one of my mother's sisters was not enthusiastic. But their objections would not have prevented me. It was my parents who were crucial.

So finally, to cut the story short, we set out to get my father's consent. My two brothers and I talked with the parish priest about what we should do to get his consent.

Q. *So your brothers supported you.*

A. They did. Two of them did, and the parish priest told them, "Tell your father if he does not support this son going to seminary, then the first brother who is teaching will be sent away from school; and the other brother who is teaching, and who passed the exam to go to Catholic Teachers Training College, will also not be admitted."

They said that to frighten my father. But when my father heard that, he didn't surrender. He said, "That's okay, if they don't want the two of you, you come back, and we will all go to farm every day. That's what we have done for centuries."

But they said to him, "No, no, we cannot do that. You are setting the clock back."

Then my father said, "Okay. If you want to throw yourself away, you can throw yourself away! You can go ahead."

Q. *He was really not very happy about your becoming a priest.*

A. No, he was not happy. But he gave his grudging approval. And for me that was enough at that time, because I knew it was painful for him at the end. The parish priest helped me buy the outfit for the seminary. My father was in no mood to bring the little money he had to buy it while he wasn't very convinced.

But then something dramatic happened. We went to seminary at Nnewi.[5] It would be about twenty miles from my home and thirteen miles from Onitsha. After three months (it was Easter time), we went home on holiday. I think we had two or three weeks' vacation.

I came home, and my father was surprised. And I said to him, "What about working on the farm? Where you are going tomorrow, we go." I saw he was surprised. Then the second day he said to me, "They were

---

[5] In 1947, he entered All Hallows Junior Seminary. He also taught there (1951–1952), having completed his Cambridge certificate course.

deceiving me then." I said, "What do you mean?" He said some people from the village came when they heard I wanted to go to the seminary and told him if I went to the seminary he would never see me again—that I would be the same as lost, and he would never see me again. He said, "Then they were deceiving me, but I see you have come back, and you are just my son as before, and we are going to farm together. They must have been deceiving me." So I told him, "It is not true that priests do not go home. It is not true. They go home. You still remain my father. In any case, priesthood doesn't come immediately, it will take another twelve or fifteen years." He said: "Well, then, if God wants this, my son, you go ahead. God will bless you."

From that day there were no more problems with him. No more. So that when I was made a priest he was very happy. And when I was being sent to Rome, as a seminarian, for theology, he was not yet a Christian, and many people said to him: "What happens now? You are an old man; your son is going away." He said, "God is there. He will go, I will be here, and he will come back."

Q. *It was his prayer.*

A. Yes, and he said his prayer for me. Then, on the day I was made bishop in 1965, the bishop who preached—a Nigerian bishop, Bishop Anthony Nwedo C.S.Sp., who knew the incident about the pencil—mentioned in the homily for my bishopric that my father offered to buy a pencil with which they would cancel my name. And my father was sitting in the front row in church! It was all very interesting.

Q. *But your father was pleased at the end.*

A. Yes, he was, and he noticed that I came home on vacations and worked with him every time. It also made me very clear when I became a bishop, and later an archbishop, that seminarians must love their parents. And if a seminarian didn't love his parents and didn't go home during vacations and help them, work with them, I gave him a tough time. A seminarian must love his parents; he must go back home at vacation time. If the parents are in a shop, he must work with them; if they are farmers, he must go to the farm with them. They must see him as a good son. If he does this, then he has his two feet on the ground, because you cannot replace parents with piety. If a person is not a good son to his parents, he is not fit to be a priest. He's not fit; there's something wrong.

Q. *Well, it's clear you loved your parents very much. Your father was happy in the end, despite his early opposition. And your mother gave her consent after initial resistance; she was happy too. But when you came back from Rome, was your mother already a Christian?*

A. She was. As you would expect, it is easier for a mother to become a Christian than for a father, because in the African Traditional Religion it is the father who offers the sacrifice to the spirits and the ancestors. To become a Christian means to forget all about those sacrifices. The father of the family was the link with the ancestors, and if it is a group of families, cousins and so on, then the oldest man is the link. So you see for them the break required a lot of courage: it wasn't their lack of appreciation for Christianity, it was the break that presented the problem, so that somebody had to reassure them that there is still a link with the ancestors.

In any case, when I was a seminarian, all those years in junior seminary and philosophy, obviously I was speaking with my parents about Christianity. My mother began then, and finally she got baptized when I was already in theology, in Rome, but she was already attending catechism when I was at home. She took the name Bernadette at baptism.

Q. *And your father? Did he become a Christian?*

A. Before I went to Rome in 1955, people said to my father: "Won't you become a Christian?" And I said the same to him. Even priests visited him. I remember an Irish priest, Father Michael Smith C.S.Sp., who was one of those teaching logic in the seminary, came to my father and said he would convince my father. And he argued and argued all day with him, a whole day using logic. And my father smiled and said, "I have heard all you said, but you know this Christianity is new. When we were small it was not there."

Finally my father said to me, "I will become a Christian when you come back from Rome and you are a priest. Then I will become a Christian." That's what he said in 1955. And then I went to Rome.[6]

---

[6] In 1955, when Francis Arinze first went to Rome, the Onitsha Archdiocese had a total Catholic population of 211,478 people and 86 priests, 81 of whom were missionaries; the other 5 were African.

Chapter 2

The Student Years in Rome and Ordination to the Priesthood

(1955–1960)

Two young Nigerians arrived at Rome's central train station in September 1955; one was Francis Arinze, the other, Paul Umeh. It was their first time outside their native land, and they found themselves in a country in which they did not speak the language and did not know the culture. But from what the cardinal recalls today, it seems to have been less traumatic than it might have been because they were in an international seminary, attending one of the pontifical international universities in the Eternal City.

My questions[1] took him back almost half a century, but his memories were surprisingly fresh.

---

[1] The interview for most of this chapter was recorded on December 9, 2000.

Q. *Your Eminence, you first arrived in Rome at the age of twenty-three, going on twenty-four. What do you remember of those days?*

A. I arrived in Rome in September 1955. I was a seminarian. I had just finished philosophy in Nigeria, in our major seminary at Enugu,[2] and my bishop, Archbishop Charles Heerey, C.S.Sp., sent me to Rome.

I was with another seminarian, Paul Umeh, from another diocese in Nigeria. We traveled by boat from Nigeria to Liverpool.

Q. *From Lagos?*

A. Yes, from Port Harcourt to Lagos and then to Liverpool. Two weeks. Then we went from Liverpool to Rome by train, if you don't mind. From Liverpool all the way to Euston, and then crossed to Dieppe from New Haven, then to Paris. And then we traveled from Paris to Turin and Rome. We were young. I would not try it now.

When we reached Rome's central station, the Stazione Termini, we were very daring. Without ever having been here before, we took bus 64, even with our luggage. And when we finally didn't know where we were going anymore, we got off the bus and began asking questions in our bad Italian. Finally we got a taxi that took us to the Collegio Urbano di Propaganda Fide.

Q. *You mean you had learned some Italian already?*

A. Well . . . a little, plus Latin. Because we had been told we were coming to Rome six months before.

We were then received at the college. We were very happy. It was not possible in those days to go to Perugia or to Florence to study Italian for three months, as it is today. There were short courses within the college—that is, the seminary of Propaganda Fide. Classes began soon after, in October, in the Urban University.[3] The lectures were in

---

[2] He did his philosophical studies (1953–1955) in Bigard Memorial Seminary, Enugu.

[3] The Urban College, Rome, was opened in the year 1627. It later became part of the Pontifical Urban University, established in 1962.

Latin, in those days. Every subject was in Latin, except some subjects like catechetics—a layman was teaching it—and Greek. But all the others were in Latin.

Q. *When your archbishop told you six months earlier that he was sending you to Rome, did the news come out of the blue to you? Where did he get the idea to send you to Rome?*

A. Who suggested it to him? I do not know, because my archbishop did not really know me in person very well. Nevertheless, I guess it could have been the rector of our junior seminary, where I had been from 1947 to 1952.

At that time, the rector was one of the Irish missionaries, Father William Brolly, and when he was sending me to the senior seminary he told me that I had done well in the junior seminary and that he would tell the archbishop that I'm the type that should be sent to Rome. He said it plainly even before I began philosophy, but I didn't pay much attention to that until I was told in 1955 by the rector of the major seminary, Father James O'Neill: "The archbishop wants to send you to Rome." He also said that the bishop of Owerri diocese was sending another seminarian, Paul Umeh, to Rome. The rector prepared us for going to Rome.

Before I went to Rome, I went to thank Archbishop Heerey in Onitsha. He didn't know who I was, and when I introduced myself, he said: "Oh, you are Francis Arinze!" He wished me well. He was a very good man.

Who else recommended me? I do not know. I would imagine that before the archbishop would decide on such a thing he would have talked to the rector of the major seminary.

Q. *When your bishop decided to send you to Rome, I presume you told Father Tansi?*

A. Yes, I did.

Q. *What did he say?*

A. I cannot remember what he said. He was already in the monastery at Mount Saint Bernard, in England. He had already been there for five years. I do not know that he had any hand in the archbishop's deciding to send me. In any case, Blessed Tansi was not the type to push himself forward, to give his view on such a thing. I think not. He would have just concentrated on his monastic life. But, of course, I wrote to him then and informed him, and he wrote me a few letters in those years in Rome, but, unfortunately, I have lost them.

Q. *So when you got to Rome you had classmates from around the world. Who were your classmates then? Is there anybody we would know today?*

A. There are some. Some of the theology classes were combined in some of the courses then, while other courses were separate. So some of those with whom I was in class, and who are now bishops, would be people such as Cardinal Wamala, in Kampala, Uganda, and Bishop Kalanda, in Fort Portal, Uganda. The two of them were one year ahead of me.

Then there was Archbishop James Odongo, also from Uganda, and Father Severino, from Tanzania—I don't know where he is now.

From my own country there was Bishop Anthony Gbuji, of Enugu. We were seminarians together and were ordained together.

From Vietnam, I remember Monsignor Albert Tran Phuc Nhan, who later became a biblical scholar. He is a priest in Vietnam, and sometimes we communicate.

And there were many others: Archbishop Barry Hickey, of Perth, Australia; Father James Moroney, from the Victoria area of Australia—I don't remember exactly which diocese.

There was Anthony Eruvelil, from India; and Bishop Joseph Pallikaparampil, the bishop of Palai; and very many others, including Archbishop Francis Shimamoto, of Nagasaki, Japan.

And there was Archbishop Emmanuel Kataliko, of Bukavu, Zaire/Congo, who suffered exile earlier this year and died suddenly on October 4, 2000. We were classmates too.

I don't want to say that all our companions became bishops, but quite a number did. At our ordination in 1958, we were altogether about forty-three seminarians from the Urban University. Many religious houses sent their students to the Urban University, too, but we were at the Urban College, that is, the seminary.[4] It was *catholic*; it was universal, even in those days.

Q. *What memories do you retain from those years in Rome?*

A. Really happy ones. We had professors who inspired us. I could

---

[4] He lived at the Collegio Urbano (the Urban College) in the years 1955–1959 and at the Collegio S. Pietro (St. Peter's College) in the years 1959–1960.

continue to name them: I will never forget Monsignor Robert Masi, who later became rector of the Apollinaris College for priests. At that time, he was a professor of sacramental theology and also taught at the Lateran University. He directed my thesis, because it was on the Holy Eucharist. He is dead now.

There was also Monsignor Antonio Piolanti, who is still very much alive, though he is getting on in age. His Latin was excellent, and he taught us dogma. He had taken over from Archbishop Pietro Parente, who wrote the textbooks we used and was then made Archbishop of Perugia and later transferred to the Congregation for the Doctrine of the Faith (then the Holy Office), as secretary. Later he became a cardinal.

Then there was Father Pietro Chiochetta, from the Comboni Missionaries; he is still alive in Verona. I have maintained very happy relations with him, even now. Father Chiochetta taught Church history. We liked his sense of humor and good Latin.

Then there was Father Bonaventura Mariani, a Franciscan: he taught introduction to Holy Scriptures, but he is dead now. And there was Father Johannes Visser, a Redemptorist and moral theologian.

They were all very inspiring. Very inspiring!

Q. *You wrote your thesis on the Eucharist?*

A. I chose as my theme a thesis on sacrifice in the Traditional Religion of the Igbo people of Nigeria, as an introduction to the catechesis of Holy Mass. It involved considering sacrifice in the Traditional Religion of my own people in Nigeria, and how the herald of the Gospel, taking note of that background, can bring them now the Christian sacrifice so that they will really welcome it, understand it as much as they can, and celebrate it with as much fruit as possible.

Q. *But to study theology well and do theological research work, I presume you needed to know foreign languages. I understand you speak German today. Did you learn it in those years as a student in Rome?*

A. Yes, as a seminarian. When we were seminarians in the Urban University, we were offered free courses in French and German, so I took both, for interest's sake. They gave evening courses at the university; they were not obligatory, but I took them. It must have been in my second or third year of theology.

Then I had a priest friend in Germany. Somebody introduced me to this parish; I went and the priest was friendly, and we became friends.

That was in 1959, a year after ordination. Then he introduced me to another priest friend of his. They were both parish priests in small village parishes, in the Archdiocese of Freiburg. So I developed the habit of going to them whenever possible, staying five days, one week, or so on. That is how I learned my German. I never studied in Germany, but I picked up something of the language each time I went there.

Q. *But I understand you speak it well?*
A. Not enough to write a formal letter, but enough to write personal letters to friends; enough to preach, if it is not a big occasion. If it were a big occasion, I would want it written down and corrected by a German speaker; but if it is just an informal occasion in a village, I would just go ahead and say Mass, and read what has to be read, and so on. That, yes.

Q. *And you can do the same in French?*
A. Yes, except that with French I have had many more opportunities, because in Africa today French and English are spoken; and there are many more opportunities to speak French than opportunities to speak German. Therefore I have more practical experience in French than in German, and I have gone to many more French-speaking countries, especially in Africa, than to German-speaking ones.

Q. *Do you speak Spanish too?*
A. Not really. I have learned the grammar a bit, but I have not had the opportunity to speak Spanish. I gave one conference in Cordoba; it was written out so I read it, and that was when I was beginning my work here in the Vatican.

I listen to the Spanish programs on Vatican Radio, but I don't really know it well. I would understand about 80 to 90 percent of what people said in Spanish, but I have not had much opportunity to speak in the language.

Q. *Finally, after three years studying in Rome you were ordained a priest.*[5] *What are your memories of that period?*
A. Ordination to the priesthood came in 1958. Very, very many events took place in that year: that was the year of the death of Pius XII.

---

[5] He was ordained subdeacon on August 15, 1958, and deacon on September 29, 1958, at Castel Gandolfo, where the Urban College had its summer residence.

He died on October 9. We were deacons then. Of course, it was such a major event—of which we had never seen the like.

Q. *Had you actually met him, or had you seen him in those years?*
A. Oh, yes, I saw him because I had come to Rome three years before. But there was no intimate contact between us; we saw him at big audiences and big celebrations. I don't think that he ever came to our Urban College in that period. It was not usual for the Pope to visit colleges so often in those days. I think it was Pope John XXIII who began it. But we saw him. We knew him as "Pastor Angelicus". He sort of seemed nearer to God than to men, and he spoke in language that was rather elevated. That is how we as seminarians looked at him.

At the time he died, Cardinal Agagianian, an Armenian, was the prefect for Propaganda Fide, as we called it; that is, prefect of the Congregation for the Evangelization of Peoples—the name that Congregation got after Vatican II. And, you know the speculation of journalists: they saw Cardinal Agagianian as "papabile".

Q. *I remember Cardinal Agagianian. I remember when he came to visit Ireland. The people gave him a great welcome. My parents went to see him and took me along. I also remember people spoke about him then as the future pope.*
A. So we seminarians were saying: "Yes, we want our cardinal to be pope." And since he was always the one who ordained the seminarians in the Urban College, we said, "Very good, our cardinal will become pope now, and then, as pope, he will ordain us." But when they went in . . . you know the usual saying: "You go in as pope, and you come out as cardinal." He came out as a cardinal. All right. They chose Cardinal Roncalli. We didn't know who he was, we seminarians. But the Italians knew, and many others knew. But we seminarians didn't know who was the patriarch of Venice. We saw the smoke and heard the announcement. We clapped, but we didn't know. I did not know.

Q. *Were you in Saint Peter's Square then?*
A. No. We were up in our college, because it is high up and you can see Saint Peter's Square very well from there. It was a good vantage point, yes. There was no need to go down to the Square; we had a clear view of the whole thing.

Q. *Soon after this, Cardinal Agagianian ordained you.*

A. The cardinal was obviously arranging to ordain us, but then we were told that he had to make a journey to the Far East, to Australia, to visit mission countries. So he said he would perform the ordinations one month early. Ordinations used to be three or four days before Christmas, but he fixed them for November 23. That was fine except that the new Pope was going to take possession of the Lateran Basilica on November 23, and Cardinal Agagianian said he had to be in the Lateran for that ceremony, and therefore the ordinations would have to be at five o'clock in the morning.

Q. *So early?*

A. Yes, at five o'clock in the morning, so that he could be in the Lateran Basilica at ten o'clock, for the papal ceremony.

The Australians did not like it, because they had visitors who had come a long way, and it was not easy for them to be in our college at five o'clock in the morning. I liked it because I did not sleep well anyway the night before; so for me five o'clock in the morning was very good. I was very happy it was early.

Q. *You did not sleep well. Why? Were you worried?*

A. No. My imagination . . . I couldn't stop my imagination. . . . I wasn't worried. I was very happy, but my imagination was working on it: priesthood, such a major event after all our retreats, after all these years. I tried to sleep, but I couldn't. So I got up and I sat. I was writing things in my spiritual notebook, thoughts that struck me that night. Sometimes I read them again.

Q. *So you still have that spiritual notebook?*

A. Yes, I have it. I have it, and all the notes I took at the retreats as a seminarian, I still have them too.

Q. *So you were ordained at that early hour in the morning.*

A. Yes. We were ordained in the chapel of the Urban College of Propaganda Fide, on November 23, 1958. We were forty in all being ordained that day. It was a beautiful ceremony. After that, of course, you know what follows.

Q. *You told me once that your parents couldn't come to the ordination.*

A. No. Nobody could come from Nigeria: it was far too expensive; they did not have the money. So there wasn't one single person coming from Nigeria for the ordination. Not one came from Nigeria. Not even one. However, there were a few Nigerians resident in Rome, not many like today. Those few resident in Rome came; the priests, some diplomats, and some other Nigerians passing through Rome; that was all.

Q. *Father Tansi could not come, but I imagine he wrote to you on that occasion?*

A. He did, but, unfortunately, I have not kept his letter. Some people have been better than I. I know a nun who is in a Carmelite monastery in Nigeria, and I received her letter in December 1997; she told me she kept all the letters that Father Tansi wrote her. I wish I had all mine.

But that time in 1958, I wrote to tell him that my ordination was going to take place. It was the custom in those days that when a young deacon was ordained a priest he would have at his First Mass a priest who was very dear to him, to be at his right hand: to assist him at Mass, so that if he made a mistake, if he forgot something, the other would be there to help out. He used to be called the "assistant priest", and he would put on a cope. Today we are more accustomed to concelebrate. So Father Tansi would have been the priest I would obviously have asked to do it. The newly ordained always chooses such a priest; it would often be his parish priest.

Father Tansi could not come either. I wrote to him and said, "You know that I would have asked you to be my assistant priest, so could you name someone to stand in for you?" He named Father Basil Morrison, who was also a Trappist but has since died. I don't remember if he belonged to Mount Saint Bernard Abbey, but he was resident in Rome at that time, and he was with me at my first Mass in the Basilica of Santa Maria Maggiore, standing in for Father Tansi.[6]

Q. *Did you go back to Nigeria soon after ordination?*

A. Yes, but not immediately. I was ordained in November 1958. Then I finished the theology course in 1959—that was four years' theology—and in those days I gained a licentiate.

---

[6] Father Arinze celebrated his First Mass in the Basilica of St. Mary Major, at the altar of Our Lady, "Salus Populi Romani", and his second Mass in the Carmelite Monastery of Carmelo Tre Madonne, Rome.

Then I was working for a doctorate in theology, and I finished it in November 1960. In those days it was possible to do that. Today it is not possible; you would have to put in two or three more years, not just one year after the licentiate, as in our time. However, in those days it was the quickest you could do it. It was possible for me to do so because my archbishop told me to do a doctorate in my second or third year of theology. So I chose my subject long before.

Q. *And what was the subject of your doctoral thesis?*
A. Sacrifice. Sacrifice in the tradition of our people. I had already chosen it in the second year of theology, and I had done a short write-up, a small thesis on sacrifice in my second or third year of theology. So I had already been working on it, consulting books and so on, long before. It was not a sudden thing at all for me, and that's why it was possible for me to finish it in a short time.

Q. *You helped out in a parish in the north of Italy, the Easter after your ordination, as we shall see later, and then you went to England in the summer of 1959, and you visited Father Tansi.*
A. After I was ordained a priest, I went to England the following year, during the summer, principally to consult books for my doctoral thesis, but, of course, I could not omit a visit to Father Tansi at Mount Saint Bernard, and I served his Mass there.

After that I returned to Rome and completed my doctorate. In November 1960, I did a defense of the thesis.[7] And immediately after that I went home.

Q. *When you were studying in Rome did you meet Pope John XXIII at any time?*
A. Intimately, no, but in a group audience, yes. We were young priests then, because we were ordained a month after he was made Pope. He visited the Urban College; he came within a year of our ordination. We were all happy, enthusiastic. And, of course, there were other audiences: the newly ordained priests were brought to him.

And I recall that at one stage, when my archbishop came to Rome, he brought us with him when he went for an audience with the Holy Father, and we got his blessing. Those are about the only times I met him.

---

[7] Francis Arinze, *Sacrifice in Igbo Religion* (Ibadan University Press, 1970).

Q. *So, what memories do you have of Pope John XXIII?*

A. I remember him as a Pope who was kind, relaxed, not afraid to depart from tradition. For instance, the very fact of his visits: he began this movement when we weren't accustomed to the Pope going to this college and that college, or to events. He did that.

Then the major event: he called Vatican II on January 25, 1959. I remember, I was a young priest then; I had just been ordained two months before. I was actually visiting a place where I had been invited for Mass. I had just celebrated Mass, and we were about to have lunch; and there was a bishop there, and it was announced, "The Pope is calling a General Ecumenical Council." I still remember the bishop saying, "Hey, *this* Pope!" I don't even remember the name of the bishop, and it doesn't matter, but what that bishop said is also what many others said, "*This* Pope!" They were not thinking of a General Ecumenical Council. But looking back now, it has all worked out well.

I think we also once heard that he gave his ring to an Anglican bishop. That is very eloquent. Here was a pope who wasn't afraid to do what he thought should be done, and who was kind, and who had a way of touching people's hearts.

Of course, Pope John XXIII, now blessed, was much deeper than people thought. People just thought of him as *nice* and *good*. He was that, but he was much more. He was much deeper, and more intelligent, than many people realized.

Q. *As a cardinal, you followed the process for his beatification through the Congregation of Saints.*

A. Yes.

Q. *And you read his life and works.*

A. Oh, yes. I cannot complain that I have not enough information. Obviously, the discussions in the Congregation would be confidential.

Q. *So, as a student you saw two Popes—Pius XII and John XXIII.*

A. You must make allowance for this: I was just a seminarian at the time of Pope Pius XII, and I was just a young priest, newly ordained, at the time of John XXIII.

So, seeing them from afar, and in our conversations and comments as seminarians and young priests, we saw it this way: that Pius XII was with God, John XXIII was with men. Of course, this is a summary judgment, because after all John XXIII was very much with God, and Pius XII was very much with men. But it is a question of the accent, the impression.

Pope John XXIII, now blessed, didn't have to say, "Do not be afraid"; his actions, reactive approach, and reactions conveyed the message. We were not nervous in his presence. But probably with Pius XII we might have been slightly nervous. That's all I would say.

Pope John XXIII once put it so beautifully in a speech, when he said: "Some people said I didn't do this, or the pope didn't do that. No pope can do everything. The pope who builds the Basilica of Saint Peter's is not the one who builds the Basilica of Saint Paul's." That means, every pope is gifted by God and is a different person. God is infinite, and no pope or bishop will mirror all the good sides of God. Each one will mirror one side, but all of them mirror Christ, the eternal Shepherd. That's my impression.

Q. *Some people speak of one as the intellectual, and the other as the not-so-intellectual. Clearly you do not see it quite that way, from what you have said.*

A. Ah. Pope John XXIII. People just call him "the good Pope". Nice smile! But of course they might miss the deeper part of his character. Remember, he was an experienced nuncio in difficult places, in Istanbul and Paris. If that is not sophisticated, I do not know what is.

Obviously, he was very intelligent, and behind all that goodness and smile is the depth of the person. His remarks might appear simple, but they are also very deep. The two things are not opposed, depth and solidity plus simplicity.

Indeed, those people who are complicated, and who cannot put it clearly and simply, I begin to suspect that they are not deep either, because the Son of God speaking to us in the Gospels, even children can follow what he is saying.

Some people, they tell me they are professors; they speak and not only do the students not understand them, but I sometimes wonder whether even they understand what they themselves are saying. But Pope John XXIII, I would liken to one who is so deep that he is also very simple. It is his fascination.

Pope Pius XII was obviously very deep, but perhaps John XXIII had more the gift of approach to people. It is just two characters. They are not the same. Even children of the same parents are not photocopies of one another.

Q. *At the time you were a student in Rome, many people used to go to visit Padre Pio. John Paul II went once. Did you ever visit him or see him?*

A. No. I never met Padre Pio. I did not go to San Giovanni Rotondo when he was alive. But when more and more was being said about him, I read much about him, but did not go there until last year—the Jubilee Year. Then I went twice: I went first with the bishop of a neighboring diocese, San Severo, in May 2000; then in August 2000, I was invited for a big ceremony, the dedication of an altar, where they inserted the altar on which he used to say Mass into another altar. I was chief celebrant at the dedication Mass. I was very happy to be there.

Q. *You also followed his cause as a member of the Congregation for the Causes of the Saints. Having read all the documentation on his life, what impression has he made on you?*

A. Very positive. He was an extraordinary person. I'm impressed especially by his love of souls, ready to be in the confessional for hours. And I'm impressed even more by his love of the Church, especially when he was given vexatious orders from Rome, when he was misunderstood, when wrong reports were sent about him to Rome. They were wrong. And I think he was told, "You will not meet the people or say Mass for them for two years"; and yet there was not one word of complaint from him. He followed the orders exactly. Is that not enough to indicate that a person is a saint? How many persons reach that height of holiness that they love the Church so much that they are able to retain their love for the Church and their faith even when ministers of the Church make a mistake in administration, and they don't go mad or say anything that they would like to retract later? That is a sign of greatness and faith, a model for us all.

Q. *Moving away from the heights of sanctity, I want to ask you a question on a much more mundane subject. When you were a student in Nigeria and in Rome, I imagine you played some sport. Did you play soccer?*

A. Yes. A good Nigerian plays soccer, without necessarily being in the World Cup. I played soccer, yes, but I wasn't a champion or anything like that. I played a bit in the junior seminary, and in the senior seminary too. And when I was in Rome, as a seminarian, I played some soccer too. I used to play right halfback.

Q. *Did you play any other sport?*

A. Lawn tennis. I began lawn tennis, really, as a young priest. I began to be interested in it in 1961. I used to go to a secondary school near the major seminary, in Enugu, because we didn't have a tennis court in the seminary at that time. Now, of course, there is a tennis court, and many of the seminarians are excellent players. But at that time, in 1961, there wasn't a court there. That is the one sport I kept up. I could not keep up soccer, not at this age! No.

Q. *Do you play other sports, too, such as swimming?*

A. No, I am not a swimmer. When I was in Castel Gandolfo as a seminarian—in those days, we went there for three months' summer holidays to a place that is now a catechists' college—we had a swimming pool, but I was only learning. So I don't know how to swim. You had better not throw me into the water!

Chapter 3

Return to Nigeria and
First Ministry as a Priest

(1960–1963)

After finishing his studies in Rome, the young Father Francis returned home to Nigeria, to his family and diocese, though not for long.

My questions evoked distant, but emotion-filled memories, including a particularly beautiful one concerning his father.

Q. *Your Eminence, did you return to Nigeria immediately after gaining your doctorate in Rome?*

A. Yes. When I completed my doctorate in Rome, November 1960, I did a defense of the thesis. And immediately after, I went home. I traveled by train to Lourdes, and after visiting the sanctuary in Lourdes, I went to Marseilles in France, and then took the boat home. It took two weeks, or maybe ten days, from Marseilles to Lagos. It was a passenger boat. Then I went by truck from Lagos to Onitsha, all within a day.

Q. *I imagine your family did not come to Lagos to welcome you, given the distance.*

A. No, and there was no need. But the people of my town arranged for those who would bring me home; they arranged that one of the drivers of a Mercedes—a type of truck in which they would have passengers and also luggage—came with the truck to the harbor of Lagos, where the big French boat that brought me home docked.

We reached Lagos in the morning, and I said Mass on the boat. Then my luggage was off-loaded; they did it all rather fast. So, by two o'clock that same afternoon, we were already on the road. The journey was 434 miles. I still remember it. We traveled on the old road from Lagos to Onitsha; today there is a better and shorter road, three hundred miles.

We traveled a good part of the night and reached Onitsha in the morning. And because Onitsha is on the banks of the River Niger and in those days there was no bridge, we went across on a ferryboat. The trucks and cars were put on, and then we crossed. It took time, but it worked.

So that day, December 8, 1960, I said Mass in the cathedral at Onitsha[1] and greeted people in the archbishop's house. It was a quiet Mass, and afterward there was breakfast in the archbishop's house, with the cathedral administrator, Father Patrick Smyth, who was very kind to me.

I was in my village that same day.

---

[1] Holy Trinity Cathedral, Onitsha.

Q. *And I'm sure you got a great welcome when you arrived home?*

A. Yes, a great welcome, as you can imagine in those days, after being away five years and now a priest. My parents were there, and my brothers and sisters—they hadn't seen me for five years. And the people were there.

Q. *So the big celebration took place in the village, not in Onitsha?*

A. Definitely. There was no celebration in Onitsha, but there was a celebration in the village, especially on the following Sunday.

Q. *What did you feel coming back home after several years abroad?*

A. You can guess; you can guess. A young man who has been away five years would be very happy to be back home; happy to see his father, mother, brothers, sisters, relatives, friends, former teachers. It was a great joy. And that young man was now a priest.

Q. *Before you left for Rome, your father had told you that he would become a Christian if you returned home as a priest. Did that happen?*

A. In December 1960, thanks to God, I came back from Rome, a priest. And I said to my father, "Remember what you said before. I am now back from Rome, a priest. All of us are Christians, all your children and my mother, all of us. It's only you now."

My father said, "It is true. I will join all of you, so that in the next world all of us will be together."

Then he learned catechism, without learning as children do. Then the parish priest examined him in catechism and said, "He has passed."

I said to the parish priest, "But did he really pass?" Father smiled and said, "He knows enough; he's not going to be Thomas Aquinas. It's enough!" Then he was baptized in 1961, and he took the name Joseph.

Q. *What did you feel on that day?*

A. Obviously I was happy, as you can imagine, and I thanked Divine Providence.

Q. *After your return to Nigeria, did you begin your ministry as a priest immediately, or what did you do?*

A. After returning home, I was appointed to teach in the major seminary[2] for two years. It was the seminary where I myself had studied.

---

[2] He taught at Bigard Memorial Seminary for two years, 1961–1962.

I was just appointed to teach; the period was not limited. I was the first Nigerian priest on the staff; all the rest were Irish missionaries. The first subject I was assigned was liturgy, for the theology section, and logic and part of philosophy, for the philosophy section.

I loved teaching, except that it didn't last too long, because toward the end of the second year the archbishop, Charles Heerey, C.S.Sp., who was always very good to me, called me and said, "You see, relations with the government about Catholic schools are very important. We absolutely need a Nigerian priest for this, because an Irish priest would be seen as not of your country, no matter how well he does. So we want a Nigerian priest."

There was an Irish priest, Father John Jordan, who did this work then. Excellently. He really built up the Catholic school system, and we cannot speak of the Catholic school system in Eastern Nigeria without saying the names of Father John Jordan and Father Cornelius Wolfe. Father Jordan is dead now, but Father Cornelius Wolfe is still alive— he must be about eighty-two years old. When I gave a conference in Steubenville, the Franciscan University in Ohio, in 1998, he was in the U.S.A. at a priests' conference. And when I was speaking to the priests, there he was in the audience. I greeted him, and I told the priests, "This is the priest missionary who was assistant education secretary for the diocese when I was in primary school, and he gave me the certificate of a good pass in religion in 1946." He was eighty years old on that day. I asked him to speak, but he was rather hesitant to speak. A very good man!

So the archbishop asked me to be in charge of Catholic schools: to be education secretary, immediately, in Enugu, the capital of Eastern Nigeria, but, also at that time, with responsibility for all the dioceses in the eastern part of Nigeria in their relations with the government.[3] That was in 1962. I began that. And Enugu was cut off from Onitsha and made a new diocese at the end of 1962.

That was the year that Cardinal Montini visited Nigeria, as archbishop of Milan. And the following year he became Pope.

Q. *Did you meet him then?*
A. Oh, yes, I did. Indeed, I was the interpreter for him for his homily in Enugu, when he spoke there. I was master of ceremonies at the

---

[3] He was regional Catholic education secretary for Eastern Nigeria.

Mass, and the archbishop told me, "The visiting cardinal is going to preach, and you had better translate for him since you know Italian."

So I told the cardinal, "There will be a translation." He said, "I'm going to speak in Italian." I said, "Yes." He asked, "Will it be translated into the people's language?" I said, "Yes." He said, "Not into English, please, into the people's language." I said, "Yes. It'll be all right." And that's what happened.

After the Mass the people were happy. But the Irish missionaries were not too happy and said, "We didn't understand the Italian, and now of the people's language we understand only part." I just smiled.

The cardinal gave me a sick-call bag, a bag for visiting the sick.

The following year he became Pope. We were, of course, very happy.

So I was working as Catholic education secretary.

Then the bishop in Enugu, Bishop John Cross Anyogu, whom I knew, said, "You studied in Rome. It would be good for you to go to Britain, just for a year, to get a degree in education, to see and study their education system, because it would help us." I was happy to do that. And so I went to the Institute of Education in London and studied there from September 1963 to June 1964. It was a brief but providential period in my life too, because there I saw Father Tansi for the last time.

Chapter 4

A Year in London

(1963–1964)

In London, Father Arinze enjoyed his study of the English educational system and gained his postgraduate certificate in education at the University of London's Institute of Education in 1964. But he also visited his spiritual mentor, Father Tansi, who was ill by this time.

I began by asking him about his stay in London.

Q. *You went to London in September 1963 and studied at the Institute of Education until June 1964. Where did you live in London?*

A. In a hostel for Catholic students near Finsbury Park (I think, or Manor House). Monsignor John Coonan was in charge overall, although he lived in another part of London; but he had another priest there. It was welcoming for students, especially from missionary countries. We lived there and went to school wherever we had to go.

I found it very fruitful to study the British educational system. I appreciated their respect for diversity, keeping up standards, but still not denying grants to church schools just because they were church schools. Those grants were not exactly equal to those given the public schools, but still reasonable encouragement, and the standards were kept up.

We were trained to do practical teaching in schools of any type, and we were welcomed in them. Later on, I found that the senior lecturer who was directing our little group, and who was very kind to me—he even gave me very high marks—didn't even believe in God. It was only when I left the Institute that I found that out. But he never showed it; he never showed any discrimination against me because I had studied in Rome. They all knew that I had studied theology in Rome, but everything worked out fine there.

Q. *What was his name?*

A. Evans. P. C. Evans. But he must be dead by now, because he was already well advanced in years then. And that's forty years ago already.

Q. *Did you keep in contact with him afterward?*

A. Yes, a few times we exchanged letters.

Q. *Did you do your teacher training practice in schools in London?*

A. Yes. When we began our course first we were sent into primary schools, to get us into the stream of things, for one or two weeks, I think. Then we would do theoretical classes, the theory of pedagogy, and so on.

At some stage we were sent to certain schools. But first, each person would indicate his area of preference, and all the professors and lecturers would divide us up into smaller groups of twenty or so. One lecturer would be in charge of a group of twenty, and these were posted in schools to teach. We were not able to start where we liked; we had simply to continue the lesson from whatever point the children had reached, and we went on from there. The lecturer would come around to analyze and supervise, and that was all part of the course.

Q. *Where did you actually teach?*

A. Oh! I have forgotten now. I only remember that I went to one school that was a community school, not particularly Christian. Just anybody went there, as it was not on a religious basis. I think I went to three schools altogether, and we did a full month in a larger one. I was sent to Stroud, in the southwest; I do not remember what type of school it was, but I spent a whole month there. I liked it.

Q. *And you met Father Tansi during that stay in England.*

A. Of course. I could not be in Britain for one year without visiting Father Tansi.

I went to visit him during Christmas in 1963.[1] Then he was not well, and one month later he died, on January 20, 1964, in Leicester Hospital.[2] They sent me a telegram saying, "He is dead. He will be buried tomorrow." I was in London, studying, so I immediately took the train to Leicester, and I was able to be at the funeral at Mount Saint Bernard Abbey. It was January 21, 1964.

So it worked out providentially for me that I was in Britain just at that time.

Q. *Then, at the end of your time in Britain you gained your degree in education and then returned to Nigeria.*

A. Yes, I came back home. It must have been in July 1964. I then continued my work as education secretary in the schools,[3] until I was made auxiliary bishop the year after, 1965.

---

[1] He visited Mount St. Bernard on December 12–14, 1963.

[2] Father Gregory Wareing, O.C.S.O., gives an account of the last week and death of Father Tansi in his booklet *A New Life of Father Cyprian Michael Iwene Tansi* (Coalville, Leicester: Mount St. Bernard Abbey, 1994).

[3] In this period, Cardinal Arinze wrote a booklet, *Partnership in Education between Church and State* (Enugu: Udes's Press, 1965).

Chapter 5

The Youngest Bishop
at Vatican II

(1965)

After returning to Nigeria, Cardinal Arinze began work as secretary for education in the diocese, but not for long. On July 6, 1965, Pope Paul VI nominated him as coadjutor bishop of Onitsha and auxiliary to Archbishop Charles Heerey, C.S.Sp. The announcement was made public on July 31, and the archbishop consecrated him bishop on August 29 that same year, in Holy Trinity Cathedral, Onitsha.

Very soon after, he went to Rome to attend the final session of the Second Vatican Council. In my interview,[1] I sought to record his memories of that event, which was so important in the life of the Catholic Church.

---

[1] The chapter is based on extracts from an interview recorded on December 9, 2000.

Q. *In 1965, Pope Paul VI named you auxiliary bishop of Onitsha. You must have been one of the youngest bishops in Africa then.*

A. At that time, I was thirty-two years old, and—apart, possibly, from some young bishop in the Communist-dominated parts of Europe—they tell me I was the youngest bishop in the whole world. The Church was taking a risk [*laughs*].

One day the Holy Father, John Paul II, said to me, "You became bishop very young." I said, "Yes, Holy Father. The Church was taking a risk."

Q. *What was his comment?*

A. He said, "It worked out well."

Q. *You were consecrated just before the final session of Vatican II began. You were consecrated bishop in Onitsha and then catapulted straight to the Vatican Council in Rome.*

A. Yes. Nobody forced me. I was happy to come. I was made bishop on August 29, 1965, and the last session of the Second Vatican Council began on September 11, just two weeks later.

Q. *So you flew to Rome this time—you didn't go by boat.*

A. Yes, there was an Alitalia flight, and many Nigerian bishops went on it. I was not alone. We all went together. I was the youngest. We were housed together in some hotel; I have forgotten the name of the hotel, but it was near the Stazione Termini. We went to the Council by bus each day. It was a wonderful experience, especially for me as a young bishop who had not worked on the documents before. As you will have noticed, most of the documents of Vatican II were finalized at the last session of the Council, whereas the work on these was done in the earlier sessions, the first three sessions. But most of the documents were approved only at the final session. So there was the signing of the documents—every bishop signed them—and the approving of the documents, on which I had not worked.

And as a young bishop how much did I know of what was in those documents? I was in admiration of many things that were being said. I was there, almost like a student. One of the bishops at the Council once asked me whether I was a seminarian [laughs]. I said, "Yes, I had been a seminarian eight years before, but I was no longer a seminarian." I liked the joke.

As you know it was at this last session, in 1965, that the following documents were approved:[2]

> on bishops;
> on religious;
> on seminary formation;
> on Catholic education;
> on the relation of the Church to other religions;
> on divine revelation;
> on the laity;
> on religious liberty;
> on the Church's missionary work;
> on priestly life and ministry;
> on the Church in the modern world.

Eleven of the sixteen documents of Vatican II were finalized at the last session of the Council.

Q. *So you had to read all of those then.*
A. I read as much as I could. Not that I made any oral intervention. I did not speak. But a few little things I wrote. I had the joy of seeing one or two words I had suggested taken into the text. I've forgotten what it was.

Q. *So you mean you actually made some amendments.*
A. Yes, but I don't remember now what it was. But I was happier more with the whole experience, listening and watching, looking at

---

[2] The cardinal also mentioned the official Latin titles of these documents: *Christus Dominus* (bishops); *Perfectae Caritatis* (religious life); *Optatam Totius* (training of priests); *Gravissimum Educationis* (Christian education); *Nostra Aetate* (relation of the Church to non-Christian religions); *Dei Verbum* (divine revelation); *Apostolicam Actuositatem* (apostolate of lay people); *Dignitatis Humanae* (religious liberty); *Ad Gentes* (the Church's missionary work); *Presbyterorum Ordinis* (the ministry and life of priests); *Gaudium et Spes* (the Church in the modern world).

those who were the timbers, the pillars, of the Church. Listening to them, getting to know them, people whose names I had heard before but whom I had not known in person.

Q. *So who stands out in your mind from that experience of Vatican II?*
A. The cardinals of Cologne (Frings), Vienna (Koenig), Brussels (Suenens). Everybody knew about those.

But there were also some on the African level: Archbishop Jean Zoa, of Yaoundé, in the Cameroon, who was then the youngest African archbishop of the first generation. He was very capable. And there were also groups of bishops who met, sometimes according to language.

In those days we began to hear the name of Archbishop Marcel Lefèbvre. No one knew then . . . we did not know he would end the way he did. But he already gave signs during that session, because whenever there was anything touching on freedom, religious freedom, or other religions, he collected all the signatures he could to oppose those.

Q. *So his position came from way back!*
A. It wasn't something that happened suddenly. He must have been thinking that this opening to other religions, the world, and other Christians would be dangerous for the Catholic faith. His concern for the Catholic faith, as I saw it, made him not trust this openness. That's how I would put it.

Q. *And how did you feel at that time about the openness?*
A. I was slightly afraid. I did not know where it would end, so that I was more comfortable with what had been than with what could be. I was not sure where this openness would lead; so I must not class myself as one of those who had a prophetic vision and saw that the whole thing would end beautifully. I was not sure. I was slightly hesitant. But I also liked the freshness, as in the liturgy. I liked that.

Q. *Is there one thing that stands out in your mind from that last session of Vatican II?*
A. What stands out in my mind is the courage of the whole Church as Church, that all of those bishops were there, with two thousand years' weight of Church history, and in trust, trusting in the Holy Spirit, they went on. That seemed to me extraordinary. Because they were conscious of being servants of that Gospel, they were not afraid.

But what struck me especially was the concluding part of the Council on December 7 and 8, 1965, and the messages that were read out then. They were so full of freshness, full of trust, full—let me say—of optimism in the good sense. Not in terms of being unrealistic, but in the sense that when you trust a person and say to that person, "I think you can do good", that person will bring out his best.

You can see this in the Council's message to women, or its message to artists, to men of culture and science, and its messages to statesmen and youth. Here was a type of message that said, "Look, the Church trusts you, and thinks that you can do a lot of good. Please do a lot of good."

That's how it sounded to me. That was goodness, as I saw it.

Q. *Was there any bad news in it?*

A. I am not sure that I, as a young bishop at that time, would have been so clear-visioned. But I must say that, at some stage, I became slightly afraid of those who were pushing openness. I thought some were pushing it too much.

Q. *Could you give an example of what you mean?*

A. I do not want to name names . . . it would not be fair. But some touched on priestly celibacy a bit, on ecumenism, and I was not sure that in their enthusiasm they took sufficient notice of repercussions and of doctrine. But this was only a perception, a type of fear you do not too easily articulate. As I said earlier, I was not sure where it would all end. That is how I would put it.

Q. *And now with the hindsight of some thirty-five years, what do you say?*

A. I would almost say the same; that my hesitation at that time has not been without ground. As you notice then, whether on ecumenism or inter-religious dialogue, or even inner unity in the Church, collegiality, or whether you call it centralization or decentralization, there is always a healthy stand. But there is always another stand, a little left-of-center, if not even dangerously near extreme left within the Church, and that has caused not a little headache within the Church, not to mention outside.

You can see the problems of unity, the problems of different doctrines occasionally, and the problems of practice, some practice not based on correct doctrine.

So while Vatican II has done a lot of good—who knows, if we didn't have it, would things not be much worse? Nevertheless, we cannot forget that there have been problems. They may not have been caused by Vatican II, but occasioned, if you wish. Or they were problems raised by people who thought they were being faithful to Vatican II, or who said they were walking in the spirit of Vatican II, or who perhaps had a further agenda, which went beyond what the Council envisaged.

Because with what the Council envisaged and said, I have no difficulty there. But interpretations can differ a lot. You would be surprised how two people can quote Vatican II as if it supported their stands, but those positions are not the same. They can be sincere, both of them. But sincerity is not the only virtue. There's another virtue—objectivity. And sincerity cannot be the criterion for truth.

Q. *And the real positive elements that have come out of Vatican II in these years, how do you see them?*

A. There's no doubt; much has come out of Vatican II to nourish the Church. So much that I can only mention some: esteem for the Word of God, and greater place given to the Word of God in the liturgy and in our personal lives; a greater commitment to Christ and the Gospel; greater openness to whatever the Holy Spirit does or gives, whether in the Church or outside the visible boundaries of the Church.

As a result of Vatican II, there is a positive attitude of much greater respect and attention to the Holy Spirit, especially in the Latin Church, if I may use that word. There is greater appreciation of cultural variety in the Church. It is not a new doctrine, but because of the success of the missionary work of the Church in much of Latin America, and also in Africa and Asia, it has taken on great importance today.

One hundred years ago, the greater part of Africa was just beginning to be evangelized. Granted, there was the early Church in North Africa and Ethiopia, and the Church has never disappeared there, even though it is now greatly reduced. Nevertheless, it is true that missionary work, in the enduring sense, in Africa, south of the Sahara, is only a matter of the last 150 years. For the Church, that is young.

The attention of the universal Church to cultural variety is really something appreciable in our times, and is a result of Vatican II.

Then there is the whole dimension of universality, which is related a bit to cultures but is not exactly the same. It is reflected, for example, in the Roman Curia itself, which is more universal than at any other time in history. That too is a consequence of Vatican II.

Then there are the Holy Father's [Pope John Paul II's] travels. He doesn't just travel; he meets people. He calls his travels pilgrimages to the people of God in the various continents, so the people know "we are the Church, universal and local".

And there is the flourishing of bishops' conferences, at the national and even at the regional levels. This too is thanks to Vatican II.

Q. *That's been a big, important step in strengthening the Church.*

A. Yes, it really is a big step forward. Even though the Catholic Church appreciates that we have a pope: we need a pope; we need a strong center, obviously. Those who do not realize that we need a strong center have no idea what happens where the Church is weak. I don't want to name countries, but I know some countries where, without a strong center, the Church would be decapitated.

The Church obviously needs a strong center, but at the same time the Pope does not replace the diocesan bishop. The diocesan bishop is the vicar of Christ for his diocese; and then he, with the other bishops, under the authority of the Pope, cares for the universal Church. Collegiality. That dimension is a major contribution from Vatican II: not a new doctrine, but a new emphasis. We should be happy with that.

And then also Vatican II has given life to the liturgy. Of course, in the liturgy people notice immediately the Holy Eucharist—that's the center, the high point. And even there much has been done.

But also there is the Divine Office, the prayer that religious and priests say in the name of the Church. Excellent work has been done on it. It's one of the best books in the liturgical reform.

There are some parts that could be looked at again in the liturgy, for example, some parts where there was too much simplification. For us, let's say for African cultures, the Mass—as it is now—looks oversimplified: genuflections, making the sign of the cross only three times, and reducing the number of bows. I once asked one of the experts, and he said, "You Africans, you were not many at that time. Most of those who took part in the commissions were Europeans and Americans, and they wanted ceremonies to be simplified. You Africans seem to like color, and you want many gestures." I said, "There's nothing wrong with color; there's nothing wrong with bows and genuflections. We human beings need these visible signs. Why do you simplify it so much?"

I would just add, as a joke, when the Eucharistic Prayers were introduced (canons two, three, and four) and the priest said Mass using Eucharistic Prayer II, the man who offered the stipend for the Mass felt that it was rather short and asked for his money back! The Mass was far too short; he didn't get value for his money. Theologically his position is not acceptable, but psychologically for him it was a bit rushed. So there are things like that which are not dogmatic; they are just arranged like that, but they could be done differently.

Q. *As I understand it, you are saying that culturally things can be different, and the liturgy can be arranged differently in the different cultures.*

A. Obviously, because it is human beings who sit and arrange how it will be celebrated. Our Lord didn't go into all the details about how Mass would be celebrated, so those can change.

Of course, there are those who go too far today, and they introduce a spontaneous liturgy: a priest comes and does his own thing. One priest does one funny thing, another does another, yet another one has a strange idea. Another one banalizes and desacralizes and comes and says, "Good morning, everybody"; instead of saying, "The Lord be with you", which has the weight of tradition, theology, scriptural implications, and Judeo-Christian background. All this is packed into that expression "The Lord be with you."

But these are peripheral, and as long as you have men on earth, you will have those who exaggerate and who say things and also do things that the Church does not approve. There is not finally a magic formula for avoiding all sorts of errors, and we cannot, because we are afraid of that, be afraid of any change.

Q. *The laity too got new impetus from Vatican II.*

A. I should have come to that too. That is a major point of Vatican II. It is still so for the apostolate of everyone in the Church. The Church is not the clergy. The clergy are part of the Church, but the Church is all of us who are baptized, and the majority are lay faithful, and their apostolate is in the Church and in the world. That is a major point of Vatican II.

It is not a new doctrine, because Saint Paul had Aquila and Priscilla and other lay people who worked with him. But the emphasis is certainly new that the lay apostolate is not helping the clergy in the clerical apostolate, but the lay people are doing their own apostolate; and the main focus of their apostolate is not even inside the parish church or parish grounds, but in the family, in science and culture, in trade and industry, in the mass media, in the legislature, and so on. That's dynamic.

And then, as Vatican II points out, there are other forms of apostolate, the religious, of course, the youth, and so on.

Q. *A lot of bishops today have not had your experience in Vatican II.*
A. That is true, obviously, because it is already thirty-five years since the Council closed in 1965.

Q. *You mentioned earlier that you had met Cardinal Montini when he visited Nigeria in 1962, but did you meet him as Pope Paul VI during the final session of Vatican II?*
A. I did, but not intimately. As a young bishop I could not hope to. I did not meet the Holy Father alone during Vatican II; but I met him together with other bishops.

It is true that, during the Synods of Bishops that followed in 1969 and 1971, it was possible to exchange a few words with him; and later too, during the Nigerian civil war, soon after Vatican II, in 1969.

Q. *As I understand it, Pope Paul VI was very important for the conclusion of the Second Vatican Council.*
A. Oh, yes. Of course he was very important. At that time as a young bishop I would not have known what was going on behind the scenes in the evening, between the cardinals who directed the Council and the Pope. I had no idea. I was too young to know about that.

Nevertheless, I could guess there were discussions when the presidents of the Council would say they would confer with the Holy Father, and then decisions were brought back to the Council. For me that was normal. Normal. Because, after all, the Pope was the president at the Council.

Q. *Were there many black African bishops at the Council?*
A. The number I cannot tell. It was not very high in those days. There were few.

Q. *If you had a Vatican Council today, you would have a completely different composition.*
A. Definitely.

Q. *You would have many native-born African and Asian bishops present.*

A. Definitely. At Vatican II, for Africa and Asia the majority were missionary bishops. Today it would be different, very different. For instance, Nigeria today with forty-eight dioceses, or prefectures apostolic, the missionary bishops might be five of the total number. So the whole equation would be changed. It is a sign of the success of the work of the missionaries. As one missionary said, "When we succeed we are no longer there." It is a sign.

Q. *Do you think that Vatican II has been fully implemented now, or is there much more to be done?*

A. Fully implemented? No. Such a major event as Vatican II could not be fully implemented in thirty-five years, no matter how much we work. But the Church has been making an effort.

You notice that twenty years after Vatican II, Pope John Paul II called an extraordinary Synod of Bishops in 1985, to look back and look forward. And at the Congress for the Laity, November 2000, he gave each of the lay faithful a copy of the documents of Vatican II, which means that it is still relevant. Go back to it!

I don't forget that soon after that congress, Jerry Coniker, the head of the Apostolate for Family Consecration, said to me, "Please, next year, we are going to work and produce videotapes on some more Vatican II documents in line with what the Holy Father told us at the Laity Congress."

I regard Vatican II as a gold mine where you can get more each time. Even with documents that seem very familiar to us, we can see much more in them. You don't have to go to major documents such as *Gaudium et Spes* (The Church in the Modern World) or *Lumen Gentium* (the document on the Church); even in smaller ones, such as *Nostra Aetate* (on other religions) or *Dignitatis Humanae* (on religious liberty), you can always discover more. It is really true that the Holy Spirit guides the Church, more so in a general ecumenical council.

So many things remain to be done. Think of that document on the liturgy,[3] and how much is said there, it is a very big agenda.

Or think of the document on missionary activity—*Ad Gentes*. If you take even one paragraph of that document, the famous paragraph 22 that

---

[3] *Sacrosanctum Concilium*—The Constitution on the Sacred Liturgy—was the first document to be promulgated by the Second Vatican Council, on December 4, 1963.

speaks of culture and says there must be the study of culture in a whole region so that it would be seen better how to articulate the faith in the language of that culture, and in the categories of that culture. That is easy to say but very difficult to do, because the Council is really asking for a local Thomas Aquinas, and a local Francis of Assisi, and a local Catherine of Siena, and a local Thérèse of Lisieux, and a local John of the Cross. In other words, it is asking that in each culture there will be people who have so imbibed the Gospel that it has become part of them; and the Gospel is able to grow, like a tree, in a way that is obviously local and yet recognizably Catholic. It takes time.

Q. *And this process can of course raise problems because, when the locals articulate it in their own way, others may not necessarily grasp the language and the concepts.*

A. Yes, it raises challenges and risks as well as problems. Even among the people of the place there will not necessarily be agreement. Some may think you have gone too far to the left, others that you have not gone far enough. Then some will say you are now introducing elements that they would consider superstitious; another will say he does not understand. Then with others the problem may be that the Church has been made too parochial, too local, and is losing the dimension of universality.

It is not enough that the Gospel be brought to one people, it is also important that that one people remain recognizably Catholic, because the two dimensions (local and universal) are not opposed. But to balance them well is not easy at all.

Take the question of dances. It is now becoming almost the fashion in Africa that during the Mass there will be some type of dance. Well, on that one, there may be different opinions. In my view, many of the dances I see at Mass are not suitable for Mass at all, but are suitable after Mass, on the soccer field or in the parish hall, where they would fit in very well, but not within the Mass. Perhaps some of these could fit in during the offertory procession, but greater care is needed in selecting a dance that would be suitable after Holy Communion or at the beginning of Mass.

I've seen places where, after the *Sanctus*, we wanted to get on with the Mass, but they brought on a whole bevy of girls and filled the whole sanctuary [*laughs*]. I said to myself: What is this all about? Won't they allow us to celebrate the Holy Eucharist? So here people can disagree. I had to control myself and behave well so that they would not see that I was altogether perplexed. These are matters where the solution is not easy at all; and two bishops can disagree, two theologians can disagree, and therefore we need to go carefully.

Q. *Therefore one must respect the different feelings.*

A. Respecting feelings is important, but also understanding what that cultural manifestation means in itself and, secondly, what effect it is likely to have on the people themselves. What it is in itself, what it means in itself originally, and what sort of effect it is likely to have, and what advantage Holy Mother Church has in introducing it.

All this can be very fine indeed, and very subtle. And some of it can be very difficult so that even very good people can disagree, which means we need to go carefully. No one individual should rush it; or arrange something on Saturday evening, force it down the throats of the people on the Sunday morning, and then turn around and call it inculturation, using the people as ecclesiastical guinea pigs on which to test his latest productions. That can do harm in the long run, so that I say sometimes that some unwise people drive in where angels fear to tread. There are so many areas that look simple, but they are not.

Q. *So it's a question of preparation and arriving at a consensus in a given community?*

A. Yes, preparation, if under preparation you include interdisciplinary study so that the theologians, the ethnologists, the literature experts, the musicians, those who are experts in the fine arts and history and in interpretation and biblical knowledge and liturgical history work together. All this must be taken into consideration because the Church has a history and a liturgical history. Weigh all that together, agonize over it, refer it to the bishops, not just to one bishop, and get the people of God to react, so that what comes out finally does credit to the people of God and will last. The work of an enthusiast, done overnight, does not last.

Q. *One of the big pushes in recent times, and on all continents, has regarded the position and role of women in society and in the Church. Vatican II opened up new horizons here.*

A. The Council did that without going into too much detail. The Council spoke more on the laity and the lay person as such, whether man or woman. That was the emphasis.

Obviously the Church and society don't stand still, and so in the last thirty-five years there has been more pronounced attention to women. Some have exaggerated, while others have been reasonable. The Pope himself has been very encouraging. He has taken some unprecedented measures. Apart from *Redemptoris Mater*,[4] in which he presents the Blessed Virgin as the model woman, he has also written a *Letter to Women*, in which he speaks of "the feminine genius".[5] No other pope ever went that far.

So we could say that we have the seeds in the Council's documents, without the details.

Q. I remember you once told me that when you were Archbishop of Onitsha you appointed a woman to the board of the seminary in your diocese.

A. Yes, because the contribution of women is irreplaceable. Therefore, in the training of future priests it was clear to me that women's contributions would be important. So on the board of the minor seminary, I had two religious sisters and two women who were mothers with many children and who were exemplary Catholics. There were also some laymen on the board, and of course there were priests, including the rector of the seminary. The priest functions for the whole Church, but the majority in the Church are lay people. And these lay men and women know a good priest when they see one. Indeed, some of them can write a better testimonial on their parish priest than the bishop can, because they are closer to him. They love the Church. Therefore, they can contribute to the formation of ministers for the Church.

Q. That was quite an advanced position in those days, wasn't it?

A. At that time it was regarded as progressive, as they called it, in 1970–1972. Today it would be regarded as normal.

At that time too, I also got some sisters, religious sisters, to teach in the minor seminary. Again it would be regarded as normal today, but at that time it was not. Not in Africa.

---

[4] Pope John Paul II's encyclical on *The Mother of the Redeemer* (*Redemptoris Mater*), published on March 25, 1987, speaks of Mary in her relation to Christ and the Church.

[5] Pope John Paul II's *Letter to Women*, published on June 29, 1995, on the occasion of the Fourth World Conference on Women, held in Beijing, the People's Republic of China. Seven years earlier, the Pope also issued the apostolic letter *On the Dignity and Vocation of Women* (*Mulieris Dignitatem*), published on August 15, 1988.

Q. *You saw at that time the importance of having women in these positions.*

A. I was convinced. I was convinced. Also with those seminarians aged eleven to eighteen, with a good woman on the staff, not too many but one or two, it helped to balance their character; and also because the priest must deal with men and women.

Q. *When the Council ended, on December 8, 1965, you went back to Nigeria, and then, I imagine, you tried to implement the Council's teaching in your diocese.*

A. Yes, but I must not give the impression that it was I who was the chief catalyst, and the one who was getting people to act. No, the Church is much bigger than I, and I am not the center. In any case, at that time I was auxiliary bishop of Onitsha.

But I have a very clear memory that when we returned home, Archbishop Heerey, C.S.Sp., to whom I was auxiliary, was a very kind man, and he was then seventy-five years of age. He said to me, "It is very good, we will now have to discuss with our priests and so on about the Council." I said to him, "Your Grace, would you want meetings of the priests in various zones of the archdiocese?" He said, "Yes", and then he asked me to conduct the meetings.[6] I was very happy to do so, and being auxiliary bishop, I wasn't overburdened with administration.

So I was happy to go through the Council's documents with the priests, because the priest has a key place in the Church.[7] The priest is nearer the people than the bishop is; he is with them every day, and especially on Sunday. He baptizes them, he catechizes them. He says Mass for them every week. He is there at their weddings. When they die, he is there at their bedside and at their funeral. If we are to have priests, or brothers or nuns, or young people well prepared, then we cannot forget the role of the priest. Vatican II said so expressly in the document on the training of seminarians. The very beginning of *Optatum Totius* says that, of all the things the Vatican Council desired to improve in the Church, the first one was the formation and training of the correct type of priests, because the priests' role is crucial. I remember that aspect.

[6] In 1965, the Catholic population of Onitsha archdiocese was 302,664 people; the archdiocese had 63 missionary priests and 14 African priests, according to the Vatican Yearbook (*Annuario Pontificio*).

[7] At this time too, Bishop Arinze wrote a booklet, *Towards Christian Unity*, published by the Archdiocese of Onitsha, 1966.

There were also a few seminars that the bishops organized across diocesan frontiers. That was the start. Then we had to get the documents. When I myself became archbishop, after the civil war, I got a copy of the Vatican II documents for them; every priest had to have a copy. I made sure of that. And for the religious houses of sisters too, I said: "One house, one copy." I also sat many times with the religious sisters, because to be informed is the first thing before further action. And then the sixteen Vatican II documents were so rich, none of us can boast that we know them all.

The Vatican II documents also inspired what I got going in the archdiocese: to have a laity council at the diocesan level, with a constitution, and then on the parish level too, again with a constitution, to have a parish council. Up to then we had committees in parishes, but there was nothing written and they went along doing what they thought best. I got it all written down. And then a pastoral council for the archdiocese as such where there would be priests, men and women religious, and the lay faithful; and, of course, a priests' council.

For every one of these I simply got people to discuss a draft constitution. A draft was made, it was distributed, and it was discussed many times, until there was general agreement. Even though I knew that as archbishop I could write it up, I knew it wouldn't be healthy. If the people involved in it discussed the constitution themselves, and they saw the reasons for every paragraph, then you would have greater hope of fruit. And I could see it worked.

It really worked. For example, on the parish councils, it was very important, as I said, that there must be a term of office, so that nobody would be a life member, always there, and you have no honorable way to change the person. So I insisted on all of them: term of office, three years; repeat, if possible, three years; after that, no. No matter how capable the person is, he must not hold the same office for a third term consecutively.

The aim was to give more people a chance to be trained as leaders, to get another style, to reduce attachment and selfishness, and personality cult, and also stagnation. Because no matter how good a person is, after some time a bit of a change is welcome to everyone. But it is difficult to ask a person to go, if there is no honorable way by which you can say according to this section of the constitution you can't have another term.

That has worked out very well, and also helped to build up leaders, because especially among the lay faithful you need to build up leaders. If not, the lay people can be many in number, but they will not be as effective as they could be, and as they should be. Also you know the usual temptation of the lay faithful, thinking that the priests will take all the initiatives and the lay faithful will obey. Not that it is the ideal at any time, but it was more or less the practice, let us say, forty years ago, in many countries. Everybody sees that has to change, and in any case in the world of today, whether you call it democracy or whether you call it people's participation, or involvement, or whatever name you call it. For us in the Church, democracy is a secular concept, but there is no doubt that the values it incorporates are precious, that the people take part in the affairs that concern them. You don't just do things for people, but let the people do it with you: then it's healthier.

Q. *It's also a different style of governing a diocese.*

A. Definitely. When I was archbishop all those years, many things were achieved; sometimes people were praising me, but I knew that it was not really I who had the original idea; some were originated by a priest, or by a layman, or a lay woman, or a sister. Whoever originated a good idea, whatever seemed good, I welcomed it and encouraged the person; and if the thing worked out well, all of us rejoiced. That person will know, in his heart, that he originated it and will realize that his suggestion was taken seriously. It helps very much. And if it fails, well, who are we? We accept that it didn't work, and we look for another solution; and I will not victimize the person for suggesting something that I supported and that led to failure; if I discourage such a person, next time they will all run away.

Q. *So that was an important step because that was how you took the Council back home.*

A. I was convinced of that, and the Vatican documents said that expressly. Indeed, they even said—I think it is paragraph 31 of *Lumen Gentium*[8]—that the clergy should allow the lay faithful that freedom which belongs to everyone in this earthly city. This means that the Council was afraid that priests would keep too much to themselves and not leave enough initiative to the lay faithful. It's very clear in that document, because the Church has suffered because of the clergy doing too much and the lay faithful not enough.

---

[8] Vatican II's Dogmatic Constitution on the Church.

Q. *So you give responsibility to the laity?*

A. Yes. Definitely. And in Nigeria it has worked well. The lay faithful, for example, the Catholic women's organizations, have worked very well, encouraged by Vatican II, and have developed written constitutions. Likewise the Laity Council at the national, ecclesiastical provincial, and diocesan levels has worked well.

It has brought a lot of good and encouraged leadership qualities in people. You would be surprised what people can do if they are given a chance, and if they are given responsibility. Some will fail, of course, but some of us clerics fail too. Some bishops fail, some priests fail—it is not only the laity who fail.

Q. *Was the Nigerian Bishops' Conference set up then, or did it come later?*

A. It was beginning in a small way at the time I was made bishop in 1965. In those days bishops' conferences were not really very strong all round the world, except in a few countries. In Africa, the Association of Member Episcopal Conferences in Eastern Africa (AMECEA) was famous, that is one of the earliest in all of Africa. Nevertheless, Vatican II really encouraged national bishops' conferences and also regional ones.

We began, too, in Nigeria, though obviously there was collaboration among the bishops before. Before Vatican II it didn't take the form of a written constitution, but Vatican II made it so, and gradually it began and was reinforced more and more with a central office that has been a credit to the Church in Nigeria. The central office or secretariat was first in Lagos and is now moving to Abuja, the federal capital. Inspired by the original vision of Vatican II, the Nigerian Bishops' Conference has been strengthened more and more with the passing of years.

Since Vatican II, the various organs of the Church, beginning with the Holy Father, have encouraged national bishops' conferences and regional ones. And this is very healthy.

Apart from the national bishops' conferences in the various countries in Africa, we have, of course, the continental symposium—the Symposium of Episcopal Conferences of Africa and Madagascar (SECAM). And we also have regional ones; up until now there have been nine of them: northern Africa, eastern Africa, Egypt and Ethiopia, southern Africa, Cameroon, central Africa, Zaire, Rwanda-Burundi. Then in West Africa there were English- and French-speaking regional conferences but, in November 2000, the bishops of these two regional conferences got together in Ouagadougou, Burkina Faso, and decided to fuse into one regional conference for West Africa.

Q. *You were there at that meeting.*
A. I was. It was a very happy event. And in spite of the barriers of language, the bishops saw that there's not such a great difference between our peoples, and some of the borders that the colonialists established divided peoples of the same ethnic group. So the bishops decided that it might be as well to have one conference for all of West Africa. This type of tendency shows the Church is alive also in our times. We thank God for all that.

Q. *Were you the first president of the Nigerian Bishops' Conference?*
A. No, I was not, by any means. When it was beginning in a small way, and that was at the time of Vatican II, Archbishop Charles Heerey, C.S.Sp., my predecessor in Onitsha, was president. Later Archbishop Ageey, of Lagos, became president, and after him Bishop Dominic Ignatius Ekandem, of Ikot Ekpene, who was made cardinal in 1976, became president. Then, after his two terms of office, I was elected in 1979 and was president for two terms, but during my second term, I was transferred to Rome.

Q. *And you were president of the conference when Pope John Paul II made his first visit to Nigeria in 1982.*
A. Yes, I was.

Q. *Did you know him at Vatican II, which you both attended?*
A. No. I was perhaps too young to have known him particularly then. He was not a cardinal then either, but Paul VI made him a cardinal soon after Vatican II, in 1967. So I did not know him at Vatican II. But I got to know him soon after at the Synods of Bishops.

Q. *The first Synod of Bishops was held in 1967;*[9] *were you at that too?*
A. Yes. I was there in 1967, in the name of the bishops of Nigeria, who elected me.

---

[9] The 1967 synod issued two documents: the first, on dangerous opinions and atheism (*Ratione habita*), on October 28, 1967; and the second, on the ministerial priesthood (*Ultimis temporibus*), on November 30, 1967.

Q. *And you attended many other synods too, I think.*

A. Yes, I attended the 1969 Synod,[10] when Nigeria was in civil war. That time the Pope named me. But all the other times I was elected by our bishops' conference, and so I attended the 1971 [11] synod and the 1977 synod, but I was not part of the 1974 synod.[12]

But I was at the 1977 synod. The 1977 synod followed the line set at the 1974 synod and gave its conclusions to the Pope. Later, Pope John Paul II issued his first post-synodal apostolic exhortation, *Catechesis in Our Time (Catechesi tradendae)*, on October 16, 1979. I got to know Cardinal Wojtyla very well, and the following year he was elected Pope. So I got to know him through the synods, not through Vatican II.

Q. *In actual fact you attended many more synods. The record shows that while you were still in Nigeria you also attended the synod in 1980. And after you came to work in the Vatican you participated in almost all the synods: the extraordinary synod of 1985; the Synod on the Laity in 1987; the synod in 1990; the first Synod on Europe in 1991, after the collapse of communism in Eastern Europe; the Synod on Africa in 1994; the Synod on Lebanon, 1995; the American Synod, 1997; the Synod on Asia, 1998.*

A. Yes, I think you are right!

---

[10] The 1969 synod focused on collegiality.

[11] The 1971 synod issued the important document on justice in the world (*Convenientes ex Universo*), on November 30, 1971.

[12] The 1974 synod, like most of those that followed, issued only an interim statement or "message". It handed its conclusions to Pope Paul VI, to issue a definitive statement in the light of the synod's deliberations. Paul VI then issued the post-synodal apostolic exhortation *Evangelization in the Modern World (Evangelii Nuntiandi)*, on December 8, 1975.

Chapter 6

The Nigerian Civil War

(1967–1970)

Nigeria gained independence in 1960. Seven years later, the civil war started and cost the lives of one million people of all ages. Most died from hunger, starvation, or illness linked to these, but many also died on the war front. It was the first of the civil wars in African countries that have bloodied the post-independence period. For the newly appointed Archbishop Arinze of Onitsha, it was a baptism by fire. He was the leading Catholic bishop in what was then known as Biafra.

Twenty-eight years after the civil war ended, I asked the cardinal for his memories of this period.[1]

---

[1] The interview took place on April 4, 1998. It was part of that long interview that I recorded soon after the beatification of Father Tansi (March 22, 1998).

Q. *I'm sure you have many vivid memories of the Nigerian civil war. I'd like to hear some of your reflections on this whole period. Perhaps we could begin with your appointment as archbishop of Onitsha. Am I right in saying that you began your ministry as archbishop on the very eve of the civil war?*

A. Yes, I was named archbishop just a week before the actual war broke out. I was made assistant bishop in August 1965. Then two years later Archbishop Heerey died, on February 7, 1967. And, on June 26, that same year, Pope Paul VI appointed me archbishop of Onitsha. A week later the civil war broke out.

We did not even have time for the usual ceremony installing a new archbishop. But we did a quick ceremony for canonical effects; there was only one other bishop present, Bishop Joseph Whelan, bishop of Owerri, and the five archdiocesan consultors. They read a document and got me to sit on the bishop's seat as archbishop. That was all, because the war was beginning. No members of my family were present. We did the big ceremony more than three years later, after the war. So it was a rough start, if one may use that expression.

Q. *Am I right in saying that when the civil war broke out you were then the leading Catholic bishop, the principal Catholic figure in what was then called Biafra?*

A. Yes, in the sense that at that time in Nigeria there were three ecclesiastical provinces: Lagos for the western part; Kaduna for the northern part; and Onitsha for the eastern part. It is that eastern part, co-extensive exactly with the ecclesiastical province, that declared itself politically Biafra. The Church had no hand in that; it was the decision of the military people. That eastern part was declared Biafra, and it was against this that the rest of the federation started the war, the civil war that lasted almost three years. The rest of the federation shrank the area of that part until it was so small that it finally surrendered.

Q. *I imagine you saw the war coming. I mean, a war doesn't come overnight. There are clear signs. The situation was deteriorating, so you must have been aware of what was going to happen.*

A. We saw it coming. We saw it coming because there were massacres of people from the eastern side in other parts of the Nigerian Federation the year before, in 1966. Before that there was a coup d'état in which people from many parts, especially the north, were killed; mostly military people, but some civilians too. So because of all these things there was killing, especially of Ibos, but also of other people.

In any case it was a military government then; one coup, and then another one. And then the military governor of that eastern part discussed with the rest, and after many months of disagreement that part, the eastern side, declared itself independent, calling itself Biafra. Therefore one could say we saw the war coming, even though everybody hoped it would not come.

Still you could see the suffering in society, the disruption, and the great gap between the military leaders. Therefore when the war began it was not a total surprise.

Q. *You knew the military leaders?*
A. Yes, but only one. The one governing our side, Colonel Ojukwu, certainly I knew that one; but the other ones I had never even met, but we just used to read about them in the papers.

Q. *What are the things that stand out in your mind from that period? I mean, three years is a long time in a war, you must also have seen a lot of things.*
A. Oh, many. . . . As an archbishop, one of my first concerns was: How does it affect the people? Before the war began there were already refugees who came back from other parts of Nigeria, and so there was a high concentration of people. One saw the suffering of the people and wondered what could be done. What could be done for them? And while there had been a lot of relief, and individuals had been contributing relief supplies (food, medicine, clothes), when the war broke out then there were many more refugees. Whenever the war touched any part of Biafra, the people ran to another part. That was one major concern.

I will never forget one Irish priest then; he is still alive—Father Anthony Byrne ("Tony" Byrne we used to call him). He was in charge of our social services at Onitsha and was a very good priest, intelligent. The idea struck me to send this priest to Rome to seek advice on what to do, and how to help the suffering people. At that time, I hadn't known about Caritas Internationalis. This priest made the contacts, and that is how the relief work began for the refugees. He later wrote a book called *Airlift to Biafra*.[2] I received the book at the end of 1997, and I read it with great interest.

He contacted many people at Caritas Internationalis, the secretariat of state, and good people in Germany. The relief work began and went on right through all that war, so much so that the Protestant agencies also joined in, and Catholic and Protestants formed what they called Joint Church Aid, bringing medicine, food items, clothes into what was then Biafra. Even by flights at night; some nights ten flights, twenty flights. On good nights when there were no bombings, forty flights from Libreville, just an hour's flight from that area; or from São Tomé, the island of Fernando Póo. That's how it all began. Generous people around the world, when they saw these pictures of starving children, gave a lot of money. So that was one major area.

Indeed, the Catholic Church's work then began to graduate from just being a welfare department in the General Catholic Secretariat in Lagos, and in the other dioceses, to become the Social Development Department. Many parents named their children *Caritas*, because they saw that it was the relief supplies that saved the lives of their children during the war.

That was one major area where the Church had to be 100 percent present; also providing for people in makeshift schools and looking after them with religious services. That was one area.

Another area concerned the missionaries. Missionaries of various ages; some older missionaries could not stand the bombing and having to run away at short notice and settle elsewhere. I encouraged those who could not stand it to leave, and they left. But most of the missionaries stayed with us and suffered with us all throughout the war. It was a wonderful witness; a wonderful witness by missionary priests and sisters. And often these missionaries were "the voice of the voiceless" when they came on vacation to Europe, because they were believed better than Nigerians or Biafrans because they were as objective as you could hope to get.

---

[2] Anthony Byrne, *Airlift to Biafra* (London, 1997).

The missionaries fulfilled a major role, even though at the end of that civil war the central government in Lagos sent away the missionaries who had stayed with the Biafrans all the way through the war. It was a big blow to the Church in what had been Biafra and a big blow to the missionaries who had spent their whole lives there. But their suffering was rewarded by God, because very soon the Church they left behind began to flourish with local vocations such as we never had before. So we talk about a boom of vocations, precisely there where the people had suffered so much.

Imagine Onitsha Archdiocese: at the beginning of that civil war in 1967, we had about eighty priests, of whom about fifty were missionaries and thirty were local priests. After the civil war all the missionaries were withdrawn; not one remained; so at that time I would have had about thirty-three priests, mostly young priests. I appointed some as parish priests of two or three parishes. Two were studying in Rome; I brought them back home immediately after theology, and I ordained them. I appointed them to be parish priests before their ordination! Their parish-ioners attended their ordination, and two weeks later they moved into the parish to run the parish. One of those priests was later selected as the promoter of the cause of Father Tansi, and he is still there; I selected him in 1978 or '79, so he has been there about twenty years doing that. They have done well.

I was really in admiration as I watched those young priests, some running two or three parishes without much experience. There were no curates. Every priest was a parish priest. But by the time I left Onitsha for Rome in 1984, we had about 150 priests in the archdiocese.

The sisters too—the Nigerian sisters—did very well (all the Irish sisters were asked to leave the area). There were very few sisters remain-ing, and some sisters who had been running small maternity clinics in the villages were now made matrons of major hospitals, and they really succeeded. They are leaders. That area is a tale of joy and heroism, which perhaps the outside world knows very little about. It gave me great joy, but it also meant a lot of work, organizing, running from place to place.

The very Onitsha, where I was archbishop, was one of the first places to be destroyed. Houses burned. People fled. Belongings were lost. I was at the Synod of Bishops in Rome in October 1967, at the time when Onitsha was overrun. But thanks to the missionaries who were there at the cathedral we didn't lose the archdiocesan records, because they brought out all the documents. We lost many of our vestments and other things, however. The archbishop's house was burned down. Three years later, in 1970, I came back to see it. It was burned. The cathedral was not burned, but it was considerably damaged.

On my return to Onitsha Archdiocese from Rome in November 1967, I fled to one place—Umuchu—but later I found that it was too far for the priests to reach. So I fled to another place, Adazi, a parish, and I just announced to the parish priest that I was coming down to make it my headquarters. He did his best.

At one moment, I decided to divide the documents and belongings and put them in six different places so that all would not be destroyed at the same time. If the war came to one area, I went there and brought out the stuff from there, and we put it in other places. We kept doing that sort of thing during the three years' war.

One day at Easter 1968, the war reached Adazi, the place that I was using as my headquarters, so we had to run away. The first bullets began to fall and killed people before the soldiers actually arrived, so you had a space of about two hours to move everything out. We were doing that sort of thing for the three years, and yet we were also organizing bishops' meetings.

There were areas not touched by the war. But our archdiocese was affected very much; though still never the whole of it, because we always had parishes in the rural areas, and I was able to move from one place to another.

Q. *So you were a bishop on the run?*
A. Yes . . . in a way it was exciting, but it is not a thing I would like to repeat!

Q. *Were you ever nearly killed?*
A. Yes. There was one day in 1968 when we were visiting the bishop in Umuahia, with the papal emissaries who had come from Caritas Internationalis to see the refugee situation. The emissaries were Monsignor George Roschau, from Secours Catholiques, in France, and Monsignor Dominic Conway, later bishop of Elphin, from Propaganda Fide, in Rome.

I brought them to Umuahia, another diocese, to visit the bishop, and there was an air raid on the city at that very time, so we were hiding under the steps of a priest's house. Our feet were shaking because buildings were being blown up in that town at that time. But I was not killed, that's why I am still around. But some were killed. I knew a priest who was killed in an air raid in the middle of Umuahia in 1968, Father Wilfred Ude-Umeobi.

Q. *Were you ever made a target, because in a sense Christianity and specifically the Catholic Church were identified with the Biafran leadership and aspirations?*

A. No, I was never singled out as a target but, particularly in the situation of an air raid, one always ran the risk of getting killed.

The war was not religious; it was mainly inter-ethnic envy and disagreements; economic hunger, because the petroleum was mainly in the area called Biafra, not exclusively but mainly. And then there were quarrels among the military men: mainly political, economic, military, not religious. There were Catholics in other parts of Nigeria too, and there were Christians in both armies, even though it was true that there were more Catholics in what was then Biafra. That was true. But to call it a war against Catholics—NO! To call it a war against Christians—NO! It was not that. Even General Gowon, who was head of the government in Lagos, was a Christian, not a Catholic, but a Christian. And it was also proved by this fact that although some churches were destroyed by the bombings, the soldiers really didn't go out to destroy churches as such. No! I suppose they threw their bombs, and they didn't know where they fell.

Also, after the war, I went with my secretary on paths we could not reach before. I met the Nigerian soldiers, and they were very good to me. They were not harsh at all, and they knew who I was. I told them who I was. One day one such soldier snatched my car from one of the brothers living with me—the Brothers of Saint Stephen—but later my car was returned that day, at nighttime. I was told later, after Biafra had been defeated, that soldiers used to snatch cars in the first two weeks after the defeat; they snatched cars to use for military purposes, and the supervisor asked the soldier: "Whose car is this?" He replied: "The archbishop's", and they told him: "Return it to him immediately!"

So they weren't out to get us. Again that time when the missionaries were rounded up to be sent away, I decided to go and see the head of state in Lagos—General Gowon. I got a flight on the military plane; it was the only one available. But some people were afraid that I might be detained. I went there. He was very good to me. He listened to me. He said it was government policy to send away the missionaries, but he was not against the Church.

Q. *But General Gowon sent the missionaries away. Did he explain to you why he did this? I imagine that you were arguing for them to stay? What really happened in that discussion with him on this issue?*

A. He said to me, "These missionaries must go. You should run the Church with your own Nigerian priests."

And then also I found out that he knew that the Catholic Church in Biafra did not identify with the political question but kept out of it, and looked after refugees. I saw he was well informed. So there was no problem for the Church as Church. It was very encouraging to me because it showed me the necessity that, when there is a conflict, bishops must be very careful to keep to the Gospel area, the mandate we have from Christ: love of one another, human rights, social assistance, refugees. Excellent. That's one area. But as for political formulae, we have no mandate from Christ. As individuals we can have opinions, and that is right, but as bishops we have no opinion.

Bishops, therefore, should not come producing political formulae for solutions of inter-ethnic and national questions. As individuals they have every right to have opinions, but if they voice that opinion it would be regarded as that of the Catholic Church, and that's serious. The bishop has to be aware that he is spiritual father for many, and the Catholic Church does not impose a political pattern on all her children. The bishop should be able to speak on Sunday to people who have different political affiliations. The people should be able to recognize in him their common father. This explains also why the Church would not like the bishop, or the priest, to engage in party politics—because it becomes difficult for that priest or bishop to be spiritual father to those who disagree politically with him.

The mandate Christ gave us is very difficult. When Christ came, he also met a political situation—the Romans were ruling the Jews—but he did not organize a resistance group. Even when he multiplied bread and fish and the people were so happy they wanted to make him their king, he ran away; he did not want this. They wanted him to be minister of economic affairs. He did not accept. His Kingdom was very different. The temptation can be very strong; it should be resisted. Then the Church can work with any regime. Whether Biafra should be independent or not; whether Nigeria should be integral or not; whether you should carve out one state, two states, three states, or two hundred states; as a bishop I have no mandate; as an individual I can have an opinion.

Q. *So when you went to General Gowon and spoke with him, you discovered that he understood this very well?*

A. Yes, and I said that to him. And then I saw that he monitored our activities in Biafra and that he knew that the bishops did not adopt what I call a political formula. So he had no difficulty with me. I left him knowing that the federal government was not against the Catholic Church as such.

Q. *Let's step back a little to the beginning of the war. What did the Church do when the war broke out? What did you do? Did you call together your priests and bishops ?*

A. I wouldn't remember every detail, but the bishops of the whole of Nigeria—both Nigeria and Biafra, perhaps thirty of us— before the war broke out, made many appeals to the military leaders to solve the problems by discussion. Many appeals. The bishops conferred at the national level in all Nigeria. That was clear; we did that all along. Then, I think, we also did it together with all the Protestant leaders.

When the military people made Biafra separate from the rest of Nigeria, we did what we could within Biafra. We were eight bishops— Bishops James Moynagh, S.P.S., John Cross Anyogu (who died in July 1967), Joseph Whelan, C.S.Sp., Brian Usanga, Anthony Nwedo, C.S.Sp., Thomas McGettrick, S.P.S., Godfrey Okoye, C.S.Sp., and myself.

We often met to discuss inner Church matters, or services to refugees, which began to increase. So when the relief flights began—Church-organized—obviously it meant much more common action within the dioceses, within what was then Biafra. Plenty of meetings, and many under difficult circumstances because sometimes we hadn't even enough gasoline—then you had to travel under harsh conditions—but it worked. Priests also held meetings, often to see how best to continue the ministry under war conditions, with which none of us had experience.

Oh, yes, we had many such meetings. Also on how to minister to soldiers, and I remember I did confirmations even in soldiers' camps.

Q. *In the military camps of the Biafran army?*

A. Yes. And we had to appoint military chaplains, and they did good work. Of these priests, one of them was killed at the war front, a very fine priest—Father Paulinus Ezike, C.S.Sp.

Q. *Did you see many people being killed?*

A. I didn't. But a military chaplain must have, because he was near the war front. I did not because I did not come so near to the war front. But I saw the wounded, people in hospital—yes; both civilian and military. I saw those, yes.

Q. *But in the bombings . . . you saw people killed?*
A. Yes, but that was after the bombings. I was never so near a place being bombed that I would see them wounded immediately . . . but in hospital, afterward, yes.

But you must know that most of the people didn't die in the bombings. The soldiers who died died at the war front. It was more the case that hunger killed many children. Hunger, lack of food . . . just that; or sickness, they were sick, and there was no proper medicine. Or both.

Q. *So you visited a lot of places where people had no food?*
A. Yes, and then to see the arrangements being made to look after them.

Q. *Do you mean that you supervised these arrangements and made sure that they functioned?*
A. Yes. I did that through priests and sisters. Every parish priest helped. Many refugees were housed in temporary schools; these schools were simple structures, some of them with walls, others with walls only halfway up, and the refugees stayed in them. Many of them were the same buildings that we used as churches. Many of them didn't have a separate church building and a separate school building; it was the same building for both. So it made that aspect of Church life come into great prominence in a way it never had before. It was the dimension of social assistance.

Q. *How many died in the war?*
A. It is difficult to tell, because there wasn't a scientific way of estimating. Certainly more people died of hunger and sickness, generally related to hunger, than died in the actual war front. But soldiers also died at the war front. I have no way of knowing the number. Some talk of about one million or more children dying, and old people. They died from hunger and sickness, or both.

Q. *What was it like to go in and minister to such people, especially to children who were dying of hunger?*

A. Among the refugees there was that sickness called *quashiorkor*. I hear the name originally came from Ghana. To see them in what we used to call sick bays (that means makeshift centers—they didn't deserve the name "hospital") where people are given partly food, partly medicine. But there were people who were definitely hungry, also sick. Often the sickness came from hunger too. It was a sorry sight to see them, especially the children, their lungs all out, and in the worst case they had got swollen limbs, swollen hands and feet. Others looked just like bare skeletons. All through it was a very painful sight.

The relief organizations, the Church ones also, did wonderful work; flying out some of the more serious cases of children to the island of Fernando Póo, and Libreville in Gabon. I understand that some of the children flown out later came back healthy, and some have become priests since then. But that is already thirty years ago.

Q. *At the time of the civil war, you attended two Synods of Bishops in Rome; the first when the war was about to begin, the second in the middle of the war.*

A. Yes. I attended the synod in October 1967, in the name of the bishops of Nigeria who elected me. That was the time the civil war was beginning in Nigeria, but, before it broke out, I was elected by the bishops' conference to represent them at the synod, and so I attended it.

In 1969, Nigeria was in civil war. I was in the Biafran part, and the bishops' conference elected a bishop from the other part. Then the Holy Father nominated me so that the bishops in the Biafran part would know something about the synod too. This time the Pope named me; but all the other times I was elected by our bishops' conference.

Q. *But the fact the Pope named you to the synod in 1969 was impor-tant, because it gave you the opportunity to brief him personally on the situation in Biafra.*

A. Yes. Well, obviously, as the civil war was still going on, I could not come to Rome and say nothing at all about the suffering of our people. Not in the synod, however. I asked for an opportunity to speak with the Holy Father's assistants, his immediate assistants, and the Holy Father himself, who did everything he could to help the suffering people.

Q. *What memory do you retain of Pope Paul VI and his attitude to the war?*

A. He was a person who was very deep and concerned about people. He showed great concern about people's sufferings.

I remember during the Nigerian civil war, during the coffee break at one of the sessions of the Synod of Bishops, he was there with all the bishops wanting to greet him.

I greeted him and said, "Holy Father, pray for our people who are suffering."

He said, "*Che cosa posso fare? Che cosa posso fare?*" (What can I do? What can I do?) I remember the expression, "*Che cosa posso fare?*" He said it two or three times. It was lovely coming from him.

Q.   *He knew the country, of course.*
A.   Yes, he had been there in 1962. But even if he hadn't been there, there was the nuncio, Archbishop Luigi Bellotti, and there were the bishops to inform him. The Holy Father had very many ways of know-ing what the real situation was. And he did everything possible to help, at every level; at the political level and, especially, at the level of assistance—helping the hungry, the refugees, the sick, the poor, the homeless, but also urging the military men responsible to find a way to resolve problems other than by violence and fighting. I had many reasons to know that.

That same year, in January or February 1969, he invited bishops from the various parts of Nigeria and Biafra; six of us in all: the three archbish-ops in the country, and three more bishops—one from each of the three provinces. He invited us to sit with the people in the Secretariat of State, and we met for about four days in the Vatican. It was a very fruitful meeting.

We had a concelebrated Mass with the Holy Father's secretary of state, Cardinal Cicognani. And, of course, the Holy Father received us in audience. This was all very healthy because the country was at civil war, and the bishops from all parts of the country came together and issued a joint appeal to their people, which was very good because it showed that the bishops didn't identify themselves with the military authorities.

After the meeting, we issued a joint statement,[3] as the civil war raged on. We made a general appeal to the people to lay down their arms. And

[3] The text of the bishops' statement was published in the Vatican's paper, *L'Osservatore Romano* (February 8, 1969), together with the text of Paul VI's talk to the three arch-bishops and three bishops representing the ecclesiastical provinces of Kaduna, Lagos, and Onitsha.

we appealed to the international organizations to help the suffering, the
hungry, and the sick. I thought it was all very good.

Q. *What were the reactions to that joint statement inside Nigeria and
Biafra?*
A. I cannot tell. The war realities absorbed all my attention.

Q. *The Pope appealed to the military men. Do you think they listened
to him?*
A. To what extent they listened, I do not know. But to some extent
they did listen because, for example, the Holy Father, through Caritas
Internationalis, was assisting the suffering people no matter on what side of
the fighting line they were. And the federal government knew that very
well. I even heard that, at the end of that civil war, when the secretary
general of Caritas Internationalis visited Nigeria, the federal government
thanked Caritas "for keeping the Biafrans alive". That means the people on
the other side, whom the government technically called "rebels", because
that was the technical name for whoever did not accept the federation—
even if you were a good person. The federal government thanked Caritas
for keeping them alive because it knew that Caritas sent food and medicines to both sides and did not discriminate against either side.

Q. *I knew that Caritas had sent aid to the Biafran side, but I didn't
know that it had also sent it to the federal side in the civil war.*
A. Ah, yes. Also to the federal side, but of course the government
was not very interested in publicizing that during the war. But I knew
that. Then, at the end of the war, in January 1970, the Holy Father made
a big appeal that all violence and revenge afterward should be avoided.
And the head of the federal government, General Gowon, did his best to
prevent any type of revenge killings.

Q. *Is General Gowon still alive, and have you met him since then?*
A. He is still alive, but no, I have not met him since 1975. Indeed,
he governed the country for quite some years after that civil war. But
later he was ousted from power in a bloodless coup d'état in 1975, while
he was traveling overseas. When he heard about the coup, he went to
England and earned a doctorate at one of the British universities. He was
a young man; he still contributes to the good of the country, and he
speaks on religion.

Q. *What scars has the civil war left in the country?*

A. The one good result it has left, I think, is that people realize that a civil war does not solve problems, but only makes them more acute. Therefore, even though Nigeria has undergone many crises in the last twenty-five or more years, Nigerians, you notice, have no longer had recourse to civil war. It does not mean that there are no more problems, but perhaps both the people and the leaders realize that a civil war is a very negative thing, very destructive.

Then, there is the aspect of poverty. After the civil war, the people in that area that was Biafra lost their savings and were given only a token £ 20 if they operated their bank accounts at all during the whole period of the civil war. So they lost their savings.

Q. *You mean the federal government took it from them as a punishment for the war?*

A. Yes. Only those who did not touch their bank accounts at all during that whole period got back everything they had before. How many were such? Very few. So that was one scar—poverty.

Secondly, it also left scars on the national level: the people in that area—Biafra—felt treated badly by the rest of the federation. I wouldn't say rejected, that would be too strong, but they felt the sense of suffering. Although General Gowon, the head of state during and after the war, did his best to reassure the people then, and he prevented any massacre after that war. That is to his credit. And also to the credit of Pope Paul VI, who often spoke on that.

Q. *Did you personally brief the Pope about the war?*

A. Not on the point of genocide.

Q. *But there were other scars too.*

A. There was also a scar on the feelings of the Igbos; in particular, that they are not allowed into the higher echelons, the higher rungs of national life, in the military and the civil service. Not because there was any law forbidding them, but probably by the fact that they were not there for three years: others were ahead, and then whoever is at the head decides who is promoted where. So that was a scar. But that scar has been healed to some extent, though not entirely. The making of new states in Nigeria since then—there used to be only three or four regions, but there are many, many more now—there are thirty-six states. I think that has helped to make development more local, so, that is something.

Q. *What lessons did the Church draw from the Nigerian civil war?*

A. The Church was reinforced in her conviction that she must be an instrument of acceptance between people of varying ethnic groups. The Church must preach justice, harmony, much like what Pope John Paul II said during his visit to Nigeria in March 1998. The Church must preach reconciliation too, because often people have something to forgive one another, something to ask forgiveness for. The Church must continue to do that. It does not mean that when we preach, everyone will live it, because not even when Christ preached did everybody live it. But we must continue to do so.

Then the Church herself must be a model of universalism, which goes beyond the frontiers of language groups or ethnic groups. Those were some lessons. Definitely.

Also the Church has to learn to do more on the side of what we now call human promotion; vocational schools; of course, ordinary grammar schools as at present, yes, but also vocational schools. Nigeria needs more of that type of training in technical matters because the tendency has been the white-collar job types, where you pass the exams, have certificates, and then look for a job. The Salesians are excellent at vocational education.

Nigerians must learn also to do things themselves and to get trained so that they don't need anyone to employ them, but they can set up their own industries. That presumes many other things: political stability, availability of electricity, water, functioning telephones, and other things, which are not all under the control of one person.

All that is necessary if there is to be development of the whole person, and of the whole people, as Pope Paul VI said in his encyclical *Populorum Progressio.*[4] All that is necessary. You notice that the social doctrine of the Church takes more and more corpus as the years go by; it's more and more vocal. The Church has become more and more vocal in matters touching all those areas of development: life, family, wages, employment, relationship between poor and rich, the destination of earthly goods. It has taken clearer and clearer shape. It's not a new doctrine, but the emphasis is definitely new.

---

[4] Pope Paul VI in his 1967 encyclical letter, *The Progress of Peoples (Populorum Progressio)*, offered a Christian vision of development.

Q. *When you look back at the civil war, are there some things that stick out in your mind now?*

A. Yes. There are some people who appreciate religion more under suffering than when they have everything nice and easy. So some people appreciated the Catholic Church more during that civil war than before, and therefore they respect religion more as a result.

Secondly, suffering brings some people nearer to God. We don't want people to suffer, but when you have everything nice and plentiful and sweet, there is a tendency to forget God. It may not be a coincidence that that area where people suffered most is the area where today we have the highest growth of priestly and religious vocations and commitment to Christianity. It may not be a coincidence.

We have a proverb in my language: "A little bird eats plenty and drinks plenty, and it says to its guardian spirit, 'I am ready for anything now, even for a fight with you.'" That is, when people are well fed and science and technology solve many of their problems, they have a tendency to forget God. We don't agree with the Communists, who say that religion is born out of need; they are wrong. But it is true that the person who is in need thinks of God more often than does the person who has everything available.

Q. *Like the man I met at one of those long gas-station lines on the outskirts of Abuja in March 1998 who said, "Only God can help us here in Nigeria."*

A. Yes, he will think of God more. He suffers more. He sees that human beings are not always able to bring him the required solution. We need God!

Perhaps it is not a coincidence that those who do agriculture, working in the fields, often talk of God more than those who work in factories, because the man who works in the field knows he depends on God for sunshine and rain—in the correct quantity—and for the seasons, regularly, so the summer or the spring should not come and then switch off again and go back to winter, which makes it difficult for some crops. In short, they realize more their dependence on God.

Many children in big cities have not even taken notice of the moon, whether it is a half-moon or a full moon; they do not look up. There are many children in big cities who have not seen a live chicken running around; they see the chicken only at table. They have not much idea of a poultry farm, or what it looks like. So who knows? Who knows? They

have not seen a spring of water, unless they went on a picnic: they have
not seen a spring, where water comes out naturally from a hillside or a
rock, and so on.

Q. *What you are telling me, really, is that the winter of the civil war in
the eastern part of the country has been followed by a kind of springtime in
the Church.*

A. I think so. I would see a connection between them; not because
we want anybody to suffer, but because suffering is one of the best
schools. It is better than reading books. And those who have suffered
have learned much more than those who have read books. Although we
also need to read books!

We have a proverb in my language: "The woman who began
setting up her household or cooking before the younger woman has
more broken earthenware vessels than the younger one." That could
mean that she has more experience, or it could mean that she has
suffered more and met more obstacles, and therefore has learned more,
is wiser than the one who is probably coming straight from school and
has all the answers ready: every point you bring up, she brings up the
solution. The older one is slower to talk because she has suffered more
and learned more.

Q. *If you were to pick out one terrible thing you saw during the civil
war, and one very beautiful or inspiring thing, what would these be?*

A. One terrible thing would be a soldier who was killed, a flourishing young man, one who was a university professor; out of zeal he went
to the war front and was killed. He was a poet too. He was Doctor
Okigbo, of the University of Nigeria, Nsukka. Also, an air raid bomb
that blasted in the center of a city, killing a priest who was doing his
normal work, making his rounds. This happened to Father Wilfred Ude-
Umeobi at Umuahia in 1968, as I mentioned earlier.

Something happy? A mother who gave birth to a baby during that
war named the baby Caritas because she received the relief supplies from
Caritas Internationalis that were filtered through the diocese, and so on.
For her Caritas meant life, otherwise she might not have been alive
anymore, so the child is called Caritas. When that child grows up, people
will have to explain the origin of the name. I told that later to Monsignor
Carlo Bayer, who was secretary general of Caritas Internationalis during
that war and afterward.

Another thing stands out. Heroism on the part of the missionaries, who, you know, stayed with the people no matter what.

And then we learned there were many things we could do without. We learned to take tea without sugar, and since then I don't take any sugar in my tea! And sometimes we hadn't even the tea; we just learned to drink water in the morning and eat some local yam—that would be something like potatoes. Drink water, because there were none of these refinements—things we once thought were necessary. And much else.

Q. *And now looking back at a distance of more than twenty-five years, you are a cardinal here in Rome. It must seem light years away from the civil war and all that you lived through.*

A. Yes, a big difference. But yet when you still see the people who had gone through that suffering, I think they have been seasoned by the suffering; and they have learned things that are not easily learned by reading books. Although we need formal schools too, life, and especially suffering, is the best school—especially learning to do without things. We think that "that" is necessary, and we feel we need "that" and "that" and "that".

But in the midst of that war we also did our best to live normal lives. With the missionaries we played lawn tennis; every Tuesday we met at a certain priest's house at Nnokwa, a little far from the war front. We gathered there and played tennis. Because you have to be alive and sane and normal before you can help the people. And if the bishop or the priest is agitated, then he disseminates that lack of peace. That too I regarded as important. And we tried to keep our seminaries going; we moved them from place to place, even during the war.

Q. *It seems to me that the Nigerian civil war heralded something in post-independence Africa that we have seen repeated in many parts of Africa because it was the first of the major armed conflicts in post-independent states of Africa. Would you agree?*

A. Yes, except that it was a full-blown civil war, and then it lasted three years and was over quickly, and there was reasonable reconciliation afterward. But Congo (Kinshasa) saw violence from the first years of independence. In Sudan the situation is very different; the suffering is much more prolonged, and there is no reconciliation yet; except for the little bits of good news that we hear from time to time. Then

Rwanda-Burundi is totally different again, it was not really a war. It was a massacre. It was a very difficult one to explain.

Then there are tensions in other parts of Africa. In Sierra Leone, it is bad. And Liberia, that was bad too. Those were civil wars, and they were really bad, and they led to a lot of killings and suffering, not to speak of destruction. Especially when you think of Sierra Leone: destruction had one round, then another round. You would almost like to say: Does man ever learn? Does one country not want to learn from another country? Animals learn by instinct. Why do men repeat historical errors already tried?

Nevertheless, Africa must trust in Jesus Christ. With better leadership, with a greater commitment to the Gospel, and with time and patience, Africa will have a happier and more stable future.

Chapter 7

Fostering Religious Life
in the Diocese

(1965–1984)

Archbishop Arinze was a pastor in the Archdiocese of Onitsha for nineteen years. The two previous chapters have given some account of his first five years of ministry as bishop there, while this chapter and the next offer a mere glimpse of what happened over the next fourteen years (1970–1984).

At the beginning of the civil war in 1967, as we have seen, the Archdiocese of Onitsha had about eighty priests; fifty of them were missionaries, the other thirty were local priests, Nigerians born in the country. But when the civil war ended, all the missionaries had to leave the country by government order; not one remained, and the archbishop was left with only thirty-three priests, mostly young, to work with him in the diocese.

The departure of the missionaries "was a big blow to the Church", the cardinal recalled in the previous chapter. "But their suffering was rewarded by God," he noted, "because very soon the Church they left behind began to flourish with vocations, such as we never had before."

That happened as the archbishop moved ahead with great apostolic zeal and determination over the next fourteen years, mobilizing the native clergy, religious, and laity of the archdiocese in the work of evangelization and community building. And, drawing on the considerable experience gained during the war in the field of social assistance to those who were suffering, the archbishop gave his full support to "social development" work in the archdiocese, helping those in need and promoting "the total development of the human person". He also set up a marriage advisory service to help couples and families.

From the end of the civil war onward, the archbishop did the work that most bishops do: he visited parishes; he met with the priests, religious, lay people, and with the Catholic lay associations; he ordained priests, confirmed children and adults; and preached the Gospel. And every year, he wrote a pastoral letter to his flock.[1] *God blessed all these efforts with considerable fruit. By the time the archbishop left for Rome in 1984, the number of Catholics had practically doubled, and "the vocations boom" was in full flood.*[2] *"God's invisible hand" was at work. The full story of these years has yet to be told.*

His main sermons, lectures, and talks from this period have since been collected and published in Nigeria.[3] *This documentation provides a good insight into his pastoral ministry and reflects the wide diversity of concern that came to his attention in those years.*

Those concerns range from Church–state relations; co-responsibility in evangelizing; the Christian and politics; prospects for ecumenism; young people; the Church and state in education; the importance of religion in education; social development through love, justice, and truth; the ministry of service; the laity; the priests; the theologian and the Church's teaching authority; religion for peace; mutual tolerance; influence of non-Christian religions on social and political life; the contribution of the Church to the development of poorer countries; building trust in modern pluralist societies; human rights; the family; marriage; abortion; poverty; corruption and disorder in society. They provide eloquent testimony to his faith and his pastoral work.

In those years too, he also participated in the work of the universal Church by attending the Synods of Bishops in Rome, and through his membership, at different times (1973–1984), in some of the Vatican offices, including the Congregations for the Doctrine of the Faith, the Evangelization of Peoples, the Causes of the Saints, and the Secretariat for Non-Christians, and the Pontifical Commission for Justice and Peace.

---

[1] His pastoral letters are *The Hour of the Laity* (1971); *More Justice for the Poor* (1972); *The Church and Nigerian Culture* (1973); *The Greatest Investment* (1974); *Spreading the Good News* (1975); *Work and the Christian* (1976); *The Christian as Leader* (1977); *The Christian and Money* (1978); *The Child Has Rights* (1979); *The Christian and the Family* (1980); *The Holy Eucharist Our Life* (1981); *The Christian and Politics* (1982); *The Christian and Chastity* (1983); *The Christian as a Citizen* (1984); *In Faith and Prayer* (1985).

[2] According to The Vatican's Yearbook (*Annuario Pontificio*) for 1984, in the Onitsha Archdiocese there were then 564,070 Catholics, out of a total population of 880,000; and 69 diocesan priests, 13 priests from religious orders; 126 women religious, and 57 men religious; and 179 seminarians doing philosophical or theological studies.

[3] These were arranged and edited by Rev. Fr. Lambert Ejiofor, Ph.D., and were published in five volumes, 1,231 pages, in "The Looking for Light Series" (Nsukka, Enugu, Nigeria: Optimal Computer Solutions Ltd., 1990), Book One, *Gospel to Society*; Book Two, *Work and Pray for Perfection*; Book Three, *Spreading the Faith*; Book Four, *Africans and Christianity*; Book Five, *Motherhood and Family Life*; *Blessed Virgin Mary*; *Christian in Christ*.

From 1979 to his coming to Rome in 1984, he was president of the Catholic Bishops' Conference of Nigeria.

One significant aspect of the archbishop's work in those years was his attention to the promotion of the various forms of religious and consecrated life in his diocese, including the founding of a religious congregation. In the present chapter, my questions focus on this work, but I first began by recalling some sad events in his life in this period.[4]

---

[4] Most of this chapter is based on extracts from the interview of April 4, 1998.

Q. *The civil war ended in 1970, and you began the normal pastoral work of a bishop in a diocese. But a year later your father, whom you loved so much, died.*

A. Yes. My father died in 1971, and my mother less than ten years later, in 1980.

Q. *You were an archbishop then, and I presume you celebrated their funerals.*

A. Oh, yes. Our people set great value on attending funerals, and friends make a big sacrifice to be there. Even today it's a wonderful witness. If a priest dies, of course, most priests, not only from his own diocese but also neighboring dioceses, will be there. But even the father of a priest, or the mother or father of a sister, you'd be surprised at the number of priests and religious who would be there, and other people too.

It is wonderful evangelization, because the people see the Church as a family. And in any case it is the tradition of our people, that, really, if you do not come to a person's funeral, it means you don't love that person.

Q. *And some of your family have died since too. I remember I was here one day when one of your brothers died.*

A. Yes. The one you mention was my brother Linus, who wanted to be a priest, the one just three years older than me. He died in 1996.

Q. *You were very close to him.*

A. Yes, of course, of course. And one of his daughters is a religious in one of the Nigerian sisters' congregations, near Onitsha. She was professed just three weeks before he died.

Q. *You mentioned religious life. In fact, apart from the ordinary work of a bishop in a diocese, visiting parishes, confirming people, preaching, and so on, you have also had very close ties with religious orders and congregations. For example, in the mid-1970s, you founded the congregation of the Brothers of Saint Stephen. Could you tell me how that came about?*

A. That was about the year 1976, when the novitiate began. But it had an earlier history.

There was a group of young men, and some not so young, at the cathedral at Onitsha, but they were not a religious congregation; they were a pious union called "Brothers Associate". They were there in 1965, when I was named auxiliary bishop. Much earlier, maybe twenty years before, there was a group of Saint Peter Claver Brothers begun by my predecessor, but later on they could not survive as a congregation, and they were merged with the Marist Brothers. Two or three of them did not join the Marist Brothers, however; they stayed on at the cathedral. Then a few more brothers came and joined them at the cathedral. They were not many—maybe five in all. They wore a type of religious habit, and they were called brothers. The public thought they were a religious order, but they were not; they were a pious union, and they led very edifying lives. Very edifying!

Their leader was one of those who went to the seminary with Father Tansi in 1927–1928. He was called Simon Okoye, but he took the name Michael. I think he must have reached the age of ninety when he died in 1994. He led a very edifying life. I think he also should be in heaven. Perhaps, one day, somebody may decide to promote his beatification cause too. He was not a priest. He was a brother. He had wanted to be a priest, but he didn't succeed. He remained a brother and led a most edifying life. He spent most of his life at the cathedral at Onitsha, assisting the priests. He was a kind of catechist. He was most reliable. He was a witness, and he inspired many people to live good Christian lives, and who knows whether he didn't do more good than some priests. Only God knows that.

When I became archbishop in 1967, I saw these men. And then some more young men told me they too wanted to become brothers. I discussed the matter with some priests: How can we have them just as a pious union? Where is their future? Suppose we get another bishop or a priest at the cathedral who says, "I don't believe in these brothers", then what happens to them?

I kept thinking about it, and toward the end of our civil war (1969–1970), I got a clear idea: they have to become a religious congregation, so that I could have the heart to take younger people in with a future promised them. I then got some priests to work on the idea; I gave them the major points and asked them to work on what they thought. Finally, after receiving and considering their report, I decided to call them the Brothers of Saint Stephen, because Saint Stephen was with the apostles and the other deacons. They were not to be deacons; but they were to be with the priests, doing whatever was possible to relieve the priests so that the priests could concentrate on other matters.

Then, I wrote the constitution. I consulted, of course, Rome too. I think it was in 1977. I sent my request to Rome, and they said, "You go ahead. When you have something like thirty or thirty-five professed brothers you tell us, and then we will approve it officially as a diocesan right congregation. And at that time you bring us a supporting letter from the Nigerian Bishops' Conference." I said, "Very well", and then I went on to accept candidates who applied.

Those who wanted to be brothers tended to be those who already had some vocation or gift: carpenter, mechanic, trader, and so on, not small boys from primary schools who, in any case, tended at the age of eleven or twelve to go on to the seminary. They would be around twenty-five years of age; they would hardly be accepted in the seminary then. Some had not done secondary school at all, but I took them all the same if they seemed serious in their desire to serve God and if they seemed successful in whatever they were doing before, such as electricity, trading, and carpentry. I took them on.

But the aim of the congregation, the chief aim, is catechetics. And their motto is "That they may know you." That is their major assignment. And then they are to be of help to the priest in whatever does not necessarily demand priestly ordination to do: such as run the parish office, teach catechism to people preparing for various sacraments, prepare people for marriage, help families, and then, eventually also, bring Holy Communion to sick people because our priests are overburdened, and they help the priest to distribute Holy Communion.

These brothers could be trained also according to special gifts: so one brother was a stenographer, another was trained in building so that we would not have to get a contractor for every church building, or priest's house, or convent and spend a lot of money. Then another brother was trained in printing, and now there is a plan to have a printing press, and brothers would be the chief people working there. That is the type of thing envisaged.

But in their constitution is also included that a few could be ordained priests for the internal service of the congregation, according to the decision of the superior general, and not because the individual wants to become a priest. It is not a congregation for priests, but priests can be designated for it; indeed, the first one was ordained in 1989 as a priest, and he is the only one so far.

When they learned that I was coming to Rome in 1984, they felt sad because they had just been approved by Rome as a diocesan right congregation in 1983, when they had thirty-five brothers. When I was coming to Rome, they did not yet have a superior general, and they were sad, so I said to them, "Okay, I will take two of you with me to Rome, and one of you will be the cook in the house, and the other one will do other jobs in the house, but both of you will be students. You will study in Roman universities, and when you finish your studies, you will come back. And then I'll take two more, and I will continue doing that until the Lord decides differently." So I have been doing that now for fourteen years, and about six of them have come in that way, for an average time of six years, though some for even more.

One of them, for example, did philosophy in the Urbanianum [the Urban University] for two years, and then theology for three years, and then he went on to study spirituality in the Angelicum[5] for two years. Now he is back home and is working in the apostolate and the novitiate. Another one studied liturgical metalwork and learned how to make chalices, ciboriums, how to gild rings, and so on. But when he went home, they found him more suitable as a superior, so he isn't doing that work. Yet another one learned the same metalwork in Germany and is still doing that at home now. Two others studied catechetics in Castel Gandolfo and the Urbanianum, and they are doing that type of work. And another one is running a vocational school.

But most often the brothers are working in parishes, as catechists. Living in twos, they run the parish; everything from catechetical work to the parish office; they are the right hand of the parish priest.

Q. *Are there many brothers in the congregation today?*
A. A little fewer than seventy. It's a difficult vocation. It's difficult because society tends not to understand them. The people ask, "Are you priests?" They say no. Then they ask, "Can you say Mass?" and they reply no. "Oh," the people then say, "is that because you did not succeed in

---

[5] The Pontifical University of St. Thomas Aquinas is also known as "the Angelicum".

passing your exams?" (Which means, you did not have enough brains to become a priest. That means, because you couldn't get the big one, you satisfied yourself with the small one)—that is the mentality of many people, and even of some priests too.

Now this is not correct as a mentality because it means that such people do not understand what the Catholic Church means by religious life, the consecrated life as a monk, as a nun, as a brother, or as a sister if they are outside monasteries; or even newer forms of consecrated life in the Church today where some have vows but they do not live in community, or even if they live in community they may not even be technically called brothers or sisters as, let us say, in the secular institutes. There are many types.

There are a variety of forms of consecrated life. Take the ordinary religious life that we know: there are the brothers of Saint Francis, who are very many: Capuchins, Friars Minor, and Conventuals—they are not necessarily priests, although many are priests. But there are others—the Brothers of the Christian Schools, the De La Salle Brothers, the Marist Brothers—who are not clerical in the sense that they don't come because they want to be priests; they come because they are attracted by that way of following Christ. It is the same with the sisters: we have the Holy Rosary Sisters, the Mercy Sisters, the so-called Blue Nuns; we have so many varieties of them. Now the sisters and the brothers take exactly the same vows, except that the sisters are women and the brothers are men.

It isn't a question of being intelligent and passing exams; it isn't that the intelligent ones become priests and those who pass fewer exams become brothers. That's not a correct way of looking at it. In Nigeria, opinion on this is changing gradually. When people got Marist Brothers running one of our best secondary schools, people said: "Ah, so he is very intelligent and brilliant." The people changed position, but they still said the same thing: "Why if you are so intelligent, were you not ordained a priest?" Very good! The answer to that is the reason why they are religious. So it is not that they are not intelligent.

There are other people who look for power in the Church, and they see the priests as having power, and the bishop as wielding even more power. He comes on Sunday, and he is president of the assembly; and everyone listens to him, even when he gives a sermon that is not very well prepared. And then there are doctors and lawyers and all sit there as his congregation, and you know, ordinary men can be childish, and some people would like that role—to be the leader of the whole group.

But if we read the Gospel and we ask ourselves, what did Christ tell us? He said: "The Son of Man came not to be served but to serve, and to give his life as a ransom for many"; and again he told us, "The Gentiles lord it over them, but with you it shall not be so!"—authority is understood as service by Christ. If a person looks on the priest as primarily someone having power and being on top, that person has not even begun to understand what priesthood is about.

Therefore religious life is a dimension, is an aspect, and is a way of following Christ that should not be missing in any church, anywhere in the world. If there were no religious brothers or sisters in a diocese, something of the life of the Church would be missing there.

We also need that witness . . . and, as one of the brothers used to say to priests, "Fathers, please, see that we also can contribute. There are some people who are afraid to come to you because they regard you as very intellectual and high up. They are worried what to say to you but, in our case, they say: 'Ah, he's just a brother, he's just one of us, he is near us, let us go to him and tell him our problems.'" Therefore the brother can give a witness that a priest cannot give, and that even half a dozen cardinals cannot give because the brother is nearer the people in a way in which the cardinal is not near them, no matter how humble he decides to be.

So the brothers have a role.[6] There isn't a single doubt about that. Also in Nigeria, there is such an intense desire to pass the examinations and acquire university degrees and brandish these, and show off, and write them before one's name. Well, then, we need religious who are not particularly brandishing degrees, not because they are a group of ignorant people, but because they are a group of people who are primarily preoccupied, not with shining as intelligent persons in front of the people, but as witnesses to Christ.

So even though the brothers have a role, one can see from what I have said that it is not easy. Not everyone will have this gift, but those who have it can do a lot of good in the Church. Some people will look down on them but, as I used to say to those Brothers of Saint Stephen: "Nobody can make you feel inferior without your permission. It is only when you yourself accept this idea that you are inferior, then that's

---

[6] The archbishop gave many retreats and spiritual conferences to priests, brothers, sisters, and lay people between 1966 and 1984, and, at the request of the Brothers of St. Stephen, these were collected in a booklet, *Alone with God*, published by the Archdiocese of Onitsha (August 29, 1986).

the time we are in trouble—all of us. But if you do not accept the idea that you are inferior, if you know who you are, if you are at peace because you have understood your vocation, then if all of your brothers and sisters do not understand your vocation, you can at least explain it to them. Even if a particular priest looks down on you, you can explain to him, presuming he is willing to listen. But the question of feeling inferior is primarily to be resolved by the person who laments and says, 'Others are looking down on me.' It is you yourself who are first to ask yourself whether you are at peace with who you are."

Suppose somebody looks down on me and says, "You are black!" I can laugh. I remember once a boy said to me, "You are black." I said, "If that is so, let us see." I said, "You are white." He said, "Yes." I said, "You are not, you are not white." I said, "See my shirt, that's white. Are you like that?" "No." I said, "See my cassock. It's black. Am I like that?" "No." So, I said, "I am not black, and you are not white." He got a shock. I said, "You are pink, and I am coffee brown, or café latte." But, I said, "Is there nothing else important about any of us, except the color of our skin?" So we both laughed, and he began to see the problem in its proper dimensions.

It is only a problem if you accept that you are inferior, that you are no use, and that you become a brother because you couldn't get anything else; it was only a consolation prize you got. If you believe that, then you should get out of the whole congregation or change your ideas. But if you know who you are and are at peace, then you are well positioned to help others and also to explain to those who ask. But it will not be a job of one day! Some will still misunderstand, but some will begin to understand.

There is nothing like a group that knows who they are, knows where they are going, and are at peace about it. Indeed, this shows the reason why many religious congregations or dioceses are not getting new vocations. It is not the only reason, because the lack of children in the family is also a major reason.

But if in an area there are not young people becoming priests or sisters or brothers, those who are already priests or sisters or brothers should look at themselves. Who knows? Perhaps they are contributing to the lack of vocations? What young person wants to join a group of people who do not seem to be happy, who do not seem to know who they are, a group of people who look agitated, a group who are not at peace, a group of people who are criticizing their superiors from morning till evening?

If the priests are criticizing their pope and their bishops, and the religious brothers and sisters are attacking their superiors and are angry with Rome and angry with the Roman Curia and so on, then do you really expect young people to commit themselves to this group for life? You are not serious!

Why is it that Mother Teresa's order has many vocations? I will not forget that, sixteen days before Mother Teresa died, I was in Calcutta, on August 20, 1997. I was there for other reasons; the bishops had invited me to that area, and I asked the archbishop of Calcutta: "I would like to say Mass in the house of Mother Teresa." He arranged it. She was at the Mass, in a wheelchair. Afterward, during breakfast, she didn't eat, but she talked. I asked her, "Mother Teresa, can you tell me why it is that many religious congregations are lamenting that they don't have enough vocations?" She gave me a very eloquent answer, "I do not know because I have not had that problem."

She was really saying three things. First, she was saying, "The Missionaries of Charity have always had plenty of young women who want to join us." Number two, "We never had problems getting people." But number three, her charity: "I do not want to judge those who do not have vocations." She does not want to pass judgment on those who are not being joined by many young people. She only makes a positive statement: that many young people are joining her order and that she never had difficulty in getting young people. As for the rest, it's up to you and me to analyze. It's most interesting.

If I were to be asked questions by those who may be promoting her cause of beatification, if I only give that witness, I would consider that I have contributed much already, because it shows her charity toward other groups. But also her clarity of vision, that is, with her sisters. She helped them to know who they are, where they are going, so that nobody can join them and say, "We do not know where we are going." Oh, they do! That may explain why they get vocations even from Germany and Britain and Italy, where people say there are not enough vocations, or the U.S.A. Why? Not just from India! Don't tell me that they are just joining from India because they have not enough work and from Nigeria because they are underdeveloped. It is not as simple as that.

Q. *I agree with you. I do not think that that is the reason. But to return to our original question, you founded this order of the Brothers of Saint Stephen. Have you founded other orders too?*

A. No! I have no intention of founding any others, just that one. No more! But there were sisters already there when I was archbishop, and I looked after them too, as much as I could. But I saw no need at all to found any other congregation.

There was just that monastery of Benedictine women, which I have already mentioned to you. I only invited an existing monastery in Rome to start a house in the archdiocese. I also invited the Capuchin Friars from Florence, and they began a house, which is now flourishing in Onitsha. But I didn't found them. I only helped them to have a home and then encouraged candidates to join them, but they are on their own.

Q. *You really have had a lot of links with religious life!*
A. Oh, yes. The Capuchins are doing very well; they are now in several dioceses in Nigeria. They have plenty of candidates. I encouraged them to have their novitiate in Nigeria. Not to bring candidates to Italy, except perhaps the first ones, so that the training would be more rooted in the place.

Q. *I was struck by the fact that you wanted to open a Cistercian monastery in the Onitsha Archdiocese. Am I correct in saying this?*
A. Yes.

Q. *Why did you feel the need for this monastery? Was it because of Father Tansi?*
A. I am not the originator. It was my immediate predecessor, Archbishop Charles Heerey, C.S.SP., Irish Spiritan, who had the idea. It was he who sent Father Tansi to the Mount Saint Bernard monastery in 1950.

Q. *But on condition that he come back to Nigeria.*
A. Yes, that was the type of understanding also with Father Mark Ulogu, who had been curate to Father Tansi at Aguleri, in 1949. The hope was that after some years they would come back to Onitsha to start a Cistercian monastery, and sure enough Mount Saint Bernard sent some monks to survey the ground in 1961 or 1962. I remember because I was teaching in Bigard Memorial Seminary; I was teaching liturgy and philosophy. And they came, and one of those who came, Father Luke Harris, is still alive. I saw him in Mount Saint Bernard in December 1997. He had been a pilot in the Royal Air Force, and he is still there in Mount Saint Bernard.

Q. *Do you go to Mount Saint Bernard every time you go to England?*

A. Well, I love to go there. Last December I went there. Indeed, the abbot said, "Come, come and tell us about Father Tansi and the arrangements for the beatification." I had gone there two years before, in 1995, when I went to England for Christmas.

The Cistercians came, invited by Archbishop Heerey, and they surveyed various parts of the Onitsha Archdiocese, but they thought the climate was a bit hot and humid for people from Britain.

Q. *I can well understand that!*

A. As monks in a monastery, they would live their whole lives there, no holidays, and no transfer. So they looked around and inspected other areas, in Jos, and in Plateau State. They liked the area, but the arrangements for land were too slow to go through.

Q. *Do you mean that obstacles were put in their way?*

A. I do not know the nature of the problem. But we heard that land acquisition was difficult.

Finally Mount Saint Bernard decided on Bamenda in the Cameroon; they decided to go there. And they did go there in 1964, soon after Father Tansi died; he was meant to be the novice master there. So they went to Bamenda, but they had not forgotten Onitsha. Meanwhile, Archbishop Heerey died in 1967. I had been his auxiliary bishop for two years (consecrated auxiliary on August 29, 1965), and I was named archbishop the same year (June 26, 1967). I wanted the Cistercians to come, not because of Father Tansi, but because I was convinced of the dimension of contemplation, prayer, sacrifice that monks contribute.

But meanwhile our civil war had begun. I could not do anything then. But when the civil war was over in 1970, and we had begun to live a more normal life in Church and society, I wrote to them. I don't remember if I wrote to Mount Saint Bernard, but I certainly wrote to Bamenda, Cameroon, where they were, and finally they asked me to come. I went there and stayed some days with them and began to ask them if they could come to start a foundation in Onitsha.

In the meantime, a Nigerian priest from Benin, later on Issele-Uku Diocese, Father Anselm Ojefua, together with the bishop of Enugu, Bishop Okoye, began a Cistercian foundation in Awhum, near Enugu.

Q. *I met some of the monks at the beatification ceremony for Father Tansi; there were many of them, and some seemed very young indeed.*

A. Yes. It's to be expected. That monastery has grown. It was not founded from another monastery; it was that priest, a very hard-working diocesan priest, and the bishop of Enugu, who was a Spiritan. This priest began to gather people, and he would visit some Cistercian monasteries in the U.S.A. and elsewhere, but it was not a daughter monastery of any other. Gradually it was looked after, I think, by Genesee Abbey in the U.S.A., because it had to be affiliated to some monastery. That has been a success; that is Awhum, near Enugu.

But still I did not succeed in having a Cistercian monastery in Onitsha. I visited the Cameroon. I did my retreat there, and they said to me, "In principle, we accept coming, but we don't have the numbers yet." Then, toward the end of the 1970s, they came, including the abbot of Bamenda.

They inspected land in Onitsha Archdiocese and finally chose Nsugbe, about six miles from Onitsha. The land was given by Nsugbe people. A certain Catholic from Nnewi was so happy that he said to me, "I will build the first buildings, which will not be the whole monastery, and donate them to you for your silver jubilee as a priest." He gave me the keys of the first buildings in 1983.

Q. *The keys of the Cistercian monastery?*

A. Yes, the monastery in Nsugbe, and the monks in Bamenda began to send monks; not a high number, because they themselves did not have so many, but in principle they approved it. It continues to grow, not as fast as that of Awhum. That then is the Cistercian monastery.

But meanwhile, of course, I plugged for other monasteries. I tried to get the Carmelites from Monselice, near Padua, and they were ready to come, but their superior general overruled them and said no. The Carmelite father general said to me, "You should wait until the Carmelite Monastery in Owerri, founded from Ireland, grows, and then it can make a foundation at Onitsha." I replied, "Look, Father, the Irish have been our missionaries, and they have done very well, but now we need a bit of diversity, so I absolutely want some from Italy now."

Q. *It's very interesting that you felt the need for diversity, to have other experiences.*

A. Yes. I myself, in any case, had done my theology in Rome (1955–1960), so I thought, "Look, I love the Irish, but I also want to add something of the Italian contribution and style." It's better so.

Meanwhile, the bishop of Enugu, Bishop Okoye, a Spiritan, who died in 1977, had tried to get Benedictine nuns to come when he was in the Diocese of Port Harcourt, another diocese. That was before our civil war. Then he transferred to Enugu one of the Nigerian nuns in a Benedictine monastery at Amoji Nike, about six miles from Enugu, near the airport, with the encouragement of Bishop Okoye.

Then there was another Nigerian, who was in a Benedictine monastery in Monte Mario, here in Rome. I spoke with them; and—to make a long story short—they consented to come. In 1978, they sent us four Benedictine nuns, three Italians, and one Nigerian. Now that monastery was begun in Umuogi, about four miles away from where the Pope beatified Father Tansi, just across the little stream. After twenty years, that monastery now has 140 nuns, and they have been able to send nuns to about four monasteries in Italy where they have few new vocations. They have also sent about six nuns to Malta. Indeed, they have begun a new monastery in the Onitsha Archdiocese in a place called Ozubalu; they opened it just before the Pope came, on the feast of Saint Paul, January 25, 1998, because they have the vocations.

Q. *Extraordinary!*

A. I am convinced of the contribution that monasteries can make and should make. The Church is not complete without monasteries.

Q. *That was really what I was trying to get at when I first asked the question, namely, your own perception of the importance of monastic life.*

A. These nuns are doing a fully contemplative life. Some run schools, but not these. They are all within their enclosures; they do manual labor; they have a farm; they have poultry; they make vestments for Mass; they make altar bread; they make cassocks for priests—and, as we have many seminarians, they never lack work. Never. In our place the cassock is just the normal dress for the priest, so these nuns never lack work.

Q. *Did you yourself ever think of joining a contemplative order?*

A. No, not really.

Chapter 8

Working for the Canonization of West Africa's First Native-Born Saint

(1974–1998)

The Blessed Father Tansi had a major impact on the young Francis Arinze. "After God", he attributes his vocation to him. When Father Arinze became archbishop, not many years after Father Tansi's death, he decided not to let the memory of this great man fade away, and for many years he worked, with considerable skill and dedication, to promote the cause of Father Tansi's canonization. He is now only a step away from realizing his goal.

I interviewed the cardinal after the Pope had issued the decree for Father Tansi's beatification, but when it was not yet clear that he would go to Nigeria to beatify him, as happened later, in March 1998.[1]

---

[1] The interview was recorded on November 12, 1996. On the basis of this interview, on the eve of Fr. Tansi's beatification, I published the article "An African Miracle" in *The Tablet*, London (February 28, 1998), pp. 276–77. On March 22, 1998, on the occasion of his second apostolic journey to Nigeria, Pope John Paul II beatified Fr. Tansi. Chapter 15 contains the cardinal's reflections after the beatification.

Q. *Your Eminence, you have helped open the way to the beatification, and the future canonization, of the man who baptized you and inspired you to become a priest. Would you tell me how this came about, and particularly why you considered him a candidate for sainthood?*

A. We used to call him Father Tansi. That was his family name, the name of his father. His baptismal name is Michael, and when he went to the monastery of Mount Saint Bernard, in England, he got the religious name "Cyprian". So now he's called Father Cyprian Michael Tansi.

He had another name too before baptism: Iwegbane or, in short, Iwene; it means, "Let anger not kill." I heard that his father was imprisoned by the British administrators, though he was innocent. And when the boy was born, the father from prison sent the name, "Let anger not kill." Every name in our language has a meaning.

He originated from a town called Aguleri. When we say "a town" in Nigeria, we mean what Europeans would call a group of villages that together would make a town in our country. Aguleri is a group of villages. The people live there; they have plenty of farmland. Actually the land is very rich. And there is a little river passing nearby, the Anambra, and so the land is very fertile.

Father Tansi originated from Aguleri, in the Archdiocese of Onitsha. Today Aguleri is in Anambra State. He was born at the beginning of the century, in September 1903. He died in England, at the age of 62–63, in 1964. Like most of us, his family was not Christian because Christianity was new at that time. His family belonged to the African Traditional Religion, what some Europeans call "animism".

But we don't like that term *animism* because Europeans first used it when they thought that people put a soul into everything—into the trees, the mountains, the rivers. But people don't really put a soul into them. It's just that they believe there is a spirit who looks after that river, a spirit who looks after that mountain, a spirit of thunder who kills people who are bad, and so on. So Europeans thought, "Ah, these people put a soul in everything", so they called the religion "animism".

There is no agreement as to what to call this religion so the people just said African Traditional Religion. In Asia they call them "tribal religions". Whatever we call them, the fact is people believe in God, one God; they believe in spirits good and bad; and they believe in ancestors, which is the happiest element of their religion.

Q. *Was this the same Traditional Religion to which your family belonged at the beginning?*
A. Yes, the same. Indeed, my home would be about twenty miles away from the home of Father Tansi. Not so far away—one could do that on foot or by bicycle. Today we have cars. Then he went to school, and through this school he became a Christian and was baptized. But he had to pass the exam in catechism to be baptized. This was a Catholic school run by the missionaries, the Irish Spiritans, the Holy Ghost Fathers, as we called them then. They did wonderful work through this school.

At that time the colonial British government concentrated on government and trade. There was oil, cocoa in some parts of Nigeria, cotton in some parts too. But the missionaries put heavy emphasis on schools and education. That actually led to all kinds of development: political, economic, cultural, and religious. Not just religious. If Nigerians asked for political independence it is because they had gone to school—primary, secondary, and university. They learned what the world is saying or doing. Then they were in a position to ask for their rights, for political independence.

Iwene Tansi became a Christian through the Catholic school, and later he did a teacher's training college course and became a teacher. It was while he was a teacher that he desired to become a priest. He is one of the earliest in the whole of Nigeria to go to the seminary.

Q. *Was he the first Nigerian to be ordained a priest?*
A. He was not the first. The first Nigerian priest was ordained in 1929, Father Paul Emecheta, from Asaba. The second was John Anyogu, who was ordained in 1930. Father Tansi and two other companions were ordained in 1937.

Q. *So he was in "the top ten"?*
A. Yes, definitely yes. The seminary in which he studied was

opened at Igbariam, not too far from Aguleri, in 1924. He was ordained a priest in the present cathedral of Onitsha in 1937, with two other companions, Monsignor Joseph Nwanegbo, who died in 1965, and Monsignor William Obelagu, who died in 1977. I knew Monsignor Obelagu best; he was my vicar general when I was archbishop of Onitsha. He was the oldest priest in the area; he was an excellent priest.

Q. *What are the significant steps in Father Tansi's life that led to his beatification?*
A. Several. First when he was a diocesan priest (1937–1950) in the Diocese of Onitsha. Then, in 1950, the Holy Year, he went to Mount Saint Bernard Trappist Monastery, in Leicester, England. He lived there for fourteen years, until his death on January 20, 1964.

Q. *Why did he move from the Diocese of Onitsha to Mount Saint Bernard?*
A. Of course, finally only God's grace can explain this. For many years he wanted to be a monk. He had read Dom Marmion's book *Christ the Ideal of the Monk* and other books, and he told the archbishop, my predecessor, that he would like to become a monk.

At that time, Archbishop Heerey was called vicar apostolic because Onitsha became an archdiocese only in 1950, the year Father Tansi went to the monastery. Archbishop Heerey was open to the idea, and he kept looking for a monastery to accept Father Tansi: Mount Mellary and others in Ireland, and some in England. Finally Mount Saint Bernard accepted Father Tansi and another Nigerian priest.

Q. *Did the other monasteries not want him?*
A. I don't know all the details, but Archbishop Heerey, my predecessor, had some difficulty in getting a monastery to accept him. In those days, in the 1940s, you can imagine what it would be for a monastery in Ireland or England to accept a Nigerian who had been a diocesan priest for nearly twelve years. I don't know the details. I was still in the junior seminary at that time. But what is certain is that Father Tansi worked as a diocesan priest in the Diocese of Onitsha from 1937 to 1950. He was known as an ascetic. He was known as a zealous priest. He was known as a great preacher and a great missionary who convinced people. So he had already the reputation for sanctity in those years. He was the first priest I ever knew.

Q. *How did you meet him?*

A. He opened our parish in 1939. He had been an assistant curate at Nnewi (1937–1939). Nnewi would be about twelve miles from my home. At that time I was a catechumen, and he signed my catechumen card. I must have been about seven years old then, going to catechism.

Then he opened what is now the Dunukofia parish in 1939, and he baptized me there in 1941. And later, as I mentioned earlier, my first confession and Communion were at his hands, and he prepared me for confirmation. He remained there until 1945, when he was transferred to Akpu, another parish. Later, in 1949, he was transferred from there to Aguleri, his hometown, always as parish priest. From there he went to the monastery.

I was ordained in 1958 and was able to visit him in 1959, toward the end of my studies in Rome, when I was a young priest. I served his Mass when I visited him then at Mount Saint Bernard. Those were the days before concelebration! I visited him again in mid-December 1963, when I was studying in London. He was not too well then, and within a month they sent me a telegram: "He is dead. He will be buried tomorrow." I took the train to Leicester, as I said earlier, and so I was able to be at the funeral, on January 21, 1964.

He had already the reputation of being a holy man in Nigeria. It would seem that in the monastery at Mount Saint Bernard the monks presumed that everyone should be a saint, so there he wasn't particularly thought of as a saint but as a good monk who had done very well. Probably the monks were more surprised at the beatification than we in Nigeria. We were not surprised at the prospect. The people at the popular level already regarded him as a saint. But perhaps in the monastery he did his best to hide himself. But not from the novice master, Father Gregory Wareing, who has written a book about him.[2] This is the book by his novice master, who died in 1994, at the age of eighty plus.

Q. *So the novice master's testimony was important for the beatification?*

A. Obviously, it was very, very important. Father Tansi was known for asceticism; he ate very little, and the person who used to cook for him in Dunukofia didn't have much work because he ate so very little. But he always looked after other people very well indeed.

---

[2] Gregory Wareing, O.C.S.O., *A New Life of Father Cyprian Michael Iwene Tansi* (Coalville, Leicester: Mount Saint Bernard Abbey, 1994).

He was a great preacher. And, as I said earlier, the number of priests and religious sisters from the area where he was parish priest is the highest in the whole region, which means the spiritual touch of the man really moved people. The families, the Christian families who were part of that ministry of his, have endured to this day. Last month, I saw one of those women whom he prepared for marriage in the 1940s, and she does not forget Father Tansi. So this is the reason why people thought that Father Tansi could be proposed as a model of the Christian life.

In his monastery too, his superiors, such as Abbot Ambrose Southey, knew very well that he was exceptional. It can happen that in a monastery the other monks may not realize that a particular member has reached a high degree of sanctity. In those days they did not talk; they made signs. They talked only to their superiors. And I imagine that he would have made an extraordinary effort to be simple and to hide himself. They had no idea what a successful parish priest he had been in Nigeria. He simply worked there in the monastery, and they noticed, and then he was professed in all simplicity. They must have been surprised when they saw some Nigerian bishops coming to be led in a retreat by Father Tansi in the monastery.

Q. *The Nigerian bishops went to visit him in Mount Saint Bernard?*
A. Yes, at least one that I know. Bishop Okoye, C.S.Sp., who died in 1977. I knew him very well because I served his first Mass in 1947.

Religious sisters visited him too. Some of those he inspired and encouraged are still alive. Not to speak of seminarians and priests. He was extraordinary as a priest, extraordinary.

Q. *Your Eminence, am I right in saying that you opened the process that led to his beatification?*
A. Yes, when I was archbishop. But the formal take-off was after I came to Rome. The priest I selected twenty years ago as promoter of the cause is still the promoter. In fact, we began the first step ten years after Father Tansi's death, in 1974.

Q. *What inspired you to open the process so soon, just ten years after his death?*
A. What happened is this. I was there as archbishop from 1967, that is, only three years after his death, until 1985. I knew of his holiness. I was convinced. I discussed with my secretary and with some older priests

who knew him. I said, "We must not let the memory of this great man perish. Why don't we have a symposium ten years after his death; a symposium on his life, and those who know him could just speak, and we would collect the documentation?" They said, "Yes, do that." So we organized a symposium in 1974.[3]

Then I came to Rome for some meeting in April 1979, and I went to the Congregation for the Causes of the Saints, and I said to the cardinal prefect, "I have a saint for you to canonize." The cardinal smiled and said, "We don't canonize just like that." I said, "Then tell me how you canonize because I don't know how you canonize, but I know that from my diocese there is a candidate for canonization." So he asked me a few questions and then said, "So he died in Nottingham diocese?" I said yes. Then he said, "Good, then that diocese has priority. It has prior rights to promote the cause, but if you write to the bishop and he waives the right then you can start." I then asked him to tell me how to start, and he told me.

In June 1979, I wrote to the bishop of Nottingham, James J. McGuinness, to request that he cede the right to promote the cause to the Onitsha Archdiocese. He graciously wrote back immediately and said, "That's all right, I waive my right. You conduct it."

So then I contacted the Cistercians. I spoke to the abbot-general of the Cistercians, Abbot Dom Ambrose Southey, who was actually abbot of Mount Saint Bernard at the time Father Tansi died, but in the meantime he had been elected abbot-general and was living in Via Laurentina, in Rome. He knew Father Tansi, and so he was in favor. Not only that, he asked Father Paolino Beltrame Quattrocchi,[4] the promoter-general of the Trappist Order, to give the Onitsha Archdiocese maximum help. That made a big difference because we had no experience in Nigeria about how to promote the causes of saints. Father Paolino gave us maximum help, and that is why the cause moved rather fast.

Q. Yes, it was fast. You opened the diocesan process in 1974, and just over twenty years later he is being beatified.

---

[3] On January 20, 1974, the archbishop celebrated a Solemn High Mass in the cathedral at Onitsha, on the tenth anniversary of the death of Fr. Tansi. The symposium was held that year too.

[4] It might be of interest to note that Fr. Paolino's own parents were the first Christian couple ever to be beatified together, for having lived a good Christian life as a couple and as parents. Their beatification took place in October 2001.

A. I opened the process, yes, but not in the formal sense. We held the first symposium in 1974 to let all those who knew about this great man speak and to begin to collect the documents.

Then I asked the priests of the Onitsha Archdiocese—because some of them didn't know him—I said, "Now we have a great man. I want to appoint one of you as the promoter; those of you who are interested inform me." They did, and I selected two, and one is still the promoter today. That is now almost twenty years ago.

But it was actually when I was already in Rome, around 1985, that my successor, Archbishop Stephen Ezeanya (who died at 3:00 A.M. this morning),[5] instituted the formal tribunal in the full canonical sense for the diocesan process. He kept that priest as the promoter of the cause, and he got wonderful advice from Father Paolino Beltrame Quattrocchi, who has continued to help all through these years. Indeed, in the eyes of the Congregation for the Causes of the Saints, Father Paolino is the promoter, and the Nigerian priest Father Emmanuel Nwosu is the assistant.

Indeed, it was Father Paolino who suggested, "Why don't you transfer Father Tansi's remains from Mount Saint Bernard back to Nigeria? If you do that, the people's devotion will increase." Meanwhile, in Nigeria, groups began calling themselves the Father Tansi solidarity groups. They began to publish a newsletter.

So—to cut a long story short—my successor, Archbishop Ezeanya, who knew Father Tansi very well and was devoted to him, opened the formal process. Even before I knew Father Tansi, he knew Father Tansi. The tribunal was set up in Onitsha, and they set to work on his case and had to ask many people about him. They also asked me, even though I was already in Rome and even though I began the process.

Then Archbishop Ezeanya arranged with Mount Saint Bernard Abbey and the bishop of Nottingham to get his remains transferred to Nigeria in October 1986. There was such enthusiasm in Onitsha and in the town of Aguleri that they wanted to keep the remains in Aguleri, but the archbishop said, "No, we'll keep the remains in the cemetery for priests near Onitsha Cathedral." It is a good sign that everybody wants to have the remains. And the parishes where he worked said, "What of us?"—which was good.

Finally, his remains were interred in Onitsha. There is a cemetery

---

[5] The date of this interview was November 12, 1996.

very near the cathedral; it is for priests and religious only, not for lay people. Every time I go home, as you can imagine, I go there to pray. It is most interesting. Not only interesting, but providential too, because it was when the remains were brought back in 1986 that the miracle took place that was finally approved ten years later in Rome, in 1996.

Q. *Could you tell me about this miracle, Your Eminence?*

A.   The miracle was this. There was a girl who had a problem in her stomach, I would not know the name of the disease. She went to many hospitals, and the doctors operated on her in the Borromeo Specialist Hospital in Onitsha, the Catholic hospital, and the best that is there. Then the doctors said to the sisters who were looking after her, "Sisters, there is no hope. We closed her up. You take her home. There is no hope."

Q. *Was she a young woman?*

A.   I cannot tell exactly her age, perhaps twenty or so. She was not yet married.

Then the sister, Sister Mary de Sales, was very sad, and the parents of the girl said to the sister, "Sister, you are responsible for our daughter. If our daughter dies, it is your work."

The religious sister didn't know what to do. Then she heard that the remains of Father Tansi were being brought back. So she gathered courage, put the girl into her car, and brought her to Onitsha. From Aguleri to Onitsha is only fifteen miles or less. This girl could not stand, she could not eat or keep any food in her stomach, and she couldn't walk. When they came to Onitsha, people were pushing all over the place to touch the remains. And the sister and the girl were pushed back. So the sister went to Monsignor Adigwe, the secretary of the archbishop, and asked him, "Allow the sick girl to touch the coffin." The priest said, "Okay. Approved." So the sister brought this girl who could not walk, and she threw herself on the coffin, and immediately she stood on her feet.

Q. *Immediately?*

A.   Yes! She couldn't walk before. They were going to have Mass in the cathedral, and she said to the sister, "Let's go to the church." The sister said, "I'll get people to help you." The girl said, "No need; I can walk." The sister did not know whether to believe her or not. They were at Mass, and she told the sister, "I'm hungry, I want to eat." She had not been eating, and she would vomit whatever she ate before. The sister said, "Wait until after Mass." Then after Mass they went to a nearby convent, and they brought her two plates of food, and she cleaned up all of it. The sister was amazed.

To make the story short: After the ceremony the sister brought her back to Aguleri. The other girls came to take her out of the car, but she walked out. And the following day she was running around with them and working as usual in a maternity clinic in the rural area. So, as you can imagine, they were surprised.

Q. *But this story must have made news in the city?*
A. The Onitsha Archdiocese didn't know how to publish it. However, they had the wisdom to come back to that hospital, and the doctors examined her and asked, "Is this the same person you brought here earlier?" And they said yes. The doctor said, "But there is nothing wrong anymore. What has happened?" That was the beginning of it.

Q. *What was the woman's name?*
A. Philomena. It's a lovely name. The family name is Emeka.

Q. *Then what happened?*
A. When Father Beltrame Quattrocchi heard about it, he advised them to document it, to ask questions, to call to the tribunal all the key people—the doctor, the sister, and so on. And they were all called because the tribunal was going on soon after. Everything combined in favor of Father Tansi. The evidence was collected both on whether Father Tansi practiced virtues to a heroic degree and on the miracle.

The Congregation for the Causes of the Saints, according to its practice, authorized that it would be valid not to set up another tribunal afterward, because they had collected the information at the most opportune time and all the relevant documents, even from when the girl paid for the first time in the hospital. All those documents were collected and brought to Rome finally.

Q. *What about the girl herself? What happened to her after this?*
A. The girl was very happy. She was cured. She continued working for the sisters. Later on she married and now has two or three children.

Once, the archbishop came to Rome with that girl and that sister;

and they had Mass with the Holy Father, and they took a photograph. We had a big lunch in my house. So it isn't just a story to tell; I saw the girl.

Then the cause went on. Some of the best priests in the diocese were put on the tribunal, and, when all the information was collected, it was weighty. It came to more than a thousand pages. And, of course, they had to go to Mount Saint Bernard to interview the monks who knew him.

Finally the process came to the Congregation for the Causes of the Saints. And here there were two major stages. First they asked, "Did this person practice the virtues to a heroic degree?" After that they verified the miracle.

For the heroic degree the congregation officials first look at the case and see whether there is the evidence of his having lived the theological virtues to a heroic degree. Then they write down their own summaries. Next they demand from the diocese all the documents they need. They then pass the documents on to their theologians/consultors, maybe seven, eight, or nine consultors. Each of them reads all the documents, which had to be printed; and then each writes up his own position and says whether he thinks this person had practiced the virtues to a heroic degree. Then they held a meeting of all those theologians/consultors, and they voted 100 percent in favor; not even one doubted.

Q. *Is this normal, or is there sometimes a division of opinion on the decision?*

A. Yes, sometimes there might be one who suspends his vote, and, rarely, one who votes definitely against. Or one would say, "It's not proved"—we would need more documents before we are sure. There might be one or even two and, in some cases, more.

Q. *But can you have a beatification on a majority vote rather than a consensus position?*

A. Yes, yes, even if one or two vote against, it can be approved, although the Holy Father is not bound by that vote. But if quite a number vote against the person, or are hesitating, who then would want to continue? You would like to clear up those points. Even if it is one person, that person may have a point. It isn't so much counting the number as the reasons. But, of course, if many have doubts, then, normally, the thing has to be delayed until the doubts are cleared, and sometimes they are not cleared for years and years.

After that vote, the case is then passed on to the meeting of the cardinals, those who are called the members of the congregation, cardinals and bishops, and they hold meetings every month. Indeed, there are two groups because there are very many candidates; one group meets one week, the other two weeks later.

In that meeting of cardinals and bishops, Father Tansi's cause was also discussed, and they examined all the documents again, every one of them. I am a member of the Congregation for the Causes of the Saints. When some of the members in the Congregation actually know the person who is being discussed, it can be that they ask this person to give his testimony. I gave my testimony. But the final decision is not made on the personal testimony, but on the arguments in front of them. Again they voted, and again he got 100 percent; everybody voted in favor.

Then the documents are passed on to the Holy Father by the cardinal prefect; and one day there is what is called "The Reading of the Decrees" in front of the Holy Father; not for one case alone but maybe for ten or fifteen, and then the Holy Father approves them. That happened too for Father Tansi. Last year, on July 11, 1995, there was the approval of the decree of Father Tansi's claim to heroic virtue.

Then the claim to a miracle went through the same stages, plus one more stage—the medical doctors. That's an extra stage for miracles. So this stage was added to that of the meetings of the theologians and the meeting of the cardinals, and that also went through in January of this year [1996], and the decree was read in front of the Holy Father on June 25, 1996.

With the completion of these two stages, the process is finished. What remains now is for the Holy Father to decide the date and the place for the beatification. That has not yet been published, so everyone is waiting for it.

Q. *Pope John Paul II must know that you knew Father Tansi. Did he say anything to you about his cause?*

A. Yes, there was a stage when I mentioned to the Holy Father that I knew this priest and that he baptized me, and so on. Obviously the Holy Father was very interested. He also asked me whether he was a martyr. I said, "No, not a martyr, but a confessor. However, a Trappist who lived faithfully forty years ago was not far from a martyr." Still I had to take care that the fact that I knew him must not now be made to influence the process. I am only one witness among many.

But you would like to know, for example, there is a man called Atamanya Robert Olisa, in Ossomala, Nigeria. He is an old man. He reached one hundred years this year [1996]. He was obviously the leading layman in the Onitsha Archdiocese forty years ago.

Then when Father Tansi was going to the monastery in 1950, by boat from Lagos to Liverpool and so on, he left his cassock in the man's house in Lagos because he stayed in that man's house before boarding the boat. This man kept the soutane and gave it to me during the Nigerian civil war in 1968, which means eighteen years after it was given to him. And he said to me in 1968, "That holy priest left this soutane with me before going to the monastery. You know, one day he may become a saint, so you as archbishop should keep it well." And I did. Then when I appointed a promoter I gave him the soutane with the same instructions. When this man was asked in the process, "Why did you keep that soutane?" he said, "I knew he was a saint." The man is still alive.

Q. *That's very impressive, indeed. Your Eminence, will this be the first Nigerian saint?*

A. Yes, yes, not only the first Nigerian but also the first in the whole of West Africa, in the fourteen countries from Cameroon to Mauritania. There is not one person beatified in the whole of West Africa! There is a missionary who worked in Senegal who was beatified, but he was French, I think—Blessed Laval—but no African has ever been beatified in this region yet.

Q. *You mean that there is not one African beatified in the whole of West Africa?*

A. Yes, I mean that. I do not say our people are not in heaven, but they have not been beatified on earth.

Q. *Why do you think this is so?*

A. You see, you go to heaven, and you are there whether the Church on earth knows you were holy or not. Obviously, there are millions and millions in heaven whose names we do not know.

We are a young Church; 120 years is young for the Catholic Church. So I take it that we have not learned how to promote the causes of our saints. The Italians know how to do it very well. The Spanish know it. The Poles know it. The Germans know it. We don't blame them for that.

We don't envy them. But we must learn from them, not only how to be holy, but also how to promote the causes of our people.

Moreover, you also need personnel to promote these causes. It means a lot of work, writing, interviewing and so on. You need a little money also, but, of course, without holiness, no personnel or money will serve. So I would say that it is normal that where the Church is new you would not have so many beatified because they were not known sufficiently or even if they were known the local Church did not yet take the steps. The Pope cannot canonize a person if there is no information put in front of him.

Q. *So, what will be the significance of this for the Church in Nigeria?*

A. Encouragement. A sort of back-up to say we are the Church, too. Do not think that saints are born in Saint Peter's Basilica, or in its sacristy. They are ordinary men and women who come from your villages. Priests, do not imagine that there is a special class of priests called to holiness; it's all of you, whether you are in the parish, or you are in the catechetical office of the diocese, or you are in the monastery. You are called to be holy whether you are a professor or whether you are a forgotten village assistant priest. All are called to be holy.

We also look forward to the time when married men and women from Nigeria, and other parts of Africa, will be beatified. The Holy Father has, in 1989, also beatified Blessed Victoria Rasoamanarivo, from Madagascar, who was a married woman and whose husband was not exactly a saint; but this woman showed him great fidelity and love.

Apart from that there is the religious sister, Nengapeta, from the Democratic Republic of Congo (formerly Zaire). And the young man Isidore Bakanja, also from what was then Zaire, who died at the age of twenty-four. He was not a religious; he was a new Christian, and he was killed because he was faithful to the Rosary and the teaching of the catechism. Not to talk of the martyrs of Uganda. So Africa can't say, "We don't have saints", but the more saints beatified or canonized, the more encouragement it will be for the local Church and for the universal Church. It is also a way of underlining the universal call to holiness.

Q. *Isn't it also a link with the traditional religious beliefs in Africa? I remember you told me Africans have great respect for the dead and for the spirits after they had died; I recall how you spoke about the cult of the dead in*

African Traditional Religion, in a way that is close to the Catholic under-standing of the communion of saints.

A. You are right. African Traditional Religion honors the dead and wants to maintain links between those who have died and those who are still on earth. It's very interesting that the Japanese also honor their ancestors very much. Christianity doesn't balk at that idea. Christianity, in the doctrine of the communion of saints, really elevates this whole human dimension.

Christianity elevates it because our faith teaches us that those who have been with us in the family of the Church, believing in the Father, Son, and Holy Spirit, sanctified by the same sacraments of baptism, confirmation, and the Holy Eucharist, when they die and reach heaven—or if they have died and are in purgatory and will reach heaven after-ward—that they do have a certain communion with the Christians who are still on earth.

So we who are on earth are not alone because we relate to our ancestors who have arrived home in heaven, and we relate with those of them who are still suffering in purgatory, and we pray for them. To those in heaven we pray; for those in purgatory we pray.

Q. *It seems to me that this would be the natural inculturation of the Gospel in Africa in the light of the traditional beliefs of the people.*

A. Very much so. Very much so! And so whatever mistakes were made in the veneration of the ancestors can be corrected and should be corrected by the veneration of the saints. Indeed, the African synod and the post-synodal document *Ecclesia in Africa—The Church in Africa*, issued by the Holy Father, ask African theologians and the Church in Africa to give more attention to how to venerate the ancestors.

Q. *What will be the political impact of this beatification in Nigeria? How do you expect the Nigerian government to react?*

A. I can only guess. If I were the people in the Nigerian govern-ment, I would be happy because it means that one of our citizens has been recognized as a model Christian. That's good. It's good news. And I would imagine that it puts Nigeria on the map. Nigeria has sometimes not figured well in the world's press and media because of the government's actions. Nigeria has figured well when the soccer team got to the World Cup in Atlanta in August 1996.

But if Nigeria can get to the top in holiness, it is better than the

World Cup in Atlanta, Georgia, though I have nothing against that either. But the beatification does elevate our spirits, and it sort of says to us that not only should we be saints, but also that we can be saints. This beatification is an eloquent lesson.

Q. *Am I right in thinking that Nigeria is still under the Congregation for the Evangelization of Peoples? If so, then it seems to me that the congregation appears not to have invested money in promoting the saints. This would seem to be the case, as this is the first beatification in all of West Africa. I would have thought that part of evangelization would also be to promote the beatification and canonization of saints in these lands.*

A. It is part of evangelization to help the local Church to promote the causes of the people who are "canonizable", if I may use that word. The Holy Father, at the African synod, said expressly, "Africa, update your martyrology after the days of Saint Augustine, Saint Cyprian, Saints Perpetua and Felicity." And he exhorted them in the same way when he went to Carthage in Tunisia.

The main work is for the local Church, really, not for the Congregation for the Evangelization of Peoples. But the local Church may also need finances to do this.

Chapter 9

From the Death of Paul VI to the First Visit of John Paul II to Nigeria

(1978–1982)

Every priest and bishop meets a wide variety of people in the course of his life, but it is not given to everyone to know three future popes before they were elected to the See of Peter. But that is what happened to the future Cardinal Arinze.

As we have already seen, Father Arinze met Cardinal Montini in Nigeria in 1962, the year before he became Pope Paul VI; then he was the guest of Bishop Luciani even before the latter became the patriarch of Venice; and he got to know Cardinal Wojtyla at the Synods of Bishops.

In the interviews,[1] I sought to get his personal insights into those three men whom, the cardinal believes, God in his providence enabled him to meet face-to-face. I began with a question touching on his understanding of God as Providence, a subject we will explore more in depth in a later chapter.

---

[1] This chapter is based on extracts from interviews on December 9 and 16, 2000, and February 16, 2001.

Q. *I know, from what you have said on other occasions, that you do not see these encounters as mere chance meetings but, really, as part of God's providence in your life. I see you have come to understand this providence more and more as your life unfolds.*

A. Yes. I have come to perceive and detect God's invisible hand, God who guides. Sometimes I meet a person, and you might think it was by chance, but I don't believe in *chance*, really. Take the example of that priest I mentioned to you, Don Florio, whom I have visited thirty-five times in Belluno. He is now about eighty-eight years old.

Now the first time I went to help him, during Easter week, 1960, it was a priest companion of mine in the Urban College, from Rhodesia—as it was called then—Father Dennis De Jong, now bishop of Ndola, in Zambia, who should have gone, but because he could not go he asked me if I would go. He was prevented from going to help in the parish during Holy Week. So I went, and because I did go and help with confessions and the ceremonies of Holy Week, the priest invited me back at other times. It looks accidental, but looking back now, I think God arranged it. Now I have visited that parish thirty-five times in forty years. They or, rather, the mayor, made me an honorary citizen of Auronzo di Cadore, in October 1982. I think all that was Divine Providence. It was through him that I knew many other people in that mountain area.

And it was on my journey to visit Don Florio that I also met Bishop Albino Luciani, who had been in the same seminary as Don Florio, but two years ahead of him. I met him even before he became patriarch of Venice, when he was still bishop of Vittorio Veneto. That was in 1969. On my way to Don Florio, I went to Vittorio Veneto during the civil war in Nigeria, in November 1969—after the Synod of Bishops—to visit some Nigerians in a secular institute. They were concerned about their relatives back home, and they arranged for me to stay with their bishop. I didn't know him before. I came in, and he said, "I am Albino Luciani", and I said, "Very good, Your Excellency, I am Francis Arinze." He was bishop then, and I was archbishop. He gave me hospitality for two days.

Q. *What kind of man was he? What was your impression? We have a picture of a smiling face.*

A. Yes, he was that, and he was gentle. Just those two days that I stayed with him, he was gentle. He had a quiet voice, not the type that seems too strong. He doesn't crush you with his presence, but you feel at home. He was very friendly. And he knew the parish priest I was going to visit, the one I told you about—Don Florio; and he sent greetings. Then soon after, he was made patriarch of Venice in 1969. Then after that, I saw him again at synods and so on.

Q. *Did you meet him many times?*

A. Not many times really. I met him at the Synod of Bishops in Rome. I can't immediately tell which synod now, because I am not sure that he attended every synod. But I met him at least in two synods between 1969–1971 and 1977–1978. I had not visited him in Venice. That's all.

Q. *So you got to know him fairly well.*

A. Yes, as well as one could in the few times we met. I do not want to give the impression that we were friends, because there was a gap between us. He was the patriarch of Venice, and I was an archbishop in Nigeria who occasionally came to Rome for a meeting.

But still he knew my name, and he knew I was a friend of Don Florio, and every time we met he said, "Send my greetings to Don Florio." And when I went to Don Florio's house I saw a photo of the patriarch with Don Florio; it was taken when the patriarch came and said Mass in the parish, because he was patriarch of all this area. Don Florio still has the photo in his sitting room.

Q. *When was the last time you saw him?*

A. It was at the funeral of Pope Paul VI. When I heard that Paul VI had died, I flew to Rome immediately. And after the Funeral Mass, I was about to go away when somebody clapped me on the back. I looked around, and it was Cardinal Luciani.

He said, "Oh, so you have come." I said, "Yes, you know that Paul VI was very kind to our people, so I had to come." He asked me, "When are you going home?" I said, "Tomorrow." He said, "So soon?" I said, "Yes, I came only for the Funeral Mass, so I go back tomorrow." He said, "All right." I said: "Your Eminence, we'll pray for all of you

as you go into the conclave." "That's all right", he said in his little
voice.

Q. *Where were you and what was your reaction when the patriarch of
Venice, Albino Luciani, was elected Pope?*
A. I was surprised. I was in a parish; I remember it very well. I was
visiting a parish, Orsumoghu, in Nigeria on that day in 1978, for confirmation. I turned on the radio, and they said: "There's a new pope." I said,
"Okay." Then they gave his name, "Albino Luciani." I said, "Is that the
one they chose?" That was my first reaction. I was surprised. I was happy,
but I was surprised. Then I thought, "I hope he will not remember me
now, and tell me to come to Rome for something." It just crossed my
mind quickly, but that was all.

Q. *So you were surprised?*
A. Yes. Although I didn't know all, how popes were actually chosen, but I was not expecting he would be pope. I saw him as a gentle
shepherd. I didn't associate him with "Pope". But I did not have strong
reasons really, just that type of feeling you have without being able to
articulate it. But a thing like this comes, and you are pleasantly surprised;
but you are not able to articulate why you are surprised.
You know there are some people, you see them, and you say, "Ah,
that will be the Pope." You know how people speculate, and they make
one dozen popes already before the real Pope is chosen. And probably
not one of those twelve they lined up will be the Pope at all. I think it's
very funny that some people take it seriously.

Q. *So before his election you didn't see this man Luciani as pope. I
suppose it was much the same with Angelo Roncalli—John XXIII—who
was also patriarch of Venice?*
A. That time we were seminarians, and we never even knew who
Roncalli was. We did not know who he was. In those days, we, seminarians, did not know. The names we used to hear included Montini,
though he was not yet a cardinal at that time. We did not know.

Q. *But you had known this man, Albino Luciani, and you never imagined him as pope.*
A. No, I did not. I'm not even sure whether I was figuring out in
my mind who could be the next Pope. I don't know whether I was doing
that; maybe I was far too busy going around my diocese.

Q. *Did you then come for his enthronement?*

A. No, I didn't. I had been in Rome just a few weeks before for the funeral of Paul VI.

Q. *Then Pope Luciani—John Paul I, as he was called—died suddenly thirty-three days after his election. What was your reaction when you heard the news of his death?*

A. Sudden death. I was surprised. I was shocked. I was pained. I said, "Oh, this good man; oh, what has happened?" I was pained, I was shocked, and then I sort of thought maybe this work was too much for him. That thought just crossed my mind, and at that time I had not yet read any of the newspaper speculations. I just thought maybe this work was too heavy for him.

Q. *But Pope Luciani has left an impression on everybody, despite his very short reign.*

A. Definitely. Thirty-three days that the world will not forget. Again I came back to my idea of God as Providence: God knows best. In Divine Providence, nothing is accidental.

Q. *You said you came to the funeral of Paul VI. Did you have a very friendly relationship with Paul VI?*

A. Not close. Nevertheless, it was he who named me bishop and archbishop. And I saw the Holy Father, Paul VI, at the conclusion of Vatican II when I was a young bishop, and at the synods—1967, 1969, 1971, and 1977 (I did not attend the 1974 synod).

Q. *But you had private meetings with him?*

A. Not really, just one brief greeting during the Nigerian civil war. In those days the *Ad limina*[2] visits were not as well arranged as now, and it was not that every bishop went one by one to the Pope, not really. I met him once in private, during the Nigerian civil war. I don't remember any other time meeting him one-to-one.

---

[2] This is the visit each bishop must make to the Pope every five years to report on his work in his diocese and the situation there. It is called *Ad limina*, short for *ad limina apostolorum* (to the thresholds of the apostles), because, during his visit, the bishop must also pray at the tombs of the Apostles Peter and Paul.

Q. *What is your lasting memory of Paul VI?*

A. A person who was very deep and concerned about people. He showed great concern about people's sufferings. As I mentioned earlier, I shall never forget his concern for all our people during the Nigerian civil war, and I shall never forget his words at the coffee break at one of the sessions of the Synod of Bishops in 1969.

As I told you earlier, he was there, surrounded by all the bishops. Everybody wanted to greet him. I greeted him and said: "Holy Father, pray for our people who are suffering." He said: "What can I do? What can I do? *Che cosa posso fare?*" I will never, ever forget those words: "*Che cosa posso fare?* (What can I do?)" He said it two or three times. It was lovely coming from him. It was typical of the man. But I have told you all this when we spoke about the Nigerian civil war.

Q. *Clearly those words have been engraved in your memory. I remember the first time you told me this story; you told it with such feeling, even after thirty years. That happened at the 1969 synod. But at later synods you met another man, Karol Cardinal Wojtyla, from Poland. You told me that you got to know him well at the 1977 Synod of Bishops.*

A. Yes.

Q. *What was your reaction when he was made Pope? Were you surprised, or were you expecting it?*

A. I was happy. I was not expecting it because I didn't work out in my mind who would be Pope. And in those days we didn't think of having a pope who was not an Italian. But when I heard the news I was in Belfast on that day, October 16, 1978.

I was in Belfast because the Irish Missionary Union had invited me to come. Each year they invited somebody from the mission countries to come and speak on missions in as many dioceses as possible. That year they invited me, and I went to many places—for example, Cork, Galway, Dublin, Armagh, Clonmacnoise—and spoke on the missions, in schools, churches, and so on. Not to raise money for Nigeria. No, no! I was invited to speak and help keep alive the mission consciousness in Ireland, for which Ireland has long been noted.

On that particular day I was in Belfast, and when I heard the name of the new Pope I said to the parish priest, "Ah, we're going to have some order in the Church. People are going to know where they stand. Because my memory of him is of a person who has very clear ideas and who is not afraid to say them. And he comes from a country where people have suffered much under Communist oppression."

That was my memory of him. And I also remembered that he always got majority votes in the synods and was voted into the council of every synod. The other synod participants voted for him every time.

Q. *That's always a good indicator.*

A. At the time nobody could say this would be the Pope, but the fact that he was being voted every time in the synod council for the next synod was a good sign. It is a sign of what others thought of him.

Q. *You met Karol Cardinal Wojtyla and got to know him at the synods.*

A. I met him at the Synods of Bishops, because he was at every synod. Not that I was close to him, but gradually attending many synods it was not possible not to notice this Polish cardinal who was being voted for the synod council every time, and who spoke in a way that I could identify with, and who showed a sort of optimistic image of Catholicism and spoke not as one of those lamenting that everything has gone to pieces, but happy.

He was clearheaded, if you like. He may be strong too in ideas, in the sense of happy and optimistic about the Church, because some people sometimes speak as if the Church were near the end, and they say the problems are too many, and there's nothing we can do about them. That's my memory of him.

Q. *And then in the 1977 synod you said you got to know him very well. That was the synod on catechesis.*

A. Yes, it was, because the post-synodal exhortation *Catechesi Tradendae* went through the hands of three popes. Yes.

I have no special memory of him now at that synod, but I remember him still being prominent in the elections for the post-synodal council. We knew each other so well that he himself knew my name.

When he was elected pope in 1978, I was in Belfast, as I said earlier. And when I came later that same year to Rome for a meeting of one of the dicasteries, before December, we went as a group to meet the Holy Father. When I was going to say my name, he said my name already. I said, "You know my name." He said, "I remember you from the Synod of Bishops." I was surprised.

Q. *You didn't come to his enthronement.*

A. No, I did not. I was still in Ireland, and the enthronement was almost immediately. He was elected on October 16, and he was enthroned, or began his papal ministry, as they say, six days later, on October 22. I was still in Ireland. I remember it well, because people were commenting on it in Dublin, and they and I were very happy on the day of that ceremony.

Q. *And when the Turkish gunman, Ali Agca, shot him in Saint Peter's Square on the evening of May 13, 1981, you were in Nigeria. What did you feel when you heard the news?*

A. I was shocked. We were all shocked. It was almost unbelievable. We prayed, we organized prayers, and we followed the information every day, as much as would filter out. We were very happy when we saw the Holy Father recovered.

Before the assassination attempt on May 13, 1981, we were already discussing his visit to Nigeria. Then later that year, when Archbishop Lourdusamy—now cardinal—visited Nigeria for one or two weeks, in his role as secretary of the Congregation for the Evangelization of Peoples, he gave us updated information about the Pope's recovery.

Then, at the end of that year, in October or November 1981, I was in Rome for another meeting. I was then president of the Nigerian Bishops' Conference, and I met the *sostituto* secretary of state, Archbishop Martínez Somalo, now cardinal, and I said, "Of course our primary concern is the Holy Father's health, but please know that whenever the Holy Father can start traveling again, Nigeria would like to be number one! We don't want to be forgotten." And so it happened, because suddenly, in December of that same year, the nuncio sent me a message and said, "Come, that visit is near. Come! You are to go to Rome with me immediately." That's how the discussions began.

Q. *When Pope John Paul II came to Nigeria in 1982, you were still president of the bishops' conference.[3] What stands out in your mind from that visit?*

A. It was a time of grace for the country. The Holy Father was very good to us. It was the first long-distance travel by the Holy Father after Ali Agca shot at him in Saint Peter's Square on May 13, 1981.

---

[3] In advance of the visit, Archbishop Arinze published a book on the history of Christianity in Nigeria, *Answering God's Call* (London: Geoffrey Chapman, 1982).

The first big journey by the Pope after that attempt was to Nigeria in February 1982. We were slightly concerned, and we didn't want to overstrain the Holy Father with the schedule. But we noticed in the discussion stage before the visit that he wanted always "more items" on the agenda, and at one time I suggested, "Holy Father, let the items be fewer!" For example, after lunch we didn't put anything on his schedule for an hour or two. He said, "What next?" I said, "Holy Father, our climate is hot. After lunch, we don't put any engagements immediately; we give you some time to rest." Whether I pronounced the word "siesta" or not, that is what I meant, and we provided for that. But during the whole visit he didn't show signs of tiredness even once.

Many things stand out in my mind about that visit.

First, the Holy Father: we had the *Ad limina* visit of the bishops of Nigeria a month before his visit to the country. It was not arranged because of the visit; at that time it was simply our turn to come, so it was very providential. As you know, on these occasions he invites all the bishops to have lunch with him, which means discussion. So he was very well informed of the situation. Very well informed. Then the schedule: he asked what the bishops would desire: Where would they want him to visit, as far as possible, within four days? Which groups to meet?

It was all like that. Even the particular meeting with the Catholic Women's Organization was added on, even though there was already the Pope's meeting with the National Laity of Nigeria. But when we spoke so much about the activities of the Catholic women, the Holy Father said, "Are you including them in a separate group to meet?" We said, "No, they are in the laity camp." I said, "Holy Father, do you want to meet them as a separate group?" He said, "Yes." So they were given a separate meeting within the National Laity gathering, and they were very happy about it; and rightly so, because they are easily the most active lay group in the country; although they do not separate themselves from the Laity Council.

Another very good side of the Pope's visit was the political. We had a civilian government at that time. The federal government was very good to the Church. Shehu Shagari, a Muslim from the north, headed it. The government was very good to us, and even gave us money to help the Catholic Church plan the visit. The government gave us one million Nigerian naira; it was, at that time, equivalent to 1.5 million

U.S. dollars.[4] The government also supplied the airplane for all the internal flights of the Holy Father, free of charge; and the helicopters too, free of charge.

Q. *That was extraordinary generosity.*

A. And nobody could accuse the government of being pro-Catholic, because the president was Muslim, the vice president was a Protestant. So it was very good.

I think the government realized that the Pope has a message for mankind, and that he is a voice that is listened to, and that he wasn't coming just for the Catholics. They saw that he could help the country, a country that is very difficult to govern, with its 240 ethnic groups, with more than a few problems, but also possibilities—quite a number. So the government realized that and was very happy about the visit and facilitated it.

We couldn't ask more from the government. The security officers were very good, and when we were making the various plans we had very many meetings with government ministers beforehand to discuss logistics. It was all very harmonious. And I noticed that it helped politicians in the various parties to talk to one another, so that, at least for five days, they seemed to be united. That was good too. It was all very inspiring.

Obviously, it helped the Church too. There's no need to say that. It helped us to work together, it helped the dioceses to plan together; because the more you plan a thing together, the greater unity you will have between you. That's clear. For example, he ordained ninety-two priests in Kaduna. These priests were deacons rallied from all the seminaries in the country. That meant a lot of preparation and harmonization. There are many aspects, but I would not like to continue the list. It was all a very happy thing; he baptized, he did confirmations, and, of course, celebrated Mass at various places.

For the Mass in Onitsha, an open space was cleared where there was nothing before, because no stadium could contain that number of people. We had been advised to make a very wide space to avoid anybody being stampeded to death, because the enthusiasm would be very high.

---

[4] At that time, the exchange rate was 1 Nigerian naira = 1.5 U.S. dollars.

Q. *Was it a different place from the one where Father Tansi was beatified?*

A. Yes. Different. It would be about four kilometers [two or three miles] away from there. Where Father Tansi was beatified is farther outside Onitsha, in the town of Oba. But where the Pope came in 1982 was on the outskirts of the growing city of Onitsha. So we got the place cleared by big companies; I went and begged them, and they helped us with machines, and the government helped.

And at the end, as soon as the Pope left, I decided that we would open a parish there, even though people were not living there, and we called it the parish of Saints John and Paul. We also called it "Iba Pope"— the Pope's podium, and people began to buy land there, and land became very expensive. And now it is very heavily populated.

In September 2000, I was there for a Mass. It is fantastic on a weekday; it is so heavily populated. People say, "This is holy ground; that's where I must go and live." It's very interesting. It's all so big now; there are many four- and six-story buildings, and there's a big convent there, and a big priests' house. They are also building a church because what they have now is too small. It is very encouraging.

Q. *Clearly the event made a big impact on the people. But what do you remember of the Pope's Mass on that spot in 1982?*

A. I remember at Mass we had a thousand people distributing Holy Communion—seven hundred seminarians and three hundred priests. I know because we had to buy the vessels; we didn't have enough ciboriums.

After the Mass, I asked the priest who was second master of ceremonies, the local priest, Monsignor Patrick Achebe, what the Pope was saying when, after giving Holy Communion to some people, he sat down. He said the Pope looked, and he saw all the seminarians and priests in white cassocks, and he was saying, "Wonderful, wonderful, wonderful." He kept saying "wonderful, wonderful", for a long time.

Q. *Was that the Pope's first major contact with the people of Africa?*

A. No, no. He first came to Africa in 1980. He went first to Zaire, the big Zaire, and then to Kenya, Ghana, Burkina Faso, and the Ivory Coast.

But 1982 was his second major visit to Africa. In Nigeria he met the priests of the country at Enugu seminary, the religious men and women at Ibadan seminary, representatives of the universities at Ibadan University, and then the laity in Kaduna and the workers in Lagos. And there were three major Masses in the three metropolitan sees: Lagos, Kaduna, and Onitsha.

Q. *The Pope came to Nigeria in 1982 and, shortly after, less than two years later, he invited you to come to work in the Vatican, and you have been here ever since.*

A. Yes.

Chapter 10

Return to Rome to Work
in the Vatican

(1984)

*In 1984, Pope John Paul II brought a number of diocesan bishops to work in the
Vatican, as a further step in the internationalization of the Roman Curia. Among
them was Archbishop Arinze, whom he appointed to head the Vatican's Secretariat
for Non-Christians, now called the Pontifical Council for Inter-Religious Dialogue.[1] The invitation came as a surprise to Archbishop Arinze, but he did not
hesitate; he accepted. In this chapter, and particularly in a later chapter, he explains
why.*

*In this chapter, he talks about how he began working in the Vatican, and what
that entailed. Our discussion opened as he left Nigeria to take up his new posting
in the Vatican, in 1984.[2]*

---

[1] Pope Paul VI set up the Secretariat for Non-Christians on May 19, 1964, with the
task of promoting studies and fostering friendly relations between the Catholic Church
and the followers of the non-Christian religions. Its charter was the Second Vatican
Council declaration *Nostra Aetate*—on the relation of the Church to non-Christian
religions. Almost a quarter of a century later, Pope John Paul II, in a reform of the
Roman Curia on June 28, 1988, changed the secretariat's name to the Pontifical Council
for Inter-Religious Dialogue and broadened its mandate.

[2] This chapter is based on extracts from two interviews recorded on December 9 and
16, 2000.

Q. *Your Eminence, you must have had mixed feelings at leaving your diocese in Nigeria. You had been enjoying life as a pastor there, and you loved your own people.*

A. Yes, of course, although "enjoying" is not the word I would use. I loved my people, and I was happy in Nigeria as archbishop of Onitsha. I was not thinking of being given any other assignment. But because the Holy Father said, "You come to Rome", I had no second thoughts. And as an archbishop in the Vatican said to me, "You were serving Jesus Christ in Onitsha; in Rome you will be serving the same Jesus Christ." So on that point I had not a doubt.

Obviously, it meant a change, not only of climate but also of colleagues. I had now to work with people I generally did not know before, who generally came from other parts of the world, with different backgrounds.

I was not afraid. Obviously, I had to learn. I had to listen. I had to watch and ask questions, and I had to ask advice. I was not in an altogether strange place, because, although I was living in Nigeria, I used to come to Rome, from time to time, for various meetings. Not only that, I had been a seminarian in Rome, and later I came to Rome, as bishop, for various meetings—it could have been for the Congregation of the Evangelization of Peoples or the Pontifical Council for Justice and Peace or the Secretariat for Non-Christians. I was a member of this Vatican dicastery before, too, but at that time, little did I think that I would work here full-time. But in those years there were always reasons to come to Rome, and I had met some people in the Vatican, but I didn't ever imagine that I would be living here one day.

I began working in the Vatican. I had to learn, and I saw that people were friendly and ready to help, whether in actual introduction to the work or in the material arrangements: where to live, furniture, and so on.

Q. *As I recall, you first lived in Palazzo San Calisto. That's the first place I met you.*

A. Yes, I was assigned an apartment there, with rooms quite big and quiet enough. I liked it. From there I could get to the office each day in twenty-five minutes, whether by car or on foot. If you greet no one on the way, coming or going, it takes twenty-five minutes. If you go by car, it takes about the same time, by the time you have got the car out of the garage and have done battle with the traffic.

After some years the possibility of living even nearer the office presented itself, and I accepted. I was given an apartment just vacated by Cardinal Garonne. Now I'm very near the office, just three minutes' walk from the house to the office. It's better.

Q. *And you have a wonderful view from your apartment now; you can see Saint Peter's Square, the Apostolic Palace, and the study window at which the Pope appears to bless the people in the Square.*

A. Yes. A wonderful view, and near Saint Peter's Basilica for ceremonies.

Q. *When you arrived as head of office, did anybody say, "This is how you should proceed." I mean, how did you know what to do? How did you set your priorities? Did you meet the Pope immediately?*

A. Yes, the Holy Father was very good to me. When I was first given the appointment, on April 5, 1984, I discussed with the substitute secretary of state—at that time it was Archbishop Martínez Somalo, now cardinal—and we agreed that I should come in May.

I came in May, and I met the Holy Father. And I also met Archbishop Martínez Somalo. And then I met the staff in this office. I met Father Marcello Zago, who was secretary at that time but later became archbishop and secretary of the Congregation for the Evangelization of Peoples. I also met Father Shirieda, undersecretary, and the rest of the staff. They were all very kind, and with them I had no difficulty, especially Father Zago, who told me how the office works.

My predecessor, Archbishop Jadot, had left recently, so I didn't have the time to sit with him. But when I had settled in, within three months, we invited him from Belgium to come and have two days with us, with the whole staff. We even had a visit outside Rome, a type of picnic. But, more important for me was to sit with him, listen to him, and get his advice. Then with Father Zago, Father Shirieda, and the others in the office, I was never abandoned. I was never lost.

From being archbishop, I realized that I was coming to an office that had been there before me. So I must not come with a Messiah complex that "I have come to make all things new." The office was there already, and the staff was there already. There were members around the world—bishops, cardinals, and so on. Then there were the consultors, people very well informed on the various religions. And my predecessors were there too: Cardinals Marella and Pignedoli and Archbishop Jadot. So I must not act as if I were beginning from year one.

I had a rich inheritance. I walked into it, and I did my best to continue along the lines indicated by my predecessors, and then to study gradually how to break new ground or to reinforce what seemed healthy from the past. There was never a major departure.

Q. *What were the priorities then?*

A. One of the priorities I had clear in my mind was to strengthen the role of the local Church in inter-religious dialogue. That means that this office of the Holy Father for inter-religious dialogue will do well to collaborate with the dioceses and with the bishops' conferences in such a way that they see inter-religious dialogue in their country as their responsibility, not ours in Rome. But our office will help them, will suggest, will occasionally give a little push, if necessary, or hold back if we think they are going too fast. Give them indications, give them publications, but the initiative is theirs so that it won't happen again as happened to me once before.

One archbishop in Africa who is very friendly to me—we had been friends before I came to Rome—said to me once: "There are Muslims in my archdiocese, and they are difficult to deal with; please come and dialogue with them." I said, "No, brother! Have you abdicated? Am I now to be the archbishop of that see? You are still the archbishop, so do not tell me to come and meet them because you don't know how to do so. No. No. You will say to me, I am meeting with the Muslims in my archdiocese, would you like to come along with me to give me suggestions and so on. But it's my own responsibility." I said to him, "If so, I will encourage our staff to come, or our consultors in your area, but I will not take over your work. You have your responsibilities."

That's one priority that was set. And we did our best in this office also to make that clear to people of other religions when they come to visit us. I won't mention any country, but if people from one religion come here and say they want very strong ties with the Vatican for inter-religious dialogue, I say, "Excellent, but the dialogue will not begin with your link with the Vatican. It will begin with your links with the Catholic Church in your country. There is a Catholic Church in your country where you come from, so meet them. When the Catholic bishops in your country tell me that your dialogue is now in fourth gear, ready to go to fifth gear, then we will get warm, but not before. Therefore, you go back so that the dialogue will have roots in the place."

If a person from a big religion, or whatever, comes here and wants to meet the Pope, we say, "Is there a bishop behind you?" He says, "No, there's no contact." Then I say, "No, we will not bring you to meet the Pope; please begin with contact with your bishop." The reason is that if we arrange a papal audience they will be photographed, and he may go back home and say, "I have met the Pope." And if the local bishop says anything, the person may say, "This bishop does not matter, I'm already in line with the Vatican." So, as you can see, in that case we do damage. But the dialogue will have roots if it begins in the place where the person lives. If we see that such people are not interested in meeting the local Church, we will gradually put them far away from us, because it means they come for political reasons or for international visibility, and that is not good enough. That's one priority area.

Therefore, if we go to any country to meet people of other religions, we always regard it as fundamental that the local Church take part. If the local Church doesn't want to take part, we will not go. We only made an exception in one place where the bishops explained that they supported us, but, for local reasons, they didn't want to send anybody lest that person suffer after we have left. It's a country where there isn't religious freedom. But that's very exceptional, very exceptional. Also, the local Church helps us not to make blunders when we go to any place, because otherwise we may make big mistakes, and then go to the airport and leave and saddle the local Church with headaches after we have left.

Another priority area we have set is contact with Catholic seminaries, universities, centers of thought, because theological reflection, good doctrine, which is the basis for inter-religious dialogue, is very important. It is not something peripheral or additional. If we have bad doctrine, we will have bad practice. If people have wrong ideas on inter-religious dialogue, then whenever people carry it out they will do things that are not in line with our faith.

We have made an effort here. A few documents have been published. One is *Dialogue and Mission*,[3] which was published at the time I was coming in. I was not responsible for that; the office was; even though I contributed as a member from Nigeria. Then *Dialogue and Proclamation*,[4] which we worked out with the Congregation for the Evangelization of Peoples, thanks to one bishop from India who once said to me, "You are dialoguing with Muslims, and Buddhists, and Hindus. Do you dialogue with the Congregation for the Evangelization of Peoples? Give us one book, the two of you, those two dicasteries. Give us one book."

Q. *An Indian bishop suggested this.*

A. Yes, and he was right. He said: "Give us one book that will say to us: the Church wants both dialogue and proclamation of Christ." He was right, and that is what we did, so that nobody will have the excuse to say, "The Church wants only dialogue today; the Church does not want proclamation of Christ to be stressed. The Church only wants nice, good relations with other believers." Nor will anybody be able to say: "The Church wants Christ to be announced and has no time for dialogue. Dialogue is only for university eggheads; we're rather busy." No. No. The Church never adopted that line. So we now have this document. That's also an area of priority. And when I do visits, even for other matters, I always say to the bishop, "If you have a major seminary, please arrange that I sit with the seminarians and staff to discuss things. And if there is a Catholic university there, I would like to give a talk there for the sake of conscientization and sharing these ideas." I generally try not to refuse when they invite me for a lecture as such, because of the necessity to spread the doctrine that is underpinning the practice of dialogue. We regard this as an important area also.

Another very important area that we have made an effort to emphasize is attention to Traditional Religions. We do so because in inter-religious dialogue usually the big religions—Islam, Hinduism, Buddhism,

---

[3] In 1984, the Secretariat for Non-Christians published a document titled *The Attitude of the Church toward the Followers of Other Religions: Reflections and Orientations on Dialogue and Mission*. It explained that inter-religious dialogue was part of the evangelizing mission of the Church.

[4] On May 19, 1991, the Pontifical Council for Inter-Religious Dialogue and the Congregation for the Evangelization of Peoples, after a very wide consultation process, jointly published the document *Dialogue and Proclamation: Reflections on Dialogue and the Proclamation of the Gospel*. It focuses on the question of the relationship between inter-religious dialogue and the proclamation of Jesus Christ.

and, of course, Judaism (though contact with Judaism is under a commission in another dicastery[5])—attract all the attention. That's correct.
Nevertheless, the people who follow these Traditional Religions are also
God's children, and the Church should give them more attention than
hitherto.

Some call these Traditional Religions "animist", but this is not the
correct word. Indeed, there is no word agreed everywhere for Traditional Religions. In Asia, they tend to call them tribal religions; in
Australia, aboriginal religions; in North America, Amerindian religions;
in Africa, we generally say African Traditional Religion.

We have found that these Traditional Religions deserve more attention than the Church has been giving them up to now. For one thing, it
is these religions that have given the Church the most converts in Africa
and Asia. These converts come from a definite cultural and religious
background, and when they come into the Catholic Church they should
not be culturally lost. The Church should do what it can to evaluate the
cultural and religious context from which they come and carefully identify elements that the Church can adopt or adapt or retouch, and also
those elements that the Church cannot accept, no matter what the
conditions. That cannot be decided a priori. It is only after study and, I
would add, sympathetic study that one can come to such conclusions.

So early on, when I took on this work, in the first three years, we
began a study of what finally became the *Pastoral Letter to Catholic Bishops
in Africa on Pastoral Attention to African Traditional Religion*, which we issued
in 1988. Later on, our members from around the world saw it and said,
"Please, it isn't only Africa. Write a similar letter, retouch it, and send it
everywhere in the world where there are people of Traditional Religions." And we did that too, in 1993.

We sent it to bishops who have such people, for example, the United
States of America. Think of the Tekakwitha Conference, called after
Kateri Tekakwitha—the Native American woman of Canadian extrac-
tion beatified by Pope John Paul II on June 22, 1980. This is a conference
of the Native Americans who are now Catholics, and she is their patron.
They want to retain their culture as Native Americans, and they have a

---

[5] The Commission for Religious Relations with Judaism is under the Pontifical
Council for the Promotion of Christian Unity. This appears as an anomaly in the field of
inter-religious relations, due to historical and other reasons. Thomas J. Reese explains
some of the background for this in his book *Inside the Vatican: The Politics and Organization
of the Catholic Church* (Cambridge, Mass.: Harvard University Press, 1996).

right to that, but they want to be Catholics too. This letter aims to encourage them.

This dialogue with Traditional Religions is not simply dialogue in the classical sense. Here we highlight inculturation, that is, giving attention to these religions and the cultures they influence with a view to a deeper planting of the Gospel among those peoples. It will interest the members of these religions who are now Christians, but it will also interest the members of these religions who still remain in these religions; and if they remain in them they also have a right to dialogue in the ordinary sense. We don't deny them that right, but we take notice of the fact that many of their followers are now Christians and that inculturation will not have serious meaning without a serious study of these religions and cultures.

We have made a big effort here in relation to Traditional Religions. We have one official now who is responsible for following this dialogue with Traditional Religions worldwide, as well as for Traditional Religions in Africa, south of the Sahara. He is Father Denis Isizoh.

I won't forget that when I met the Shintoists in Japan, I said to them: "I come from a background of African Traditional Religion, and I see some similarities: you pay attention to ancestors, you look on trees, forests, rivers not just as trees and forests, but you see a spirit, a power behind them. And you have a type of elevated respect for trees and forests, not because you think a tree has a spirit, but you are really reverencing the one who made those trees and those rivers; and in that you are very near to my people's background religion."

For that reason, I find myself much more at ease with Shintoists than I would find myself with Buddhists, for example. I'm only speaking about a type of what touches the soul, not that I don't value persons. It is very interesting. Not to mention the tribal religions I met in Taiwan, in eastern Taiwan, in Hualien. They had dances that resemble very much the dances of my people. It's very interesting.

All these are religions that generally do not trace their religion to a book or to one founder. They are religions that I would call "the human soul looking for God". Looking for God so that rain, sun, moon, trees, rivers all convey a message to the people. Seasons too, for they are generally agricultural people, and they have a way of being near to God so that when Christianity comes it looks like the midday sun to people who were looking for light at four o'clock in the morning. It's most interesting. It's no surprise that Christianity has had many converts from the Traditional Religions. It's no surprise.

Q. *What do the followers of Traditional Religions say to you when you tell them that you once were like them and that you can, in a way, understand their souls, as it were?*

A. I tell them that I myself come from a background of Traditional Religion, and that I later became a Christian. And I tell them that I do not feel that Christianity has deprived me of anything, but that what my father and his father and his forefathers were looking for, I have found.

Not that Christianity is a better edition of the Traditional Religions. No! Christianity is new, a new reality; it is from heaven, supernatural, not a development of the natural.

Nevertheless, grace builds on nature and does not destroy nature. After all, God gives his gifts as he wills, and the Word of God also is generous, as Saint Justin Martyr or Saint Irenaeus said. Many others too said the same, right down to Pope John Paul II, who said that God gives his grace also outside the visible boundaries of the Church, and there we find the seeds of the Word, seeds of contemplation, precious things, both religious and human, in these Traditional Religions. All this encourages us that inter-religious dialogue is not a secondary school children's debate, nor is it an academic exercise. It is actually part of our witnessing to Christ the Savior.

Q. *As you have explained, the Catholic Church recognizes that the Holy Spirit is somehow active in other religions in various ways and is opening people's minds to the Being who is beyond this world. When the Church promotes inter-religious dialogue, is it seeking to lead people to baptism, to baptize people? Is that the end goal, or is it more complex than that?*

A. It is more complex than that. I would approach it in the same way that Pope John Paul II did in chapter 5 of his encyclical letter *Redemptoris Missio*,[6] published in 1990, in which he speaks of the ways of mission, that is, the various ways in which the Church carries out the mandate given her by Christ.

As Saint Mark records in the last chapter of his Gospel, Christ told the apostles just before he went back to heaven (and so at a supreme moment), "Go into the whole world; preach the Gospel to every creature. Those who believe and are baptized will be saved; those who refuse to believe will be condemned." So Christ sent the Church to bring his

---

[6] Pope John Paul II's encyclical *Redemptoris Missio*—The Mission of the Redeemer—is devoted to "the permanent validity of the Christian mission" and was published on December 7, 1990. In it, he calls for a new evangelization.

good news of salvation to every human being. That's the work of the whole Church. Sometimes we call it the mission of the Church, what Christ sent the Church for, or we can call it evangelization, which is the spreading of the good news of Jesus Christ. But that evangelization "is not done in one act alone", as Pope Paul VI said in *Evangelii Nuntiandi*, the document that he issued after the 1974 synod on evangelization.

In *Redemptoris Missio*, chapter 5, Pope John Paul II names what he calls "the ways of mission". They are the various ways in which the Church carries out the mandate given her by Christ, and I can list them off by heart. First, witness in the name of Christ without words, just by living.

Q. *You mean like the Trappist monks at Tibhirine, in Algeria, or Charles de Foucauld?*

A. Yes. Like those monks, and also like Charles de Foucauld in the desert. Just living the Christian life without preaching to anybody. Just witness to Christ—prayer, asceticism, love of others; help the sick; show love to those who are poor; do service or human promotion, like Mother Teresa and her sisters. They see somebody sick or hungry—they don't give a lecture in theology—they simply clean the person, give the person shelter, food, a bed. They are already evangelizing. They are doing it in the name of Christ. They are not just social workers. People know they are sisters and the reason why they are doing it. They are doing it in the name of Christ; it is not something additional to their Christianity: it is very much a part of it.

Then obviously the mission is also carried out by preaching Christ, by announcing Christ, and by catechesis. Preach so that people will accept the Gospel. If they freely accept, then they are baptized. They are then inserted into the Church, and there is the nurturing of the local community. All that is evangelization.

Then there is inculturation, planting the Gospel in a deeper way. And the Pope then says inter-religious dialogue is one of the ways of evangelization. So too is human promotion, charity work, and assistance, as I mentioned earlier. All of this is evangelization. So when the Church does any of these, the Church is doing them in the name of Christ.

If therefore I meet Muslims, Buddhists, Hindus, I do not do it as an academician from a university, discussing ideas, like a philosopher. I do not do it as a social worker. They know I am a cardinal who believes in Jesus Christ, so I am meeting them in the name of the Catholic Church.

More immediately, I am sent by the Pope and then, in the wider context, as one motivated by my faith. That much is clear. I never hide my religious identity card. That's why those Christians who meet other believers and don't want their identity to be known—I think they are making a mistake.

Are we hiding anything? Are we hiding that we are Christians? Why do we meet other believers?

Q. *But what is the immediate aim of this dialogue?*
A. I would say mutual listening, mutual encouragement, understanding the other. Then, hopefully, collaboration in some work—as, for example, justice, peace, defending the family, society, training of children, drugs—what do we do about this? And about AIDS. It is all that, but much more. It must also foster our being enriched in our love of God, and our seeking the will of God. That is the vertical dimension.

Is that whole activity done because that person must be baptized, and if the person doesn't want baptism then I'm no longer interested? No! It isn't as simple as that.

I meet them as my witness to Christ, and the immediate aim is what I have said: encounter, collaboration, promotion of good works, growth in my faith, growth for the other person in love of God and in seeking God's will. What will the result be? I don't know. The result depends on Divine Providence, divine grace, and the response of each individual: that person, me, and other people. God can use it in ways he knows best, but, whatever it is, it is all under the general umbrella of the mission of the Church.

Every activity of the Church, including inter-religious dialogue, is in the final analysis oriented toward bringing people to God, through Jesus Christ, the one and only Savior.

When some hear of mission, they think only of proclamation. I use "mission" in the sense of the total thing for which Christ sent the Church—"Go into the whole world and preach the Gospel to every creature." Of course, the final hope is that we will all reach heaven and see God as he is. And within the Church, in the world today, if people want to get the benefits of redemption in their fullness, they would have to become members, actual members of the Church.

God's plan of salvation, as Vatican II tells us in paragraph 16 of *Lumen Gentium*—the document on the Church—also includes people who are not actually members of the Church. There are conditions, however: if it is not their fault that they are not members of the Church, if they are open to divine action, if they are ready to do anything their conscience tells them God wants and to avoid what their conscience tells them is not right. Only God can judge all that. But if they are open, God will not deny them the grace necessary for salvation. If their religious contacts with Christians facilitate all that, then all to the good.

But let not those who read our words think that inter-religious dialogue necessarily means discussion. No. It can mean just a friendly visit to another person. It can mean just friendly contact. I visit, let us say, Syria or Japan or Indonesia, and the bishop there arranges that I meet local religious leaders. We exchange good feelings, greetings, good wishes, and that's all. And I encourage the local Christians to be friendly with them. That's good, and it does not necessarily mean a discussion. Or say I visit a leprosy control clinic run by Christians and Muslims in a certain country, and I give them full marks for their working together.[7]

Q. *In what country is this leprosy control clinic run by Christians and Muslims?*

A. It is in one country where Muslims are in the majority. Christians and Muslims run a leprosy clinic. They get the doctors, and they get the nurses. Excellent. I encourage them. That's good. All that is included in what we call inter-religious dialogue. By doing that they showed love of their neighbor. God can use all that to bless them in ways that I do not know. It is a work of faith and hope.

Q. *So the starting point, really, is the recognition that all of these are God's children.*

A. Yes. They are all created by the same God, and all of them are redeemed by the same Christ, and all of them are called to the same heaven. All of us are called to the same heaven, not to another heaven. God wants everyone to be saved. Since that is so, we must take every human being seriously.

---

[7] Of relevance to this general theme is the Aquinas Lecture given by Cardinal Arinze at the Catholic Institute of West Africa, Port Harcourt, February 6, 1988, on *Progress in Christian-Muslim Relations Worldwide* (Nigeria, Jos, Plateau State: Augustinian Publications, 1988).

Q. *That opens a lot of horizons, really, for many people, because people had the impression in the past, and to an extent still today, that there is only one gate to heaven, as it were.*

A. Well, if by gate they mean Christ, they are right. Christ is the only gate to heaven. That means that whoever is saved is saved because of the grace of Christ. But a person may not have become an actual member of the Church with a name in the baptismal register. You just think of all those good people in Africa before the missionaries came, for centuries.

Q. *Are you also thinking of your own ancestors?*

A. Yes. They never saw a priest, never ever. Are you saying that not one of them would be in heaven? You are not serious, because Saint Paul told Timothy, "God wants everyone to be saved and to come to the knowledge of the truth." God will have his own way to judge those who through no fault of their own did not know Christ or the Church, but who are open to his action, who are of goodwill, and who follow their consciences. All those "ifs" are quite a number. It is not easy, but only God will judge that, so that no one will be condemned when it is not his fault. Only God will judge that. Then if the person finally is saved it will be because of Jesus Christ, who died on the Cross, even though the person didn't know that Christ was his Savior. The person will know it on the last day.

Q. *Speaking about the possibility of coming to know Christ, I found one statement in Vatican II's document on the Church in the modern world* (Gaudium et Spes) *quite striking; it said, Christians too have some responsibility for atheism in the world insofar as by their lives "they conceal rather than reveal the authentic face of God and religion."*

A. That is true. If we Christians do not give good witness, we do damage, we do harm, because if people do not see us as good followers of Christ it will obscure what they think of Christ. I heard that Mahatma Gandhi used to say he had great esteem for Christ but for some Christians no, because they were not so faithful to Christ. We hope that is not true.

But if, as Vatican II says, one reason for atheism is that some Christians are not good witnesses of Christ, then every one of us has to watch that. If we give scandal, if we don't live according to the teaching of Christ, we damage not only ourselves, but also other people who might have, through our good witness, believed in Christ.

Q. *When you came here to head this Vatican office, I was already living in Rome, and I remember that not everybody shared this push for inter-religious dialogue. I still hear that some bishops, priests, and lay people do not grasp, or even agree with, what this dialogue is about. Did you find that, too?*

A. I did, to some extent. Of course, I might not be in contact with some who have those doubts. But I was in contact with a few.

I did not regard it as abnormal, because it takes some time to digest what Vatican II has said. It takes time because a Catholic—and he can even be a bishop—may be hesitant, thinking that this thing they call dialogue is dangerous because it risks correct doctrine. And, out of concern for correct doctrine and the integrity of the Catholic faith, the person is hesitant to embrace dialogue. Secondly, the person may have seen some who, in the name of dialogue, do things that are not really the type that Vatican II wanted, some who do dialogue their own way, who do it with wrong ideas that turn some people off.

So I regard it as one of the duties of this dicastery to keep on conscientizing within the Church, especially beginning within the Church,[8] among bishops first of all, because bishops are key people. If a bishop is convinced, he can share it with his priests.

If bishops come for an *Ad limina* visit[9] we generally invite them to our office, especially if they come from a country where the majority are people of other religions. We, the whole staff of our office, sit with the bishops for one to two hours: we listen to them, they listen to us, and we share ideas. It is very important. If a bishop has the tendency to regard dialogue as some kind of hobby for those who have time, it is our duty gradually to present reasons as to why it is not optional, why the bishop is really bound to be interested in inter-religious dialogue, and in the correct spirit. It takes time.

Q. *It's interesting you should say that. Some time ago, I heard something similar from Cardinal Cassidy[10] on the subject of Christian unity. He*

---

[8] A selection of the cardinal's talks, given during his first five years as head of this Vatican office for dialogue with other religions, has been published: Francis Cardinal Arinze, *Church in Dialogue: Walking with Other Believers* (San Francisco: Ignatius Press, 1990).

[9] This is the visit each bishop must make every five years to the pope to report on his work in his diocese and the situation there. See note 2, chapter 9.

[10] Edward Cardinal Idris Cassidy was then president of the Pontifical Council for the Promotion of Christian Unity, the Vatican office engaged in the dialogue and search for unity among Christians.

said his office has to dialogue with bishops and bring them on board in the quest for Christian unity and help them understand and share the direction the Church is following.

A. It is to be expected, and it is our work to do that. It is also our work to show in practice that inter-religious dialogue does not soft-pedal proclaiming the Gospel, that it does not discourage the missionary from proposing faith in Jesus Christ to other people. That is very important.

Q. *Do you see that as a real danger?*

A. Yes, it is a real danger because there are some who, in the name of dialogue, do not want us to talk of conversion to Christ anymore; they don't want us to propose Christianity to anybody. They almost want us to encourage the Muslims to be good Muslims, the Buddhists to be good Buddhists, and the Hindus to be good Hindus; and after that they think our job is done. Such people give the impression that the Church can choose whether to stay with dialogue or to stay with proclamation. And they think they should dialogue, and it is fine, and they are spreading the Kingdom of God in that way.

It sounds innocent, but it is not innocent, and Vatican II did not say that. Because in paragraph 2 of *Nostra Aetate*—the document on the Church and other religions—the Council said, "Although the Church esteems whatever is good or true or noble in the other religions, the Church preaches Jesus Christ as the way, the truth and the life and that only in him do people find the fullness of religious truth and life." That's *Nostra Aetate*—the Vatican II document on the relation of the Church to other religions—that is not yet *Ad Gentes*, the Vatican II document on the Church's missionary activity. The same Vatican II that issued *Nostra Aetate* also issued *Ad Gentes* and *Lumen Gentium*—the document on the Church.

We make it clear that we do not buy the erroneous theological stand of those who push dialogue at the expense of proclamation. That stand is wrong, as *Redemptoris Missio*, the Pope's encyclical *The Mission of the Redeemer*, states very clearly. I have found that when those who are hesitant about dialogue realize that our office is saying all this, that it is presenting the total mission of the Church, then they are reassured.

A Young Cardinal

Pope John Paul II created twenty-eight new cardinals in a public consistory in the Vatican, on May 25, 1985. Cardinal Arinze was one of them. He had been just one year in the Vatican, and when he was made cardinal, he was then one of the youngest cardinals in the Church; only Cardinals López Trujillo (Colombia) and Meisner (Germany) were younger than he.

He received the news that he was to be made cardinal on April 22, 1985, and two days later the Pope made the public announcement.

I asked him how he was given the news.[1]

---

[1] This chapter is based on extracts from the interview recorded on December 16, 2000.

151

Q. *Did the Pope phone you to tell you that he was making you a cardinal? Or, what happened?*

A. I was told that the cardinal secretary of state, Agostino Cardinal Casaroli, wanted to see me. It was not often that this happened; indeed, it was the first time that he wanted to see me. I asked myself, "Have I done anything wrong? What has happened? I am surprised." Anyway, I went. But when I was going in, I saw another archbishop coming out, so I wondered.

In any case, in a short time it became clear what he was calling me for. He said, "The Holy Father is making new cardinals, and you are one of them, and it will be announced in two days' time. Until then you say it to nobody. Clear?" I said, "Clear."

Q. *You weren't asked whether you accepted or not?*

A. Well, I suppose it was implied in my being called. If I had said, "No, no, no, let the Holy Father go on, but cancel my name immediately. I'll give you a red pen with which to cancel my name." It would have been interesting [*laughs*]; but I did not do that.

Q. *Does it happen that somebody refuses to accept the nomination?*

A. I don't know. I have no idea. But it would be a bit funny, indeed, if the Pope said, "I want to make you a cardinal", and the person said, "No, Holy Father. No, thank you." I think that person would be funny.

But from all we have discussed already, you can imagine my own stand. I am not going to do any politicking to be made a cardinal, but if I am asked to be a cardinal, I am not going to say, "No, no, I am not worthy." Who is worthy? [2]

---

[2] The cardinal is referring to an earlier interview, on April 4, 1998, in which he reveals his own thinking on this whole matter. But, as a consequence of the reorganization of the various interviews, the relevant part of that interview is to be found in the next chapter.

Q. *Were you surprised at the news?*

A. You know, it is usual for people to say they are very surprised, they never expected that. I say, "Now, take it easy." If today many people are speculating that the Pope is going to make new cardinals because they know the number there normally should be, and they know that many have died, now they look around and say: "Is he the archbishop of New York, or Venice, or Washington? Or is he the head of this or that dicastery in the Roman Curia?" Well, if the Pope takes one or two or three of them to be cardinal, it is not a total surprise. If any of these says, "I am totally surprised", I would like to say to him, "Are you really serious?"

But still the Holy Father was free. He does not make every head of a dicastery a cardinal. My predecessor in this office was not a cardinal.

Q. *You mean Archbishop Jadot?*

A. Yes. He worked here for four years, and I was here for just one year, even less. So there was no question of saying, "Oh, yes, I presume I am going to be a cardinal."

Q. *How are cardinals made?*

A. I don't know. I only know in my case that I was called and told, "You will be a cardinal. Two days' time. To be announced." I'm just dramatizing it.

Q. *Sure. But doesn't the Pope consult existing cardinals about whom he is going to choose?*

A. I have never been consulted. So I don't know whom the Pope consults. I did not ask, and I did not inquire. Nor shall I inquire. But I only know that the Holy Father has full right to name as cardinal anybody he wishes. That's number one. And number two, no one has a right to demand, "I should be on the list." No, that would not be reasonable. It follows obviously that the Holy Father can consult anybody he wishes. I must presume that. I cannot believe that the Holy Father consults nobody, that he just makes his list without consulting one single person. I can't believe that.

Q. *So you have never been consulted?*

A. No. Nor am I asking to be consulted [*laughs*].

Q. *Not long ago, a fellow African cardinal, Bernardin Gantin, the dean of the College of Cardinals, spoke on the fact that there are many European cardinals, but not so many from Africa or Asia.*[3] *After the last consistory (1998), there were about seventeen cardinals from Africa and a somewhat smaller number from Asia. I understand that you feel you should not raise this question with the Pope, but is it not important that the Church in Africa, and in Asia for that matter, be well represented in the College of Cardinals? Today, Europe seems to have a surfeit of cardinals.*

A. I do not want to go into this question, except to say that implied in what you have said is that every part of the world should be represented, especially as the Church is spreading in the world today. Beyond that I do not want to go, because I don't want to look as if I am politicking or pressuring. I don't like that. A journalist can go into that.

Q. *You have worked closely with the Pope in these years. What particular insight has it given you to the man and to the role of the papacy in the modern world?*

A. Oh, that's a bigger question now. I will have to be very brief here. Obviously the Holy Father is a person of great faith, and great love, and great heart. He has also very clear ideas. And he's a good listener; he does not cut any of us short. None of us can say, "I wanted to tell something to the Holy Father, but he did not want to hear it." So I feel free when I meet the Holy Father to say what I think, and this is very encouraging for our work.

Even when he invites us to lunch, the secretary, the undersecretary, and the president of the council, we know that he wants to know about our work. And he listens and asks questions, and we put before him our plans, and we get his reactions. So it's all very encouraging.

Q. *So he really listens to you.*
A. Not only listens, but is involved.

At first when we went . . . in my first year here, we had seven points to raise with him, and I agreed with the secretary that we would try to

---

[3] Bernardin Cardinal Gantin, dean of the College of Cardinals and formerly prefect of the Congregation for Bishops (1984–1998), made his remarks in answer to a question in an interview with the Italian Catholic monthly magazine *Trenta Giorni*, May 1999. (The magazine is also published in English.) He suggested that the concept of "cardinalatial sees" should be "relativized", and that the red hat should be given more to the person than to the see, as happens today in Africa and Asia, where "cardinalatial sees, as such, do not exist."

get these points across. We put the papers in our pockets, and we sat down.

The Holy Father raised one point, on his own. We discussed it. He raised another one, on his own. We discussed it too. He continued in this way until he had cleared five of the seven points in our pockets, and there remained only two to raise with him. It meant to us that he is very interested in the work, not just in general.

Therefore, when he called us the next time, we wrote up the points on a sheet of paper, and as soon as he said prayers to start the meal, we put a copy in front of him, in front of his secretary, and every one of us. And that's lunch, you know. And we went through all the points. And I have been doing that for the past fifteen years.

Q. *So, what has that taught you about the man?*

A. He is 100 percent devoted to the work of God. He doesn't have time for anything else.

But he's also able to joke, like when he said to me one day at lunch, "Your soup is now cold"; and then he said, "Why not bring him another bowl!" So he even pays attention to the temperature of the soup in my bowl! And he appreciates a joke too. But we don't spend the whole time joking. We discuss issues.

What more do you want from a pope? We know he decides, but he listens to us, he takes us seriously. If we have any contribution, we make it.

Q. *Have you ever asked for an audience, saying you wanted to talk about something specific with him?*

A. Yes. Every time I have asked to see the Holy Father I have gotten an appointment. The bishop who arranges the meetings would only ask me, "Please, is it very urgent? Is it a question of one or two days? Or can it wait one week?" That's the only detail we discuss. Which means I got it every time.

I don't overdo it. If there are things that I don't have to see the Pope about, then I don't ask to see him just for the joy of seeing him, because I know he has much work to do. Most of the things we settle with the Secretariat of State by letter, or with another dicastery.

But when I think I want to see him alone, I have the opportunity. And, in any case, he calls us periodically. He calls each dicastery in this way, generally over lunch.

Q. *What insight has all this given you into the role of the papacy in the world?*

A. The Holy Father coordinates the apostolate, he encourages it, he empowers. He is there to be Christ for us; as the prophet Isaiah said of the Messiah, "The smoking flax he will not extinguish; the bruised reed he will not break." He's not there to quench the spirit, but to encourage. He gives leadership. He's there as the manifestation of Christ's love for us.

And Pope John Paul II gives so much of himself, from morning till evening, beginning with allowing people to come to his daily Mass. How many times does he eat alone with his secretary? I don't know. But there is no pope who has hosted so many people at his table—almost all the bishops of the world. And when you say eating with the Pope, do not imagine you just go there and sit and eat. It is to meet and discuss about the apostolate in a pleasant atmosphere.

Q. *A working meal, in other words.*

A. Yes, yes. The time is not wasted in small talk, which is what we expect. It's good. And then you know that you have one or one and a half hours with him. If you went to his office, you would have fifteen minutes, because he can't give one hour to everybody in the office. If he did that, he would only see few people in a day.

Q. *What other aspects or events stand out for you in this pontificate?*

A. Many. First, the Holy Father sees himself as Vicar of Christ and not just as a bureaucrat sitting in the Vatican City. He visits the parishes of Rome; now he's visiting the 291st parish; then he visits the dioceses of Italy as no pope has done up to now. Now, that is really impressive.

And then no pope has been seen by so many people; people as far away as Australia, New Zealand, and Papua New Guinea, Argentina and Kenya, Japan and Korea. Everywhere you go they say, "When the Pope was here." So that's something. It helps the local Church to see itself as part of the universal Church. It is that same universal Church present in Quebec and Washington, D.C., Lima and Caracas, New Delhi and Wellington, Cairo and Ankara. It's the same Church. There's nothing exactly like that. As one Protestant in the U.S.A. said, "Your Pope knows how to pope." [*Laughs.*] Very clear, that.

Then the Holy Father meets people. He often says: "Man is the way for the Church." He doesn't meet only Catholics or only bishops, priests, and religious. It is the human being—and therefore the people of culture and science, the people of other religions, the government leaders—each of them feels the Pope is for them. At one moment, the youth will feel the Pope is just for them, he's "the Pope for the youth". But the families too will think that the Pope is only for them; and the people of culture and science feel, "This is our Pope." Seminarians feel the Pope is theirs, and you notice, too, that the university students, at least in Rome, think likewise; and he has a Mass for the inauguration of the academic year. It's wonderful. It is something really special that each of them feels the Pope is entirely for them. It means he is really a pastor, near the people. That is also very impressive.

Then there's the Pope's human touch, even within the Roman Curia. It isn't just in the office. The Pope's secretary telephones the cardinal head of the dicastery and says, "What about lunch tomorrow, with the secretary and the undersecretary?" And we know what that means. It means that the Holy Father wants to meet you to discuss with him how the work is going. During the discussion we also eat, but we know that eating isn't the main thing. We can eat at home. But to meet the Pope for one or one and a half hours, that is something. And he is really interested in the work. That is extraordinary. He is very well informed.

Since he knows so many languages, and bishops from around the world come for *Ad limina* visits, almost every bishop has had lunch or supper with him. You can realize what this means; it means he is very well informed, indeed. It also means that many bishops have the opportunity to say what they think straight to the Pope, not through this or that office. If they don't want to say it, then they have themselves to blame, but they had the opportunity. It really is extraordinary. You ask yourself: Is it one person doing all of that or are there several? That is really something.

Q. *In fact, what you are saying is that he has blazed a trail on how to live and exercise the papacy.*

A. Definitely. Of course, every pope cannot do that. Every pope will have to be authentic. So if one day we have another pope who doesn't do exactly what this present Pope is doing, nobody should complain, because God didn't create only one type of pope.

But there is no doubt: he has made a wonderful mark.

Q. *And you yourself, as cardinal and head of one of the Vatican offices, what is your personal experience of the Pope?*

A. I feel that if I want to see the Holy Father, I can see the Holy Father. I can never complain and say I wanted to see the Holy Father but they did not permit me to see him. It has never happened. I do not ask to see him every month because there is no need. But when there is really need, then I request and I get the audience. What more do I want?

Q. *Could you pick up the phone and call him?*
A. No, we don't telephone the Pope. I've never tried it.

Q. *But has he telephoned you?*
A. No. But, equivalently, yes, because his secretary does that. There is his secretary, Bishop Stanislaw, and when he phones we know it is from the Pope. We don't expect the Pope himself personally to phone.

Also, in a few cases, apart from writing, I have, in an emergency, contacted the Pope's secretary, and it has always been an excellent reception. For example, when that priest, Don Florio, who was eighty years old, came to Rome, I phoned the Pope's secretary—it was exceptional—to request that he attend the Pope's Mass, and it was agreed. But I would not do it too often; it could become an abuse.

Q. *Has he read your recent book, which was published in German?*[4]
A. I don't know, but I have given the Holy Father the book, and he looked at it quickly. So I shall not ask him afterward, "Have you read it, Holy Father?" That would be too much!

Q. *You have been a member of many Vatican dicasteries over these years, including the Congregation for the Doctrine of the Faith, the Congregation for the Evangelization of Peoples, the Causes of Saints, and many others. What reflections have you drawn from this experience? What's your own reading from what you have seen and experienced?*
A. The Church is a mystery. It's divine and human. You will notice that in the Credo we say: "I believe in God, Father, Son and Holy Spirit. . . . I believe in the Catholic Church, one, holy, catholic, apostolic. . . . I believe in the resurrection of the dead . . . the forgiveness of sins."

So the Church is also an object of belief. Not an imaginary Church, but the actual Church that exists. As when our Savior was on earth, divine and human, some refused to believe that he was God because they

[4] Brucken Bauen, *Francis Kardinal Arinze in Gesprach mit Helmut S. Ruppert* (Augsburg: Sankt-Ulrich-Verlag, 2000).

thought they knew him. They thought they knew Nazareth. They thought they knew where he came from. He himself once said, "You do not know where I come from", that is, you do not know me. He asked the apostles, "Who do people say that I am?" and they said: "Some say you are John the Baptist, others Elijah. . . ." "But you, who do you say I am?"

So with the Church too, we can see the divine elements: we can see the sacraments; we see especially the Holy Eucharist. We see how the faith has come down through the centuries. We see the martyrs who died for Christ. We see the virgins, the monks, the nuns, and all the people who are sacrificing their lives. And that is glorious. But we also see Judas Iscariots. We also see even some bishops who became heretics along Church history, such as Nestorius. We also see children of the Church who did a lot of damage from inside, and we also see today lay people, men and women, priests, occasionally bishops, who give a very wrong image of the Church and who do not live according to the Gospel.

When the Holy Father led the whole Church in the "*mea culpa*" ceremony[5] on March 12, 2000, he was saying some children of the Church have not shown good witness to Christ and have done damage to Christ and the Church and mankind, and for all those we are very sorry and sad, and we ask God's forgiveness.

This is the Church in which we believe. So I am aware working in the Roman Curia that I am a human being, the people with whom I work here—all of them are human beings—and also those in all the other dicasteries. But the wonder of it is that in the midst of all human weaknesses, and occasionally pride, vanity, even careerism here and there, the mission of the Redeemer goes on.

Remember that even two apostles in the Gospel got their mother to lobby for the ministry of internal affairs and the ministry of finance, and Christ didn't approve at all. And do you imagine that the other ten apostles were any better? No proof that they were better, because they gave John and James a tough time, and Christ had to call all of them to a spiritual conference and tell them, "You don't understand the spirit of the Son of Man. The Gentiles lord it over them, but with you, no! no! no! Authority is to be service. The Son of Man came to serve, and not to be served."

---

[5] The cardinal is referring to the "Request for Pardon" ceremony held in Saint Peter's Basilica, in which the Pope asked God's forgiveness for the wrongs done by "sons and daughters" of the Catholic Church over the centuries, not only to other Christians, but also to other believers.

In the Church, therefore, there is no forgetting the lesson from our Savior. It would be wonderful if everybody were a first-class saint, but, as I am not a first-class saint, what right have I to ask that everybody working in the Roman Curia should become a first-class saint? Have I become one myself?

This is the Church in which we believe. I am not looking for another Church. I love this Church, and I believe in this Church. I am aware that everything is not perfect; we must make a bigger effort, and I begin with myself. As somebody once said: Let there be peace in the world, and let it begin with me.

Q. *Your fellow African cardinal, Bernardin Gantin, dean of the College of Cardinals, has spoken about the careerism he saw during his term of office as prefect of the Congregation for Bishops.[6] In your experience, is it a big issue?*

A. I do not know the proportions myself.

Q. *But it is a reality.*

A. Yes. But is it a surprise? As I said earlier, if Christ trained the apostles for three years in the best seminary that ever existed, and two of them wanted the top places, and the other ten were not any better, are we really thinking that we will do better than Christ did in training? So careerism is a human weakness, and, I think, until the angels blow the last trumpet, there will be people who will try to use an ecclesiastical position as a ladder for self-promotion or for promotion of their friends.

To what extent does that go on, I do not know, but neither am I overly anxious even to know. I just want to do my work quietly, but I need not be so naïve as to believe that nobody would care whether he was promoted or not. It would be a surprise if nobody cared. If you had three thousand people and none of them cared, it would be excellent. If none of them cared whether they were promoted or not, it would be very good, but we are not in heaven yet!

Q. *So it's a question of balancing, perhaps, a person's ambition with the good of the Church.*

A. For myself, it's rather clear to me what attitude I should adopt, and we have discussed that before.[7]

---

[6] Cardinal Gantin's interview in *Trenta Giorni*, May 1999. See footnote 3 above.
[7] The material to which the cardinal refers is to be found in the next chapter.

Q. *Yes, we have discussed it in some depth, and your own position is very clear.*

A. If God wants me to be here, then I am happy. If he wants me to be there in that place, I am happy again. But I will not maneuver; I will not do politicking; I will not try to arrange my future because I trust God and those God has placed over me. So, without worrying about tomorrow, I do the work I am assigned today.

If everybody does that we will have a much simpler formula, and many people will not be suffering. But some people become architects of their own misery because they do not have things they desire and think they want, and they want it badly either for themselves or for their friends. I do not support that mental or spiritual posture. It is a pity if some have that.

I am not sent as the cosmic force to solve all such problems, nor have I a Messiah's complex that I am going to solve it for all such people. No. But I try to do what I can myself, in the little area that I have, like the Brothers of Saint Stephen whom I have in Nigeria. I share that mentality with them, and the posture we should adopt before God, so as not to complicate our spiritual machinery and so as not to spoil the work of God, because we are able to spoil God's work, unfortunately.

Q. *So that's really how you acted, as archbishop of Onitsha, when you appointed priests, moved priests or other people. Is that the way you approached the task?*

A. Yes. I tried to look at it that way. As for appointments of priests: I would sit with consultors who examined what would be the best place to appoint this priest. What is the best place for him and, more important, for the people? Because we are ordained for the people. And when it became clear we moved along that line. But I always discussed with the individual priest and said, "If the assignment we are about to give you is not suitable for you, please come along to me and give me your reasons. If you think it is bad for the people of God, or bad for you, please come forward." He may be right, and if he gives a reason that looks objective, I say Okay. I will reexamine it with the consultors. We reexamine it and change it, because maybe we didn't have enough information before, and we were going to make an unwise decision.

But one thing is clear, even if we made an unwise decision, if that individual after exposing his reasons totally accepts the decision, God will look after that person, even when the superiors' decision is not the best. God will still look after that person.

And another thing is clear to me too: if anyone attacks the superiors, or maneuvers and does politicking, there is no guarantee that God will be with that person, because we are no longer sure the person is doing God's will. Why should God be bound to give you grace to carry out the task into which you maneuvered yourself, which God never wanted for you in the first place, and which you got by politicking? Then you turn around and ask God to give you the grace. God could say, "Look, my friend, who got you into that corner anyhow? You got yourself into a mess; you are the architect of your own misery."

Q. *I was struck in reading one of your talks—I think it was in 1971 to the lay apostolate or pastoral council in Onitsha—where, working with the concept of Church as family, you said if there are problems within the Church, let's talk about them among ourselves, as a family would, but let's not go outside and hang out the dirty linen, as it were, in front of the public.*

A. Yes, that is true.

Q. *So the way you approach the Church is with this concept, this mental framework or understanding of the family. You see the Church as family.*

A. Yes, and I would still say the same today. We must not say that everything is perfect in the Church. Everything is not perfect because we are pedestrians, we are pilgrims on earth, and some of us are holier than others, but all of us have defects—every one of us!

So many things could have been done better. Therefore, without pretending that everything has been done in the very best possible way, we cannot admit that there is no room for improvement, because—yes! there is always room for improvement. We can discuss then, but with love for the Church, with faith in the Church, with love for the superiors and respect for them. I would say even sympathy, because to be at the head is not a picnic; it is not enjoyment. Those at the head have a lot of headaches, so they deserve love and sympathy, even before we give them obedience. Indeed, if a person loves the superiors and sympathizes with them, obedience would become less difficult, much less difficult.

But those at the head must leave it possible for people to discuss things freely, and not punish those who say that everything is not perfect, so that they will be encouraged to discuss it within the Church, with love for the Church. A good family member does not go to outsiders to discuss the problems of his family. A good family member does not go to outsiders and tell people, "You know my mother is not very kind and fights with my father sometimes; my father is very harsh to my mother." A good son or daughter does not say that outside the family. But within the family, that child has a nice way to bring up a point to be discussed. A good family member does not tell outsiders, "You know our house is leaking, our family is in trouble. The roof—we didn't repair it." A person who loves his family doesn't do that. He discusses it within the family, so also in the Church. The more we do that, the better the Church will go; to say that everything is not going well does not mean we don't love the Church.

But if a person thinks something is not going well in the Church, and the first thing he does is to call the TV or the newspaper or the radio and tell the whole world, then I begin to ask myself, "Does this child love his mother?" If so, why go to the marketplace to discuss the defects of your mother? Or what you hold to be the defects of your mother, because they may not even be defects, but you think they are defects. Even so, why don't you do it lovingly in the family?

Q. *And what if the person says, "I'm afraid of my mother, and I can't say it to her?"*

A. I would say, there may be something wrong with you, or something wrong with your mother, or both of you; but in any case it will not justify your going outside to discuss it. If you are afraid of your mother, there is already something wrong. But have you no brothers? Have you no sisters? Have you no father? Is there no other approach? Let it be in the family; it must be possible.

But we must also admit that, even when we have done our best, some people will still misunderstand us, including people in the Church. And two saints can misunderstand one another and disagree. You notice, in the Acts of the Apostles, John Mark didn't go with Barnabas and Paul on the first missionary journey; when the going was difficult, he withdrew, and Paul didn't like it at all. And then, when they were going to do another journey, John Mark wanted to join them, and Paul said, "No, because when we were going the first time and when it was difficult, he withdrew, he's a coward. And now that we are following the beaten track, he wants to join us. He will not join us!" And Barnabas said, "He will

join us", and Paul said: "He will not join us." And they separated, and
Barnabas took John Mark and went a different way to preach, and Paul
took Timothy and went his own way to preach. And all of them ended
up in heaven! All this shows that even good people can disagree, and even
saints who reach heaven may have their defects. There is no guarantee
that every saint was a saint on earth from the word *go*. No! Some saints
were very irascible, but they kept making big efforts to control their
temper.

So in the Church, two good bishops can disagree. Two good cardinals can disagree. Of course! You must have heard of Cardinal Ferrari of
Milan. They said he was against the Pope's holding onto the Papal States,
when he was archbishop of Milan. He was against the Papal States
because it was distracting the Pope from doing his spiritual mission in the
world. And some people in the Roman Curia said, "This cardinal is not
faithful to the Pope", and they marginalized him, and they didn't allow
him to meet the Pope anymore. That's what we heard. Later he died. He
has been beatified, which means an apology had been made. He was
right, but he was misunderstood.

But there was not only Cardinal Ferrari, now blessed, there was also
Galileo. He said the earth was actually moving, the sun is not moving at
all; and the theologians said he was wrong, and he was punished, but he
was right.

And yet we love the Church, even though mistakes are made by
Church officials. Yes. This is the only Church we have. Christ could have
sent angels to run the whole Church; no need for bishops and the Pope,
but he didn't do that. He knows why he chose us men, and then that's
that.

Q. *In my years reporting Church affairs here in Rome, and in some other
countries, I have met theologians, and even bishops, who feel they can't speak
forthrightly, or who are afraid to speak. I don't know whether it is due to a lack
of courage on their part, but they feel they can't speak freely. I remember once
being on a TV program in Naples with theologians, and coming back on the
train to Rome we talked a lot, and at one point I said to them, "The things you
have said to me now, have you written them somewhere? Can I read them
somewhere?" They said: "No, no, we can't write those things because if we do
we'll lose our teaching positions." What do you say to people like this?*

A. It would be too rash for me to go into any summary judgment
without knowing enough about such cases.

In brief, however, in a more general way, I can say this. First, they must not be forbidden to think or to say what they think. Secondly, they must be willing, somehow, to share their thoughts with some people in the Church and also with some people who have a kind of share in the decision-making process. Thirdly, they must be willing to accept that if, after they have said what they think, those who are officially charged with looking after what the Church is teaching say finally to them, "We think you should modify that, or that, or this", they must be willing to absorb that, even if that judgment is not finally infallible. Because it may well be that those who examined it, to the best of their lights, think that such a phrase or position should be modified. But it may be that after twenty or thirty years it would be found that neither the first nor the second position was totally right, or that the theologian was 80 percent or 90 percent or even 100 percent right. It's possible. That means that within the Church we must also be ready to be misunderstood.

A person can be right, but not be understood. Some people can be geniuses: they see a point but they are ahead of their time, and they are not sufficiently appreciated. It can happen. If a person is not prepared even to be misunderstood, he is unrealistic.

Here there is a temptation: that all those who make a mistake claim themselves as giants ahead of their time, who are not understood, and they pity those who did not understand them and look down on them. That is a temptation. It is very difficult to be a judge in one's own case. You know the old fallacy in logic that was taught to us when we were doing logic:

> *Great men have been misunderstood,*
> *I am misunderstood,*
> *therefore I am a great man.*

Or

> *Great men have been ridiculed or marginalized,*
> *I am ridiculed,*
> *which proves that I am a great man.*

It doesn't always follow. It is true that some great men have been ridiculed, some of them, including Saint Thomas Aquinas, at some stage, even by the local bishop—but later on he was proved right. Although great men have been ridiculed, fools also have been ridiculed. And it may well be that, although you are ridiculed, you may not belong to the group of great men but to the group of fools, even if they are few. So it doesn't prove it.

The fact that what you say is not accepted does not necessarily prove that you are a genius, ahead of your time. Maybe you are, maybe you are not. But what we expect from you is the humility and the realism to listen, to voice your view, to listen and to accept if it is said that you are wrong. Please, accept it, even if you do not understand. At least accept that you cannot be a judge in your own case. For the rest, you leave it to God and to time.

Humility is a necessary commodity. It is not the same as obscurantism. It is not the same as saying that the official line is the only line that is true and anything that differs from that official line is false. The Church has never said that. No. No. The Church even distinguishes between an authoritative statement and an infallible statement. They are not the same. The Church says only that the theologians must respect what the authority says. It does not say that whatever authority says must be held as the only truth. Because even Vatican II says that "The truth cannot impose itself except by virtue of its own truth, as it makes its entrance into the mind at once quietly and with power."[8]

But the individual must distinguish between being condemned— and he may be wrong, or he may be right, or partially wrong and partially right—and rebelling against the lawful authority in the Church. I remember one religious—this time a sister—not because of doctrine, but because of some disciplinary action, said to me, "I will not fight my superior, even when I don't agree with what that superior did or said, because if I fight the superior I do not think that God will remain with me." Full marks. Full marks.

Q. *Like Al Gore and the Supreme Court!*
A. No [*laughs*]. No, that is totally different. I'm in the area of faith, and because of my faith I respect the superior. I will not fight against my superior. While in political and social matters that's wise. And also in soccer, the referee blows the whistle and says, "You're offside." For the sake of peace we accept that, otherwise they throw bottles on the soccer field, so we accept the decision of the referee as final. But it may well be

---

[8] *Dignitatis Humanae* (the document on religious liberty), no. 1.

that when they take a photograph or a video and look at the video or the photo, they may find that the referee was wrong and the player was not offside. There we accept the referee's decision for disciplinary reasons and good order.

But for us in theology and in the Church, it just isn't as simple as that. It is more our faith, our love of God and our faith in the Church, which includes the Church as divine and human. The human element can fall short, and we admit that. So even if my superior is not the holiest or the wisest or even the most prudent, I still respect the authority of God in that superior. I will not fight the superior, I will not ridicule the superior, I will not mock the superior, I will not sabotage the authority of the superior because, if I do that, I cannot reasonably expect God to be with me and protect me.

On the other hand, the superior has a grave responsibility before God. Humility and fairness are virtues that should mark the superior.

Q. *I've met theologians who have felt in all conscience that what they have written they believe in their heart to be true, and if they are asked to say that they don't hold this, they feel it is a violation of their conscience. If somebody has studied and written something and at the end of the day feels, "Really, in my heart, I can't understand where I am wrong. I can't see where I am wrong; how can I say I don't hold this position?" What would you say to such a person?*

A. Of course you have the right to expose all your arguments to the Church superiors. That position is respectful. It does not mean that a person be obsequious or servile, in the sense of lacking in courage. Respectful silence, yes, would be honorable. It is not duplicity.

But conscience, while it is the criterion of what we must immediately do, cannot be the final criterion for theological truth; otherwise everyone would say, "My conscience tells me that is right, so it doesn't matter what the Pope says. I will follow my conscience." If we acted like that, everybody would become his own pontiff. Christ set up the Church so that we would have a visible teaching authority to guide us on questions regarding faith and morals.

It is not the conscience of every theologian that guides us in faith and morals. If a theologian wants to set up conscience against the official Church teaching authority, that's a big undertaking. It would be safer for that theologian to say, "My view is what I have written. Since the authority set up by Christ says it is not correct, I am ready to submit. I won't write further along my line; I will keep silent. I will not oppose the official teaching line." At least that much.

If you are right, God and history will look after you. It may be long after you and I are dead, but if you want to fight the issue and rebel today, even if your stand were right, I think it would be an offense against faith and humility. Because a person can be misunderstood, and some theologians have been condemned even by bishops, but later on they were found to be correct.

Q. *Sure. We have seen some such cases this century.*
A. Yes. So an individual who is not ready to be misunderstood is unrealistic. Because the person is asking for angels to run the Church, and Christ did not choose angels. He could have, but he didn't.

Q. *For many years now you've been a member of the Congregation for the Doctrine of the Faith. What have you seen in your dealings with different theologians? You may not have met them face-to-face, but at least you have had reports on them; you've listened to the feedback. What have you learned?*
A. Effort to articulate our faith must continue, and the Church needs theologians, and they have an important role. The teaching authority of the Church has a different role. They are not opposed obviously, because the theologians work very much with the teaching authority of the Church. If a theologian has as much knowledge as possible, but also humility and realism, then I think things will work out well. So that even if the theologian is misunderstood, and that's already saying a lot, the theologian with spiritual equipment will know the correct posture to take.

Q. *Thank you for answering these questions, but with your agreement I would like to move on to another topic.*
A. Yes.

Q. *When the Pope, in his 1995 landmark encyclical on ecumenism,* Ut Unum Sint,[9] *asked Christian leaders to help him rethink how the papacy is exercised, in your view, what was he asking for?*
A. I myself can only figure out . . . not that I have any inside information on that. I can only figure out from the actual documents that he

---

[9] The encyclical was published on May 25, 1995, and is the first in the post-Vatican II period to be dedicated primarily to the ecumenical movement.

has said, "Give me ideas; if you think there are other ways of exercising the primacy, I am open to discussing them."

Q. *Have you given him any ideas?*
A. No, not me personally.

Q. *Why not? Did you feel that you had no ideas to offer?*
A. Oh, no! Not that I have no idea, but I am thinking that the Pontifical Council for Christian Unity, which refers to other Christians, and some other offices from around the world would give some ideas. If I develop any ideas, I shall have avenues to bring them forward.

Q. *What do you see as the future of Christian unity? It's been one of the things that the Pope has been pushing hard for.*
A. Christian unity is very necessary.[10] It is not easy to see how soon it will happen, and how it will come about. But God knows. The problems, obviously, are many. But it is not the will of Christ that Christians be divided. We must keep praying and working for union.

Q. *I remember you once said to me that you thought it was easier for Christians to unite in Africa than in Europe, since the African Christians had not lived through the historical battles that were fought on this continent.*
A. Yes. Instead of "easier", I might say "less difficult". I think this because Christians in Africa are in any case young in terms of history, and so they don't have the heavy weight of historical traditions as in Russia, in Germany, or in Switzerland or Britain, where many things are mixed up with national sensitivities that make it all the more difficult. But God's Spirit is there. In Africa there is not such a weight of history. I say this without wanting to suggest that Africans are better Christians. And obviously we don't want to do Church unity by continents. But each continent should contribute. And the Africans, since sometimes we have in the same family a member of African Traditional Religion, a member who is a Christian, and occasionally even a Muslim, it should be less difficult for us to contribute from that angle. That's what I mean.

---

[10] Cardinal Arinze, when he was a bishop in Nigeria in 1966, wrote a booklet (*Towards Christian Unity*) on the quest for Christian unity, published by the Onitsha Archdiocese.

Chapter 12

God's Providence in Life

Pope John Paul II visited Nigeria for the second time in March 1998; this time to preside at the beatification of Father Tansi, the first native-born Nigerian—and indeed the first native-born person in the whole of West Africa's fourteen countries, from Cameroon to Mauritania—to be declared blessed by the Church.

Cardinal Arinze accompanied the Pope for this unique event in the history of Christianity in Nigeria. One could see the joy on his face throughout those days, and whenever the Pope mentioned his name at the public ceremonies at Oba, near Onitsha (more than two million people), and at Kubwa, near Abuja (700,000), the crowd cheered loudly because they knew he had played a major role in making this day possible.

It was a moment filled with many memories for the cardinal, a time of reflection. Not long after his return from Nigeria, on April 4, 1998, I interviewed him at his office in Rome, to capture his deeper emotions and reflections while they were still fresh. What follows is the most personally revealing part of that interview and, perhaps, of this entire book.

Q. *Your Eminence, let me begin with a rather personal question: it is about God's providence in your own life. I would like to know how you see that God's providence has worked in your life. It seems obvious to me that an event like the beatification of Father Tansi would surely make you reflect deeply on how God works through you. It was you who decided not to let the memory of Father Tansi fall into oblivion; and it was you who opened the path to his beatification. So you have seen that God has worked through you in some way, and the people in Nigeria too knew that you had a hand in bringing the Pope back to them. I saw this for myself in Onitsha and Abuja. So it seems clear to me that God's providence has been at work in your life. How do you read it?*

A. Well . . . Divine Providence works in many ways that are beyond us. There is a prayer that Mother Teresa said often or, rather, a phrase she used often: "May God help us not to spoil his work!" If only we do not spoil God's work, he will use others and us in his plan, which we need not understand.

I suppose some things we think we did, but God knows that it isn't really we who did them; it is he, but perhaps we didn't spoil his plan. It is a very sad thing that we are able to spoil God's plan and prevent it from unfolding as the Lord God would want it. Even though God is above all of us, he has condescended to allow us to contribute.

So in his own ways he brings us to be alive just at that time. Perhaps if I were born ten years before, or ten years after, the events would all have been different. So all of us should acknowledge this, not with many words but just with adoration of Divine Providence, and rejoice when God uses us in some way.

The fact therefore that I knew Father Tansi, and that my successor as archbishop of Onitsha, Archbishop Ezeanya, also knew very much about Father Tansi (which made him very happy and anxious to continue promoting the cause), that made a lot of difference. And some of the priests of the tribunal, they too had known Father Tansi. I know one priest, Father Celestine Obi, who comes from the very place where

Father Tansi had been a parish priest; he would have been very young then, but he would have known him, at least as a small boy. In all these ways, at least, Divine Providence worked.

Then the bishops of Nigeria came to Rome for their *Ad limina* visit in 1995, when the cause of Father Tansi had almost been completed, and they, as a group, asked the Holy Father if he would come to Nigeria for the beatification, and they followed it up in writing. And I know that the president and the vice president of the Nigerian Bishops' Conference went to the Secretariat of State several times in the last three years. So it was not a thing that happened suddenly, nor was it a thing that was, let us say, effected by any one person. Many people contributed. The people would also have their thought that I may have contributed somehow, but I will not go into that!

Q. *I see you are very conscious of God's providence working in your life.*
A. Yes, yes. I will never forget one Nigerian priest, one of those ordained with Father Tansi, the same day—he was Monsignor Nwanegbo, who died in 1965. When I was just a young priest, in December 1960, I came to visit him soon after my return from Rome. I said, "Monsignor, I am sorry; I should have been here an hour ago, but I was delayed in leaving home. I'm sorry." He said to me, "You don't know what would have happened to you if you had left home at that time. You don't know whether God delayed your departure and saved you from an accident." We don't know. I won't forget that advice. He was one of our first priests.

There are many things that God arranges on our way, individuals who come into our lives. If I am sitting here today, who knows? How is it explained? Only God knows the combination of events. Sometimes we say a person is lucky. I never apply to myself the word "luck". No, I say it is providential, because it isn't really blind fate or fortune or a blind combination of events. It is God directing all.

The one thing all of us should be attentive to is not to spoil God's plan, if only we didn't do that, which means positively trying to respond to what God wants of us. That's why one reflection I put together on one hundred years of Christianity in Africa—it was the year the Pope came to Nigeria, 1982—I titled *Answering God's Call;*[1] answering God's call in the sense of the call to the Gospel for Nigerians. Answering it.

---

[1] Archbishop Francis Arinze, *Answering God's Call* (London: Geoffrey Chapman, 1982).

If only we would answer God's call. He always takes the initiative. He will arrange the rest. And I could go into little details in my life, but there is no need. And some of them would be too personal. But I am very aware of individuals whom Divine Providence has used to make me be where I am, or what I am, or know what I know, or to save me from this thing, or that one. Some I would never know. Some I would know.

So, I strongly believe in Divine Providence; I strongly believe that God has us almost "in the palm of his hand", as the prophet Isaiah (cf. Is 49:15–16) would say, and that nothing escapes him.

Q. *So when you pray, what do you pray? Do you pray to be open to God's plan? Do you pray and thank God for his providence? Or what?*

A. All this. To thank God for his care of me, of others; to beg God for light to know what he wants of me; for strength to do it; for perseverance, not to get tired of doing it. All the time aware that he knows what he wants of me. He is not guessing. He also knows what I can do, so he won't want of me what I am not able to do.

Therefore, for example, when the Holy Father was planning to bring me to Rome, I did not know it. But I was asked by Archbishop—now cardinal—Eduardo Martínez Somalo, whom the Holy Father delegated. He said the Holy Father was thinking of bringing people to Rome, about ten archbishops, and he would choose two or three or four to work in the Roman Curia. I was then archbishop of Onitsha. "Would I accept?"

I said, "I have no option, whatever the Holy Father wants." He said, "Yes, but he wanted to know what your choice would be." I said, "No. I have no choice." He said, "No choice?" He wanted to know if I preferred to remain as archbishop of Onitsha or to move to Rome. I said, "I prefer neither. I don't prefer one or the other. I am quite happy where I am, and if the Holy Father calls me to Rome I am quite happy there also, and if he decides that I should be somewhere else that is neither of these two, I would be quite happy again there. But I will not choose even one."

He said to me, "But which is better for the Church: that you stay where you are, or that you go to Rome?" I answered, "I cannot be a judge in my own case. Actually, I don't know which is better for the Church. I have no idea whether it is better for the Church that I stay where I am or I be called to Rome. I do not know. But one thing I know, that wherever the Holy Father puts me I will be happy. So tell the Holy

Father not to worry how I feel, and to be sure that I will be happy anywhere he puts me, or if he leaves me where I am, that he has no difficulty." So he asked me whether I was ready to put all that in writing. I said, "I have no difficulty. If you want, I will put it in writing." He said, "Do so, and bring it another day." I did so. I brought it another day. Then after a month I got the paper: "The Holy Father asks you to work in the Secretariat for Non-Christians." I had no idea where the Holy Father was going to put me. He asked whether I consented. I said, "I have already given the answer before, so asking me is totally unnecessary." So that is how I came here!

So if I have any difficulty in my work, as I have—everybody will have some difficulty in his assignment no matter where—I just go into the chapel, and I have no difficulty in praying to our Lord. I say, "Lord Jesus, you appointed me to this. I didn't ask. I didn't refuse. I didn't do politicking in order to be assigned here. Therefore I have a right to get grace from you to do this work." And I am sure he will listen to such a prayer!

We have a proverb in my language, the elder who tells a boy to catch a rat. There's a type of rat in my place called *Nkakwu*, not an ordinary rat; and this rat smells very much, even when alive.

Q. *A kind of skunk?*
A. Maybe. So the elder who tells the boy to catch a skunk will have to give him water to wash his hands afterward, because the boy didn't even know that this little animal smells so much, and the boy in all innocence obeyed the elder and caught the animal. The elder has the obligation to give him water to wash his hands.

So if I relax totally in the hands of Divine Providence, I don't resist God. I don't fear Divine Providence because I know that God is not arranging to kill me. God is arranging for my good in the greater plan for his glory. So why should I be afraid of what God wants?

The same idea I tried to insist with the Brothers of Saint Stephen, that congregation that Divine Providence began through me. I said to them, "Please do not pressure your superiors to give you this or that or that or that. Do not insist on what you want. Don't ask for anything. Allow your superiors to give you an assignment. Don't put them in a corner. If you see that some harm will come to the Church if you accept an employment, then tell them the whole thing in all frankness; hide nothing. If you think you are not able to do a job, tell them and tell them your reason. But after telling them, be totally at peace; if after that they say, 'You are going to do this', accept it, and God will look after you.

"But the moment you begin to push your own will, and say what you want, and do politicking and get this one to talk for you, and the other one to pressure and talk for you, that moment you are no longer sure that you are doing the will of God. Perhaps you are now doing your own will, which you obtained by getting your superiors in a corner. Then we are not sure you are doing God's will, and why should God be bound to give you grace to escape from the predicament into which you have maneuvered yourself?"

For example, when we were called to Rome that time, including Archbishop Ryan of Dublin.

Q. *Archbishop Dermot Ryan?*

A. Yes, and also Cardinal Etchegaray and Archbishop Fagiolo—now cardinal of Chieti-Vasto, in Italy. Within six months or one year, Archbishop Ryan died. I said to myself, "Ah, you see, Divine Providence. We don't know what God has in mind." Suppose the Pope called him from Dublin, and suppose he refused, and if God knew very well that he would die, suppose he refused? But he did not; he came. God plans everything. We don't know. Suppose he had refused, and then he died; God could ask, "Who is that who has come before me?" And he would say, "I am the archbishop of Dublin." God could say, "Archbishop of what? Isn't that the fellow I wanted to transfer to Rome, and he maneuvered, and didn't want to go? I don't know what you have been doing for the last six months. You have been doing your own will. I had no hand in it all; I only permitted it because you wanted it." I only take this as an example.

So I am always afraid of pressuring so that I get an assignment, because I am no longer sure that it is the will of God. I think it is very dangerous in the spiritual life. Whereas when the superiors are totally free to give assignments, then I am surer that I am doing the will of God, not my own will. And I am surer that God will give me the grace, and that he will never give me an assignment above my power.

Q. *Is this how you saw it when the Pope appointed you bishop for the first time?*

A. Yes, the same thing. It was 1965. I was Catholic education secretary at Enugu. The nuncio, Archbishop Bellotti, called me to Lagos to the nunciature,[2] and said, "The Holy Father wants you to be the auxiliary bishop to the archbishop of Onitsha." I looked at him and said, "Excellency, there must have been a mistake." He was shaken. He said, "What do you mean?" I said, "You must have come to the wrong person; maybe there was a mistake in the name." He said, "What do you mean?" Then I named one priest whom I thought would be the bishop, because at that time there was a rumor that a bishop would be appointed, so I named one priest. I said, "It must be this name you mean to call, and you called me by mistake." He was shaken. He asked me, "Are you Francis Arinze?" I said, "I am." He said, "Then it is you; it is not a mistake." That was the nuncio from Verona; he has since died. He said, "So you are the person." I said, "Are you sure that it is me that the Holy Father wants?" He said, "Yes." I said, "Okay, if the Holy Father wants it, then I accept." I didn't argue anymore because I thought if Divine Providence wants it, God must have something in mind that I don't understand.

Q. *Where did you start with this understanding of Divine Providence?*
A. I cannot tell. I don't remember. But that has been very clear to me. I have tried to share it with others, because I have seen too many people, priests, religious sisters, who have become, as I often put it, "architects of their own misery", because they are pushing their own wills in subtle ways. They are not trusting Divine Providence enough, so they are struggling, trying to get what they want in little things, and that's the beginning of misery and they remain "spiritual dwarfs". They won't grow because we are not really sure that they are not doing their own will in subtle ways. So how can they be sure they are doing God's will? As Mother Teresa says, "May God help us not to spoil his work."

Q. *And was this also how you started out in your vocation to the priesthood?*
A. I cannot really analyze myself that much to be able to tell when this idea [of Divine Providence] became clear to me. I cannot tell whether it was when I was fourteen years of age. I cannot tell. But what I know is that it was clear to me at the time I was named bishop in 1965, and it was clear to me when I was made archbishop two years later. It was

---

[2] On July 6, 1965, Pope Paul VI named Father Arinze titular bishop of Fissiana and auxiliary to Archbishop Charles Heerey. On July 14, Father Arinze was called to the nunciature in Lagos and informed of this and asked if he would accept. The announcement was made public on July 31, 1965.

clear to me, and it has guided me and given me a type of peace of mind so that I am not afraid. For example, coming to Rome to the Curia was a big change for me from being archbishop of Onitsha. It was a big change but, as Archbishop Martínez Somalo (now cardinal) told me in Rome, "You were serving Christ in Onitsha; the same Christ is in the Vatican." And it has worked out exactly so.

And looking back I am very happy and don't regret a single thing. I heard that some priests were surprised that I accepted the assignment to come to Rome. Well, those priests have to revise their whole approach. Their approach is wrong, definitely wrong. It is not correct.

I cannot understand how a bishop, once the Pope, having examined and prayed and consulted, says, "I think I will give you this assignment," could have the guts to say, "No, I shall not accept." But what are you going to accept after that? For the rest I would be afraid to go before God, because he can say, "You have been doing your own will; you have not been doing my will. You have not been open to my action; you have been spoiling my work. You have not allowed me to use you. You were afraid of my plan. You don't trust me. You don't love me then. You don't realize that I love you. You feel like a slave. Not good." And a priest or a religious or a baptized Catholic who constructs his own spiritual life by seeking what he wants is on the wrong track, really. That person may not commit any major sin, but he must have a truncated, or delayed, growth.

Q. *I am very glad that I have focused on this question; I did so because I think it is worth trying to understand what is really behind a person's life.*

A. You have asked all these questions about this concept! When I meet the Brothers of Saint Stephen next time I will go into greater depth with them, because I think it is one of the reasons for misery for many people in their spiritual life. They make it all very complicated by pushing their own will; they spoil everything, and that is one reason why many are not happy. It is not because they don't possess this or that or that, or because they are not posted here or there or there. No! It's they who are spoiling their own lives. And now it's clearer to me when you have almost forced me to analyze it. So I will now stay longer on this point with them when I meet them next September, God willing.

Q. *I personally think this is a fundamental concept. It makes me reflect on what happens to us in the educational process. When you go to school, they tell you to develop your critical sense, and so the educational pattern that most of us go through is one in which you are told to make decisions, to try to follow your conscience, once you understand what it is your conscience is saying. It is very easy to be doing one's own will, as you say, but it is not so simple to discern clearly when you are moving into doing your own will rather than God's will. The way you are suggesting seems very clear to me, but you leave the decisions to others—your superiors.*

A. Of course, there are occasions, circumstances, where it is not easy to know God's will, where it is not possible to ask the superiors to decide; they cannot decide on all details. So all of us go through that agony: everyone—parish priest, religious, bishop, cardinal, father of a family, mother of a family, individual persons. There are many points on which we cannot ask our superiors to decide for us. We take the ordinary means: we pray; we study the situation and try to be as objective as possible; we ask advice of those we know.

And we are not afraid to ask advice of people who we fear may have a different opinion from ours; otherwise we are like that king in the Book of Kings[3] when Jehoshaphat, the king of Judah, was asked by the king of Israel, I think, "Let's go to war." And the king said, "Is there no prophet we can consult whether it is the will of God?" He said, "Well, there are my prophets." But he said, "Is there no prophet of Yahweh?" He said, "There is one, Micaiah, but I don't want to contact him because he always prophesies unpleasant things." But the other king said, "Don't speak like that"; and so they called Micaiah and asked him, "Are we to go to this war or are we not?" He said, "Yes, go! You will win." But they said, "Look, we ask you in the name of Yahweh to tell us the truth." Then Micaiah said, "Since you want the Word of the Lord, the Lord says this: I saw them, and the very many false prophets, and the devil said, 'Who will bring the king there so that they will die at the war front?' So go home!" So that means, Micaiah said, "The Lord says, 'Do not go to this war because you will be beaten.'" And the king said to the other one, "Didn't I tell you that he never prophesies any good about me?" The king went to war, and he was killed, of course. There he was, afraid to consult, afraid to consult the one prophet of the Lord. And when he got that consultation, he did not like what was said, and therefore he did not accept it.

We are often like that: we are afraid to consult the man of God, the person who is well informed, because we fear that the advice from that

---

[3] 1 Kings 22:1–40.

person may not be in line with what we want to do. Self again! And when we hear such advice, ah! then we rationalize, and we look for others to ask so that they will say a different thing. It can happen even to religious. Many religious today say they are doing discernment, and by that they mean, "Ah, the superior wants us to do something we don't want to do, so we hold a meeting in which everybody gives his opinion, and so the more people that give an opinion against that the better." All that in the hope that the superior will be so tired and sick and disgusted or perhaps afraid—they frighten the superior! So the superior changes his position and goes along with what many of them want, and they call it discernment! It really is a group deception; they are deceiving themselves because they are afraid of the truth. That's what we all have to watch out for.

It's like when a person wants to do a thing, he can always get a text of Vatican II, especially *Gaudium et Spes*—the document on the Church in the modern world—to support his case. It's like this: suppose a person wants to drink wine—there is a section of Scripture that would seem to justify it; while for those who are against drinking wine, there is another section of Scripture that would seem to justify that too. Not because the Scriptures are ambiguous, but because the individual is retouching the text a bit and is changing the interpretation to suit what he wants to do. He is afraid to be challenged by the whole book as it is, by reality as it is; he is afraid to live with reality. He wants to live in a dream world made by himself. So he is the architect of his own misery, and there is no hope until he decides to take the full plunge, that is, to trust in Divine Providence.

So, to summarize: I would say sometimes the superiors cannot decide for us, because it is not their role to decide on every detail. We have to decide, but we must not be afraid to consult and to listen to good advice, even when that advice does not please us.

For example, I am president of the Pontifical Council for Inter-Religious Dialogue. I cannot ask the Holy Father to decide on every point; it is not right. There must be some decisions that I have to make, but I have to be careful to look for the wisest route, to seek good information, to look for sound advice, even from people whom I may not naturally like. And when something seems clear from the information in front of us, or from the people who are well informed or serious, or from the number who think the same way—all honest people—all those are indications of the will of God; we go along with that. We must not ask for mathematical certainty, but we must be ready, at any time we see the will of God to be different, to change and, if necessary, to apologize.

It helped me very much when I was an archbishop . . . although I had consultors and I took them very seriously, the priests knew and the lay people too—women, everyone—that if they brought me any information that looked serious that I took them seriously, and I would not mind changing my policy if what looked objective indicated another way. Why not? If a bishop does that, people will cooperate more because they will see that their advice is taken seriously.

It does not mean that I take the advice of whoever sat last on the chair, because acting in that way you become an object of ridicule. You would have some firm points, but it would also mean that on many things I thought I knew, I now see that I didn't know. So it doesn't mean doubting everything, but it means being open to looking for God's will and not always being sure what God wants.

I know that Father Michael Scanlan, president of the Franciscan Steubenville University, in Ohio, wrote a book titled *What Does God Want?* Such a book is necessary because many people think they know what God wants. Not always!

The person who does God's will is always at peace. He isn't a person agitated or disturbed. What is going to agitate him? That interior peace is very much based on knowing that you are doing God's will, and therefore you are safe.

If you had a pilot who is regarded as one of the best pilots of Alitalia, and the aircraft is one of the best, and the mechanics are the best, and everything is well, then, so far as human trust is concerned, you sit as a passenger, and you relax. If you are still worried, well, you are always nervous. That's human trust. But when we trust God, it's so much more.

Q. *On your spiritual journey through life, Father Tansi must have given you much advice or counsel over the quarter of a century you knew him. What piece of his advice or counsel remains in your mind today?*

A. I cannot remember his exact words in this matter, but the general advice that would have become a sediment, the fossilization of his many words, would be this: "Be serious in your response to God." Or what he himself says in another place, "If you are giving yourself to God, you might as well give yourself entirely to God." These are not the exact words, but something like that.

So that when Professor Isichei wrote his biography—she is from New Zealand, but was a professor in Jos at that time—she entitled the book *Entirely for God*.[4] That is, Father Tansi was thoroughgoing, and his response to God's call was without looking back: it was wholehearted. He wasn't becoming a priest halfway. And when he became a monk, I understand that he said to his novice master, "Father, if we must do this thing, we might as well do it properly. Do not spare me." Or something like that. This was really his style. He was not going to accept half measures, or those who say "yes, but. . . ." They say yes now, and then they say no tomorrow. Then they qualify it; then they hedge again and dodge and complain and so on.

I never saw Father Tansi complaining. Never. He must have felt the cold in Mount Saint Bernard, but I am not aware that he ever complained. It may well be that his last sickness went far before those near him realized it was serious. I am sure that if he had been there to see what was being arranged for his beatification, I am sure he would have said, "Look, it is not really necessary. There is no need." Often he would say, "It is all right", when actually he was suffering.

So it's a message that remains in me as something of him and from him, that a person who lives by half measures, whether a priest or a religious sister or a married person or simply a baptized person, Father Tansi would say, "Look, that is not all right at all."

Q. *I notice that your own motto is "May the Kingdom of Christ flourish"—"Regnum Christi floreat."*

A. Yes, that's what I took as bishop in 1965.

Q. *Why?*

A. I saw my assignment as bishop as being at the service of Christ and his Kingdom. That is all summed up in the feast of Christ the King, or even by Palm Sunday. The people were throwing their clothes in front for Christ on the donkey to ride upon. They were showing him that they were putting everything at his feet; they accepted him as their King; they gave him that which they had. They trusted him. They were not keeping back anything from him.

That is what the bishop is there to promote—that all may know Christ. Indeed, that's the motto I gave the Brothers of Saint Stephen,

---

[4] *Entirely for God: The Life of Michael Iwene Tansi*, by Elizabeth Isichei (Kalamazoo, Mich., and London: Macmillan Education, 1980).

"That they may know you." It was from when Christ said, "This is eternal life that they may know you, the one true God, and Jesus Christ whom you have sent." If all the world would know him, would trust him, would accept him as universal King, King of kings, King of all hearts, not a king dominating, but the King who is really the center, to whom we go, in whom we finish.

Q. *In those early years as a seminarian in Rome, and since then, what spiritual author or theologian has influenced you? Or has there been one?*

A. During our theology course, the major theological textbook in dogma was of Archbishop (later Cardinal) Parente, and the major moral and pastoral one was by the Redemptorists, presented by Father Visser. Those gave us a major orientation in life, and that has carried me quite a distance.

From the point of view of spiritual authors, from my ordination onward I have tried to keep very close to the documents from the various popes; starting especially with Pius XII, John XXIII, and so on. Especially the encyclicals, particularly those that refer to the priestly life or ministry, because there one is on safe ground: it's not an opinion. It's guidance. That's what I would say has oriented me most: the pontifical documents and the major event—Vatican II, which looms so large over the past forty years, and is a mine never exhausted.

That is what I would say guided me.

And then, in the last seven years, the *Catechism of the Catholic Church*, which I appreciate so much that even for my daily prayer I take a section, sometimes only a half-page, and reflect on it, and pray on it. Even today I've done the same, because I think it contains so much, and there one is on safe ground, not on the hypothesis of somebody's speculation. Why spend so much time and energy on hypotheses, on theories, when you have safe ground?

Q. *In various interviews with you over these past years, I have been struck by the fact that so often you come out with biblical stories. And listening to you, I have wondered how much the Bible has been part of your spirituality and study from the beginning?*

A. Study? Of course we were taught in the introduction to the Bible some scientific analysis, and then for the actual introduction we had as our professor Monsignor Salvatore Garofalo, from Naples, the great biblical expert, a great pastor and biblical scholar. He died about four years ago. He was really great. He gave us a love of the Holy Bible, not because we were biblical scholars. No, I make no pretense to knowledge like those in the Biblical Institute. Not that. But, Bible for life, yes! Especially, he commented on the Gospel according to Saint John, and he said to us, "Now I have introduced you to a love of the Bible; you go on with the rest."

So I try, without pretending any time to be a biblical scholar. I just read. I try as far as possible to read the Bible for fifteen minutes a day.

Q. *The whole Bible?*
A. Yes, I read each day, for fifteen minutes, without discriminating among the books of the Bible, just from cover to cover. Occasionally, I would skip some parts, like Leviticus, where it talks of the types of vestments the sons of Aaron would be wearing, this one so many cubits, depth, and so on. Well, I would skip some parts like that; otherwise, I would just read for fifteen minutes, and I try to do this in the chapel, in front of the Blessed Sacrament. Of course, if I am traveling, that is not possible; but on ordinary days fifteen minutes, because it is better that than the commentaries. Although sometimes I read commentaries too, especially when I am asked to speak on a particular part. But it is not generally the commentaries, but the book itself. After all, if the Lord God has spoken to us through the prophets and, in the fullness of time, through his Son in the New Testament, why are we looking for second-ary books then when we have his direct Word?

Q. *You have been reading the Bible like this for many years, I imagine?*
A. Since my seminary days. Because in the seminary we were ad-vised to read each day fifteen minutes of Holy Scripture and fifteen minutes of spiritual reading every day. And I have tried to do this, but I do not succeed every day. Sometimes events crowd it out, but I try. Each day. And it helps very much. And if a priest is to preach, and it is not the Word of God he gives the people, then he is giving them secondary material.

Q. *You do this reading on top of your prayers?*
A. Yes. This is on top of my prayers. We were also advised in the seminary to pray for thirty minutes each day and, if possible, in chapel. Some people would say that all this is very rigid and regimented. Well, you can say that. But we eat three times a day, and we do not consider it

monotonous, and we continue that for many years, some for seventy years, some for ninety. So I try as far as possible to do it. Even if I am traveling in the airplane, I try to do it there.

That reading of Scripture is not too much, especially when you consider how much time we give to the newspapers, to say nothing of the TV. Where there is a will, there is a way. If a person considers a thing important, he will make time for it, but when you don't consider a thing important then you will say: "I'm very busy today; this will be done another day." That's a sign of what you do not consider to be a priority.

Q. *As you mentioned earlier, Father Tansi used to say, "One has to be serious about God", or one has to take God seriously.*

A. Yes. If you are going to serve God, you might as well be entirely for him. When he went to the Monastery of Mount Saint Bernard to be a novice, after working for thirteen years as a parish priest, he said to his novice master: "Father, if this thing is to be done, let it be done properly. Do not spare me." It's the right spirit.

Q. *I would like to ask you something more personal: I noticed in the little chapel of your apartment, you have the crucifix of Saint Francis of Assisi. You had your own African name, but you chose the name Francis at baptism. I wondered if you had actually reflected a lot on Saint Francis of Assisi?*

A. I must not pretend that I had reflected a lot about Saint Francis at my baptism. But I continued to be fascinated by him. Saint Francis is obviously very striking as one who was carried away by the mystery of Christ. He was a follower of Christ who hadn't any excess luggage; whatever few clothes he had from his father he gave back and followed Christ with nothing. So his is a type of wholehearted following of Christ, with no regrets. He stands out.

And also Saint Francis of Assisi was fascinating for his openness to the human person, including Muslims. You will notice that people of many religions feel attracted to Assisi. Even when we had the Assembly of Religions in the Vatican, in October 1999, everybody wanted to go on the planned one-day pilgrimage to Assisi; they all wanted to go to the place where Saint Francis lived and died. When the Buddhists and Shintoists in Japan heard of the earthquake in Assisi in 1997, some of them sent money for the repair of the buildings. They did so on their own initiative, without anybody asking them.

Saint Francis was opposed to the crusades at that time. He went to meet the Sultan at Damietta. The crusades are a very complicated thing, and, as you know, Saint Catherine of Siena was in favor of the crusades, but Saint Francis was against them. His approach to the Muslims was so fascinating that the Franciscans remained friends of the Muslims, and in many majority Muslim countries they are still welcome. The Franciscans have remained the custodians of the Holy Places in the Holy Land as a result of this. This saint is altogether extraordinary.

Q. *So would it be fair to say that you have sought to identify your own spirituality with that of Saint Francis of Assisi?*

A. I do not know whether I have gone a long distance in identifying with him, but I look up to him. I wish I would have some little chips of his spirituality, some sprinkling of his deep waters.

There is no doubt that he helps us to follow Christ; and for us in the Pontifical Council for Inter-Religious Dialogue he has helped us to realize more that the human person is our way forward. Pope John Paul II often says, "Man is the way for the Church." Of course. Christ is "the Way, the Truth, and the Life", but it is through our fellowman that we show that love of Christ and reach Christ. And Saint Francis has done this magnificently.

That may explain part of the attraction that he has, not only for Christians, but also for other believers.

Q. *Now as you look back over more than forty years in the priesthood, what are your feelings?*

A. Gratitude to God, and a sense of adoration before the mystery of God's choice. The ways of God are beyond us. Who would have told me forty-three years ago that I would live so many years in the priesthood? Gratitude to God, adoration and fear before the mystery of Divine Providence, but, at the same time, trust and joy at so many graces, so many opportunities, so many people I have met—not whom I have met, but whom God has put on my way all these years.

Q. *Why do you say "fear"?*

A. Oh! How can we be sure that we have responded to God's grace adequately? Hasn't every one of us fallen short in generosity to God's grace? Which of us can say I have been faithful to God's grace every day, all my years? I cannot say that, and I don't imagine many others can say that. So every one of us will have occasions to say, "I have not been

100 percent generous with God, who called me." So when I say "fear", I use it in that sense, but not as an overriding state of mind. My overriding state of mind is one of joy and gratitude.

Q. *What is the image of God that you have developed in your mind and heart over these years?*

A. I see God as Providence, God who has arranged our future. The question is whether we will do our part, but his part is sure. He has arranged my future. I don't have to arrange my future myself. He looks after me. In his hands I am safe. So with him I am secure. He is my guardian. He is my help. This is for me a major way I look at God. You can say *Creator*—it's true, but that looks philosophical. For me, *Providence* is nearer, and it includes creation, preservation, and everything else.

Chapter 13

Building Bridges in Morocco, Assisi, and Algeria

The cardinal's work is by definition one of building bridges between Christians and the followers of the other world religions. He has visited many countries, on all continents, to promote this work, sometimes with the Pope, more often alone or with staff members from his office.

In this chapter,[1] the cardinal speaks about three very different events in which he was involved and which were—each in its own way—significant in the history of relations between the Catholic Church and other religions and which history may come to regard as important bridges on that road to inter-religious harmony and cooperation.

The first was the Pope's extraordinary visit to Casablanca, Morocco, in 1985. It was his first visit to a country with a Muslim majority. The cardinal accompanied him on this visit, which had a wider significance in terms of the Catholic Church's outreach to Islam.

The second was the historic meeting in Assisi, in 1986, when the leaders of the major world religions came together, at the Pope's invitation, and fasted and prayed for world peace at a time when it seemed seriously threatened. The cardinal and his office staff helped organize that event. Here, he looks back and reflects on the meeting that is considered as one of the great "prophetic" events of the papacy of John Paul II.

The third event was the funeral of the seven Trappist monks who were kidnapped from their monastery in the Atlas Mountains, in Algeria, in 1996, where they had lived in dialogue with the Muslims in the area. Two months later they were executed. This tragedy took place during the terrible conflict that erupted in Algeria after the military took power in a coup d'état on January 11, 1992, and

---

[1] This chapter is based on extracts from interviews that were recorded on December 9 and 16, 2000.

suspended the elections when the Islamic party looked set for victory. Some fifty thousand people were reportedly killed in the following four years of violence, including women, children, elderly people, and eighteen priests and religious. An Islamic armed group was alleged to have killed the monks on the morning of May 21, 1996. The full truth of their tragic death has yet to be discovered.

The Pope asked Cardinal Arinze to represent him at the funeral of the monks. But just before he arrived in Algiers, the ninety-two-year-old Algerian cardinal, Leon Duval, a great friend of the monks, died; he was heartbroken at the killing of the monks, which "crucified" him, he said. He had championed the cause of Algerian self-determination and was affectionately nicknamed "Muhammad" Duval by the country's Muslims. His coffin was placed alongside those of the monks in the basilica, as the cardinal celebrated the Requiem Mass on June 2, 1996.

In this chapter, Arinze speaks of reactions to the tragic killing of the monks and takes the discussion a step further.

We began our conversation by talking about the Pope's visit to Casablanca, Morocco.

Q. *In 1985, just over a year after coming to the Vatican, you accompanied the Pope to Morocco on that historic visit. Was that the first foreign trip that you made with the Pope?*

A. It was. In that visit, however, the Holy Father visited other places too, he did not visit only Morocco. He visited places in West Africa— Togo, Ivory Coast, Cameroon, Central African Republic, (the former) Zaire, and then went to Nairobi, Kenya, to conclude the Eucharistic Congress. And when that was concluded, he flew straight to Morocco. At that stage I joined his entourage.

I was not in the entire papal trip, but only on the last part to visit Morocco, because it's an Islamic country officially. I was in Nairobi at the Eucharistic Congress for all the days of the congress. I had other duties at the congress. I was in the Holy Father's entourage for the last part of his African trip, the visit to Morocco. I'll never forget it, August 19, 1985.

Q. *What do you remember of it? Did you help plan it?*

A. I remember that well. Our dicastery helped in the preparations, yes, not just me.

For instance, we had to give our own opinion on what subjects the Pope could speak, because the king of Morocco had invited the Pope to come to Morocco, and the Holy Father had said to him, "For what reason? Your country is Muslim; whom shall I meet?"

The king said, "You are a moral voice in the world. I will gather the Muslim youth, and you will speak to them." And the Holy Father said, "Yes, I will come."

It was primarily the king of Morocco, who is regarded as a successor of the successors of Muhammad, who invited the Pope. He is actually called "Commander of the Faithful" for the Muslims. He is highly respected. The Pope accepted the official invitation to address the Muslim youth. The Holy Father, of course, met the Catholic community too, and said Mass for them and delivered an appropriate homily.

Q. *But the Catholic community in Morocco is very small.*

A. Small, yes. All foreigners, because the law of Morocco doesn't allow citizens to become Christians, but foreigners can be Christians and practice freely.

On the streets they wrote: "*Welcome, Holy Father, to the land of Islam*", in French.

I noticed that there were very many people on the streets to greet the Pope, very many people. There was not a dull moment between the airport and the city, and from the king's palace to the stadium.

The Holy Father, of course, greeted the king and all his entourage. You know their national dress in Morocco—they almost look like Benedictines in their beautiful white attire with a little white head cover, really like the monks.

Then the most impressive moment was when the Pope spoke to eighty thousand Muslim youth in the Casablanca stadium. I counted the exits, twenty-four exits in the big stadium. The youth were all dressed in white, eighty thousand of them lined up. I tried to count the lines until I could count no more.

There were of course many people present who were not so young, including President Leopold Senghor, then president of Senegal. He is a great African; and he has a sense of the value of history. He recognized that history was being made: here was the Pope invited to an officially Islamic country to address, not Catholics, but the Muslims.

The Pope spoke for about forty-five minutes, in French. The youth clapped and clapped. And they clapped at the correct moment. It wasn't something orchestrated, as sometimes happens—at least in my country—where politicians when campaigning for elections hire a group of unemployed young people for the occasion to applaud whatever they say, even when they say something below the permissible level of nonsense. But these young people clapping for the Pope were not "prepped" on when to clap, or how to clap. It was spontaneous. It was genuine. It was really great.

And the speech the Pope made still remains most relevant. I remembered it three weeks ago when I was preparing a talk that I have to give next February [2001]. I still find it so fresh and took some quotations from it. It showed that when we make an appeal to the human soul and to some of the highest ideals of Christianity and Islam, it is surprising on what points we can and do agree.

That was a very remarkable day. It was a visit of only six or seven hours, but it was important. The Pope began the visit soon after lunch and finished it around eight o'clock that night. Then we boarded the plane and returned to Rome. In terms of history, it remains a milestone.

Q. *And what were the Pope's own feelings about that visit?*

A. Well, I can say only a little; I cannot get into the Holy Father's mind. I think the Holy Father was happy about it, and he does quote from that Casablanca speech from time to time.

Q. *People consider his Casablanca speech a landmark in Christian–Muslim relations; a frontier speech.*

A. Definitely. Moreover, I do not know anybody who opposed the Pope's going there. And if anybody thought the Holy Father wasn't open, that visit was the answer.

Q. *As I understand it, this speech pushed the frontiers of dialogue to where they had not been before. And there was a lot of courage involved in the visit and in the speech.*

A. Definitely. There was a lot of courage involved on the part of the Holy Father in accepting the invitation, but there was also a lot of courage involved on the part of the king in inviting the Pope to address the Muslim youth. Both sides are to be congratulated.

And then the Holy Father, who cannot be regarded as not loving Catholic doctrine, because of Vatican II, had an open heart to meet the followers of Islam. It is all one piece because you notice that Vatican II, which had no hesitation in articulating what the Church thinks she is (*Lumen Gentium*), also because she knows who she is and what her mission is (*Ad Gentes*), had no hesitation in saying that this same Church sees it as part of her mission to meet every human being, whether it be in the whole world (*Gaudium et Spes*) or people of other religions (*Nostra Aetate*) or other Christians (*Unitatis Redintegratio*).

It is all one piece; it isn't a question of "but"; it is a question of "therefore". It is because the Church knows who she is—and hasn't any doubt about that—that she can, without complex and without unnecessary fear, meet every human being.

Q. *It was with this same spirit of openness that the Pope invited the leaders of the major world religions to that historic meeting held at Assisi in Italy on October 27, 1986, to pray and fast for peace in the world. You had an*

important role to play in helping organize that meeting, which is widely
regarded as one of the great "prophetic" acts of John Paul II's pontificate.[2]

A. Yes, it was a courageous decision on the part of the Holy Father
to invite people of many religions, in the International Year of Peace,
to come to Assisi to fast and pray for peace. Not to discuss, but to fast
and pray.

I do not want to give the impression that I was one of the people
who did it. No. No. But our office, the Pontifical Council for Inter-
Religious Dialogue, together with the Pontifical Council for the Promotion of Christian Unity—other Christians counted for half of those
present—and the Pontifical Council for Justice and Peace, together with
the Secretariat of State, organized the event. So you see there were four
Vatican offices involved, and Roger Cardinal Etchegaray was the chairman. Our office contributed, and I contributed too, but as part of the
office. That's the context. The Holy Father entrusted the work to these
four Vatican dicasteries.

Q. *Am I right in understanding that the idea for this meeting was the*
Pope's own?

A. Yes. It was his idea. We worked out the details as to how it would
be done. It was, as they say in Italian, "*inedito*", unprecedented. There was
no precedent on which we had to go.

We took care, for example, to make sure that there was no appear-
ance of one prayer by all the religions. So we arranged a separate place of
prayer for each religion, not for a common prayer by all religions. There
was a period of one and a half hours for each religion to pray. All the
Christians were together in the cathedral of Assisi: ecumenical prayer,
because prayer depends on belief, faith. If we don't believe the same
thing, we cannot have the same prayer. That part was clear.

And even at the last part of the act, in front of the Basilica of Saint
Francis, each religion was given a few minutes to pray, through a few
representatives. It was not inter-religious prayer. The others stood in
reverent attention, as four or five people from each religion went to a big
stand and prayed for a short time publicly and then returned to their
seats. And then the Pope spoke. Care was taken for that part of the event,
as for the rest.

But when you have a big event like that, there will be a mistake

---

[2] A book has been published on this historic event: *Assisi, World Day of Prayer for Peace,*
October 27, 1986 (Rome: Pontifical Commission *Justitia et Pax*, 1987).

somewhere. In Assisi, there was one place where a church was allocated to the Buddhists, and we didn't know until afterward that the Buddhists had a statute of Buddha and placed it on what they considered to be a table but was in fact an altar. They put the statue on the altar and did their thing. Now some people far away immediately condemned the whole event in Assisi because of that, but they took it out of context because, first of all, the Buddhists did not do it to spite us—they didn't know what an altar meant for us. And, secondly, it was our fault: we should not have allocated a church at all to the Buddhists; we should have allocated a hall. So there we learned. We would not do it again; we would not allocate a church to the Buddhists or to the Muslims; we would give them a hall, not a church. Thirdly, we should have assigned one of our officials to be with them. Actually, we did ask someone to be there, but the person was not there at that time. These are small points, but in every big event there will be some mistake like that, but that in no way damages the whole event. The whole event was positive. There was not a doubt about that, and those Buddhists are our friends, and they meant no insult to us. I say this because some people heard that and ran away with the idea that this was the typical event in Assisi.

The major event was that the Holy Father was putting in front of the whole world the idea that to look for peace we need, of course, the United Nations, we need governments and negotiations, but we also need religion. We need prayer. We need the religious dimension, and the religions of the world have something to contribute to peace. That's what he was underlining.

Later on, in his encyclical *Centesimus Annus*,[3] he said the same thing, that he believes that the various religions have an important contribution to make to peace, to the construction of peace. In Assisi, he said, "Either we walk together, or we all suffer together in the world." We are like people in the same boat. That's what he was underlining. I think the world got that message.

Q. *Yes, but the Pope had to defend himself publicly over the Assisi meeting. There were some rumblings in the Roman Curia, and elsewhere in*

---

[3] Pope John Paul II's encyclical *Centesimus Annus* (On the centenary of *Rerum Novarum*) commemorates Pope Leo XIII's social encyclical, *Rerum Novarum*. It goes on to analyze the situation at the end of 1989 and the beginning of 1990 in Eastern and Central Europe, following the collapse of Communism there, but before the collapse of the Communist Party in the Soviet Union.

*Church circles, after the Assisi event, and the Pope defended that meeting in
his Christmas address to the Roman Curia in December 1986.*

A. There were rumblings. Whether you call it defending himself,
or explaining for those who were ready to listen, the Holy Father,
really, expounded and explained the theology behind the Assisi event.
Yes, you are right in the sense that his major Christmas speech of
December 22, 1986, was the theological exposition of the doctrine
underpinning the Assisi event. For someone of goodwill who wants to
know: Why did the event take place? What took place? What did it
mean? Why did the Pope want it and support it?—that's where to go.
Read the whole speech.[4]

In brief, the Pope is saying that there is only one Creator of all
mankind—God; there is only one divine plan of salvation for all, and that
is in Jesus Christ, who died on the Cross for all; there's one human nature
in all of us; and the final destiny of everyone is to see God as he is in
heaven, and that destiny is the same for all. These are common to all
men, and these are fundamental before ever we talk of differences of race
or religion or otherwise.

The Church recognizes these facts, underlines them, in inviting
people of many religions to come together to pray; and every authentic
prayer comes from the Holy Spirit. In this speech,[5] the Pope speaks not
of every prayer, but of every authentic prayer. This means that it isn't
only Christians who can pray: Jews can pray too, Muslims can pray,
people of Traditional Religion can pray.

The Pope didn't put it in so many words, but that's what it means. It
means that when people of other religions are making efforts to be in
contact with God, the Transcendent, we Christians do not laugh at
them. We don't smile. We take them seriously. Not because we regard
one religion to be as good as another. Certainly not, that would be
relativism. But because we think that whatever is true or noble or
authentic in another religion is a gift from God. That means the people
of other religions pray. This is so even though there may be errors in their
religions here and there, and there will be because human nature is what
it is, and there is original sin, and religious truth is difficult to get at, even
for Christians.

Even though there are shadows in those religions, nevertheless, there

[4] John Paul II, Address to the Roman Curia, *Acta Apostolicae Sedis*, Rome, 1987, no. 79,
1082–90.
[5] Ibid.

are elements that are good, if only you come near enough to those religions to understand them. Nobody is always wrong. Even a clock that does not move, like that one on the wall over there, will be right twice a day. [The clock in the cardinal's room for visitors had stopped.] How much more men who move, who think, who know what it means to be honest, to be generous, to tell the truth, to be kind to another person, to do something gratuitously for another person because of God, in whom they believe. And there are such people in Traditional Religions, in Judaism and Islam. So we must believe that God also gives his gifts outside the Church.

Q. *So when there is something authentic in the prayer and in the actions of people of other religions, this surely is from God.*
A. Somehow we will eventually have to trace it back to God.

Q. *So Christians don't disregard it.*
A. No, we do not disregard it. Indeed, our regard for man is also part of our respect for God. For God, and for what God is working in these people.

Q. *So inter-religious dialogue is also a voyage of discovery of God in people.*
A. Also that. Not because we have any doubt that we have the truth in the Church, but because we can admire what divine grace has done for people who don't even know the Church. If I look at people of African Traditional Religion, I can admire a lot of goodness in them that was there not because they were Christians. They don't even have contact with Christianity.

Q. *And there is also a lot of truth there, too.*
A. Yes, truth and goodness. So that should make us, let me say, humble, before the facts. If it is a fact, it is a fact. But we don't have a single doubt about Christianity and its novelty, and the fullness of revelation in Christ. It is full; it is definitive. Nothing to be added.

Q. *But what of the fullness of revelation that we will come to understand, to experience, at the end of time?*
A. Yes . . . not that I have captured it fully myself. But this revelation is full in Christ, and in the revelation he has given his Church. But

in no way do I pretend that I have understood it fully myself, or that I am fully inserted in it, or that I am now a Christian 100 percent. That would be presumptuous of me. I am always making progress, and I should always make progress. I can always understand more, more, more, and more and more. And so I should.

And the Church as a whole, too, will always understand more and more of what God has revealed. Not because God is revealing new things; rather, he is leading the Church to higher levels of understanding of the mystery of Christ. And at the same time we can also admire the workings of God in other people, in people of other religions.

Q. *So when the Pope had to try and explain this in that Christmas speech of 1986, he was really combatting a mentality that did not realize that this discovery had to go on, to continue in some way.*

A. Yes. Those who, without saying so, seem to think that all goodness, truth, virtue, honesty, gratuitous love is in the Church but not outside her don't seem to realize that there are some people who are really kind, but they are not Christians, also some who tell the truth, some who are chaste but are not Christians. So we can discover this, and when we discover it we thank God, we praise God, we encourage those people, we work with them. They may have an element of their culture that Christianity thinks is really good. We work with them.

When we talk of inter-religious collaboration, it can be in defense of the family. Everybody knows there are many differences between Christianity and Islam; nevertheless, at the United Nations World Conference on Population and Development in Cairo, in 1994, the Holy See's delegation, together with the delegations from many majority Muslim countries, worked together to defend family values and especially to fight the ideas of introducing abortion and promiscuity and what they call the "new forms of family life", such as two homosexuals living together being approved as a family. We joined together to say, "No, we don't want this."

At Cairo, there were some Muslims from their own background and some Christians from theirs sharing some values regarding the family. Not every value, but some. And we worked together to that extent. That is inter-religious collaboration. You don't have to agree on everything before you can work together. You don't have to approve the other religion in its totality before you accept that its followers are doing good work on this point, or that point, or another point.

Q. *Earlier we spoke about Archbishop Marcel Lefèbvre, and you said that already at Vatican II you had noticed his reaction to openness in the inter-religious and ecumenical dialogue. But for him, and his followers, the Assisi event was the last straw, and after that meeting they broke with the Pope.*

A. Yes, they were really breaking away before that, but the Assisi event must have made them throw up both hands, if I may say so.

Q. *So their final break came as a result of a fundamental misunderstanding of the Assisi meeting?*

A. I do not pretend to know all the reasons why they broke away. But definitely they did not understand Assisi.

And if I were able to get Archbishop Lefèbvre—God rest his soul—or his followers to sit with me, I would ask them, "Have you ever met a really good Muslim? Have you ever met a really good Hindu who is really kind and honest? Have you ever met a follower of African Traditional Religion who obviously is chaste, who gratuitously does something good for another person, and who actually prays in the morning?"

I would ask them, "Have you any idea of the type of prayer my grandfather used to say in the morning when he got up? When he prayed to 'the God of heaven, who made heaven and earth'. And then he prayed to God and said, 'Give me life, for me, my wife, and my children. Preserve us.' Have you any idea of the prayer my father said for me when I was going to Rome in 1955, and he was not yet a Christian? He became a Christian afterward. His prayer was beautiful."

Q. *What prayer did your father say for you?*

A. He said: "God will be with you. He will be before you. He will be after you. No harm will come on you. I will be here. God will lead you back here again. He will bless you." What more do you want in a prayer?

Q. *He said that prayer when you were leaving for Rome?*

A. Yes. Yes. It is a prayer. In the Traditional Religion of our people, the parents pray over their children when the children are going on a long journey. They pray for them.

So I would say to Archbishop Lefèbvre and his followers, "You do not perhaps realize that outside the visible boundaries of the Church there are elements that are good or noble, even attractive, in other religions. You probably have not come into real contact with them. So you thought that only in Christianity was there any truth, or honesty, or chastity, or gratuitous love. So you didn't realize that the world is much bigger than you knew." I would say to them, in the words of Hamlet, "There are more things in heaven and . . . earth than are dreamt of in your philosophy" [I.5]. The world is much bigger. God is infinite, and he has given his gifts to the various peoples.

I would say to them, "Do you realize the amount of goodness in the Greek philosophers who didn't know Christ?" Somebody dedicated a book to the Pope, I don't remember which book, and he wrote: "To the Vicar of the One whom the Greek philosopher saw from far away." I would say, "Are you saying that everything that Aristotle and Plato said was all 'no good'? Not an inkling of the truth in what they said? You are not serious! And, remember, they were not Christian, they had no contact with Christians, and it was before Christ. So there must be some goodness there, some minimum goodness. The early Fathers of the Church saw that, why do you not see it in the twentieth century?"

Q. *Do you really think that with that kind of reflection the followers of Archbishop Lefèbvre would be able to come to understand and accept this?*
A. You see, in matters religious it isn't argument, it isn't debate, that prevails. Finally, God's grace will have to work in people's hearts, because you don't change a person's religious stand by argument. However, arguments can help. But it is finally up to God's grace and the human heart. The human heart is a mystery. But I think one quality we all need very much is humility, that we are able to kneel in front of God, who is a reality, whether that God speaks to me through a Christian, or even in other ways, or through other believers, or through the sunshine, or through the rain, or through the trees.

Q. *What you have said certainly gives much food for thought. But so too does the next tragic event on which I would like to have your reflections. You went to Algeria to celebrate the Requiem Mass for the seven Trappist monks who were kidnapped from their monastery and murdered in 1996, but you found yourself also presiding at the funeral of the great Cardinal Duval, who died shortly after hearing news of their deaths.*
A. Yes. That was on June 2, 1996.

Q. *I assume you knew Cardinal Duval?*
A. Oh, very well. I knew him at meetings of the African bishops,

when I was still an archbishop in Nigeria. I remember him because he was a very honorable man, and not just because he was tall. He had very high ideals and very high ideas, and he was friendly.

Q. *Did you know the Trappist monks at the monastery of Notre Dame de l'Atlas, in Tibhirine?*
A. Not intimately, but I had visited them in 1986. That year I visited Algeria for about ten days; I went by car from Algiers to visit that monastery for a day.

Q. *What did you think at that time? I mean, in 1986, nobody imagined that they would be killed.*
A. No. We had no idea of the violence that would break out in the country later. But I realized then that the monks were really very courageous. They were living in the midst of a Muslim population, and I was told that the people were very friendly to them and that some Muslims even came for spiritual meditation and prayer on their own—not because they wanted to be Christian but they could see that the monks had a spiritual affinity, nearness, message for them. And also one of the monks was a medical doctor, and he was very kind to the people.

Q. *When you heard the news of their kidnapping and their killing, two months later, on May 21, what did you feel?*
A. Devastated. Devastated. I had hoped that even if they were kidnapped, that those who kidnapped them would not harm them, out of respect for the supernatural, for the Transcendent, out of the respect for God that genuine Islam does have.
Genuine Islam tells Muslims not to harm the monks and the religious personnel. Not that it is right to harm anybody, but it says that expressly. So it is clear that, by Muslim standards, those who killed them are not even good Muslims at all. The Qur'an has very great respect for monks. It tells Muslims something like that. "The Jews and the Christians are those nearest to you because they have monks, and they are not proud." So it was most disappointing, most painful.
But even if it was such a disaster, there was also the very, very deep spiritual side. The monks as a whole, that group, they really loved the people. The monks knew they were in danger. They could have left that place. They were not obliged to stay; they chose to stay. We understand that several times over the years, as the danger grew, they had

discernment meetings among themselves: Would they leave? Would they go? Every monk was free to go to another monastery. They all chose to stay. We understand that they were even offered soldiers to guard them, and they examined the idea and said, "You see the people themselves don't have guards, so we don't want armed protection."

We understand that these people of violence who kill and kidnap had visited them before. The monks were ready, as men, to be near them, to give them food or medicine, but not arms; and they would not keep arms for them so as not to be involved in the violence. The monks had a very clear message.

But, of course, the greatest testament is that document of the prior of the monastery, Father Christian-Marie de Chergé.[6] That document is a document coming from a person of very high spiritual stature. Before such a spirit, I feel very small. Here is a person who is much higher than I am in matters touching God and love of others. As if he knew, he even forgave whoever might kill them and begged the rest of the world in no way to look down on such people. Practically said, he hoped to be in heaven with that person. That's what we look for in the beatification of martyrs.

Q. *Do you really foresee that one day these seven monks will be beatified?*
A. That's my hope, because it seems to me that they qualify. But, of course, I do not beatify people just because I have this opinion, but my own contribution in the cause for their beatification would be positive.

Q. *Did the Pope want to go to the funeral?*
A. I do not know whether the Holy Father wanted to go. I would not have expected him to go; it is not usual. But the Holy Father sent me officially.

Q. *He actually asked you to go?*
A. Oh, yes. It was not just that I wanted to go, but the Holy Father said, "You go and represent me. Go and celebrate the Mass." That part was clear. Then, just before the funeral day, Cardinal Duval died. But at the time the Holy Father sent me to say the Mass for the monks, the cardinal was still alive. Sick and old, yes, but still alive. He died in between.

---

[6] The last testament of Father Christian-Marie de Chergé has been published in many languages and is a lasting witness to Christian love.

Q. *So he knew you were coming.*

A. He must have known. I had not yet reached Algeria when he died, because I had another meeting in Cairo, and it was there that I heard that he had died. I had already written the homily,[7] so I began then to add a good section on him, because then it was agreed to have the funerals together, his and that of the seven monks.

In a way it was like his saying, "Oh, have they killed all seven of you? I shall die with you; I want to be buried with you." He had begun that monastery, so it meant more to him than to you and me.

It was a ceremony eloquent in itself.

Q. *The ceremony was held in the Basilique du Notre-Dame d'Afrique, in Algiers.*

A. Yes, in the Basilica of Our Lady of Africa, built by Cardinal Lavigerie, the founder of the White Fathers, a beautiful church by the seaside. I understand that Muslims come there to pray because there is a beautiful statue of Our Lady in there, and I heard that, when it was built, a Muslim either donated or decorated the canopy over Our Lady's statue because, as you know, the Qur'an mentions Our Lady [spelled Marium or Maryam] thirty-four times. She is the only woman mentioned in the Qur'an, and always mentioned with high respect and honor.

Q. *So when you got to the Church, were there many people gathered for the funeral?*

A. It was packed. But many, I understand, were either military people or not necessarily Christian. I was told that many of the people there were Muslims who came out of great respect for Cardinal Duval and the monks.

Q. *But were the bodies of the monks there in the basilica?*

A. We did not open the coffins ourselves. Only later on I heard that it was not the entire bodies. Whether it was just their heads, I do not

---

[7] Cardinal Arinze delivered his homily in French, during the solemn Requiem Mass in the Basilica of Our Lady of Africa, in Algiers, on June 2, 1996. Its title conveyed his message, *Souffrance, Amour, et Reconciliation* (Suffering, Love, and Reconciliation). He told the congregation, "God does not love violence. It is not by assassinating people that one promotes justice and peace, social order and religion. God is the God of life, not of death." "These tragic events", he said, "do not compromise Muslim-Christian relations; on the contrary, they highlight the need to promote them."

know, nor did I ask that kind of question. The occasion was far too solemn for me to ask such a question.

Q. *But some of the bodies were there in the Basilica?*
A. The seven coffins of the monks were brought there, as well as the coffin of Cardinal Duval. I dared not ask any question. I just got on with the ceremony.

Q. *What were your feelings as you looked down at those coffins, as you presided at the Funeral Mass for them?*
A. Difficult to express in words. I felt, here is Christian love without frontiers; Christian love reaching the heroic. Here is also the paradox of people of violence killing the very people who loved them, killing the very people who are bringing them development, who are bringing them light, solidarity. Killing the very people who should not be touched. Nobody should be killed. But of all the people who should not be killed, the monks were surely number one. It was sad. It was a proof that violence is blind. Violence cannot be the answer to problems, no matter how real the problems.

It was also part of the mystery of the Cross and the mystery of suffering. Why these innocent seven? What of all the evil people who have brought so much sorrow to the world? On Calvary we know who was on the Cross. Why should he be on the Cross? He, the most innocent person who ever walked on this earth?

So I thought of all that.

Then there was also the important event of the death of Cardinal Duval, archbishop emeritus of Algiers, a few days earlier. His coffin was in the midst of those of the seven monks. It was an eloquent celebration.

Then I thought of the Catholic bishops, priests, and religious who remained in the country in the midst of this daily danger of dying. Indeed, two months after that, one of them, Bishop Claverie, the bishop of Oran, was blown up with his driver in his house in Oran.[8] He was a Dominican bishop and was even born in Algeria. "How sad!" I said. "Oh my Africa, so sad. Why do you kill those who love you?" Men of violence need to think again.

But the witness given by Christians in a country in agony, such as Algeria, that witness is very powerful. I am told that, contrary to what

---

[8] Bishop Pierre Claverie was killed on the evening of August 1, 1996, along with his driver, an Algerian Muslim.

some think, the sad events in Algeria in these years have strengthened the link between Christians and Muslims in Algeria, because the Muslims reason and say, "Look, these bishops, priests, and sisters have stayed with us in our difficult years; they love us."

It is all very eloquent.

Q. *So the Cistercian monks in Algeria, Charles de Foucauld,*[9] *and people like that have given a particular witness, have shown a particular way to dialogue with Muslims and with people of other religions.*

A. Yes, and it's a very valid way. When we say inter-religious dialogue, we do not necessarily mean discussion. Just being with people, living with them, working with them, and even just assisting them, like the monk who was a medical doctor—doing all that is dialogue. Instead of saying inter-religious dialogue, we could also say inter-religious relations, inter-religious contacts, inter-religious collaboration.

The experts speak of four types of dialogue: dialogue of life, that is, contact at the level of daily life, without necessarily discussing religion; dialogue of work: social work, doing works together, such as I mentioned earlier, where Christians and Muslims run a leprosy clinic together without discussing religion; dialogue of discourse, discussion more between experts and theologians; and dialogue of exchange of religious experience, as when Catholic monks and Buddhist monks meet and visit one another, just to see and understand how the others live.

So it is clear that dialogue need not just mean discussion. When therefore the Trappist monks were there, praying and fasting, promoting the health of the people, developing agriculture, being friendly, seeking to better human life, that is also a way of saying they loved the people. If you are there, especially if the people are poor, and you share their joys and sorrows and projects and hopes, that's good. You are there in the name of Christ.

Inter-religious contacts for us are not secular, or academic, exercises. We are doing them in the name of Christ, and we do them as witnesses of Christ. It is part of our Christianity, not something added on, not something optional, peripheral, or marginal. It is very much part of our religion.[10]

---

[9] Charles de Foucauld (1858–1916) lived as a hermit in the Sahara desert, among Muslim people. He was killed there in 1916.

[10] See Francis Cardinal Arinze, *Meeting Other Believers* (Nairobi: Paulines Publications Africa, 1997). He describes the book as "a record of personal experiences and reflections. Almost like a long conversation . . . they spell out my convictions on inter-religious dialogue."

It is like asking Mother Teresa, "When you pick up those poor people at the roadside, you clean them up, you wash them, and you give them something to eat, is that evangelization?" Of course it is! Evangelization[11] is not only when you teach catechism, though that is the high point of evangelization; or when a professor in the Pontifical Gregorian University gives a forty-five-minute lecture on the Incarnation of the Word of God, or when you give a lecture in a big hall on "Christianity and the World Today", that is, of course, evangelization. But so too it is evangelization when you are near the sick, or the poor, without discussing any religion at all; you just show them the love of Christ.

When Our Savior was on earth, sometimes he was teaching, sometimes he didn't teach by words but he did a miracle. He saw the people hungry and took five loaves and two fishes and multiplied them for the hungry. They ate, were happy; they were no longer hungry. He was spreading the Word of God. Again he cured the sick, he raised the dead to life—the son of the widow of Nain raised to life. That's very eloquent. Or take the marriage feast of Cana in Galilee: the wine ran short. His Mother said to him, "They have no wine." Christ turned six jars of water into excellent wine; today we would say Champagne. That's good. He's really saying that marriage is good and that he wants people to be happy, and there's nothing wrong with wine and marriage. So that's good. And the miracle, being a sign, also had deeper symbolism.

When we say evangelization, we mean everything Christ sent the Church for. Whether it is the sister in the hospital helping the Ebola victims and probably contracting it herself and dying in northern Uganda or in the Congo—that is quite something, even if she doesn't mention the name of our Lord Jesus Christ. Or whether it is those helping the refugees in the Sudan, or those assisting the orphans from Rwanda, that is evangelization. It is also inter-religious contact. Such contacts for us are not secular exercises.

I would put it this way. Pope John Paul II, in his encyclical on the mission of the Redeemer, *Redemptoris Missio*, in chapter 5, speaks of the ways of mission, that is, the different ways the Church carries out the mandate given her by Christ—what Christ sent the Church for. And he lists them: witness to Christ, silent witness; teaching the Gospel, catechesis, conversion, baptism, establishing a local Catholic com-

---

[11] See Francis Cardinal Arinze, *The Essence of Evangelisation: The Supreme Value of Knowing Jesus Christ* (Dublin: Veritas, 1990).

munity, inculturation; then inter-religious dialogue; service, human promotion, charity—the sort of thing Mother Teresa and her sisters do—or the sort of thing religious do in hospitals, or they do in organizing cooperatives. All that. All of that is what Christ sent the Church for: to build up therefore the Kingdom of God among the people. Inter-religious dialogue is one element. It is not the most important, but it is one of the elements. That is why *Redemptoris Missio* says in paragraph 55 that inter-religious dialogue is part of the evangelizing mission of the Church.

Q. *I'm impressed by your memory. You quote all the texts and references from the documents. You must have a great memory.*

A. No, not necessarily a great memory. It's just that these are the key areas that mean so much for the whole work we're doing here. Otherwise I shouldn't be sitting here at all!

Q. *Through your work, you have met some of the great contemporary spiritual leaders of other religions: the Dalai Lama, the Sheikh Al-Azhar, Niwano of Japan, and so on.*

A. Yes, I have met many of them.

Q. *I'm sure that each of them, in his own way, feels convinced that he is in contact with the Supreme Being, God, or whatever he chooses to call the Being on whom humanity depends and with whom its future lies. After meeting these spiritual leaders, do you ever leave wondering whether they have indeed found God in their own way, and whether the God in whom you believe and pray to is in reality the same God in whom they believe, even if in different ways? What have these encounters taught you? What have you learned from them? At times you must surely have been impressed by their faith and their spirituality?*

A. No doubt. No doubt. And it is impossible not to ask oneself such questions. God's grace must be working beyond what we realize. Every good gift must be traceable back to God, to the Holy Spirit, to God's grace in people. It is not all clear to us, but then we don't have to understand everything.

We are small. We must not pretend that our little brains can understand completely how God's grace works. But what is clear is that there is goodness, nobility, honesty, truth—not only in the Church, but also outside. We would be rather proud, and also unrealistic and unaware of what exists, if we thought that Christians were the only ones who were honest or noble or true or chaste or able to love others gratuitously.

Granted that only in Christ have we the fullness of religious truth. As even Vatican II says in *Nostra Aetate*, paragraph 2: while the Church appreciates whatever is true, noble, good in other religions, the Church nevertheless must preach Jesus Christ as the Way, the Truth, and the Life, and that only in him do we find the fullness of religious truth and life.

The Council does not say that outside the Church there is no religious life or truth, only that within the Church we have it in fullness. And as *Dominus Jesus* would say later, and John Paul II says, only in the Church do we have the fullness of the means to salvation. But only the fullness: it does not say that elements don't exist outside the visible boundaries of the Catholic Church.

I saw that when I met, for instance, the Sheikh Al-Azhar. Or even when I met a less well-known Muslim, called Ali, who, I understand, is now dead. I visited Faisalabad, Pakistan, in 1988, and the local bishop brought me to meet Ali. I was really impressed. Ali was not a sheikh or imam, he was just a Muslim on his own. He had a library full of copies of the Qur'an, and people came to him for spiritual advice. He had young people as disciples, I understand; some stayed two weeks, some a month, some a year, as they wished. I understand that political leaders went to him for advice, but he was not a politician.

This man, Ali, spoke words of wisdom. He was very friendly to me. They spread flowers on my way. We sat down. You would think that the two of us were twins who had always shared life. And he was a Muslim, and I a Catholic. He was very friendly. I was surprised. I said to myself, "This man will go to heaven. There is God's grace working in him." So here was a person who, in my view, left himself open to God's action in him. He followed the Light as much as he could, so he would have drawn some high ideas also from his own religion. Everything would not be perfect, but God would have his own way of giving light and grace to such a person.

That's the sort of thing we mean by saying that God's grace is given also outside the visible boundaries of the Church.

Q. *Might it not also be true, in a sense, that if any of us thinks we have the concept of God so clearly worked out in our mind, that, really, we don't believe in God because God cannot be boxed in that way?*

A. We believe in God, and we don't have any doubt about that, and what our faith articulates really refers to something real. The statement of our faith is not a fruitless articulation of what we know nothing about. That would be unacceptable. So the Creed, that is, the symbol of the faith, the statement of the faith that we have inherited from Christ, through the apostles, gives us something real. So when we say we believe in "God, the Father Almighty, and in Jesus Christ, his only Son . . . God from God, Light from Light, true God from true God, begotten not made . . ."—these are the solid rock on which we stand.

Nevertheless, we must realize too that our faith terminates not in propositions, but in God. So that finally it is God we believe in, not in propositions. But since we are human beings, and since the faith had to be handed down, it has to be articulated in human language. Even when God took on human nature, he spoke to us in human language, limited as human language may be.

But probably what you want to say, and it is correct, is that we must not think that because we can articulate our faith in the Creed that we therefore have a comprehensive knowledge of who God is.

Q. *That is precisely what I meant by my question.*

A. No, we must not think we have a comprehensive knowledge of God, because whatever we say—and I think it was Saint Augustine who said it—"We know more what God is not, than what God is. We know more what he is not, than what he is."

Apart from the articulation of our faith, which we have inherited and which remains sacred in the symbols or in the Creed, there is also the apophatic tradition, that is, that in front of God we are "more in silence than in words". And whatever we know about God is small when compared to the reality of God; that what we know is analogical, that it is articulated in our weak human language.

That means, we must not think that we have comprehended who God is, as if God were simply like one of us who can be explained. Not so. God is much more than what we think he is. Nevertheless, what our faith tells us is real, and it is not defective, but we must realize that it does not say everything about God.

In the Church we have the fullness of what God has revealed, and it is definitive through Christ, and there will be no other revelation. Nevertheless, we as individuals, and the Church as a whole, can grow in our contact with that mystery, and we should grow. In that sense, Saint

Francis of Assisi would know much more deeply who God is than you and I, because he is nearer to God; he has grown more.

It isn't a question of my reciting the catechism, even if I know the 2,865 paragraphs in the *Catechism of the Catholic Church*. Even if I knew all that, it would not mean that I now know more about God than Saint Catherine of Siena, who never studied in any school and couldn't write, but because she was near God, God gifted her with greater wisdom. So she knew God more than we.

Q. *My original question was prompted by your reaction to Ali, the Muslim. His faith clearly impressed you, and your words about him confirm that God is, in the final analysis, still a mystery to us men, including Christians. I sometimes think that when you see these very spiritual people of whatever religion, such as Ali, you feel that somehow they may have got an insight into that Mystery, beyond what we have ever been able to articulate.*

A. We must admit that. It can be so. However, we do not forget that Christ revealed to us many mysteries.

Q. *Even in the Christian understanding, we are still struggling to understand Christ.*

A. Definitely. And we sometimes think we understand him, but we are still very far away.

Q. *We say we have the fullness of revelation, and yet at the end of time we know that there will be a full revelation in a way that we had never imagined.*

A. When we say we have the fullness of revelation, we must go carefully. The fullness of revelation has been given to mankind in Jesus Christ, and he has entrusted this to his Church. But that does not mean that every one of us in the Church knows God fully. We would not be so proud. We only know a little. We can grow.

It does not even mean that the Church as a whole does not grow. The Church grows in that knowledge of God, and in the knowledge of revelation, and as the ages roll by, the Church—by prayer, by reflection, by reading the lives of the saints and the early teachers or Fathers of the Church, and by the assistance of the Holy Spirit—comes to a better understanding of some parts of our faith. So the whole Church grows; much more do individuals grow.

Q. *When one thinks of those monks in Algeria, theirs was a very powerful message to the world. So too was Mother Teresa's, so too was Charles de Foucauld's. It is as if their message goes beyond what has been put into words.*

A. That is true. That is true. Remember the prophets of the Old Testament were called *men of God*. It is said that somebody once went to Saint John Mary Vianney and, after their meeting, he came away saying, *I have seen God in a man*. That is, I have been with somebody who is nearer God than most of us mortals. A person could be a professor of theology, with two or three doctorates, but not perhaps be as near to God as a village farmer who has attained a higher level of knowledge of God.

Q. *Those who will read this will say your words speak to their own experience, more so than documents that seem to affirm with great certainty and clarity but, at times, do not reach the hearts of people.*

A. To say that one individual can be nearer to God than another does not mean that the Church should abandon her duty to articulate the faith. We notice that from the early years of the Church, from the second, third, and fourth centuries, the bishops, coming together with the Pope or his delegate, felt it their duty to say, "This is what we believe, we believe, we believe." That is the origin of the *Credo*.

It is the duty of the teaching authority of the Church to articulate that faith, that is, to state it in human language, also using philosophical terms or concepts, because the faith has to be handed down. If we handed down the faith only by silent witness, but not by a simple word, you would soon find that the child growing up does not know in what faith he is being initiated. That's why the *credos* were often tied to baptism. The person is being baptized into the faith of that community as articulated. The articulation of the faith retains its importance, otherwise we will soon become a type of spiritual group in which nobody knows what he believes, nobody can articulate it, nobody knows what to hand down, and nobody can say to anyone, "You are not believing what our ancestors in the faith handed down to us."

Because in the days of the apostles, Saint Peter and Saint Paul, we are told that Saint Peter said, "There are several things Paul wrote that are difficult to understand and that some abuse to their own destruction." Saint Paul was very strict on what people were to believe. He told the Galatians, "If anyone preaches a Gospel to you different from the one we have preached to you, let him be anathema. So you are to believe what has been handed down to you, and not to believe anything else." This means that they were also very careful about the articulation of the faith even in the days of Saint Paul.

How much more so, later on, when the Church had met Greek and Roman philosophy, and the faith had to be expressed in those terms. How much more so also when some began to say there are two persons in Christ, so the Church was compelled to express herself on this question; or again when people said Christ was not God, then the Councils of Nicaea and Constantinople had to say no: "He is God from God, Light from Light, true God from true God, begotten not made, one in substance with the Father, and through him all things were made." All that articulation came with time.

Q. What you say is very clear, but in recent times, many people have gotten the impression that different messages are coming from different Vatican departments. What do you say to those people who say they hear one message coming from the Pontifical Council for Inter-Religious Dialogue and seemingly a different message from the Congregation for the Doctrine of the Faith, as expressed in particular in Dominus Jesus,[12] *the document you mentioned a little earlier.*

A. I would say to them: "Go easy! Please understand what that document, *Dominus Jesus,* wants to say. What it wants to say is this: Catholics who meet other Christians (ecumenism), or Catholics who meet the followers of other religions (inter-religious dialogue), please realize what our religious identity is, what it is that we believe about Jesus Christ and his Church, so that you may be well equipped to meet other Christians or believers in other religions. That is, without a clear self-identity, we are taking a risk in meeting other people."

The document is preoccupied with the identity of Jesus Christ, the one and only Savior of all mankind, and the assignment he has given his Church to be the reality through which people can get salvation in the ordinary way—for the Church is the ordinary way to salvation.

The document goes on to say that in that Church we have the fullness of the means to salvation; nevertheless, there are elements of truth and goodness outside that Church, and God's plan of salvation includes not only Catholics and other Christians, but also Jews, Muslims,

---

[12] The Declaration *Dominus Jesus: On the Unicity and Salvific Universality of Jesus Christ and the Church* was issued by the Congregation for the Doctrine of the Faith (Vatican City: Libreria Editrice Vaticana, September 2000).

Buddhists, and all others. But there are conditions, it points out, referring to the documents of Vatican II and to *Redemptoris Missio.*

Its main preoccupation, however, was to state the Catholic identity, the minimum below which we should not go for the sake of ecumenism, or for the sake of good inter-religious relations. It is therefore not opposed to the documents from our Pontifical Council for Inter-Religious Dialogue. We will admit that the styles can be different. Yes, because the Congregation for the Doctrine of the Faith is charged with safeguarding Catholic doctrine and telling Catholics that beyond this you are no longer believing what the Church believes. This is like saying, you cannot score a goal from here because you are offside. That's its work, to defend the Catholic faith, and to express it, and to say when a particular position is no longer in line with the Catholic faith.

Whereas the work, the assignment for the Pontifical Council for Inter-Religious Dialogue, is to meet the people of other religions, to establish contact with them, to try to understand them, and to see how to present our Catholic faith to them while they present what they believe to us. It is a different type of assignment. It is not actually a surprise if the language is different, or the style, but the truth expressed is not different.

Also, I want to mention that I am a member of the Congregation for the Doctrine of the Faith, and I also contributed to the writing of *Dominus Jesus*, so I cannot say: "I did not know anything about that document; it is discouraging to us." No, it is not discouraging to us—which does not mean that a phrase here, or a sentence there, could not have been worded differently. These are statements written by men; they are not written by angels. So they could be made better.

Q. *So, with hindsight, would you have rewritten this document in a different way?*

A. Some phrases, yes. Not the truth expressed in them, but the way they are put. Yes.

Q. *So you can understand why people would feel that they sense there are contradictory messages coming out from the Vatican, as more than one spiritual leader of another Christian community has said.*

A. I can understand that. But there are no contradictory messages coming out. I also want to add that some people ran away with newspaper headlines, and they have not read the actual document. So that's important too. People must not stop at the headlines; they should take the document and read it in a calm way.

Q. *I suppose one of the problems is in the interpretation of the text, because no document is the last word, and every document fits into a context often of other documents that have gone before it, and it has to be read also in the light of those that have preceded it. If one forgets the background, then one risks misreading the text.*

A. Yes, that is important also. It is important. If you just take two or three sentences and run away with these, then they can give a wrong picture. This also applies to the documents of our pontifical council, if you take only one part and you run away with that. Suppose you say: "God also gives his grace outside the visible boundaries of the Catholic Church." That is true, but it does not say everything, and you have to put this statement alongside the other one that says: "Only in the Church have we the fullness of the means to salvation"; otherwise you discourage people from preaching Christ to anyone.

Vatican II is careful. Even in the same *Lumen Gentium*, paragraph 16, where it says that God's plan of salvation includes also the Jews, the Muslims, and everyone of goodwill, Vatican II does not stop there but goes on to say that because of the difficulty of arriving at religious truth, and because of human weakness and the deceit of the devil, religious truth is really difficult for people, and, therefore, people make mistakes, and they have religious errors. And, therefore, the Church painstakingly pursues her missionary work, that is, to share with others the fullness of the means of salvation within the Church. There you have the whole thing stated.

And then also, occasionally, a translation in one language is not exactly faithful to the original. That happened with *Dominus Jesus*. The original text might have been actually much more balanced than a particular translation.

But I think the harder part, the greater cause of misunderstanding, is people running away with newspaper headlines. Whenever people say to me, "*Dominus Jesus* said this or that", I generally ask, "Please, have you read the whole document?" If people say, "Not really", then I will say, "You are not ready to discuss it because you have not read the document."

Once, a Muslim said to me, "Your document *Dominus Jesus* . . ." I said to him, "Look, that document is stating Catholic doctrine on salvation for us, salvation for you, salvation for others. Please, when shall we get your own statement as Muslims, what you yourself believe is salvation for you, for us Christians—what do you call us? And for Jews, and for people of Traditional Religions, and your own belief on Buddhists and salvation? So that we can discuss your document and ours together." He said, "Our own will be very simple." I said, "Very good, but write it. Do not presume that what Catholic theologians and bishops and cardinals have thought over for weeks and weeks and weeks, and the Pope has approved, is easily dismissed. You just sit back, and without reading the document, but only what the journalist summarizes, you run away with that, and we begin discussing that. You see it is not a fair ground to begin the discussion."

But for a person who has read the whole document carefully, then I would be ready to discuss, and if a person suggests that this sentence could have been formulated a bit differently, if it is really so, I shall admit it.

Q. *But certain aspects were left out, some people say.*

A. It is possible, because it is a human work. It's not Holy Scripture, where we can't add; it is a human work, and the document cannot go into every point.

Q. *What lessons have you taken from the reactions to this document?*

A. One of the lessons is that there are some within the Church who didn't have a correct theology, and therefore the document touched a sore point. And it is just as well in that case. Secondly, the document can become the occasion, after all this talk, for greater reflection, and that's good. Then the reactions of people can also make all the Vatican dicasteries that have any type of contribution to offer on this matter to ask themselves whether their own homework, and their own inner consultation, should have been any different. These are internal reflections that we cannot avoid making.

Chapter 14

Reflections on the Synod
for Africa

(1994)

A new chapter in the history of Christianity in Africa was opened on April 10,
1994, when Pope John Paul II presided at the joyous liturgy in Saint Peter's
Basilica, Rome, for the inauguration of the Synod of Bishops for Africa.

The four-week-long synod (April 10 to May 8) focused on the Church and her
evangelizing mission in Africa at the close of the millennium. It examined
questions of fundamental importance to the Church and the peoples in the fifty-
four countries of the continent, which then had a population of some seven hundred
million people, of whom one hundred million were Catholics.[1] *These included*
questions related to justice and peace, the dialogue with Islam and with African
Traditional Religion, the proclamation and inculturation of the Gospel, and the
dialogue among the Christian Churches.

The Pope appointed Cardinal Arinze one of the three president delegates to
chair the sessions. But by the end of the synod, the Pope was in the hospital,[2]
and he asked Cardinal Arinze to preside in his name at the closing celebration on
May 8.

The cardinal later accompanied the Pope to Africa in 1995 for the closing of the
synod and the presentation of its conclusions, gathered together in the apostolic
exhortation The Church in Africa (Ecclesia in Africa). On that journey, the Pope
visited three countries: Cameroon, South Africa, and Kenya, and later, in 1996,
still in the synod context, he also went to Tunisia.

---

[1] The figures are approximate and rounded up, but they are based on the fact that, at
the end of 1992, Africa had a population of 684.6 million people, of whom 95.6 million
were Catholic (Holy See's Statistics for 1992). By the end of 2001, Africa's population was
an estimated 812 million people, of whom 135.6 were Catholic, according to the Holy
See's *Statistics Yearbook*, published in June 2003.

[2] The Pope fell and was hospitalized, with a fracture in his right femur, from April 29
to May 27, 1994.

I had interviewed the cardinal prior to the synod[3] *and had filed reports on the entire synod. But soon after the close of the synod,*[4] *I again requested an interview with him to capture his memories and insights of that event while they were still fresh. He agreed, and we met on May 25, 1994. This chapter is mainly based on that interview, supplemented by extracts from an interview on December 9, 2000.*

I began by asking the cardinal about the closing ceremony in Saint Peter's Basilica, at which he had presided on May 8.

---

[3] I published articles based on that interview, first in the international Catholic weekly, *The Tablet* (London, March 1994), and in *Catholic Asian News* (Kuala Lumpur, Malaysia, April 1994). The full text of the interview—Gerard O'Connell, "Arinze on the African Synod"—was published in *Inside the Vatican* (New Hope, Ky, April 1994).

[4] I filed, or contributed to, reports on the synod for *The Tablet* (London) and *The Universe* (Manchester), in the period April–May 1994.

Q. *The Pope was in the hospital for the close of the African synod, and he asked you to preside at the closing ceremony. This was something unusual and significant: an African cardinal presiding, in the place of the Pope, over the close of the first-ever African synod. It was a great honor, obviously, but I'd like to know what your deeper feelings were on that day.*

A.   Yes, a great honor, definitely. You will please note that we were three cardinal president delegates, because the Pope is the president of every synod, but he generally gets three cardinals to run the business, in turn, to be the chairmen in the meetings. And all three of us were Africans: Paulos Cardinal Tzadua, of Addis Ababa, Ethiopia; Christian Cardinal Tumi, of Duala, Cameroon; and myself.

So the Holy Father decided to ask me. He could have asked anybody else; he could have asked the dean of the College of Cardinals, or the secretary of state, or any of the three of us, but he decided to ask me. How the Holy Father came to that decision, I do not know. But it was obviously a great honor for me, and in any case the Pope was giving honor to Africa, which was celebrating the synod. I did not regard it as overly personal, but a great honor. Definitely.

Q. *But what did you feel as you sat there under Bernini's baldacchino, in front of the high altar in Saint Peter's Basilica, where the Pope normally sits?*

A.   I felt a bit small in front of that illustrious assembly, because there were quite a number of bishops and cardinals present, and not only Africans but also those from the Roman Curia. But everybody knew that I was just reading the Pope's homily; it was not my homily, and everybody knew that.

And also there are many events that the Holy Father would have to do but, for one reason or another, he cannot, and so he asks a cardinal to do it in his place. It's just normal: envoys to Eucharistic congresses, to centenary celebrations, and so on.

More particularly, this was in his own basilica, and it was a synod where he would normally attend, but he was in the hospital and had to ask somebody else.

Q. *And what was your memory of that celebration in Saint Peter's?*

A. My memory of it is a very happy one. I read the Holy Father's homily and felt what a sense of honor and of history it was, still realizing that I was just a bishop from a village in Nigeria. So that's it.

Q. *Did you report to the Pope after the ceremony?*

A. Yes, but the Holy Father, even though in the hospital, followed it on TV, I think.

Q. *He watched it on TV?*

A. Yes. When I saw him later, he was in a very good mood, and he told me he had followed it.

Q. *Apart from that extraordinary moment, what other personal memory do you treasure from that historic event?*

A. My memory of the synod is that of representatives of the Church in Africa—and also from elsewhere, but mainly Africans—gathered with the Holy Father, reflecting together on evangelization in Africa.

My memory is very clear on the bishops. After the first day or two, and a bit of "who-will-speak-first" hesitation, they came out in all freedom and in all frankness, giving their various views; all were concerned about evangelization in Africa, the successes, the weak points and failures, the tasks to be done.

My memory of this synod is of a group of people all concerned about the Gospel of Jesus Christ. Nobody was angry with anybody. We were not agreed on everything; we could not be agreed, otherwise there would be no discussion. But that's the whole point of discussion: that individuals express how they see a problem and what they think is the solution—if they have any. Because some problems are rather difficult; it's not easy to come forward with a solution, but we can still identify the problem. And the very willingness to listen for hours each day is really very positive. I have attended many synods before, but for me this was one of the most fulfilling.

Q. *In what sense?*

A. In the sense that I observed harmony reigning. As I said earlier, I didn't notice people against anybody, or angry with anybody. But I noticed people concerned with situations, with suffering, even with cases of extreme poverty, not to mention the massacre that was going on in Rwanda at that same time. The situation in Rwanda was one that the synod participants could not avoid thinking about and asking themselves questions about.

I was happy because the atmosphere was one of sharing and listening, receiving and giving. I thought that the Holy Spirit was working; not that he doesn't work in other synods, but he really worked hard this time, if I may put it so.

Q. *In the past you've been at meetings in Africa when you were head of the Nigerian Bishops' Conference, and you've met with your brother bishops in Africa on other occasions before; did you notice some particular development here in the lines of communication and communion among the bishops?*

A. Obviously, in the synod, because of the high number of participants, there has to be. In an episcopal conference of twenty, thirty, or forty people there is greater opportunity to speak much more, so, that limitation was noticeable in the synod in the initial presentation of papers, although in the discussion groups there was plenty of time to talk.

In a few cases the bishops had the opportunity to react immediately to a document, such as the presentation by Monsignor Diarmuid Martin on the United Nations meeting that was to be held in Cairo the following September.[5] The bishops were also able to react immediately to the presentation of the Message of the Synod, which finally ended up being seventy-one paragraphs. More than fifty synod Fathers spoke here, and you would have loved to have been there.

You could see one person get up and say, "I think the message, and the wording is too difficult. I think the whole thing should be set aside and a separate message written, so that the people in my diocese can understand it." Then another person would get up and say, "I think the problem is not really the language, but it is a bit long." Another would

---

[5] Monsignor Diarmuid Martin, secretary of the Pontifical Council for Justice and Peace, presented a report, on April 28, 1994, to the special assembly for Africa of the Synod of Bishops, on the final session of the preparatory committee for the Cairo International Conference on Population and Development. The full text of his report is to be found in *Serving the Human Family: Holy See at the Major United Nations Conferences* (New York: The Path to Peace Foundation, 1997).

say, "It's not the length I'm worried about; it's the style. I would prefer a simpler statement." The others got up and suggested modifications in one section or another. It was really very interesting, and very refreshing. For those who had not attended synods before, they feared that finally we might have no message at the end of the day. No such thing, of course—the commission members had just to forget all about sleep for the next three days, and then we got a good message, properly amended.

There was freshness of contribution, and good humor too. But the humor didn't always come from the African members; there were also— I cannot name people—but there was one cardinal, and he was so humorous. And he gave quick answers, and he got everybody awake and got everybody in a really good mood.

I would say that one really remarkable thing that I saw here was the freshness of reaction. Another, I would say, was the discipline in attending, day-in, day-out—though that applies to every synod.

Then again, many of the bishops had not attended general synods before. Only seven of the bishops had attended all the sessions of Vatican II, and only about nine bishops had attended at least one session of Vatican II. So you can see that the African episcopate is rather young. So this freshness at the synod, who knows? Part of it is African style; part of it is that many are under fifty, or are at most under sixty, years of age. Those who were older than sixty were certainly a minority.

Q. *Was there any particular speech or intervention that particularly impressed you, and made you reflect afterward?*

A. Yes. Most of the speakers spoke on inculturation and, predictably, of course, the question of theology—African theology—came up. And if we are to have African theology, then we must have African philosophy too.

One speaker even got onto those concepts in philosophy and theology that Christianity has regarded as rather crucial, such as "nature", "essence", "substance", "person". So when we argue in our human language, and we are trying to express what it is we believe in, we speak about one God, three Persons, and how the second Person took a human nature, and so on. Well, one of the synod Fathers went into all that, and it was very interesting. I understood later that this synod Father had written a thesis in his early days on such matters. Fair enough. You can't have an African theology without African philosophy.

But you asked me what struck me most. One moment I can't forget was when Cardinal Poupard, the president of the Pontifical Council for Culture, got up and said something like this: "But Christianity, you know, has its history. And it will always have something Semitic, you know, because of its Jewish background; and it will always have something of Greek thought, because of its development here; and it will always have something Roman because of its history and its first life there. Of course it has to be inculturated, but you cannot deny the past."

That is what I put earlier in very simple language when I said that we in Africa, in developing inculturated formulations of our beliefs, must not act as if Jesus Christ died last week. It is actually two thousand years since he came on earth, and Christianity has de facto developed, acquiring a rich patrimony—philosophical, theological, liturgical, canonical, and so on. Every part of the Church will have to take note of that. But it will also make a big effort to become local. So that struck me. It wasn't a denial of the necessity of inculturation. Cardinal Poupard did not deny this; he was only addressing that growth which is also normal. Even a grown-up is the same person who was a baby fifty years ago, but he is developing without renouncing his past. That struck me.

Another moment that struck me was when Cardinal Thiandoum, reading his summary report at the beginning of the synod, and addressing the subject of inculturation and rites, spoke of them as a "right", in the sense of "r-i-g-h-t", not a concession. And there were reactions; very healthy reactions. Some thought it an abuse of the text, but the synod did not deny the central fact. That too was very healthy. That is, to develop inculturation in terms of rite, whether you think of "rite" with the small "r"—how you baptize, how you celebrate a marriage, whether you have additional ceremonies at the ordination of a priest; or whether you think of Rite in the big sense with a capital "R"—such as, of a whole family, theological patrimony, canon law patrimony, patrimony of spirituality—just as we speak of the Alexandrian Rite or the Greek Orthodox Rite. Whichever sense you mean, the doors are not closed to Africa, and the synod regarded the doors as open. That seems to me very healthy.

Q. *You've touched on something that I have heard very many people say was one of the very important results of the African synod, namely, that "no doors were closed to future development, and many doors were opened."*

A. I think that insight is correct. It wasn't a synod that came here to close doors and lock them. Obviously, there were definite points on which the synod put its foot down, like speaking on inculturation in reference to marriage. The question of monogamy is there, and that's that. There's nothing to discuss, except how to help those involved in polygamous situations to become more fully Christian, but probably we will come to that later.

Q. *Yes, I want to return to that at a later point. But I would first like to focus on the question of an African theology. What can we expect over the next years in this field?*

A. The synod encouraged African theologians to work hard at developing African theology, but it did not suggest that this would be easy.

It appeared, for example, even when one of the papers spoke of God as "ancestor". And fireworks arose, at least in the discussion group where I was, and in several others too. Some rejected it outright, and said "an ancestor" is a person of our race who lived, died, and is now in honorable memory. And they said, we couldn't apply that to God; and some said we could not even apply it to Christ. Others said no, we couldn't speak of Christ as "ancestor" in the African sense of the word. But some were not too sure at all. If anything, that was an indication of how difficult it is to develop an African theology. But it wasn't a denial of it.

The synod appreciated the necessity of development of an African theology and requested African theologians to work hard at it. It even went further. It asked them to make a big effort to develop the concept of "Church as family", without rejecting the other dimensions of the mystery of the Church, because one concept does not say it all.

The synod was also realistic and spoke of the necessity of Catholic universities and higher ecclesiastical institutes in Africa, because inculturation is not an easy matter to be put together on Saturday evening and forced down the throats of the people on Sunday morning, as if they were part of an experiment; it's not just a question of somebody's ideas, or somebody who has a fertile imagination. That would only do harm, both to the Christian communities and to the Christian name. The synod understood that we need these higher institutes if we are to have an inculturation that will do honor to the Church, to Africa, to Christianity; an inculturation that will evolve patterns that will last, and that will stand on their own anywhere in the world, in the international assemblies of theologians, ethnologists, anthropologists, literary experts, and scholars in the fine arts. To achieve this we need these higher institutes of education. Absolutely.

The synod even went to such details as to say that these institutes should not be denied the students they need, the staff they need, and the necessary finances. In this matter the synod couldn't really do more. No one would expect the synod itself to produce cultural patterns, but only to encourage those who were doing it.

The synod also asked the theologians to do all this in union with their pastors. Obviously. A particular bishop could be a theologian too, but a bishop is not necessarily a theologian in the technical sense. But that they should work together and help one another the synod had no doubt whatsoever.

Indeed, the variety of the theologians working in the synod was also very encouraging. There were twenty of them, and they were called "technical experts". Three of them were religious sisters: one of them, I think, is the former head of the Regina Mundi Institute in Rome; another is a sister from a theologate in one country in Africa; and the third sister was from the communications field. And three of the priests were from the Higher Institutes in Africa. All that was very encouraging.

Q. *In some African theology, as we've discussed before, the concept of "ancestor" is used, seeing God or Christ as "ancestor". You mentioned that the question arose during the synod. What was the synod's final conclusion on this question of "ancestor", seeing God and Christ as "ancestor"?*

A. The concept is there. There is always a great belief in Africa that there is a link between those still living in this world and those who have lived and passed on to the spirit land, as we call it in Africa. They would be our fathers and mothers who lived honorable lives, who died, and the final funeral rites were performed in their honor, and they have now reached the happy spirit land. And they are believed to be still linked, in touch with their children and children's children who are still on earth. So they influence for good; it may be for the harvest, children, good health, prosperity in trade, or otherwise, depending on the various traditions among the peoples of Africa, because the concept is not monolithic.

This remains. And there is the veneration of these ancestors. These ancestors are always distinguished from the spirits that were never bodily spirits—the good spirits and the bad spirits. The ancestors were regarded as different and were never identified with God, the Creator, the Almighty, the One who is above, the One who made "up" and "down"; they were never identified with him. Most of these forms of African Tradition Religion and culture honored God, and then the spirits, and also the ancestors.

Many theologians in Africa, making an effort to come up with an African theology, ask, "How shall we present God?" Some thought he could be presented as "Primordial Ancestor". Others thought: no, let it be just Christ who is "ancestor", since Christ was a man, and he even suffered and died and rose again. So that's it.

Certainly the synod's main document does not refer to God as ancestor. As for Christ, I am not sure. I think it didn't, but I would have to look carefully. I think it did not. But it did reserve a section on ancestor veneration and did something more courageous than anything I have seen so far.

Q. *Perhaps you could explain a little more what you mean?*

A. It was in one of the propositions—although the propositions are still a confidential document. One of the propositions spoke definitely on "ancestor veneration", saying that in African communities the ancestors do occupy a place of honor, regarded as part of those who are still living, in the way I more or less explained earlier. And therefore the synod wanted the Church in each area to study what form this "ancestor veneration" really takes and to work out how Christians can honor these ancestors. It will never be the cult or adoration that we offer to God. It is almost unnecessary to say that, but still the synod said this.

The bishops also knew, at least in some discussion groups, that the Catholic Church in Japan—where ancestor worship is regarded as very much a part of Japanese culture—has worked out directives to help Christians on how to honor their ancestors. If you think of such ceremonies in Africa as wine libations . . . when an African in the Traditional Religion drinks wine, he doesn't just drink but he pours a few drops on the ground first, and that is meant to be absorbed by the earth, and in that way the ancestors are honored. "You drink first, and after you then we come."

Q. *In this concept of ancestors, are all who died classified as ancestors, or only those who have lived honorable lives, as you call it?*

A. It may differ from culture to culture. Among my own people in Nigeria, not all who die would be honored as ancestors. Definitely those who lived lives that were not honorable would not be ranked among the ancestors; for example, if a person had been a thief, or if a person committed suicide. Then there would be superstitions too. If a person died of smallpox or a very infectious disease, the people would believe that the person had committed some sin, and therefore is being punished for it, and so, that person would not be ranked along with the ancestors. But those who lived lives that were honorable, and who died and had the final ceremonies performed for them, were so ranked. But never babies or children; the ancestors would always be grown-ups.

So you see that now when we want to bring an African to the Christian concept of the saints, and the unity of the Christians still on earth with those who are already in heaven, the Church cannot accept wholesale the African belief and style of ancestor veneration. Very much would have to be studied, retouched, changed, corrected, rejected.

But still there is here, in the African Traditional Religion, a real providential preparation for the whole doctrine of the communion of saints. This doctrine tells us that those who are in heaven, those who are in purgatory—still suffering but who can be helped by us on earth—and we who live on earth have a type of togetherness in Christ. There is a providential preparation for this doctrine in the African Traditional Religion.

Q. *As you have explained it, this ancestor veneration in the African Traditional Religion offers a great insight into the Christian understanding of the communion of saints.*

A. It does. It does offer this. And that is really why the synod is asking the local Church to study this.

A Christian agent of the Gospel does not solve the problem in Africa by saying this ancestor worship is pagan, so please forget it and now learn to become Christian. That is not the correct procedure, because that is like rejecting the providential preparation of the people for Christianity. It is like saying your religious past is totally useless; we do not take it into account; now we do everything new. That is not the correct approach.

The correct approach is to take note of what the religious past was—the positive, the less positive, the downright negative—and then see what response Christianity can make to it. Christianity will still remain new; nothing will take away its novelty. That Jesus Christ, the Son of God, became a man is new. That he gives us a share in his divinity is new. That grace is the life of God in us is new. That in Christianity we get that new life in Christ is new.

Nevertheless, that there is some type of link between those who have arrived home in heaven, those who are suffering in purgatory, and those who are still on the move on earth . . . there is something in the past in Africa that does help Africans somehow to come to accept that Christian doctrine and life. That is the area of inculturation.

Q. *But there is this other question of the spirit world; did the synod discuss that too?*

A. The synod also thought about that, because to approach Africans and to take no notice at all of their beliefs in the spirits, good and bad, benevolent and malevolent, would be unrealistic; one would have to take note of that.

Many synod Fathers also mentioned that the approach to healing in Africa is a holistic one; that is, when the person is sick, the African does not just take note of, let's say, the scientific dimension, what the modern hospitals in Rome, Paris, New York, or London would be looking at. The African would take note of that, yes; but also of more. The African would want to be sure that there isn't some bad spirit that has something against him or some ancestor who is angry with the person because he violated the laws of the land.

For instance, among my own people, if a person stole yams—yam is the fundamental crop of the people—it is believed that he would get a big punishment from the spirits and the ancestors; and especially from the spirit of the land, which would not permit someone to subvert the whole economic structure of the area by stealing the fundamental food item, even if the quantity stolen was rather small. That's all very interesting.

If an individual believes, "I offended; I committed an abomination", then more is needed than medicine.

An abomination could be stealing yams; it could be a woman climbing a tree in the Traditional Religion; it could be incest; it could be killing a person who is not from his clan, or who is from his clan. In Christianity different judgments are made on these. An abomination could also be allowing animals to give birth to young ones without assistance—if you tie a goat to a tree when it is going to have a young one, that is considered an abomination in my culture. That's how they look at it.

If the individual believes he committed an abomination, it would not be enough to give him the prescribed medicine, which the doctor in the super, model hospital has recommended. Much more is needed. The casting away of fears, the bringing of the individual to repentance—where Christianity would accept that there was moral guilt and where there was not—to remove from the individual the fear of the unknown spirits, the unknown forces of evil. That's what we would call a total approach to the human person, a holistic approach.

The synod is recommending something like that. Not new. It's therefore encouraging initiatives along those lines.

Q. *I think the synod suggested at one stage that in this field witchcraft could be dangerous to the peace.*

A. It can be dangerous to the peace. But the synod did not go into detail on that. One can think of areas. Africa is so large. There are areas where people live in fear of old people; there are areas where the people live in fear of witches; other areas where they live in fear of unknown forces. They have all kinds of fears. Christianity cannot abandon them to this state; it has to come to meet the situation of the people. Here the Gospel of Christ is the Gospel of liberation in the best sense of the word.

Even if we do not believe in witchcraft, and I do not believe in it, but if some people in fact believe in it—then when we have to approach such people, we should not approach them as if they don't believe in it. At the very least, we must help them so that they begin to realize that some of their fears are not well founded.

But then perhaps some of their fears are well founded. Very good. For example, if a person is wicked in the village, if a person does things to others that are really mean, that person has good reason to be disturbed, and Christianity should help him to realize his fault, to repent, and to change.

In cases where it is a question of physical suffering, which comes even to the greatest saints, Christianity has to help Africans to realize that suffering, carrying the cross, is part of Christianity; that suffering does not mean every time that the individual has committed a sin. Remember the passage of Sacred Scripture, where the apostles ask Jesus, "Lord, who has sinned, this man or his parents, that he was born blind?" Christ said, "Neither he nor his parents sinned. He was born blind so the works of God might be revealed in him" [Jn 9:2–3]. So Africans also have to learn that.

I am not saying that everything is good on that point. There are some cases where Africans regard suffering as always due to bad spirits, or to a person's sins, or to unknown forces. They need this new, liberating doctrine of Good Friday.

Q. *This question of the spirit world seems alien to many people in the modern industrialized societies. The Western world, the industrialized world, seems to have lost an awareness of the spirit world. Would it be correct to say that this greater awareness of the spirit world is one of the contributions that African Christianity can make to the evangelization of people in the industrialized societies?*

A. I think I can say yes to that question. That is, the African belief that man is not the highest form of existence under God; that there are some forces above us, but below God, that we call spirits—good spirits and bad spirits; and that the bad spirits can actually do harm to men; they can cause confusion, even sickness. It is not a foolish belief. It is true. Indeed, Christianity tells us the good spirits are angels, bad spirits are devils; and it also tells us that the devil has more power than men and can do harm to us. The devil can even cause a car accident; he can cause a short-circuit with the electricity; the devil can cause confusion; he can sow the spirit of disunity in a parish, in a religious family, or in an ordinary family of husband, wife, and children. We cannot ignore that.

It is a pity that some people in the Western, developed countries think that it is a sign of progress not to believe in the devil. They think that the devil is an object of superstition or unscientific civilization or inhuman forces; that it is man who makes up the devil. Well, somebody should inform them that they are wrong.

The devil is there, and he is alive and well and operating. You will notice the growing number of people who seek fortune-tellers in Italy, France, Germany, the U.S.A., and other countries. Then, the belief in reincarnation is increasing too, as is the belief in those who read the stars and those who say that they can tell the future. There is even some talk of Satanism, and they come out with what Africans don't do: they say they are offering worship to the devil. That's a terrible situation. If anybody wanted a proof that the devil exists, there it is.

By all means let's have science, but there are some things that the scientist cannot analyze in his laboratory, such as the devil, angels, indeed, the whole spirit world. Africa could contribute something here. It isn't naïve. Even though there are superstitions in Africa, in the midst of all that there is that sense of the supernatural, the existence of forces that are above man but below God the Almighty.

Q. *Could we turn to another area of inculturation, that of marriage and the marriage rites? Several bishops said, Catholics in many parts of Africa do not receive the sacraments because the Church does not recognize the African forms of marriage in which they participate. The synod suggested that there be a commission to study this whole question of marriage, but it didn't really come up with an answer.*

A. That is true. I think the synod has gone as far as could be expected in one month. That is, the synod Fathers expressed concern that, as some said, there are really three celebrations of marriage.

One celebration is according to the local customs, and people would never normally omit them, and they need not be superstitious. Here, there may be elements that are superstitious that Christianity could not accept, but that would not apply to most of these customs.

Then there is the statutory or modern government form of marriage; it could be in the registry office, or other civil form accepted by civil law.

The third celebration is the specifically Christian celebration, generally in the presence of the priest and two witnesses. I say generally, because canon law provides for other forms.

The concern of the synod Fathers was that the individuals—the young man and young woman getting married, and even their relatives, once the traditional ceremonies are completed—more or less regard the couple as man and wife, and they regard the Church celebrations as a sort of . . . well, they do it because the Church says so—those who are often not well informed—or they regard it as a beautiful finishing touch. But we are not sure that they consider that it is necessary for the validity of their marriage.

As for the civil celebration of marriage, some realize the implications if they have problems later on with regard to having to contest a case in the high court. Not that they pray for that, but just in case, especially when the woman could be rejected by the man, and she is not paid anything: she is abandoned. If the marriage is celebrated according to civil law, a lawyer would at least bring the man to court to answer a few questions, and he might get the man to pay so much each month.

The general indication of the synod was that whatever could be done should be done to simplify the form for the people; if possible, so that it be only one form; it asked if there is a way in which the Church celebration could be made to become one with the traditional celebration. The synod therefore said, let's have a group study the question.

It isn't a way to avoid a decision. No, no! It is the realization that it isn't necessarily in Rome that the problem would be solved; most of it could be solved on the spot, by the local Church, which could mean a whole cultural area where there is one and the same type of celebration. Or it might be resolved in one or more dioceses in a country, depending on the situation. The dioceses would really have to examine it together; in many cases they already could do it and refer to Rome only if necessary. That's the sort of study the synod envisaged. It is not the case, therefore, that once you set up one commission in Rome, there is no more problem in all of Africa. That would be oversimplification, because the customs vary so much.

It was clear to the synod that if a Christian is to marry, the marriage must be a Christian marriage. The only question is, what form? And here there's a wide possibility, even within the Church's canon law, and if any local Churches, in any country of Africa, feel there is some necessity to go beyond a particular point or other of existing canon law, it is for them to articulate it. But they cannot articulate it, unless they first study the question. Nobody can do this work for them; they have to do it themselves.

However, there are major milestones that cannot be moved. Obviously, the synod maintained monogamy, for example, and therefore does not approve polygamy—in any case! But it said it's another matter, the question of the pastoral way to help those who are involved in a polygamous situation, many of them not through their own fault. When they got into such situations, they didn't know. This applies to those who were not Christians then. The synod is not condemning individuals, one by one, but the Church cannot accept polygamy at all. And the Church is most compassionate in seeking ways to help those involved in such situations to accept the full challenge of the Gospel.

Q. *Would it then be correct to say that the Church is pushing for the break-up of polygamous marriage situations?*

A. The Church has never approved polygamous marriages. In Africa, some men married two wives—or three, four, or five wives—before they wanted to become Christians, or before the women wanted to become Christians. There is nothing new in what the synod has said. The pastoral practice has been that if the woman wants to come to the sacraments—baptism, confession, Holy Communion, and so on—then she cannot still be approved as the second, third, fourth, or fifth wife of the man. If the man wants to come to the sacraments, the same thing holds. So the polygamous situation has to be faced in such a way that the man is married to one woman only, but he retains the strict duty in justice to maintain all these women and their children. These others are to be treated with justice and with respect.

Q. *If I understand you correctly, this means that the civil implications of polygamous marriages would be recognized by the Church as implications of justice.*

A. Yes, justice in the sense that he has to maintain these women and their children, unless, of course, in particular circumstances they didn't need that. Then there has to be some provision so that he doesn't regard them as his wives anymore, and also the local Catholic community doesn't regard them as such. This is not something to be worked out in Rome. When I was archbishop in the diocese that is how we did it.

The same holds true for a Christian. If a Christian was married to a woman, and later on took a second wife, or even a third and fourth, in his case, there is nothing to discuss at all. He already has a wife, married in the Church. He now has to provide for the others in strict justice. But they must live separately. He makes a declaration in church to this effect, but he must maintain them and their children. Some have de facto *done* that, and in an honorable way. And then all of them become free for the sacraments.

The Church cannot accept polygamy; but the Church has compassion for those involved in polygamous situations and seeks a way to provide for them all in strict justice and charity. Not only justice, but also charity. But the Church cannot approve polygamy, in any case. No.

Where they do not accept the full challenge of the Gospel, they are encouraged to continue coming to church and taking part in religious activities, but they will not be admitted to the sacraments because it would become double standard.

Q. *Turning to another question, that of the basic ecclesiology, or understanding of the Church, that emerged from the synod. As I read it, the synod endorsed the understanding of "Church as family" as the one best suited for Africa.*

A. Yes. The synod very much liked that approach as a presentation of the mystery of the Church to Africa, because the family delivers a powerful message to Africans. The synod said that the concept "Church as family" is one of the best ways to present the mystery of the Church to Africans, and it asked theologians to work hard in developing it.

The synod also acknowledged that it isn't the only way to present the mystery of the Church. That mystery is far too rich to be exhausted in one concept; there are other concepts—People of God, Mystical Body of Christ, House of God, New Jerusalem, and so on—and these too must go on. But the Church as family—yes!

Q. *This concept seems particularly relevant and significant because of the problems emerging in Africa from excessive ethnocentrism and tribalism.*

A. You are right. In Africa we have people belonging to many language groups, or tribes—if you want to call them so, although one of the discussion groups said, "This term tribalism, if it is to be applied only to Africans, we do not accept it; but if it would be applied to Europeans and Americans and Asians, then we will accept it."

However, to come back to the main question, it is a fact that in Africa we have people of many differing ethnic backgrounds, or language groups, or tribes. In Nigeria alone, we have at least 250 language groups, which are also tribes. Therefore, if we are to have a sense of one nation, or one state, among all these people, if we are to have in the Church a sense of family, a sense of unity, a sense of the Church as communion— which is a theological concept much stressed in our times—then the Church must come to terms with this problem posed by tribalism, by the excessive accent on ethnic belonging.

This problem is one of the headaches of Africa. I don't need to name countries. It's not the whole explanation of the wars in Africa, but it has been an element, and that's undeniable. It has also done damage to the political unity of many parts of Africa.

The synod saw that the concept of "Church as family" would help to heal the excesses, the wounds inflicted by tribalism. The synod even went further and said that in looking for a candidate to be made a bishop, the ethnic group he belongs to should not become a priority.

Q. *Has that been a big factor in the past?*

A. In some parts of Africa, yes. A pity! But "yes" is the answer. There are some parts of Africa where, really, the best candidate who could deliver the goods may not be acceptable because he does not originate from the majority group in that diocese. It deprives that diocese of the best candidate in the situation, and somebody else is put there. It is not necessarily the fault of this person or that person, but this situation is a problem—let me call it a challenge.

The Church has not surrendered in the face of that problem. There are de facto, even in my own country, appointments of bishops outside their language areas, where they do not know any of the languages spoken in that place, and they are Nigerian! And so they learn the language. That is the sort of thing the synod is encouraging, not for the love of "getting someone from outside", if you may use that expression, but to show that the Church is a family, and in that family none of us is a stranger, none of us is an expatriate. If we develop more the sense of family, it will help us in the Church as a whole, and not only in the appointment of bishops.

The synod also praised religious congregations in Africa because they seem to succeed in a wonderful way in getting people from different ethnic backgrounds and getting them to function as a religious family. It was thinking of congregations of sisters, especially, because the sisters are more numerous. But there are also priests, such as the Apostles of Jesus, who have their generalate in Nairobi. In Nigeria, we have the National Missionary Seminary, the Society of Saint Paul; and it has people from differing backgrounds, and this too is a bit of a success story.

Q. *This means that in a very real sense the religious orders, like the missionaries, have paved the way for what the Church should become in many parts of Africa.*

A. Yes, in a way they have done that, and credit should be given to them. And it was given in the synod. If it didn't appear in the final document, it would be because everything can't appear there, but it was said in the groups—yes!

And if you think of the normal diocese, it would have its own seminarians from the place, and it's just normal that those seminarians would be ordained for that diocese. They are diocesan priests. It's to be expected that a religious order, or congregation, not being tied to one place, would take in candidates from a much wider area. And that's very healthy.

Q. *There was a lot of talk in the synod about the role of missionaries and the contribution they had made to the evangelization of Africa, and there was also talk about what the future is for missionaries in this continent. Could you summarize what was the main drift of the discussion?*

A. I think the main drift can be put this way. The synod thanked God for the work done by the missionaries in Africa. There was even a review of the evangelization in Africa, and the giants of this evangelization were mentioned, such as Cardinal Lavigerie, Bishop Daniel Comboni, and people such as Libermann and Bishop Shanahan. I'm going to forget some names now, but people such as those were mentioned.

Q. *You mean the names that were mentioned in the Pope's homily that you read at the closing Eucharistic celebration.*

A. Yes, also those. And the various religious families were mentioned in the synod discussions too. That was one beautiful passage in the synod. Indeed, the synod not only thanked God Almighty for the work of the missionaries, but it also thanked the missionaries for the sacrifices they had made in personnel and also in material means.

Secondly, the synod expressed joy at having the missionaries with us in Africa today. The synod did not think that the era of missionary work was finished in Africa, even though it desired that more and more people in Africa would take a great part in the work of evangelization, so that the Church in Africa—or the churches, as we say, in other words, the dioceses—and the Church in the various countries would grow up finally and not be just a mission-country Church, or Church of mission, but would become a Church on mission. That is, a Church doing missionary work herself, within her own country to begin with; then in other parts of Africa as well; and even beyond the confines of the continent. It said the Church in Africa must not wait until we have enough personnel locally; the Church in Africa has to learn to be doing it now.

The synod was aware that this is already being done in some places. Indeed, the very presence at the synod of the superiors generals of major religious orders that have houses in Africa was already eloquent. But there were also superiors generals and provincials of congregations founded in Africa. Prominent among them was the superior general of the Apostles of Jesus, a priests' missionary congregation. So that was good.

The approach therefore was that the Church in Africa must do more to propagate herself within each country, within the continent, and also to share in the greater missionary concern of the Church worldwide, including even the service of the Holy See, in the diplomatic service, or in the dicasteries of the Vatican, and including what we call *Fidei Donum* priests, that is, diocesan priests who go to another diocese within their country, or outside their country, for an agreed length of years. This would be agreed between themselves, their bishop, and the bishop of the receiving diocese.

And also the synod discussed the idea of an exchange of personnel, that some countries in Europe or America could send priests to Africa, and Africa could send some to them. In that way we exchange better in the Church.

The synod also emphasized that the Church in Africa also has to learn gradually to maintain herself from the financial point of view, without denying that Africa will continue to need financial help from outside, but the synod didn't accept it as a permanent state; that would not do honor to Africa.

Q. *So for the missionary orders, and for the missionaries who go to Africa, as I understand it, the synod simply wants them to work in greater harmony with the local Church.*

A. Yes, that was emphasized. But there was another aspect too. The large missionary orders and congregations that are actually working in Africa, including those that began the evangelization in particular areas, examined, together with the synod Fathers, the cases of religious congregations from outside Africa that would like to go to Africa, to take what they call vocations. That is, to take young men and women to join them, particularly in Europe, and perhaps also in North America.

The synod did not reject the idea, because we must communicate in the Church, but it emphasized the necessity of doing it together with the local Church. Indeed, the synod went so far as to say that congregations that have no houses in Africa should not generally be encouraged to go there and take some candidates and go off to another country unless they have discussed it and agreed on it with the bishop of the place.

This means the synod wants greater cooperation within the Church. But the synod did not become myopic, parochial; the synod does not say that Africans must stay in Africa and must not be in orders or congregations somewhere outside Africa. That would be far too rigid. The synod said no such thing.

Q. *The synod spoke about the Church in Africa being "on mission". Does this also involve a redefinition of the link between the Congregation for the Evangelization of Peoples and the local African Churches, because for a long time many of the African Churches have been considered "Churches of mission". It would seem that the synod has set down a marker and said the Church in Africa is moving from a "Church of mission" to a Church "on mission".*

A. There is nothing that would prevent a diocese, or a country, in Africa that, from an organizational point of view, is under the general umbrella of the Congregation for the Evangelization of Peoples, rather than under the Congregation for Bishops or the Congregation for the Oriental Churches, from engaging in mission work. Not only is there nothing to stop it; rather, it should engage in mission work.

Therefore, dioceses in Africa must not wait and say, "We will do missionary work when we are no longer under the Congregation for the Evangelization of Peoples." That would be wrong, because the Vatican II document on missionary work says that these young Churches must begin missionary work even before they get enough of their own personnel—clergy, religious, lay people, volunteers (*Ad Gentes*, 20). So that's one thing.

On the other hand, you have raised an important point on which the synod could not be expected to go into detail. That is, it is quite legitimate to ask, when does a diocese qualify to be transferred from the Congregation for the Evangelization of Peoples to the Congregation for the Oriental Churches or the Congregation for Bishops? That is an open question; and on that people can have different opinions.

Q. *But was it discussed at the synod?*

A. Not in the plenary sessions, but perhaps in some discussion groups. I don't think such a detail figured in the final document. But surely the whole open spirit of the synod has encouraged such discussion to continue, and I don't think anybody should stop anybody from discussing such matters.

Indeed, the question of finance should not be allowed to occupy too major a place. After all, a Church could be poor in money and yet could be up-and-coming in having missionaries.

Q. *Turning to another matter, I was particularly struck by the emphasis given to the Scriptures—the Bible—by the African synod. It seems to me to have given more attention to this than other synods hitherto; it seemed to give a more central place to the Scriptures than, for example, the first European synod. Is that impression correct?*

A. Well, I'm not sure that I'm ready to compare and contrast the European and the African synods. But if you talk about the two of them, the African was for a much longer time in preparation, while the European was much shorter in preparation; so I would not like to compare the two in that sense.

The reference to Holy Scripture in the African synod has been a very happy one. It has appeared in every synod, but in this synod in a remarkable way. It was a very happy thing. I do not know whether I have the full explanation for it. Who knows whether it is because many of those who had a hand in writing the documents are themselves very immersed in Holy Scripture? Possibly. I know some, but I would not name them. I know some who are former students of the Biblical Institute in Rome— the Biblicum—so it's possible. But, even without frequenting the Biblicum, it's those who make a document that influence it finally.

And then again, the Bible is very much loved in Africa; the people want to read the Bible. They want it translated. The synod went into great detail on the Bible, and said: "Please do translations of the Bible, and let them be ecumenical translations if possible. And put the Bible into the hands of the people. Make copies at a cost that the people can buy them, because many people in Africa are poor. People love the Bible, and if you do not organize Bible reading, teaching of the Bible, and so on for them, somebody else will do it, and then you may be surprised at what happens with the little group."

Love for the Bible is very strong in Africa. The Symposium of Episcopal Conferences of Africa and Madagascar (SECAM) already gives great attention to the Bible, and, I think, it has assigned one or two people full-time on this task for the past twenty years.

Q. *I want to ask a question about the implementation of the synod, because I see the synod has come up with very many proposals, and the key to its success is, of course, its implementation; whether on such questions as the study that's necessary, say, on African Traditional Religions, inculturation, the question of the ancestors, an African theology, the liturgy, and so on. You're a member of the council for the implementation of the synod; what process do you foresee?*

A. The bishops themselves at the synod elected nine members of the council, one for each regional grouping of bishops' conferences in Africa, and then the Holy Father nominated three more. That council has not yet met, but it will meet eventually and will work as such councils do after all other synods. It will do its part, but it must not be expected that it is that council that will bring the synod to the grassroots in Africa. It could not do it. It will do a certain amount though, for example, if the Holy Father asks it to help with the post-synodal exhortation. The Holy Father may also ask it to make suggestions on how to celebrate the concluding phase of the synod, in which he will go to several centers in Africa yet to be announced. If the Holy Father asks, the council will obviously make suggestions.

But the council cannot replace the structures of the Church in Africa; the major structures such as the diocese, the bishops' conference in each country, or perhaps the regional conferences in some large countries. And then perhaps too a certain amount can be done by regional bishops' conferences in Eastern Africa, Northern Africa, Southern Africa, Western Africa and Central Africa.

Then there is the second forum, at the continental level. One would imagine that each of these comes in somewhere in the implementation process. But nobody can replace the key ones—the dioceses, the bishops' conference in each country, and SECAM. Even without forming new commissions, they already have their agenda from the synod itself. And since the president of every national bishops' conference was an ex-officio member of the synod, and the president of every regional grouping of bishops' conferences in Africa was also a member, and the bishops' conference in each country elected bishops to participate in the synod, then no country in Africa has anybody to blame but itself if, when they go back home, they take the documents and file them nicely and then nothing happens, and they just wait for the Pope's post-synodal exhortation.

One single document cannot do everything for them; it can help, it can give indications. But finally it is the Church on the spot that has to do the work, and the hope and expectation is that it is the diocese, the national bishops' conference, and SECAM that would sit, reflect, plan, and set up more structures, if they consider them necessary for the implementation of the synod.

Q. *Do you think that SECAM should build more structures at the continental level?*

A. I would not immediately go for new structures. I would be for the executives of SECAM sitting down, examining, and asking themselves what can be entrusted to the structures they already have, because if structures are made before the work is examined, then it's not really healthy. It is always better to see whether an existing Church structure can do what is desirable. If so, let it do it. The great temptation is to create commissions too fast. And in Africa, you know, there are financial constrictions; there is difficulty about travel—even within the same country; and then there is not always an abundance of personnel. So Africa must not live beyond its means. Nevertheless, these constrictions must not be allowed to drive the synod to the filing cabinet. That would be a great pity.

All this means that, in some countries, in the next few years, you will see a real flourishing of evangelization, and in some countries much less. It depends on the key people. But no country should sit back and expect a miracle to be done for it from somewhere, or from nowhere. That would be a pity.

Q. *I would like to ask about the synod's stance on justice. Justice was the concern most frequently mentioned at the synod, even before inculturation. The Rwandan crisis seemed to run parallel to the synod. And the justice message that came out at the end of the synod was very strong. How much of an interlink was there between that message and the fact that the synod Fathers were faced daily by the terrible situation in Rwanda, one of the most Christian countries of the continent?*

A. It is true that the terrible disaster in Rwanda was going on at the same time as the synod. Upsetting, yes! But it wasn't that Rwanda was being discussed every day at the synod. On the other hand, no participant could have been unaware of it and, whether expressly or each person reflecting, nobody could avoid asking himself, "How could this happen? Has any mistake been made? Where? What should be done now, so that this will never happen again?"

It was not, however, only the situation in Rwanda that the synod participants were thinking about. There are also problems of justice and peace in many other countries. You notice, the synod's message also mentions Sudan, Liberia, Angola, and Somalia. But not all was bad news. There was also South Africa, and the elections were going on at the same time as the synod.

So I would say that the synod, with considerable courage and frankness, was making an effort not to be unilateral and partial. On the one hand, the synod encouraged dialogue between the North and the South in the world. It asked the richer nations in Europe and America to reduce, at least, or, if possible, to write off the foreign debt that is crushing many African countries, and other countries too. The synod also asked that the arms trade—scandalous!—be stopped; and definitely stopped in those areas in conflict.

But the synod did not put all the fault and blame on Europe and America. No. The synod also asked African statesmen and politicians to put the emphasis, not on huge military expenditures, but on education, roads, medical services, and institutions, food and agriculture for their people. The synod also said that quite a number of Africans have embezzled money from their own countries and banked it overseas, and it asked all those involved to find some way to repatriate that money to countries that are already poor.

The synod also asked that the question of ethnic heritage not be allowed to damage politics and national unity in Africa.

Again, the synod Fathers spoke on discrimination and sufferings meted out to women and children, and asked that special study groups be set up to examine these problems. They also said each bishops' conference should have a desk for women's affairs; that is very good.

In that general approach, you can see already that it isn't just Rwanda that the synod Fathers were thinking about.

Q. *I presume that each bishops' conference is also to have its own justice and peace commission?*

A. Oh, yes! Definitely. Definitely! Most conferences already have such commissions. And the question of refugees was also given attention. Africa has an all-time high number of refugees. It has the dubious distinction of having first place in the world as the continent with the greatest number of refugees and displaced persons. These people suffer, they are hungry, and they die. Their crops are destroyed.

And there are fratricidal wars going on in many countries. The synod did not keep silent. It made an effort to be objective in its assessment of the situation.

It also said that bishops and priests must live simpler lifestyles—let us say, in terms of their type of car, house, and so on, though it didn't go into such details—so that they can speak with greater credibility to people who are already poor.

It also asked whether bishops and priests are educating people sufficiently in the justice and peace dimension of evangelization, because it is very much a part of evangelization.

Q. *I was personally very impressed by the total message that came out of the synod. But I was surprised that the synod singled out the torture chambers in Africa, asking the heads of state to close them.*

A. It was mentioned. It could be because many such people are often without a voice; there is nobody to speak for them.

The synod also said that the news media in America and Europe should present Africa also positively and not always in a bad light. But it also said the governments in Africa should give greater freedom to the press. That means also freedom to criticize the government: and to criticize the use of torture when it is really happening, because in some countries in Africa torture is going on, but you dare not write about it or speak about it. There would be trouble for the person who did speak about it. That's perhaps why the synod singled it out.

Q. *It's a very welcome statement.*
A. Very welcome. Yes, very welcome.

Q. *As for the whole area of dialogue, inter-religious dialogue and ecumenical dialogue, the synod emphasized the importance of this, and focused particularly on the dialogue with Islam. What do you see as the basic insights of the synod on this whole subject?*

A. The synod stressed the necessity of Christians and Muslims meeting, listening to one another, working together. There was nothing new in that. But the synod also desired that there be greater formation in the Christian community, greater formation of Christians to equip them to understand the Muslims and to meet them. It even went on to speak of institutes in Africa for this purpose.

Q. *You yourself proposed such institutes when you spoke at the synod.*

A. Yes, and many who spoke in the synod were very receptive to this idea. They said it was good. It does not mean other big institutes. Nobody has yet studied how it could be. It could very well be part of an existing higher institute; it doesn't have to begin from scratch. It could also be in many places. Africa doesn't pretend to be rich in money. But the idea has been welcomed. In short, there is a need for such formation.

The synod also emphasised the need for formation of all pastoral agents for this dialogue; bishops, priests, religious men and women, and the lay faithful. Not one type for all, but something that continues:

formation of Christians in the area of dialogue to equip them better to promote dialogue.

Q. *This formation is envisaged both in the ecumenical field—to help Christians in the dialogue with other Christians—and in the inter-religious dialogue, particularly with Muslims.*

A. Yes, and also to understand the African Traditional Religion. There are three branches of dialogue here.

Q. *The question of facing fundamentalism in Islam came up a number of times in the synod. How would you summarize the synod's perception of this problem?*

A. I would use the following terms: Concern, because it is not a healthy development, whether in Islam or in any other religion. Then the bishops stressed the importance of the principle of fairness, justice— justice for this person, justice for the other person. They also put the emphasis on the need for religious freedom; that even if one religion is the religion of the majority in a country, those who have another religion must be allowed full rights of citizenship, freedom of expression, and freedom of cult, freedom of worship.

The synod, of course, has no means to enforce it in every country, nor is it the wish of the synod to enforce it, but people would expect the synod to give indications. The synod has made the effort as far as I can see. Also, there are a few Christian fundamentalists. It isn't only the Muslims who have fundamentalists. Some of the sects, the Christian sects, are fundamentalists, and we could not approve of this type of exaggeration, because it generally contains injustice done to others, whether consciously or not.

Q. *So the absence of the spirit of dialogue is really in contradiction with the spirit of the Gospel.*

A. Yes. The absence of the spirit of dialogue is part of what makes religious fundamentalism unacceptable, because it contains a refusal to be open to others, and therefore it easily leads to injustice against others, even when the fundamentalist is not aware of it.

Sincerity is not enough; it is not the only virtue. There is another virtue called justice. There's another called reciprocity: you have your rights, I have my rights. I give you freedom in my place to practice your religion; you give me freedom in your place to practice my religion. I recognize your rights; you also have the duty to recognize my rights. Yes, dialogue is not a one-way street, and religious freedom should apply not in only some countries, but in all countries.

Q. *You have listened to many of the Fathers at the synod speaking on Islam. What was the impression that you came away with?*

A. Many bishops are concerned that the situation in their country is one of tension between Muslims and Christians. They wish that the Muslims would be much more open to Christians. Many bishops said that. No bishop would suggest that Christians be closed to Muslims, but many bishops expressed the wish that Muslims would accept Christians, more than they are doing today.

Q. *About a year after the close of the synod* [6] *you accompanied the Pope to Africa for the conclusion of the synod and the presentation of the apostolic exhortation.*

A. That is true. It was the first of the continental synods, and the Holy Father followed the indications of the bishops of Africa. Because, you know, some people had wanted the synod celebrated in Africa in the first place, and some wanted it celebrated in Rome. So before the synod, the Holy Father invited all the cardinals of Africa to come to Rome, and he asked us, "Where do you want it to be held?"

Q. *You mean he took your opinion on this?*

A. Yes, he asked the cardinals of Africa—I think we were fourteen or so—"Where do you want the synod? Secondly, when do you want it?" And he followed what we said, what we had indicated.

Q. *So it was the cardinals of Africa who indicated Rome as the site for the synod?*

A. Yes. Although some cardinals said they wanted it celebrated in Africa; some were for Africa. Some said they wanted it celebrated in Rome. It wasn't one opinion for everybody.

Q. *But the majority were for holding it in Rome?*

A. Yes, a greater number were for Rome, although they also saw the value of celebrating it in Africa. But the majority were for Rome for many reasons.

---

[6] This last part of the interview was recorded on December 9, 2000, long after the Pope's visit to Africa.

We discussed it before: if it were in Rome, the Holy Father could take part every day, and the cardinals of the Roman Curia would be involved. If it were in Africa for one month, it would be too much to expect them to be there for one month. Thirdly, the news media would get the information quicker and share it more realistically, and there would be less opportunity for distraction in children climbing trees, and underdevelopment, and monkeys in the forest, and African dances; and they would concentrate on what we are discussing, and the whole world would hear the voice of Africa better. Moreover, we wouldn't get complicated and bogged down in the local politics of one African country or the other. For many of those reasons, and also because we would be showing that we are the Catholic Church, we are not just doing an African thing somewhere down there in a village.

The Holy Father listened to all, and at the end said: "Very good. Let's do both. Let's have the working session in Rome, and after I'll go to some countries in Africa to bring the results." So before the synod ended, we, the three cardinal president delegates, asked the bishops, "Where do you want the Pope to go in Africa?" And they voted by secret ballot. The Pope chose the three places that got the highest votes: Cameroon, South Africa, and Kenya. That meant Yaoundé, Johannesburg, and Nairobi. He followed exactly what the bishops had voted, but this was not announced because it would have complicated contact with the governments. The Pope could not go to any country without the government being willing long before.

Those three places got the highest votes, and so no African country can complain and say, "We should have been chosen; why was the other chosen?" My response, "You didn't get the majority vote; ask the African bishops who voted. These are the three places they voted for, so you just keep silent." That's what happened.

The Holy Father does not normally take very many cardinals with him on his travels, but that one was an exception. On that journey, he took the three president delegates of the synod, plus the secretary general of the synod, Cardinal Schotte; plus Cardinal Gantin, the dean of the College of Cardinals and an African; plus the cardinal secretary of state. It was an objective criterion.

Q. *What personal memories do you have of that epic journey?*
A. Joy of the Church in Africa at the synod. The Church in Africa welcomed this document—the *Apostolic Exhortation on the Church in*

Africa—and said, "This is our document." Most of the participants at the synod, bishops, priests, and lay faithful, came to one of those centers. They must have recognized themselves in the post-synodal document.

Although it is the Pope's document, it is drawn up with the synod in mind and draws on the propositions the bishops made at the synod. The council for the post-synodal phase is elected by the synod; and it works, and gives its opinion to the Holy Father in the making of such a document. So if anything can be called collegial, it is such a document, even though it remains the Pope's document. And so it is for every other synod.

The people recognized themselves in it. Moreover, the local Church was associated with the celebration phase, as were other Christians, such as the Protestants and Anglicans. And in one or two places, even the Muslims were involved. And, of course, the people as a whole, who are the most important of all—99 percent of the people in the Church are lay faithful—celebrated. The huge numbers that came to all three places were a sign of their regarding this synod as theirs. That whole celebration phase seems to have established a tradition for the other continental synods.

Q. *That was the first continental synod that was actually launched in the territory of the continent.*

A. Yes, although there was a European synod in 1991, after the fall of Communism in Eastern Europe; that was an emergency type of synod. There was a second European synod in autumn 1999.

The African synod set the pattern for the American synod and all other such synods. After the African synod there was no longer any discussion as to where the continental synods would be held. It was already taken for granted that they would be held in Rome, generally for one month.

After the American synod the Pope went to Mexico, to the Shrine of Our Lady of Guadalupe, to publicize the American synod. Likewise he went to Lebanon to publicize the Lebanese synod, even though it was devoted to one country only. And he went to New Delhi for the conclusion of the Asian synod. Now the Synod for Oceania is concluded, and the Pope will go to some place in Oceania for the final celebration. As for the European synod, he won't lack places to publicize that event.

It's very good. It makes us Africans happy that the pattern that was established for the African synod wasn't bad. See how all the others followed it. Even the title of the post-synodal document, *Ecclesia in Africa* (The Church in Africa), was followed for the others; and so we get *Ecclesia in America* (The Church in America), *Ecclesia in Asia* (The Church in Asia), and so on. Also, the fact that the Holy Father signed the document in Yaoundé set a pattern for others, because normally documents would be "given in Saint Peter's" or "given in Castel Gandolfo". For Africa it was signed in Yaoundé; for the Americas it was signed in Mexico City; and for Asia in New Delhi. That's history.

Q. *On that journey, you met President Nelson Mandela in South Africa.*

A. I did, but not alone. There was a big function in the president's house, and many people were there. But at least I had enough time to greet him and Doctor de Klerk, together, at that function; and I held the hands of the two of them, and I said: "Thank you, both of you, for what you have contributed in working together."

Q. *Was it your first meeting with Mandela?*

A. It was . . . although, let me correct myself; it was my second time meeting him. Because the first time, he came to see the Holy Father soon after he was released from prison, before he was elected president. He came, but I didn't meet him in a formal way.

It happened that I had a private audience with the Holy Father after Mandela, so Mandela was coming out from his audience, and then I was going in, and the Holy Father smiled and introduced me to Mandela. Just that. Brief. That was my first time meeting him, and it was in the Pope's own audience room!

Q. *The Pope introduced you?*

A. Yes. He said to Mandela, "This is one of my cardinals. He's Cardinal Arinze . . ."

Q. *Do you remember what Mandela said to you then?*

A. I don't remember exactly what he said, but whatever he said was pleasant.

So the only other time I ever met him was when the Holy Father was in Pretoria and Johannesburg in 1995.

Q. *He's a great man.*

A. Definitely. He does honor to Africa. Think of his more than twenty-six years in prison, and when he came out, there was no bitterness, no harshness, and no extremism. And he appreciated the necessity of Europeans and Africans, no matter what their background, working together. Africa needs that.

Q. *Besides that trip to Africa, you also went on other trips with the Pope. I think you went to Tunisia.*

A. Yes, it was in April 1996, and it was still in the context of the African synod. It was a trip only to Tunisia, and then back to Rome, all in the same day. Obviously, there was a major celebration, a Solemn Mass. And then the Holy Father was received in the presidential palace, and there were many Muslims there, and the Holy Father gave a major discourse to the Muslims, and so on. He even said to them, "This is Cardinal Arinze; he is my man for contact with Muslims." And the president also spoke beautifully, and some of the Muslim leaders did, too.

Of course he met the bishops of the whole area, the Episcopal Conferences of North Africa (CERNA)—it was not just the bishops of Tunisia—there were also the bishops of Algeria, Libya, and so on.

Then he went to the places of the martyrdom of Saints Felicity and Perpetua and Saint Cyprian, the great bishop of North Africa. It was all very eloquent.

Q. *Had you been there before?*

A. Yes, once before. I think it was in 1986; I went to Tunisia to take part in a Christian–Muslim dialogue at the University of Tunis. There's a research center there, CERES, I think they call it.

Q. *What does a visit to a country like that mean, say, a visit by the Pope or, say, a visit that you yourself might make as part of the work of your office?*

A. Some visits are rather short, like that papal visit, but they are full of symbolism.

Other visits that I might make, as president of the pontifical council, could be for a conference, but I would take the occasion to meet other religious leaders, to meet the leaders of the Catholic Church, not only the bishops, but also the priests, if possible, and leading lay people, and sit with them.

If they have a diocesan commission, or national one, for contact with Muslims or African Traditional Religions—or other religions, if it is in Asia—obviously it would be part of my work to meet them. If they have a major seminary, I generally ask to say Mass there and talk with the seminarians and staff on inter-religious dialogue. If they have a monastery, I would normally like to visit it, say Mass there, and ask the monks or nuns for their prayers and sacrifices. That is the sort of thing done on these visits.

Q. *As you look down the road, five or seven years from now, what is your dream for the Church in Africa? What is your dream for the Church in Nigeria where you were once a pastor? What kind of Church would you like to see in the light of what has emerged from the synod?*

A. If I may put it in a few words, I would like to see a Church with a renewed freshness in announcing Christ; a Church that does not forget that the majority of Africans do not yet know Christ and would accept him if only somebody brought the good news to them.

Secondly, I would like to see a Church that also has, as a priority, the ongoing formation of all leaders in the Church; a formation not done once and for all; a formation for bishops, priests, religious, and the lay faithful; particularly, a formation for the lay faithful, religious, and priests who are in key positions, because they influence others. You might like to know that the synod also said there should be what the French call "recyclage" for bishops, "aggiornamento", "updating", for bishops. So if they said it for bishops, you can imagine they would want it for others too.

Then, I would like to see a Church more dynamic in mission work within the confines of the same diocese, in areas not fully evangelized; and in the same country, and outside their own country too, in Africa. That is, to encourage trends that have already begun. I would want the local Church to see mission work as a normal part of being Christian, and even if the religious congregations are sending missionaries to that country, the local Church should be involved somehow in mission sending.

I would also like to see the Church in Africa gradually develop its own way of providing material and money to Church personnel, and not only receiving. That's one of the best ways we can thank those who have been giving us this help in the last 150 years.

I would like in Nigeria, and therefore in Africa too, that Christians and Muslims live together with much greater collaboration, and that they see that there's room for one another in the society.

I would also like to see a society where there's much more justice and peace than we have today, and where refugees and displaced people are only in the dictionaries. Of course it may not be achieved immediately, but we must aspire to it.

I would also like to see a Church with diocesan radio stations. I would like to see that by the end of this decade, that is to say, by the end of this twentieth century. Radio stations not necessarily caring for a whole nation, but caring for a diocese or several dioceses, too, because many Africans have their transistors and may not read their daily paper—although papers remain important, too.

Maybe that already is much!

Chapter 15

The Beatification of Father Tansi in Nigeria

(1998)

Pope John Paul II traveled to Nigeria, from March 21 to 23, 1998, for the beatification of Father Tansi; he was accompanied by Cardinal Arinze, the man who had done so much to make this day possible. It was the Pope's thirteenth trip to Africa. He had already visited forty-one of the continent's fifty-four countries, including Nigeria—Africa's most populous state, with more than one hundred million people.

This second visit to Nigeria was "an act of heroic love", Archbishop Albert Obiefuna, of Onitsha, said, acknowledging the sacrifice the Pope made in coming to beatify the man who is not only the first native-born Nigerian, and West African, to be so honored by the Church, but also "the first priest to be beatified in Africa, South of the Sahara, in modern times".[1]

"I come as a friend, as one who is deeply concerned for the destiny of your country and of the whole of Africa", he said on his arrival at Abuja airport, in a nationally televised address. He said he had come primarily to beatify Father Tansi, whose testimony "is important at this moment in Nigeria's history".

Throughout his visit the Pope was given a tumultuous welcome, as millions turned out to pray with him and greet him. General Sanni Abacha, the head of state, members of the government, and the country's Christian leaders came to welcome him. And on the evening after the beatification, with Cardinal Arinze standing at his side, he met the country's thirty-four most important Muslim leaders, including the sultan of Sokoto, who greeted him as "a man of God".

---

[1] Cardinal Arinze in *L'Osservatore Romano*, March 27, 1998. The Vatican paper interviewed him in Onitsha after the beatification ceremony on March 22.

His visit took place at a particularly difficult political, social, and economic[2] *moment for the country, then under military rule. Aware of this, he spoke the truth, the healing truth, and skillfully used the life and testimony of Father Tansi to convey his message, holding him up as a model of integrity for all Nigerians.*

In his six homilies and addresses,[3] *the Pope called for respect for the dignity of every person and respect for the human rights and fundamental freedoms of all Nigerians. He encouraged them to root out corruption, end intimidation, live upright lives, and implement social and political change through a return to democracy and civilian rule. He called for the release of political prisoners, or prisoners of conscience—though he did not call them that—and appealed for national unity and harmony. The Catholic Church had already taken a strong stance on these issues; his words supported that stance.*

On Sunday morning, March 22, at Oba, near Onitsha, the Pope declared Father Tansi "Blessed", as Cardinal Arinze looked on. That announcement set off an explosion of unbelievable joy among the more than two million people present. They sang and danced as the drums sounded and the cannons boomed. For the cardinal too, it was a moment of intense emotion and profound joy.[4]

Here, in a short extract from the longer interview recorded soon after that visit,[5] *the cardinal speaks about the significance of the beatification.*

---

[2] The country was then in a deep economic crisis, with mass poverty and unemployment. The economic crisis was clearly evident from the official exchange rate: the naira, the Nigerian currency, in March 1998 was quoted at 80 (or 85) naira = 1 U.S. dollar, whereas, when the Pope came in 1982, 1 naira = 1.5 U.S. dollars.

[3] The full English text of the Pope's speeches was published in *L'Osservatore Romano,* March 26, 1998, supplement no. 70.

[4] In the interview with *L'Osservatore Romano,* published on March 27, 1998, but given on the day of the beatification, Cardinal Arinze spoke of his feelings that morning: "I feel gratitude to God who uses us as his instruments. I feel joy that these events happen in our day. I also feel small in front of the great events of History, which I cannot pretend to digest immediately. I feel a duty to say thank you to the Holy Father for this new act of extraordinary generosity to Nigeria and to Africa."

[5] The interview was recorded on April 4, 1998.

Q. *Your Eminence, I was struck by the fact that so many people in Nigeria said they are proud of Father Tansi. I saw they felt a genuine pride in having their own saint. It seems as if they have a new sense of belonging to the Church because of this. Is that so?*

A. Yes. They are right. They are right. We know that the saints from anywhere in the world are our brothers and sisters in the faith, but when there is one chosen from among your own people, that same truth comes home as it didn't before.

It is similar to when the Pope visited Nigeria in 1982; one priest in a moment of joy said, "We are, Onitsha is, the center of the Church for six hours today", because the Pope was there for six hours. It helps a person to feel he belongs: we are not strangers. Nobody ever said we were strangers, but this event brings it home.

It is really the same thing again that we have come back to, when a person of your own race, your own people, is beatified or canonized, one feels the Church as "ours", more than one felt it before. It's not a new truth, but it is a new awareness, a new feeling, a new joy that this universal family spreads all around the world. It is not that Nigerians thought there were no Nigerians in heaven before! But when the Catholic Church so recognizes one and so honors that one that the Vicar of Christ comes all the way from Rome to do the ceremony there where the priest worked, then that truth comes home in a different way. The truth would have been the same before, but the resonance, the psychological message, is so very different.

Q. *When I spoke to Father Paolino Beltrame Quattrochi at the beatification ceremony at Oba and asked him what he thought about this day, he said, "I am very glad to see this day. I have been very keen on having it here; if it had been in Rome, you would have had two hundred rich Nigerians come to the ceremony, but now look around you and see how many have come. . . ."*

A. Yes, he is right, he is right, and he has been saying that for years. He is correct, and the Holy Father obviously knows all that too. The Holy Father is not a child; he has the perception of a pastor.

Q. *As I see it now, the missionaries have almost stopped coming to Nigeria. The Church there is strong now and is beginning to have her own saints. I have the impression that the Pope's visit for the beatification has taken on so much importance because it marks the coming of age of the Nigerian Church. You've often spoken about the Church in Nigeria as a young Church, but now it has many vocations, it is sending its own missionaries to other countries, and it has its own Blessed Father Tansi, recognized by the universal Church. Isn't all this a sign of the coming of age of the Nigerian Church?*

A. Yes, that is true. That can be said. As the Holy Father said in his audience on March 25, two days after he returned from Nigeria: "This is the first Nigerian to be beatified", and "it is natural to think of him as the proto-martyr of the nation: not because he was martyred, but in the sense that he offered an unswerving witness of love, spending his whole life in the service of God and of his brothers and sisters." [6] A martyr is a witness and although Father Tansi wasn't killed for Christ in the sense of blood testimony, nevertheless he lived entirely for God. And he is one of the first Nigerian-born priests to answer the call, so in a way we can say that he is like one of the founding fathers of Christianity in our place.

Yes, he is one of the earliest priests who taught us how to respond to the call of the faith. So for the history of the Nigerian Church this is not a small event; it is a very eloquent event. We can even call it a watershed, we can call it a coming of age, we can call it a landmark—whichever way we want to look at it. But the historian who will assess it in future will probably see much more in it than we now do. But it is an indication that the Church in that area must be taken seriously. For anyone who didn't know it before, it might be good for him to take a look at it now.

There must be something there if a priest ordained in 1937 was beatified in such a short time. Remember, the first missionaries came to Onitsha in 1885, and here is a priest who lived the practice of the virtues in such a heroic way, and then the miracle took place at the very time that his remains were brought back to Onitsha from England in 1986. That's something extraordinary. It is intervention on the part of Divine Provi-

---

[6] The full text of the Pope's personal reflection on this visit to Nigeria was published in *L'Osservatore Romano*, English weekly edition, April 1, 1998, p. 11.

dence. It isn't just hard work on the part of the promoter of his cause: because if God decided not to do a miracle, you could write as many books as you like, you could speak and hold conferences, but there would be no beatification if there were no miracle. So it goes beyond anything that men can put together.

It becomes a sign of Divine Providence in that area, and it cannot go without historical and other resonance in many directions. One of those I am hoping for most is in the lives of priests, because Father Tansi becomes a model, a local and officially approved model.

Q. *So the Pope in responding also read it as a sign of God's providence here and took this opportunity.*

A. As an analysis of what may have led the Holy Father to the decision to do it, I would agree with the analysis. The Holy Father didn't tell me, but it must have been so. We cannot be mistaken to imagine that it must have been one of the considerations the Holy Father made; because he certainly did make a sacrifice in going to Nigeria for this beatification. And then whether you consider the time, whether you consider the amount of work he has, whether you consider his health, or whether you consider the heat in Nigeria, it was a sacrifice.[7] All that is eloquent.

Q. *But it would seem, too, that the Pope was sending a message to the world, which in recent years has treated Nigeria politically, if not commercially, as a pariah state.*

A. That is true, because there is no person of world prominence as great as the Pope; and that he, at this very time, visits Nigeria is significant. Not only because the country is in the news headlines for the three days, and with perhaps analysis afterward, but also because serious-thinking people around the world must ask themselves at a cool moment: the Holy Father is a serious person, is a man of God; he must have his reasons for going there; there must be something he saw that others, perhaps, did not see. So that would be good for Nigeria. Also it would help people to see that the Holy Father does not allow himself to become a prisoner of political or commercial considerations.

The Holy Father does not say that everything is perfect in Nigeria. His speeches make this clear, very clear. But he showed love for the

---

[7] The temperature at the beatification ceremony was 100 degrees, and the humidity had almost reached 100 percent.

people. His speeches too show a clear distinction between the people and perhaps systems of economy or government, or politics, or whatever, or association among people of different ethnic groups.

Q. *It seems to me that all this comes from his understanding that God is the Lord of human history, as the prophet Isaiah tells us. The Pope interpreted the developments in Eastern European political life in such a way. Indeed, he sees that God works in history through people, and especially in these great historical moments.*

A. We must thank God that the Holy Father is not a child in these matters, or indeed other matters. He sees more than we think he sees, and, I believe, he would have reasons that we may not even know and that we have no right to try to know. But the actual position he has taken becomes a public position. Individuals can analyze as they wish. I think the reflection on his visit will continue to be positive.

The Holy Father is a master in many senses, even before he became Pope, but more so now, as a result of the experience that he has accumulated over twenty years as Pope. And which Pope has been as well informed as this Pope—whether as to languages or countries visited or those who have spoken with him? Most of the bishops have sat with him at lunch in his house, and many others who are not bishops. And what kind of governments has he not dealt with, before he was Pope and since becoming Pope?

So if you approach it only from the human angle, before speaking of the graces of God and so on, he is already a very special type of person. But when you add the spiritual dimension of his work, that he is Bishop of Rome and Bishop of the whole Church and Vicar of Christ, then there is something more.

This was his eighty-second journey outside Italy, not to mention the journeys inside Italy. Well, I would like to ask anyone whether there is any other Pope who has anything near that record and whether, therefore, there is any reason why we should not take very seriously every major act of his. That's very clear to everyone, except perhaps to a person who is so biased that he doesn't even want to look at rather obvious events. An event might take place, and we might not see all the dimensions of it, but we are expected to reflect on it. One person will see more dimensions than another, but everyone can see some dimension.

Chapter 16

Pastoral Activities

In the interviews on which this chapter is based,[1] *I sought to gain an insight into how the cardinal's year is divided up. I learned something more about his past and present activities, including his visits to India and a particular pro-family involvement in the U.S.A.*

As I began the interview with the cardinal on December 16, 2000, the phone rang. It was Father Gianfranco Girotti, O.F.M., one of the chaplains at Regina Coeli prison. The cardinal was due to celebrate Mass there next day, and the chaplain needed to finalize some aspects of the visit. Subsequently, I discovered that the cardinal has celebrated Mass for the prisoners almost every year since coming to the Vatican in 1985, just as he had done earlier in Onitsha, when he was archbishop. I found out, too, that he had used all the money he was given on the twenty-fifth anniversary of his ordination for the building of a new chapel inside the prison in Onitsha. As part of the inauguration celebrations for the opening of the new chapel, the prisoners played a soccer match in his honor.

The chapter begins with my asking him about his visit to the Rome prison.

---

[1] This chapter is based on extracts from interviews recorded on December 16, 2000, and February 16, 2001.

Q. *I understand that every year since you have been working in the Vatican, you have visited the Regina Coeli [Queen of Heaven] prison to say Mass?*

A. Oh, yes. Almost every year I say Mass there. I like to do that. I just ask to do it. I don't go every Sunday, just once a year. But when I was in Nigeria, every Christmas my second Mass was in a prison. And they knew that. Every year, on Christmas Day. Always.

Q. *Why did you do this?*

A. To give them a little joy. Those people are detained there, and they are so sad. So on Christmas Day I would go there to the prison in Onitsha, and they would be so happy. Not only for the Mass, but also because they would sing Christmas carols, and then I would visit all those locked up who couldn't come out; and the choir followed me from section to section, singing. We went through the whole prison and brought them Christmas joy. The officers told me that after each visit they would have very good order in the prison for some days.

Q. *And when you came to Rome you expressed the wish to do exactly the same?*

A. I couldn't get the choir to go around the whole prison! It was much easier in my own country. But at least I contacted the chaplain.

Q. *The chaplain in Regina Coeli prison, which is not far from the Vatican?*

A. Yes, and then the chaplain is very happy always to arrange the visit. If I could come more often, he would be quite happy. This chaplain works in the Congregation for the Doctrine of the Faith; he is undersecretary there.

Q. *You mean the chaplain of Regina Coeli prison is the undersecretary of the Congregation for the Doctrine of the Faith?*

A. To be exact, there is a chief chaplain, who is full-time. But the chaplain I contacted, who is undersecretary to the Congregation for the Doctrine of the Faith, is his assistant and is not full-time. He's undersecretary and knows about doctrine, and he is a priest who appreciates his priesthood and does this extra work. He's a Franciscan, and he does very good work there. He lives in the generalate of the Conventuals, in the Church of the Twelve Apostles. So many of the Vatican officials do work that the public doesn't immediately notice; they think we are just ecclesiastical bureaucrats.

Q. *What prompted you the first time to visit a prison? When did you make your first prison visit?*
A. Well, it was in my own country, but I cannot now recall exactly the first time that I visited the prison. But I knew that is a dimension of human life that can easily be forgotten in our rush, in the rush of every day. These people, especially those who are detained and whose cases have not yet been heard, some of them languish there for months, and some even for years.

We have in my own country and here too, obviously, a regular chaplain who attends to them. In Nigeria, we generally have religious sisters who visit them, teach catechism, look after their material needs—little things, like soap, medicines, contacts with relatives. But I used to go there occasionally to encourage the work of the chaplains, to show the prisoners that the Church does not forget them, to affirm that they also are human beings and that society looks forward to the time that they come out and can contribute again.

As Church we must also note that not all of them are necessarily guilty. Some of them could be accused wrongly; some of them could be there for little traffic offenses. They are wrong, yes, but it is not really a very grave matter from the point of view of moral theology. And even if they were guilty, even if they had killed people, they are still human beings. If the priest is not near them, who will be? So I thought that the best language for saying all that is not really talking but going there on Christmas Day.

They knew that the archbishop would always come for their morning Mass on Christmas Day. The other two Masses I would say in the cathedral, but always one for the prisoners, and this made them happy.

Q. *Is it a big prison?*

A. Oh, yes. I cannot say how many people would be there now, but it was overcrowded, because the facilities even then were no longer sufficient. With modern times, and the pressure in the big cities and the temptations, especially for young people to try to make money in a quick way, unfortunately many of them end up in prison.

Q. *I myself visited the security wing of San Quentin prison in California many years ago, and as I came out of it I had one overriding reflection—with such prisons, we men have created a hell on earth.*

A. It's terrible, terrible. In my own country they suffer a lot from the inhuman conditions: a room meant for three or four prisoners has twenty or thirty or even forty persons in it; the hygienic conditions—rudimentary!

So to be with them, and remind myself that before God I don't know who is better. God knows. I could have been there, who knows.

They appreciated my visits. I noticed that they even have catechists among the prisoners. Then there are those who are in charge of the singing—they organize it. It may not compete with the Sistine choir, but they sing.

Q. *And here in Rome what have you found?*

A. Obviously, my contact with the prisoners in Rome could not be as close as that in my own country, where I was archbishop. But at least I came there and said Mass for them and spoke in as simple a way as I could. I notice that there are people from many countries in prison here, not just Italians, and not excluding some from the African continent, and some from Latin America. By my being there they can also see that they are remembered. And the chaplain and his assistants—some of whom are religious sisters, some are volunteers from various Catholic parishes and associations—they also feel encouraged, not so much by what I say but by the fact of coming.

Q. *I understand that one-third of the prisoners in Italy are from outside the European Union.*

A. I did not know that the figure was that high.

Q. *What you have said about your prison work answers part of the question I had originally planned to ask you. I had intended to ask whether you had wanted to do pastoral work when you first arrived in Rome, given that you had been a pastor for nineteen years in Nigeria.*

A. In the beginning, when I first came, I made an effort through the Vicariate of Rome to see if there would be a church where I could go every Sunday to say Mass. When I was assigned a church as a cardinal, a titular church, I realized it was not a parish church because there are so many churches in that part of Rome, in the historical center of the city. So they wouldn't have Mass there every Sunday.

Q. *What is your titular church?*
A. San Giovanni della Pigna. It's between Largo Argentina and the Chiesa di Santa Maria Sopra Minerva; it's near the Pantheon area. That's where the Vicariate of Rome was, and that church has a thousand years of life. It's a beautiful little church. Today, it is run by priests who are in the Opera Romana Pellegrinaggi. It is also a kind of cultural center for Italians.

In any case, my original plan to have a church, through the Vicariate, where I could go every Sunday did not exactly work out. But, looking back, now I think perhaps I was trying to undertake too much when I first came. Because, as the years roll by, I realize that in any given year about one-third of the Sundays are given to papal ceremonies, not only during the Jubilee Year—that's extraordinary—but even in an ordinary year it's about one-third of the Sundays. Then perhaps for another one-quarter, or one-third, of the Sundays, I am outside Rome altogether because of travels, conferences, and some holidays in the summer. Then a few more Sundays I would still have free, and physically I could go, but I also find that the increasing workload in the various dicasteries, and not only the one in which I work—I am a member of about ten other dicasteries—demand hours and hours of quiet work, alone. Then we have office every day, Monday to Saturday, so, that Sunday does go by rather fast. And, if one has to present a position paper in any of these meetings, it means putting in about two full days of work to prepare it well.

So, in short, there is no church now where I go every Sunday. But about one-fifth of my Sundays are given to invitations, in Italy generally, as one diocese or another is celebrating something, and so on.

Q. *I see you travel a lot for your work. Sometimes you accompany the Pope, as you did to Casablanca, Morocco, in 1985, or to Khartoum, the Sudan, in 1993. But more often you travel alone or with members of your staff to countries on all continents. It seems to be part of your ongoing effort to build* *understanding, encourage dialogue, and promote cooperation between Christians and the followers of other religions. I would just like to ask you about one country that you have visited—India. Not long after the visit to Morocco, the Pope went to India for the first time, at the end of January 1986, and he visited Mother Teresa's hospice in Calcutta. Did you accompany him on that trip too?*

A. No, I would have liked to have been there, but you must not think that I would be on every papal trip. I would have loved to have been there then, especially as most people are Hindus or they are Muslims or they are Sikhs. I was not there, but obviously we followed it as much as we could.

Q. *But I am right in saying that you have been to India?*
A. Oh, yes. I have been there very many times. At least six times!

Q. *What has struck you about this enormous country, which is almost a continent in its own way?*
A. India is really big. They tell us that the population of India is higher than that of all the fifty-four countries of Africa put together. India has a higher population than all of Africa.

Q. *India has more than one billion people; and, according to United Nations predictions, it could even have a larger population than China by the year 2025.*
A. Yes. That is a fact, and it is extraordinary. Every country is important, but, when we come to Asia, the two biggest countries are China and India.

But India stands out as a democracy, as a country that accepts plurality—different from Pakistan, which really cut itself off from India because the Muslims wanted it declared an Islamic state. But Mahatma Gandhi, obviously convinced of Hinduism, nevertheless was so farsighted as to say, "Look, my fellow Indians, in religious matters you will have to leave people free. Therefore this country will be for every religion, not just for one." So that's one fact. It does not mean that every Hindu today is a good follower of Mahatma Gandhi. There are some who are definitely not good followers of Mahatma Gandhi because they are not open to other religions; they don't accommodate other religious traditions. They think that every Indian has to be a Hindu, and they oppose the right of man to religious freedom.

If an Indian wants to be a Christian and is convinced, not forced, not maneuvered, not exploited because of poverty, then that person has the right to become a Christian. If a person is exploited because of poverty, for a scholarship, and is told, "If you become a Christian, I will give you a scholarship", then that's proselytism, and we condemn that. But if a person freely wants to listen to the Christian message and freely wants to become a Christian, then that person has the right to become a Christian. And Christians also have the duty—not only the right but also the duty—to share the Gospel with anybody who wants freely to embrace it, because the Gospel is not our private property for us to keep to ourselves. It is Christ's good news, and we don't have the right to bottle it up in our pocket.

One of the things about India that attracts me is the plurality, the diversity. I am also struck by the spiritual dimension of India in the midst of all the Hinduism, which may not always have very clear doctrine. It isn't as if the Hindus have a congregation for doctrine that articulates what they believe. Not really. Nevertheless, you notice a type of appreciation of the spiritual, appreciation of the intangible reality, the Transcendent. It even appears in the Indian dances. They are slightly different from the African dances. For me, an African, the Indian dance strikes me as something with a lot of finesse in it. There's a lot of symbolism built in, even in the movement of the fingers, the movement of the hands, the feet. There's a lot of meaning in it. And they also value flowers, not just growing them but even in how the flowers are arranged, how incense is used, their bows, and so on.

This is a type of spiritual patrimony that Christianity also evaluates and respects, because you know the dividing line between the natural and the supernatural is not always so clear and, in any case, the supernatural does not destroy the natural. And the Spirit of God can, in the various cultures and rites, spread the seeds of the Word of God, as Vatican II and *Redemptoris Missio*[2] state. This is what Saint Eusebius of Caesarea called "preparation for the Gospel". The Indians are open to divine revelation. I am very struck by that.

Of course, I am also struck by the high population in India. At a railway station people were coming out in droves, and I asked the bishop, "Is there a riot?" He said, "No, it's just normal; people are just coming

---

[2] Pope John Paul II published the encyclical *Redemptoris Missio* on December 7, 1990. It emphasizes the permanent validity and urgency of missions and develops the theology of mission.

off the train." Everywhere I looked, I saw people all over the place. I asked myself: How do they have enough food? How do they have enough water? The trains are full, full, full to capacity, and the trains are made in India. It's very impressive.

Q. *Did you visit Mahatma Gandhi's tomb?*
A. Yes, I did. I visited the monument in Delhi; and I also met one of the disciples of Mahatma Gandhi, a woman called Usha Mehta. She was among those who attended our inter-religious assembly in Saint Peter's Square in October 1999. She has since died.

Q. *Oh, I didn't know that she had died.*
A. Yes, she died this year, 2000. God will accept her soul because she was a great soul, and she spoke very well. You could see the greatness of her mind. A Hindu whose thought was of such a high level you could not but admire the working of God in such a person.

Q. *What did she say to you about Gandhi?*
A. Not to me particularly, but from her witness, which she expressed plainly in Saint Peter's Square, it came out clearly that large-heartedness of Gandhi, that not being afraid of what God might be working in other people—which is one of the reasons for respecting the religious freedom of other people. The area of conscience has to be respected.

You remember, when she spoke publicly that day, she said to the Holy Father, "I want to apologize for the lack of openness of some people in India to Christianity. You are welcome in India." The Holy Father was due to go to India a week after that.[3]

We need such great people, and they still exist on earth.

Q. *You mentioned the poverty in India. What were your reflections on this?*
A. The poverty of the people is noticeable. Not everybody, of course. But it was noticeable, especially in the big cities such as Mumbai [Bombay] or Kolkata [Calcutta]. You can see the background to Mother Teresa's work. She saw so much suffering: people lying on the side of the

---

[3] Pope John Paul II went to India and Georgia from November 5 to 9, 1999, and presented the apostolic exhortation *Ecclesia in Asia* (the Church in Asia) in Delhi on November 6.

street—they had no house really—and she showed them Christianity, not by lectures but by action.

Q. *What do you say to those people who push the population programs and say the answer is to reduce population?*

A. I am not an economist, so I have no theory of the relationship between population and development, economic development. But we are on secure ground when first we value a human being as being more important than the gross national product or a bank account. That's number one.

And number two, we have to hold that God does not enjoy our misery, our poverty. Therefore it must be possible that the people existing on earth can be fed and live reasonably human lives. The parents have the duty to educate the children they bring into this world; so if parents bring children into this world but do not care for them, the parents would then be lacking in their duty. Therefore, the Catholic Church cannot be for irresponsible parenthood.

The problem arises when one asks what method will the spouses adopt in order to space the coming of children—because the word "birth control" already sounds harsh, as if we human beings control birth. But if people spoke of "spacing of children", the problem would be by what method? It must be a method that respects human dignity and respects the law of God.

The Catholic Church has articulated it so well: there is the natural method that good doctors approve wholeheartedly, that costs no money but costs discipline, and it brings respect for the women themselves and for their husbands. And then there are the wrong methods by which, to prevent a child from being conceived or born, people inter-fere with the action of husband and wife. That is the part that the Church says is against God's arrangement, and therefore it is wrong. Not as Church law but as interpretation of divine law, which is appli-cable to all.

Then there is the bigger question of whether the world has enough food for all the people. I am not an economist, but Paul VI said, "If the bread at table is not enough for the guests, you don't solve the problem by killing some of the guests, but by increasing the bread at table." Is it really true that we have not enough food in the world? Are there not some rich countries where some farmers are paid so they will not produce? And is not wheat or corn dumped into the sea, or butter and tomatoes and fruits destroyed? Some of this produce is destroyed to keep up the market prices, so they say.

Moreover, modern science can do a lot, so that it is often a question of political will. Will those who make the major decisions be willing to share? Will they be willing to put science at the disposal of agriculture to produce food, so that it will reach those who need it? Will they be willing to share? Will they be willing to rate individuals above a bank account? Will they be willing to reduce military expenditure and increase investment in agriculture? These are practical problems.

I have heard some experts say that high population does not necessarily mean lack of development. The United States of America does not have a low population; it has a high economy, and who will say they are not developed?

Q. *Italy too has a high population for the size of the country.*

A. For the size of the territory, yes; but the families in Italy no longer have many children. Last year, I heard some saying that they actually need immigrants now for some manual jobs, because they don't have enough young people. And others say that for the older people who are on pension now, there are not now enough young people earning and paying contributions to guarantee that their pensions will be paid in the future. This happens when men want to take God's place and dictate that one family will have only one child. Stop. And if there are two, then they say: too many! Now that's a bit harsh, and it's not as natural as it might seem.

Q. *This is an actual policy in China.*

A. Yes. We cannot support that. And they will soon find that there will be plenty of imbalances in society.

Q. *But in Italy there is a negative birth rate.*

A. Yes, in Italy the society is not reproducing itself, and they turn around and say they are unhappy about immigrants. Water will seek its own level. If the buildings are there and the jobs are there, but you haven't enough people to do the work, do you tell me they will not come from somewhere else? You see, these are practical questions. However, the state should find some way to help families that have many children.

Q. *Much of your time is taken on foreign trips, but you said earlier that about one-fifth of your Sundays are given to invitations, generally in Italy, as one diocese or another is celebrating some feast or event.*

A. Yes, dioceses here and there invite me. So it's normal, and it's not only I who get invited; others get invited too. One accepts those that one can accept. These are generally special celebrations, maybe a diocesan feast, maybe a saint's day, maybe an anniversary, maybe the ordination of a priest.

Next February 2001, for example, I will be in the Diocese of Rimini. The bishop there is especially interested in my giving a major talk on relations with Muslims. Then there will be a Mass in the parish church on Sunday, and there will be other contacts with the people. There are also Nigerian religious sisters working in that area. So there is never a dull moment in our lives.

Q. *And apart from your work in this office, I have seen that you have been active in two other areas in these years in Rome, namely, the Eucharistic Congresses and the family movement—particularly in the U.S.A. Let us first take a quick look at the Eucharistic Congress. How did you get involved in that?*

A. The Holy Father appointed me, more than ten years ago, to be a member of the International Committee for the Eucharistic Congress here in the Vatican. That committee oversees the major lines of these events, while the local committee in each country in which the congress will be celebrated looks after all the other aspects. So I have attended a number of them; from Nairobi in 1985 to Seville, 1993; Wrocław, 1997; and, most recently, here in Rome, 2000.

Q. *What has your involvement in this work taught you?*

A. We are about twelve people in the international committee, not only bishops and cardinals, but also lay people. A cardinal is always the chairman. The committee seeks to help each host country prepare well for the Eucharistic Congress. It can do this because of all the experience it has gathered. It is also the link with the Holy Father. And it gives advice on themes, theologians, and suggestions for program arrangements. Sometimes we are asked to give a talk, and in any case we attend, and we gain new experience, and we can also give suggestions.

Q. *But you have been even more involved with the family movement for many years, particularly in the U.S.A. How did that involvement begin?*

A. Well, the family apostolate in the U.S.A. is an organization set up by a man and his wife, Jerry and Gwen Coniker, who have thirteen children, most of these now married. They began an association called the Apostolate for Family Consecration, in 1975.

They told me that they first went around the United States giving talks against abortion, but later found it was not the most effective way to work. So they went to Fatima with their whole family and lived there for two years, and after that began this apostolate. That was about twenty-five years ago.

Q. *Did you meet them then?*
A. No. I met them here in Rome. After spending two years in Fatima, they started this association, and then they came to Rome when I was already working here. That must have been about fifteen years ago; that's when I first heard of them, because they used to come to Rome to meet some cardinals and bishops, including Cardinals Ciappi, Lourdusamy, López Trujillo, and Gagnon, and Archbishop John Foley.

They came and asked me to be one of the bishops on the advisory council of their association. I said, "I don't know anything about this association." They then gave me the list of names on the advisory council and invited me to come and visit them if I was ever in the area of Chicago where they lived. I said, "You have many bishops already; please leave me alone." But they weren't taking no for an answer.

Then when I went to some meeting near Chicago—South Bend, to be more exact.

Q. *Indiana. You mean Notre Dame University?*
A. Yes, Notre Dame University. I was there in May 1988, and they invited me to their place in Kenosha, Wisconsin, and they interviewed me because they put heavy emphasis on videocassettes for catechesis of the family. And there it all began.

They said, "Look, the way you explain and answer those questions is the kind of answer we want. So we want you to come another time." And they were not going to leave me alone.

When I didn't come, they came to Rome for something else and interviewed me here. Then they said they had a catechism for the family written for them by a great theologian, and they asked me if I could answer their questions about that too. So I did, and finally we did up to thirty videotapes on this catechism, which they turned into twenty-two audiotapes, front and back, and two tapes of introduction. That's how it all started.

Q. *After that beginning you continued your collaboration with them. Could you explain what happened then?*

A. Gradually then—to cut a long story short—they invited me each year to work for them, generally for five to six days. We make about fifty videocassettes in their studios, over five days. So that of the 15,000 videocassettes they have in their studio now, I have worked on about 1,000 or more of them.

It's very hard work. They indicate the document about a year in advance. For instance, we have covered most of the encyclicals of Pope John Paul II, and the post-synodal exhortations, and some documents of Vatican II. Jerry Coniker says, for example, "Next year we want you to work on the apostolic exhortation *Ecclesia in America—The Church in America*." We will make fifteen tapes on that, or on the Pope's encyclical on suffering, or on his post-synodal exhortation on the laity. And then I have to work through the document and prepare, section-by-section, questions for him. I must be faithful to the Pope's document.

Then I send him the questions, and when I go there we go into the studio; and we not only go through the questions I wrote down, but we also have a conversation. The aim is to discuss the Pope's document in such a way that those following it will simply love the document, and they will say, "I want to buy a copy immediately. I will not go to sleep until I read a copy." That's the aim of it. But because these documents can be difficult for people, a bit distant, we also make a few jokes. The main thing is to present the Pope's teaching in a very attractive way.

And they make audiotapes too! Many Americans travel long distances, and it is difficult for them to read, so they pop the tape into the player and listen as they travel. At home, they get the families in the neighborhood together; they go to the home of one family and turn on the videotape. It lasts about twenty minutes. Then they switch it off and discuss the topic with the help of a trained person. Then they sing, they pray, and sometimes they do a holy hour in the local church, if they convince the parish priest. In that way they have spread to about two-thirds of the dioceses of the United States.

Q. *Two-thirds of the dioceses of the United States! That's a lot of dioceses.*

A. Yes. And they have a group of young men and women, about thirty of them, not with vows, but with commitments that come very near to vows. They are not religious, but they are almost like religious. They would be called a community of apostolic life. They live together, a very austere life. They pray, one or one and a half hours before Mass every morning. They do not drink wine. They have a rather rigid life, and they only live for this apostolate. They have nothing else they are aspiring to, only to promote the family.

Jerry Coniker bought a former seminary in Steubenville, Ohio. It is about nine hundred acres, with buildings. He has families come there. Some stay about two days, some one week. They have built and set up more buildings; they have even little cabins for families; one family per house, with bunk beds. And those families who don't want to pay for that come in campers.

It's extraordinary what is happening there. Extraordinary. They pray. They don't attack anybody—priest, bishop, pope, or theologian. They are not interested in attacking anybody. They are interested only in propagating Catholic doctrine, solid doctrine, nothing more. They have Eucharistic Adoration. There are priests who come from all around and are available to hear confessions. When you see a thing like that, you just marvel.

So I go there one week every summer. Their condition is that they do not give a speaker even one dollar. You must do it all gratis. For all the tapes, you must sign that you will not claim one dollar. It's all gratis, for free. I do it because I am convinced of what they are doing.

Q. *But what do the American bishops say to you? Are they not concerned?*

A. They are not—they are happy. They, the Conikers and the Family Apostolate, have many supporters among the bishops. Cardinal O'Connor of New York, who died earlier this year, was their great supporter. Cardinal Bevilacqua in Philadelphia supports them, as do Cardinal George in Chicago and Cardinal Stafford when he was Archbishop of Denver, Colorado, and bishops such as Wuerl in Pittsburgh and Sheldon in Steubenville.

Of course, not every bishop is enthusiastic. You can't expect that. Some priests say, "Look, you are doing the work of the bishops. Who sent you to preach?" But now the Apostolate for Family Consecration has its own TV network running twenty-four hours a day. It is called Familyland Television Network.

Q. *In the U.S.A.?*
A. There, in that institute, they have their own TV station. They have these young men and women who know how to operate these TV cameras and so on. Extraordinary.

Q. *But where do they get the money for all this?*
A. Just friends. Friends give them money. When they had the Jubilee of Families here in Rome, Jerry Coniker came with his whole clan.

Q. *I saw them. I was there. I recall there were many of them.*
A. Yes, he came with his whole clan, most of his fifty-one children and grandchildren. So it's most interesting, most impressive. Some only talk of negative things, but this is very positive.

Now they have a big center in Manila. Cardinal Sin is so happy with it. They have one or two communities of women; they call them Catholic Corps. The Apostolate for Family Consecration is spreading. Cardinal Sin adopted their catechism as the diocesan catechism. They also have a very big center near Mexico City. There's a Spanish woman there who has translated these tapes and who conducts TV programs.

They have even translated some tapes into Chinese.

Q. *And I presume they have translated your tapes into Spanish and Chinese?*
A. Yes. Some.

Q. *Have you been to Mexico and the Philippines?*
A. I have been to the Philippines, yes, when the Holy Father went there in 1995; and earlier for a biblical congress in 1989. But I have never been to Mexico.

Q. *What other projects have you done with them?*
A. They have wanted me to speak on the *Catechism of the Catholic Church*, taking huge chunks, sections. I don't speak as an expert. They want me to speak on Saint John's Gospel and Saint Luke's Gospel. I read the biblical commentaries and try; just sharing, without trying to be a biblical scholar. That's how I came into that.

Q. *And you do all this because you are convinced of the value and importance of the family.*

A. Obviously. The family is the key to many other areas of development. I am very convinced of this. Indeed, I have gotten bishop friends from Nigeria to come there, and they have taken away many tapes. One sent a priest to study the system, to see what he could do. And the diocesan director of catechetics from my own home area has visited twice, and many others. So gradually many bishops, such as the Indians and Australians, visit, and they see what these can contribute.

Q. *Would they be classified as a kind of new movement, or what?*
A. You know, these good things begin in the Church, and later on you arrange a name for them, like the Focolare Movement and so on. But they are under the general umbrella of the Pontifical Council for the Laity, because it is a lay activity; it is not a clerical activity. But the clerics think they are doing a good job and support them.

It's extraordinarily good work. You see why I go there every year, because I'm so convinced of what they are doing. I am not paid anything, except the plane ticket, or part of it. They can give me their tapes: all the tapes I want. They give me as many as I am willing to take, because I take them and donate them to people. In that way people know about them.

Q. *So this is another kind of mission that you are engaged in?*
A. Yes, it is an extracurricular activity. I call it extracurricular because it has nothing to do with inter-religious dialogue.

Q. *But I imagine that you talk about inter-religious dialogue and such in your catechesis with these people.*
A. Occasionally they ask me about inter-religious dialogue while I am making those tapes, but that's not the central area. And I share their values on the family with people of other religions, but, really, when they invite me there they are not thinking about the Pontifical Council for Inter-Religious Dialogue at all.

When I go, we just converse. I don't have to look over my shoulder to ask how will the Muslims accept this, or the Buddhists. But then, as you can see, when a person is convinced of a thing, he will say the same whether he is with Christians or with others. There may be very different emphasis. If I am speaking to a group of seminarians in a theological faculty, surely the language will be different from when I speak in a church on Sunday or when I meet a group at the inter-religious summit in New York. But still the basic truth is the same.

Q. *Does this work have any ecumenical dimension to it?*

A. Not particularly there. They don't make a special effort to be ecumenical. They are simply reflecting on the Catholic family and the Catholic faith. They are not against ecumenism, but it is not their major emphasis. If a Protestant comes, they don't mind, but generally it is the Catholics who come.

Q. *You travel a lot for your work at the Vatican; you do this extra work too, but I'm sure your life is not all work. You take vacations too. Apart from returning to Nigeria for a vacation, you go to places such as Austria, too. I remember I once met you at Fiumicino airport, and you told me you had been visiting a priest friend there.*

A. Yes, I have a priest friend living near the Czech border.

Q. *And I understand that you also go to London on vacation, and you have done some work in a parish there.*

A. Yes, I go to London, and I shall go there again this year, God willing.

Q. *To which parish?*

A. Kilburn. However, it is not primarily because of the parish that I go there, but because of a Nigerian family that has a house there within the parish. And I go there, not primarily to help the parish priest, but to rest with the Nigerians, whom I have known for thirty years or more. But, of course, I'm available to the parish priest for Mass.

Q. *Well, from all you have said, I can see that you still do quite a bit of pastoral ministry.*

A. Well, a priest or a bishop is not really off duty in the full sense of the word, even during what we call vacation. He can always be available to the people. That's what we are ordained for. Nobody is ordained a priest or a bishop for himself.

Q. *But apart from work and ministry, I hear you still play tennis.*

A. Oh, yes. I try to play at least once a week and, if possible, twice, because if you are healthy there are many things you can do. If you are sick, then there are many things you will not be able to do. Health is important, and sport is not really time wasted in that sense.

Q. *Do you have a tennis partner?*

A. Those who live in my house: the priest plays, and also the religious brothers—two of them, the Brothers of Saint Stephen. And if they are not available to play, there will always be someone else, such as a Nigerian priest working in Rome with whom I can agree on a time for a game; just thirty or forty minutes of exercise, without trying to be champions, just to get some exercise. I play a little table tennis too, but it is really lawn tennis that I prefer now, because in thirty minutes you can get a game and you need only one partner.

Q. *Do you do a lot of walking?*

A. Not really walking for the sake of walking. But to get to a place, yes, if it is not too far, I go on foot for exercise. That's all.

Q. *Africans are known as lovers of music and dance. I take it that you like music?*

A. Yes, when I was in the seminary I liked to play the harmonium. I didn't really learn the organ because it was much easier for us to have the harmonium; the organ would cost much more. As a seminarian, in philosophy, I also played sometimes in chapel at Mass, or at Benediction. But now there is no opportunity to play, and I have no instrument in the house.

The music I love now is only in cassettes; I put on some cassettes while I'm doing something that does not need too much concentration. That, yes. I love the music of the Focolarini—the Gen Verde and the Gen Rosso—I've plenty of their songs, plenty of them; and at a moment when I'm not in deep concentration, I put them on. And then people give me all kinds of cassettes.

Q. *Do you like classical music, or do you prefer the more lively non-classical music?*

A. Without my being any kind of sophisticated lover of Beethoven or Bach or other such composers, I am probably happier with the type of music that the young people have, but not what they call rock music; for me that's too high-decibel, too much noise. I prefer or, rather, the music I love most is the Gen Verde, which the Focolarini show-people sing. That I like very much, and also the type of simple music tuned to a Nigerian language, which has been increasing in the Church in Nigeria over the last forty years. We have people who have studied music who can now sing the psalms in the local language, respecting the tonal nature of the language, so that it touches the heart of the people. Some amateurs too compose pieces, whether in English or Igbo, and I like these too.

Q. *What about European or American music?*
A. Not much, except the usual songs that would be sung in church. Those I would follow, but I have not much contact with secular music. Not much.

Q. *And you like singing too?*
A. Yes. I was a member of the choir in the Urban College, as seminarian. And I like to sing the Latin Mass.
[NOTE: *At this point, the cardinal, who was a member of the Central Committee for the Jubilee Year, had to leave to celebrate Mass in Saint Peter's Square for the Jubilee of Rome's taxi drivers, on December 9, 2000. I went to the Mass, attended by about ten thousand people there, including pilgrims from many countries. The cardinal celebrated at the altar in the Square at which the Pope normally presides for the major open-air ceremonies. After the Mass we resumed our conversation, starting from that event.*]

Q. *It is quite extraordinary to see such a vast number of people attending Mass in Saint Peter's Square on an ordinary Saturday morning. I noticed there was a large group of taxi drivers present.*
A. Yes, it was their Jubilee day, but you are right: it is really extraordinary that so many people come.

Q. *Have you celebrated many of these Masses in the Square?*
A. No, this is the first time that I have been asked to be the main celebrant in Saint Peter's Square. But, you know, it's not every day that one celebrates there. I am surprised. I just got a telephone call yesterday: they said many people were coming, and they generally want a cardinal, where possible, as main celebrant, and, since I'm on the Committee for the Jubilee, they asked me.

Q. *But how does it feel to celebrate the Mass there with so many people in front of you?*
A. It reminds me just that Divine Providence governs the whole world and the Church, and we are only instruments. We come and go. But it is a great honor for us, and a great responsibility that God involves

us in any way at all in his saving work in the Church and in the world, not
to mention to this extent.

Q. *It's extraordinary indeed to see all those people: children, young
people, old people, everybody was following the Mass. They were participating
actively, and they could see and hear well on the two maxi-screens.*

A. Thanks must also go to those who prepare all this: the micro-
phone people, the technicians, and the master of ceremonies. Everything
is well arranged. When those who belong to other religions come and
see all this, I just wonder what is going on in their minds. Something
must be going on.

Q. *I find it quite amazing. It's the Spirit that moves all those people to
come, to travel long distances to come here.*

A. It's very eloquent. It shows there is something in the Church.

Q. *You have seen all these pilgrims come here throughout the Jubilee
Year—you can see them very well from your apartment. What has struck
you about this Jubilee Year?*

A. People. The Pope's idea and hope have been realized. People's
recommitment to the faith, people express their faith. They are ready to
make sacrifices for it. They are not afraid to show that faith. They are
ready to sacrifice time, money, and talent and come here.

Take the Jubilee for parliamentarians, for example. There were all
types of parliamentarians present, the real cream too, including some
who were not Catholics either. Mikhail Gorbachev was there, for example. That makes us think.

I just think of the three wise men from the East who came to adore
the Lord Jesus in Bethlehem. They were a symbol of all men bringing
their gifts, different gifts, gold, frankincense, and myrrh. They came to
adore the Lord Jesus, who is the Lord of lords, the Master of events, the
Center of world history, and the One who came, as Saint John says, "to
gather together the scattered children of God" from the North and the
South, the East and the West.

Likewise in the Jubilee Year, they came from all parts, they gathered
here in Saint Peter's Square within those colonnades that, like arms,
spread out to welcome all mankind. It does encourage us. Definitely.
And because I live near Saint Peter's Square, I can see the pilgrims
coming each morning, and I can see the last ones to leave in the evening.

They really pray. I can see the people cleaning up, arranging the seats. Excellent. The people's commitment is excellent. Sometimes they fill Via della Conciliazione. It is truly extraordinary.

When the youth came in August for the World Youth Day, I saw them beginning to file through the Holy Door at six thirty in the morning, and that door was still open at six or seven o'clock in the evening. But even until ten o'clock at night they were still going through. That should make us think.

Q. *Certainly the echoes of this Jubilee have reached far and wide.*

A. Yes. I expect that even after the Jubilee Year, all of us will have to reflect and ask ourselves, what has this meant for the Church? What fruit remains? What message does it give us? That means it is so rich. It is like a very rich meal: you cannot digest it all immediately. Or like a wonderful speech, you have to take it in sections and reflect gradually. But it does give us an agenda for the next few years, I would say. It is not just a celebration that passes.

Some people, you know, before the Jubilee began, said the events are too many, all this gathering of people all the time. It is easy to say that, but when you watch these people and their commitment, one by one—and some of them have not come twice, just once—then shouldn't we thank God?

Q. *I was deeply moved some days ago in Saint Peter's Basilica, as I watched people going through the Holy Door on their knees.*

A. On their knees?

Q. *Yes, on their knees.*

A. And I haven't even done that. That should encourage us, definitely.

Chapter 17

From Mount Sinai to
the United Nations

*The Pope made his Jubilee pilgrimage to Mount Sinai, Egypt, in February 2000,
and also visited the Al-Azhar, the world's main Sunni Muslim Center, in Cairo.
Cardinal Arinze accompanied him and in the first part of this chapter recalls those
events. In the light of that experience he goes on to speak about the present-day
relations between Muslims and Christians in Nigeria and the wider question of
the role of religions in working for peace and combatting poverty.*

*Later that year, the Pope asked the cardinal to represent him at the World Peace
Summit of Religious and Spiritual Leaders, which opened at the United Nations
Headquarters, New York, on August 28, 2000. In this chapter he gives his
reflections on that meeting too.*

*The discussion then broadens out as we talk and moves rapidly from "the clash
of civilizations" to the situation in the Middle East, from the lack of religious
freedom in Saudi Arabia and China to the situation in Europe and Africa today,
and the role of religion in all of this.*

I began[1] with questions on the Pope's pilgrimage to Mount Sinai, in Egypt.

---

[1] This chapter is based on extracts from interviews recorded on December 16, 2000,
and February 16, 2001.

Q. *Earlier this year, you accompanied the Pope on his pilgrimage to Mount Sinai.*

A. That is true. In the Holy Father's Jubilee pilgrimages, Egypt could not be missing. And it was beautiful. That was in February 2000.

The main reason for the Holy Father's going there was to go and pray at Mount Sinai, where God gave Moses the Ten Commandments, and that was the high point of the pilgrimage. That was on Saturday, February 26. It was extraordinary. I had never gone to Sinai before. Rocks and mountains plenty, but trees—very few. I began to understand why the people of Israel complained and said to Moses, "You brought us to this desert place. No water to drink. You want us all to die here?" Moses must have had a rough time.

There is a monastery of Orthodox monks at the foot of the mountain. The Holy Father did not go up the mountain. It would have taken too long. The monastery, I understand, has been there for centuries, and although Islam dominates the whole region, it was never destroyed. So it is a credit to the monks. The monastery has some of the old documents and manuscripts of the Bible and of some other books. The Holy Father spent a lot of time there; he prayed there, and he spoke. That was the height of the visit. Indeed, I hardly had time for words. I hardly wanted to talk to anybody. I wanted just to be watching, to be thinking and to be reflecting, and praying.

The journey from Cairo airport was by special C130, the type of tough aircraft meant for soldiers, and tough because the airport at Sinai is not able to take jets. It worked out well. Sinai was the height of the visit to Egypt. But, of course, there were other activities.

The first day, on arrival, the Holy Father was received by the president of Egypt, President Mubarak; and they had discussions at the airport building. It was a very good setting.

Q. *Were you present at those discussions, or was it a one-on-one meeting between President Mubarak and the Pope?*

A. I was there. At one stage it was one-on-one, otherwise we—the cardinals—were present.

Then the next major event was the reception by the Al-Azhar, the Sheikh Al-Azhar, the highest authority in Sunni Islam; that means for more than 90 percent of Muslims of the world.

Q. *The Sheikh Al-Azhar is a kind of Muslim pope, as it were?*
A. Well . . . to say pope would not be exact, because they don't have jurisdiction in the way we have it in the Catholic Church. But the Al-Azhar University and Institution—because it is more than a university—also has a wing for the training of those who will spread Islam in other countries. The Al-Azhar is the number one moral authority in Sunni Islam. When it pronounces a judgment on a matter of what Muslims believe, the others would not argue with it. It is a very important institution, also because of its age and the honor it is given in Islam. It is more than a thousand years old.

The Sheikh Al-Azhar, who is the supreme authority there, and all his assistants received the Pope in their new building. And I heard that it was not the custom to clap, to applaud, but in this case they applauded the Pope, and there were real, regular friendly smiles and greetings, and speeches, both formal and informal. And they arranged the tables at which we were to sit, and the Muslim authorities arranged it beautifully: one Christian, one Muslim, and all spread around. It was really beautiful.

The Holy Father had also a one-on-one discussion with the Sheikh Al-Azhar, and a bishop who knew Arabic translated. I did not go to that meeting.

Somebody in Egypt told me that the people followed that whole event on TV and got a very strong message. Even if they didn't understand all that the Sheikh and the Pope were saying, they did see and observe. It was for them very eloquent: it showed that Christians and Muslims can meet, and they need not fight one another. It showed they can respect one another, they can even listen to one another, and they can exchange smiles. That's already eloquent.

After all, papal visits can be brief, but there are fine points; they indicate the line along which people should continue to go. Indeed, after that meeting, when later we—that is, our pontifical council—met the representatives of Al-Azhar, they suggested that we should declare February 24 the annual Christian–Muslim dialogue day, and that our annual meeting should, if possible, be on that day every year. Normally we meet once a year; one year in Cairo, another year in Rome.

Q. *So the Pope's visit to the Al-Azhar, and his meeting with the sheikh there, meant so much to these Muslims that they want to meet your office every year on February 24?*
A. It was their suggestion, and of course we support it. Next year, 2001, we will try to have our meeting on that day in Rome, or Cairo.[2]

Q. *Islam is strong in many parts of Africa. You come from Nigeria, a country where Islam is strong, especially in the north. Most Nigerian Muslims are Sunni Muslims, and here you are at the heartland of the spiritual authority of Sunni Muslims, at a time when Muslims are pushing their claims in your country. What did you feel then?*
A. I felt encouragement. I felt like saying something to Nigerian Muslims. You know that was the very time we were having violence in Kaduna, because of the Sharia, which some Muslims wanted to introduce; and it sparked violence in which people were killed. It was very sad. At the same time, even the Holy Father made a statement about it from Cairo. So I felt like bringing all Nigerian Muslims there to say, "Look at this. Draw your conclusions. Don't you think it is possible for Christians and Muslims to exist in harmony? Can't you see that? Why must there be struggle? Why must there be forcing of Muslim law on the legal status of your state? Why don't you live the values of your Sharia, without forcing them into state law?"

Q. *Why do you think this is happening in Nigeria?*
A. When I asked a Nigerian Muslim leader, "Is this Sharia your project; is it the project of your Muslim leaders?" He said, "No, it is the politicians."

Q. *So it is not the Muslim religious leaders of Nigeria who want the Sharia in this way?*
A. No. It is not. It is the politicians, from the areas where there are many Muslims, who pushed the Sharia for their own reasons; political reasons, not religious ones. It's very sad.

---

[2] The meeting in February 2001 actually took place in Cairo.

Q. *How do you see this situation evolving? Where is it all going to end?*

A. Difficult to know how it will be concluded, given that serious Muslim leaders, religious leaders, know that it is not their project. They do not always say that in public, because they would be marginalized. And you know politicians have a way of winning the masses; so the masses think, "Ah, this politician loves Islam, loves Islam." So they are very likely to vote for him at the next election. That's what a politician understands. It's very sad. At what a cost, with so many dead, with so much animosity? Confrontation! Is that the price the country must pay for you to win the election? It's very sad. You asked me how it will be concluded? I don't know. I keep on praying and hoping that enough leaders will arise, both Christian and Muslim, who, out of love for their people and out of belief that harmony is possible, will find a better solution. And please note, there are more Christians than Muslims in Nigeria.

Q. *People say that Nigerian President Obasanjo doesn't want the Sharia, but he is not able to get his way. What do you think?*

A. I would not like to go into my opinion on that one. It is too local for us to include in this book.

Q. *You are in Rome, but you often think of what is happening in your home country. If you had the possibility of sending a message to the Church and to the Muslims in Nigeria, what would it be?*

A. Both Christians and Muslims, I would say, you have enough leaders who see clearly. These leaders have a duty; please work together out of love for the people, out of sincere belief that harmony is possible between Christians and Muslims, and out of a clear vision that this Sharia thing is not primarily a religious project. Out of these convictions, please save our people from further suffering. Find a way in which we can come out of this difficulty, which is totally unnecessary.

I asked a good Muslim leader, "Do you believe that a good Muslim can live the values of the Sharia without insisting that it must be built into the state legal system?" He said, "Of course!" It is also proved by the fact that many countries in the world, with majority Muslim populations, do not insist on the Sharia in the state system. And especially the good Muslims—they can live the values of the Sharia without it being in the state legal system.

Religion should not be used as a weapon to crush other believers. It is a pity that this happens.

Q. *But we see something like this in Pakistan.*

A. Perhaps. And perhaps even in India, if some extremists are using Hinduism for reasons that are not really religious but political, it is very sad. The religious leaders have a duty to enlighten their co-religionists so that they would see where an agenda is not really a religious agenda but a political one. And you will notice, when it comes to people being killed, it is often the poor and the defenseless who are killed, but the real organizers and originators have their own way of keeping safe. It's very sad. Not one person should be killed in order to advance the agenda of some politician. Not one person's house should be burned. There must be another solution.

Q. *You are touching on the whole question of religion and peace here. I know you have given a lot of thought and study to this question, and over the years you have been engaged a lot with the World Conference on Religion and Peace on this subject. You have also seen religion being misused for political goals. In the present-day world, some forty major armed conflicts are being waged, and, in your own continent alone, there are sixteen such major conflicts. What role do you see religion playing in the quest for peace worldwide?*

A. I think religion has an important role to play for the building and maintenance of peace, and for the raising of people's awareness about this whole matter. Because long before it becomes a question of armaments, war begins in the human heart. It begins with hatred, rancor, unwilling-ness to admit fault and ask for forgiveness, the desire for revenge, with the claiming of territory that does not really belong to one but to the other, with the seeking of redress for historical wrongs by, perhaps, vendetta. All that arises in the human heart.

If religion does not help to convert the human heart in these areas, the weapons will not fall from the hands of the warlords or the belliger-ents or the terrorists or the militias or the soldiers. So the first duty of religion is conversion of the human heart; and that is not just a pious statement, it is a question of inculcating the core virtue of justice. That means the recognition of the rights of another person, then acceptance of others with their differences, the appreciation of the others, and real love for others, not something sentimental but esteem for the other for being a person. If religion does not inculcate that, who will inculcate it?

Who will inculcate admitting wrong if you are wrong, as the Pope did admit on March 12, 2000, the "*mea-culpa* Sunday", as some called it.

Religion will also teach us forgiveness. If a person has offended you, you must not try to get revenge. All the religions teach forgiveness, all of them. Buddhists say you don't solve harm with more harm, violence with more violence. Not to mention the Gospel of Jesus Christ: Christ says, "Do not avenge evil, leave it to the Father", and Saint Paul says, "Repay evil with good, and then you will heap red hot coals on the head of your enemies." So too all the other religions teach forgiveness.

Who will teach people how to be gratuitous in love of others? Religion has that duty: enlightenment, conversion of heart, justice and fundamental virtues, but also the whole area of harmony, accepting that you can live with others and share the goods of the earth.

Much of violence and war is because of greed and unjust claims to things of the earth. Religion teaches us that God is the Creator, and the goods of the earth are meant for all, not just for a few. If religion doesn't orient our heart in that way, who will do it? Will politics? Will armies?

It is religion that will teach people how to be friendly. All the religions teach that: the Golden Rule. We discovered that the Golden Rule is taught by Christianity, Judaism, Islam, Hinduism, Buddhism, Confucianism, and African Traditional Religion.[3] If all the religions of the world observed the Golden Rule for two weeks, we would have a small paradise on earth for two weeks.

So religion has an important role in the promotion of peace and in the maintenance of peace. I do not say that only religion has a role. There is a role for the United Nations. There is a role for governments. There is a role for negotiations. That is obvious. All this, but not without the religious dimension.

Q. *Many people looking at the world today, and looking back over past history, point to the fact that Europe was heavily Christianized, and yet we had the two biggest and worst conflicts in human history in Europe.*

A. That is true.

---

[3] The love of our neighbor, which Christianity professes as the golden rule of moral conduct (cf. Mt 7:12, "Do to others whatever you would have them do to you. This is the law and the prophets."), is also part of the doctrinal patrimony of other great world religions. The cardinal refers to this in his book *Church in Dialogue: Walking with Other Believers* (San Francisco: Ignatius Press, 1990), pp. 201–2.

Q. *They say Rwanda was a really Christianized country, and yet there was genocide there in 1994. How does one explain all this? Is it that religion is failing in its task? Is it that the powers of evil are so active in the world? What does one say?*

A. Finally, evil is difficult to explain, or to explain away, and the human heart is capable of evil. Even some of the best of men are capable of evil. Original sin is obviously a fact, so much so that in spite of baptism and years of Christianity, man can still wreak so much havoc on his fellowman; being like a wolf to his fellowman.

It is true that, in spite of religion, people have engaged in violence and killing. It is not because of religion that they engaged in that, because to the extent that the person promotes violence and killing, to that extent the person is not a good member of any religion. Because genuine religion teaches love of others, respect for others, justice, and forgiveness. That's the road to peace. But it is also true that, in spite of the fact that people have Christianity, they have engaged in violence and killing, as happened in Europe, and to that extent they have not been faithful to the Gospel.

We can say the same thing about Rwanda. Most disappointing. Missionaries cannot help asking themselves: Has evangelization failed in this country, which is to a great extent Christian, Catholic even? How is it the people were able to engage in such inhumanity, being like wolves to their fellow men, or worse than wolves, because the wolf kills the one person it is going to eat, but here they kill many people they are not going to eat.

It is very agonizing, but we will not despair because, beyond religion, what magic have we for the conversion of the human heart and for reconciliation, for repentance and forgiveness? We must continue. But even some of the good people can turn to actions that go against all their religion has been saying for years. Finally, it is difficult for us to analyze why men engage in evil.

Q. *The Pope speaks a lot, and he has done so for many years, on the ongoing conflict in the world between the powers of good and the powers of evil.*

A. A reality! Every one of us knows it, even by looking into our own hearts. Saint Paul said: "Though the will to do what is good is in me, the performance is not, with the result that instead of doing the good things that I want to do, I carry out the sinful things that I do not want" [Rom 7:18–19]. So we all know what we should do, but we also look into our hearts and see that we are tempted to do the very thing that we should not do; and some of us sometimes fail.

Q. *In your own life, you have seen the powers of evil at work, also during the civil war in Nigeria, but at the same time you have also seen the outpouring of good by many people. Do you think the forces for good in the rest of the world are helping the peoples of Africa enough in the sixteen conflicts that are currently being waged in various African countries?*

A. Enough? No. Good forces at work, yes! Evil forces at work, also! Sometimes when there is a war we must not summarily condemn all the people, even those at the head, because some of them are under heavy pressure—maybe from their own citizens, some maybe from other governments, or maybe from multinational companies, or local companies. It can all be very complicated. Maybe sometimes a head of state, or political leader, who seems to be a reasonable person, is in a very difficult position in which he makes decisions he would not like to make. The causes can be many, and I would not pretend to understand the causes of all these wars.

But one thing is clear: there are good forces at work. And, even in some of the worst wars, we see so much virtue in so many people: those who give their lives, those who sacrifice themselves to look after the refugees who are near the war front—there will be nurses, there will be priests among them, and some of them will lose their lives. Then there are those who give money and relief supplies.

Then we also see those who traffic in arms, who see war as a golden opportunity to make money. And there are those who look on the minerals of that country as a thing to be exploited, no matter what the cost in human lives, property and fields destroyed, houses burned—they don't care as long as they have those minerals.

So many forces at work and, as you know, the world is so complicated today that what may look like a local war has all kinds of interests in other continents, some of them open, others hidden.

Q. *How much is poverty the problem? We see great poverty expanding in the world today, and the gap between rich and poor is becoming bigger day by day, and for many people this increasing poverty is a recipe for more conflict.*

A. Yes, poverty is one of the elements of conflict. If a person is hungry and sick and has no house, that person easily becomes angry and can join a revolution because he doesn't have much to lose if there is rioting, if there is general grapple and grab, he doesn't have much to lose.

It has been noticed also that where there is a lot of poverty, or oppression, or repression of the poor, and corruption in public life, the fundamentalist sects and the religious extremists who produce a simple formula to solve all the problems once and for all have easy success. This is so because people are already sick and tired of bad government, corruption, sickness, so they are ready to follow anyone producing a simple formula by which you will wipe out all those who practice corruption, wipe out all those who conduct bad government, and install for themselves the kingdom of heaven within two weeks. They will jump at the possibility because they are so tired already, so exasperated, they are ready for anything. The extremists have a field day in such a situation.

Therefore poverty should be combatted, for these reasons also, and the Catholic Church makes a big effort here. We do not want people to remain poor. Certainly not! Although handouts are useful and provide relief, it is better still to help people to get out of situations of poverty so that they can make their own decisions and live a better and more worthy human life. Someone once said that if people have work, if they have reasonable education and are happily married and have nice homes, then they are not likely to join a revolution where there will be burning and killing and looting.

Poverty must be overcome, not just because we don't want wars but, even more, to honor God, who created us and gave the goods of the earth for the enjoyment of all. Poverty must be combatted because it is not right, or just, that 80 percent of what the world produces is consumed by 20 percent of mankind, while the other 80 percent of mankind are left squabbling over the remaining 20 percent of what the earth has to offer.

This is becoming more and more a global challenge, not just a local one, because sometimes even the cost or the price for coffee, palm oil, rice, or cocoa may not necessarily be decided in the country where they are produced. Maybe the decision on the price is made in Berlin or London or Washington, D.C., or Paris or Rome, so that the poor countries, the developing countries, are not totally free. They may have national sovereignty, but they may not have economic sovereignty.

Here the whole question of solidarity emerges: *solidarity*—a topic on which the Holy Father often speaks. *Solidarity* means the interdependence of peoples, not merely tolerated, but accepted and lived.

Q. *This was why the 1971 Synod on Justice, in which you participated, emphasized that the work for justice was "an integral part of preaching the Gospel".*

A. Exactly. It is part of the Gospel. It is not something additional, it is not something peripheral, and it is not something that we will do if there is time. It is part of the Gospel.

If people are hungry and sick, if they have no home and they have no work, and their family is in disarray, are you seriously expecting them to come to High Mass sung in Latin on Sunday? When they are not living a decent human life, a life that is worthy of human beings, then religion becomes much more difficult and looks somewhat academic for them.

Q. *This fight against poverty is one of the ways that all religions can work together.*

A. Definitely. The World Conference on Religion and Peace is a proof that people of many religions, without necessarily discussing what they believe but drawing from the high ideals of their various religions, can really join hands to tackle definite projects, to help others to live more worthy human lives.

Q. *Professor Samuel Huntington, in his thesis on the clash of civilizations,[4] envisaged a clash between Muslims and Christians as one of the scenarios for the future. Do you see this as likely, or can it be avoided?*

A. It is a scenario that can take place if care is not taken, but it is also a scenario that can be avoided. It does not have to be. It need not be. If people are careless, if people are selfish, if people are heartless, if people are without love for others, then it can happen, but it need not happen. We don't want it to be a prophecy that then precipitates its own fulfillment. This means that while we realize that a cultural clash can take place, it is our duty to ensure that it does not take place.

If Huntington's aim is to alarm us so that we make sure it does not take place, then I give him high marks. But if his belief is that it will take

---

[4] Samuel P. Huntington first published his ideas in an article on "The Clash of Civilizations", in the 1993 summer edition of the journal *Foreign Affairs*. He later developed his thesis in a book, *The Clash of Civilizations and The Remaking of World Order* (London: Simon and Schuster, 1997).

place, and that no matter what we do it will take place, then I disagree with him. It is our duty to make sure that it does not take place.[5] But we don't write him off by saying that it cannot happen.

Q. *One place where we see a clash right now is in the Middle East, in the Holy Land. How do you read that situation?*

A. The problem there, of course, is many-sided. Religion is not the only problem. There is the political problem, the economic problem, the human problem, the historical problem—history and the memories of the past, relics of colonialism.

But religion does come in, too, more so as there are three major religions in the Holy Land. Judaism was always there; then Christianity arrived when Christ came; and Islam came six or seven centuries afterward. But, de facto, the three religions have to learn to accept one another, and the religious leaders have a very difficult role to play: they dare not adopt just a political stand. We can understand when a politician has a political program, but a religious leader should have a much wider panorama, so that influencing from their point of view, and everyone contributing—religious leaders, political leaders, economists and statesmen—all of them should help because there is the possibility for a solution. It is a defeat for mankind when violence goes on, and killing.

Q. *You have been to the Holy Land.*

A. Many times, and I hope to be there again in ten days' time,[6] in Jerusalem, from Monday to Saturday, with meetings, lectures on Muslim-Christian relations, meetings with Muslim leaders and with Catholic leaders and with other Christian leaders, then a lecture in the University of Bethlehem and, of course, Mass and prayer in the holy places.

Q. *Will you meet Jewish leaders too when you go there?*

A. Not I, because we have a separate commission for religious relations with the Jews, and Cardinal Cassidy is in charge of that, and he will go there soon, though not in the same week. But they know well that it is the whole Catholic Church that is carrying on these dialogues, but through different offices.

---

[5] See Cardinal Francis Arinze's lecture "Christian-Muslim Relations in the 21st Century" (Center for Muslim-Christian Relations, History and International Affairs; Edmund A. Walsh School of Foreign Service, Georgetown University: Occasional Paper Series, 1998).

[6] End of February 2001.

Q. *I recall that a year ago, in 1999, you got a medal from the leader of a Jewish organization.*

A. Indeed, I was given a medal a year ago from the International Association for Christians and Jews, based in London, by Sir Sigmund Steinberg, who is the head of that organization. He gave me a medal at the Israeli Embassy in Rome, for the promotion of inter-religious relations, not specifically of Christian–Jewish relations. I appreciated it very much.

Q. *More recently, you took part in the Millennium World Peace Summit of Religious and Spiritual Leaders, which opened in the General Assembly Hall, at the United Nations Headquarters, in New York, on August 28, 2000. Senior religious leaders representing some seventy-five different faiths and traditions from every world region participated in that event. Could you tell me what happened?*

A. Yes. It took place in the United Nations building for the first two days, and then at the Waldorf-Astoria Hotel for the other two days. About a thousand people took part, representing the world's major religions and faith traditions.

But there were some things that were not so clear, for example, who exactly put this together? What was their aim? And why were there 350 Hindus from India in that colloquium; how is that explained? Who paid for them? And why? But without having full answers to all the questions, it was a fact that people of many religions were there, and it was also a sign that they wanted somehow to work together.

Q. *You were the head of the Vatican delegation and represented the Holy See at the summit.*

A. There really was no Holy See delegation as such. Everyone came in answer to a personal invitation. They invited the Holy Father, and the Holy Father said: "Cardinal Arinze will attend, and he will read my message", and I did that.

They invited me too, and I also read my own contribution. Many other people too read their contributions, although everybody could not speak at the plenary session. We had workshops too, however, and all could speak there. But in a meeting of one thousand people for four days you can see that there is a limit to how much discussion you can have. Nevertheless, some good was achieved.

But in such meetings, the contribution is often more in the way of messages and the main thing it says to the world, rather than in the fine print. Its main message was this: leading people of many religions are here, they want to contribute to a better world, and they don't want war. That's not bad.

Q. *So you met the secretary general of the United Nations, Kofi Annan, at the summit.*

A. Oh, yes, very much so. The meeting brought me as close to him as I would have ever desired, including a lunch that lasted more than one hour, which he hosted. I met him again when he invited a smaller group of leaders to talk with him in his office, and again we met when he spoke to us in the plenary session. He really made himself available, and we thanked him for that. It was clear that he was happy with the meeting.

Q. *I understand that at one of the workshops you took quite a forthright stand. Could you tell me what happened?*

A. You are right. There was a workshop on poverty, and I had spoken in the plenary session before this, because I was invited to speak. In fact, the chairman was a Jew, and he asked me to speak. So I spoke on poverty, the sort of thing we were discussing before: that we should make every effort to eliminate poverty and to help the poor get out of their situation of poverty, and that poverty can also precipitate other evils, such as revolutions and destruction of property, and cause one group to fight another.

In the workshop on poverty, some from India spoke, and they said that in India the Catholic Church proposes Christianity to Indians, and they are opposed to that. They said the Catholic Church should not propose Christianity to any Indian, and that for the same reason they are against the Church working among the poor in India, because they fear that if the Church works among the poor, some of those poor will want to become Christians. And therefore they are against the Church working among the poor. They said, "Go away with your money." They also said that when the Pope visited Delhi in November 1999, to publicize the results of the Asian synod, they heard him say that in the third millennium the religion of Jesus Christ will be offered to Asia in a big way, and they are opposed to that. When they finished, I put up my hand to speak.

Q. *You mean you asked for the floor, to respond?*

A. Yes, but it took me some time before I succeeded in getting the chairman to give me the floor, as many others wanted to speak too. I made three points: "The Catholic Church proposes Christianity to some Indians." I said, "Yes, but not only to Indians, but also to other Asians, to Africans, to Nigerians, and to other people all round the world, on all five continents, because the Church was sent by Christ to bring his good news to every person. But we do it respecting the freedom of everybody, we never impose, we only propose, and the Catholic Church condemns proselytism, or forced conversion."

"In answer to the second question on the Church working among the poor," I said, "the Church works among the poor, as Mother Teresa did, and with hospitals and schools on all continents and in all countries, because that is part of the religion of Jesus Christ, who also looked after the poor, and gave them food, and healed the sick. The Church will do that and will continue to do that. She doesn't do it so that they will necessarily become Christians; so even if the poor say they are not Christians, and they don't want to become Christians, the Church will still help them because they are human beings. And the Church looks on every human being as created by God and, in the name of Jesus Christ, she will come near every person."

I said, "The Church does not help the poor on condition that they become Christians; this would be proselytism, and we condemn that. But if the poor freely want to become Christians, then those poor people have the right to become Christians, and we Christians have not only the right but also the duty to share Christianity with them. So, we will not promise not to propose Christianity to the poor, or to the rich, but it will not be the condition for giving them rice, or school teaching, or medical care, but because doing those things is part of our religion."

"But," I said, "if you forbid every Indian to become a Christian, or if you prevent even one Indian from becoming a Christian, then you are unreasonable, and you are going against article 18 of the Universal Declaration of Human Rights, approved by the United Nations in 1948."

At that point an Indian got up and said, "What do you mean by that?"

Q. *You mean one of the Hindus got up?*
A. Yes. So I said to the chairman, "Please protect me; this man is not allowing me to speak. When he spoke, I listened. Now I speak, and he heckles me." Then I made my third point. I said, "You said, the Pope said in the third millennium, Asia will be for Christ." I said,

"What's wrong with that? The Catholic Church wants to propose the religion of Jesus Christ not only to Asia, but also to Africa and Europe, America and Oceania—nothing different for Asia. But only propose, not impose. If all your people want to be Christians, they have the right to be so. If one of them wants to be a Christian, that person has the right to be so. But you do not have the right to stop even one person from being a Christian."

Then there were fireworks!

Q. *What was the reaction afterward? How did the other persons present react?*

A. Some people were in favor; others were against the Indian. It was rather hot. It was most interesting. I enjoyed it.

And during the coffee break, some Hindus came and said to me, "Please don't think that those Hindus represent all of us. Let's agree on something." I said, "You have Indian homework to do; it isn't universal at all. Here at the United Nations they know what freedom is; if you don't know what freedom is, you had better settle it in India yourselves. You have some Indian priests and laymen; you have some Indian Hindus: sit among yourselves and settle it in your home country, but don't pour hot water on the whole world here because you have some problem in India, and you are angry about something." That's how it went.

Q. *Did Kofi Annan say anything to you about this? Was he present at the meeting when this happened?*

A. No, he was not present at that stage, as this was a workshop, not the plenary session.

Q. *But you could say the same thing in Saudi Arabia.*

A. If only they invited me to go there, I would say the same.

Q. *You mean they haven't allowed you to go to Saudi Arabia?*

A. No, not that I have ever asked. But I have not attended any conference yet in Saudi Arabia.

Q. *But some from your office have been able to go there.*

A. Yes, some of my predecessors. Cardinal Pignedoli, at one stage, did go to Saudi Arabia, about twenty-three years ago. But one thing is clear; it is the principle of religious freedom that is at stake. This principle is valid wherever there is a human being. It is not only valid in Italy and France, in the U.S.A. and Canada; it is also valid in Nigeria and Pakistan. It is valid in India and Japan, and it is valid in the United Arab Emirates and Saudi Arabia. It is valid in every country where there is a human being.

Q. *Let me understand this question better: the Saudi Arabian government has never issued you an invitation to go to that country?*
A. No. But let's look at it this way: I don't visit countries because the government issues invitations. It is normally our inter-religious partner who invites us. It's not exactly the government, so I don't blame governments for this.

Q. *But the Saudi Arabian religious groups, your partners in the dialogue, have come here at your invitation.*
A. Yes.

Q. *But they have never invited you back.*
A. No. They have not arranged a meeting in Saudi Arabia. When it was their turn to arrange a meeting, they decided where they wanted it to be, and we went there. If they decide on Saudi Arabia, I would gladly go there. If they decide on Cairo, I will go there. If they decide on Paris, I will go there too.

Q. *But your message will be clear: no country, and no religion in that country, should prevent a citizen of that country from becoming a follower of a religion, or from changing from one religion to another.*
A. That is the Catholic stand, and we don't make any secret of it. On the day when the mosque was opened in Rome, June 21, 1995—it was a Wednesday—and at the general audience in the Vatican the Holy Father said, "A mosque is being opened today in Rome, and I am happy that the Muslims have the right to religious freedom, and that they can exercise it in the very city where the successor of Peter lives. But, unfortunately, there are some Muslim countries where we cannot say the same about people of other religions. The world is still waiting, at the end of the second millennium, for this openness to the human person so that in every country the right to religious freedom will be not only allowed, but also practiced." The Pope said this on the day the mosque was opened.

Q. *That year, before the mosque was opened, I remember going to the Coliseum on Good Friday for the Stations of the Cross led by the Pope, and some people were distributing leaflets saying: "We shouldn't allow a mosque to be opened in Rome until Saudi Arabia allows us to build and open a Christian church in their city." Saudi Arabia gave most of the money for the building of the Rome mosque, but it does not respect religious freedom in its own territory. What do you say to it?*

A. What I say is this: "You have a mosque in Rome, and the Catholic Church thinks that if there are Muslims here they have a right to religious freedom. But where is our church in Saudi Arabia? Because if there are Christians in Saudi Arabia, as there are, then they too have a right to religious freedom."

Q. *I understand that there are more than half a million Christians in Saudi Arabia.*

A. There are, and they are working for the country. Some are pilots, some are nurses, and others are medical doctors, domestic helpers, and so on. In short, they are human beings, and therefore they have the right to religious freedom. That is the Catholic stand, and it is an honest stand. We don't hide anything, and we don't change our doctrine according to political correctness—"when it is politically difficult we suppress the doctrine, when it is easier we come out with it." The Catholic Church does not do that.

Q. *What do you say to a country such as China, which allows religion but also wants to control religion?*

A. Obviously, I am not talking with the representatives of the government of China, but if I were to sit with them, I would not lack things to say. I would say this, "Do not be afraid to allow the human soul to open itself freely to God the Creator. Do not be afraid of religion. Do not be afraid of Jesus Christ; he will not only not do harm to your country, but he will also be for the good of your country and your people, for the peace of your country and your harmony. Do not be afraid of religion. Actually, you need it. You need it more than you realize. It will help you build up the human person. You will have much more harmony. You will have much less tension. And you will have better citizens. They will have a higher level of human life. They will be freer. Christ himself has told us: 'You will know the truth, and the truth will make you free.' So do not be afraid."

Q. *So you see fear as the factor behind this wish to control religion, or the wish to block people from changing from one religion to another?*

A. I think so. I think that fear must be one of the factors at work here. Not the only one though, because the whole ideology that would be atheistic is already something that we are not accustomed to. We don't live in that kind of climate.

But if a person at a government leadership or an individual or personal level were to say to me, "I do not believe in God; I don't believe in religion", I would say to that person, "Don't be afraid." Moreover, "Do not repress your own citizens. Allow them to express themselves as human beings. You will not lose; your country will not lose. Your ideology—atheistic—may lose. Oh, yes! But since I do not believe in atheism, I do not believe in an atheistic ideology, and I would not suggest that you should keep up an atheistic ideology, because I believe in fact that God exists. But if you don't believe that God exists, at least allow those who so believe to live. Allow them free exercise of their religion, just as you want free exercise; allow them that much."

Q. *Moving on from this question, I would like to know a little about your views on Europe today. You have spent many years in Europe, and you have seen the European culture and society at close hand over many years. You came here in the 1950s and studied, and you studied in London for a year in the 1960s, and over the past sixteen years you have traveled widely in Europe and gained more insight into it. What do you see as the positive and negative aspects of this European scene? What are your impressions?*

A. Everyone will have a different impression. As I come from Nigeria, some of my positive impressions would be that science and technology are very well developed in Europe; traditions are basically influenced by the Christian matrix, the Christian past of Europe, such as the values of democracy. Elections are held, and the one who wins takes over, while the one who loses accepts—that is excellent. No tradition of change of democratic power by violence, which is important. Then there is the functioning of the services—telephone, water, electricity, roads, and airways—which are not to be taken for granted all around the world. Then there is accountability by people in public office: they can be asked questions.

There is a sense of solidarity. See how many European countries move as soon as there is an earthquake, maybe in India or San Salvador; they immediately send teams, some even with police dogs, and money is collected in churches, in railway stations and airports, and by newspapers too. It is very good.

Then the Christian traditions of Europe are rich and many. Not only the sanctuaries, the monasteries, but also the major religious orders, which of them doesn't have its original root in Europe? Then the more recent religious families and congregations were founded in Europe in the last two hundred years. Without those missionaries of Divine Providence, without the missionaries from Ireland—especially the Spiritans— I would not be sitting here today. So that's beyond doubt.

And then there is the commitment of the people to Christianity. People really make sacrifices; some are rather poor, but they give. I was impressed in Germany by the *Kindermissionswerk*, the work for missions by children, the Holy Childhood Association centered in Aachen; they really organize, and little children learn to give for the missions. I will not forget when I was a young priest, and an altar boy, nine or ten years old, gave me one German mark and said I was to send it to my bishop for the training of priests in Nigeria. He had heard we had not enough money to train our priests. I asked how he got the one mark, and he said, "Savings". People gave him money in pfennigs, and he kept them until he reached one mark, and he gave it to me. So that's really something, and it's not just the rich people; it's organized, it is not automatic.

That is also very impressive in Europe. So too is the amount of sacrifice made to promote evangelization elsewhere. Even though Christianity began in the Middle East—or, really, western Asia, which Europeans call the Middle East—nevertheless Christianity has settled down in Europe so that most missionaries in the history of the Church have come from Europe hitherto. But the situation is changing a bit now. So these are some of the very positive things.

As for the more negative ones: there's worry about the family—the family almost seems to be under attack, I would say. The image of woman is badly damaged by those who speak as if being a mother, or bearing a child, were oppression and not the glory of woman. Then in families: they think one child is enough; two, they say, is too many; four—they begin to ask questions. So there I think is a problem. The nuclear family is important, but it's not good when the relatives, cousins, nephews are somehow not thought of so much; it's more the small unit. We Africans, we are accustomed to the wider family, what we call "the extended family".

Liturgical celebrations are good; however, sometimes, as an African I

wish they would be livelier. Not that people should dance at Mass—
some people think Africans always dance at Mass. Not true. But that
there should be some way the people show that they are happy about the
celebration, and that they are sharing. Choirs, excellent! They do well,
but they should not monopolize the singing so that the people are
marginalized, as if they came to an orchestral recital: the choir performs
and then we clap for them afterward. That is a problem.

Because there are not enough, or not so many, children in the family,
and because the mass media sometimes desacralize the family or marriage
or family values, then the number of young people who want to become
priests or sisters or monks or nuns is getting lower than the needs of
society and the Church would indicate. That is also an area of worry.

One point I would mention as an African: it is that many Europeans
don't know enough about Africa. They speak of Africa as if it were one
country; they just call us Africans. But if I call all of you Europeans,
whether you are Irish or Italian or Norwegian or German; all of you are
Europeans, that is true but . . . I noticed when the World Cup was on,
and when Cameroon was doing very well, they used to call them Africans—"the African team"—but when they were winning, the commen-
tators began to call them Cameroonians. They began to realize that there
are fifty-four countries in Africa. It is not just one country down there.
But many Europeans still speak as if Africa were one country. For instance, you will hear people who should know better saying, "Oh, there
was an international congress in Rome: there were Indians and Filipinos,
there were British, and there were also Africans." All there! And they do
not see the mistake. Africa is not just one country alongside the countries
mentioned; it is a continent.

Also, it is not fair that when Africa comes to mind on the political
and mass media levels, there's always something negative in the context,
such as a military coup or somebody killing somebody or starving children or AIDS patients. Then they highlight Africa, but not much is said
when it comes to positive things. If AIDS is mentioned, immediately an
African AIDS patient is shown, but they never show us the AIDS patients
from any other continent. Is that really so? It is true that there are AIDS
patients in Africa, but there are such patients also in other continents.

So that sort of thing makes an African a bit uncomfortable, and it
actually makes some of our students adopt extreme positions that are not
necessary.

But obviously the nature of my work, if nothing else, shows me that in this world every people has positive and negative elements, and no people has the monopoly of all the good qualities. God is too infinite for any one people to exhaust his goodness. Not even the saints can do that. No saint will exhaust God's goodness; one saint reflects one aspect of God, another one reflects another. So too with all the nations of the world: we have an orchestra, and it is more beautiful that way.

Q. *Have you seen a change in Europe in terms of religious faith from the 1950s to the present day? You have worked in parishes in Italy, Germany, Austria, and Britain, and other places, and you have traveled much. What is your reading of this reality?*

A. Obviously, there is a change, and it is not the fault of any one person. It's simply that science and technology and the mass media, which have developed tremendously over the past forty years, make information readily available. Their power to show and to influence in a subtle way is much more than anything we had fifty years ago, particularly TV. But they can present an unreal world to a young person: all in color, all dressed up beautifully, in nice cars and smiling, whereas real life is just a little harsher than that.

Therefore the challenge to serious religion is this: Must we confine religion to poor and underdeveloped societies? No. Development is a gift from God; science and technology are good. The Bible tells us, "God looked on all that he had made and found it very good." But the challenge is how religion is to live in a technologically and scientifically well-developed society. That is the challenge here today, and that challenge will come to other parts of the world too, sooner or later. But it will come to all of us. That's the challenge.

The same thing is true in the whole area of medicine: bioethics— genetic engineering, as they call it: all the challenges it poses, some of them directly moral and theological, others social, others cultural. Religion has to face all these challenges.

Also the ease of travel, the jet, means more meetings of peoples and cultures and religions. This posits more challenges than we had fifty years ago, when most people traveled by boat.

Q. *As you have so often said yourself on other occasions, the economic differences pose great challenges at many levels, as we see between Eastern and Western Europe, and between the rich and so-called developed countries and the poor countries on the road to greater development.*

A. Definitely, with the influence countries have on one another. As already observed, the price of primary products—cocoa, palm oil, peanuts, bananas, to mention a few—is often not settled in the country where they are produced, but in other countries. The multinational and the economic influences of one country on another are such that no country is now left on its own.

There might be a war somewhere in Africa, but the interested parties may not only be those Africans immediately visible. There will be companies interested in one mineral here, another mineral there. There may be another country interested in having an influence in that area, and not leaving it all to that other country that colonized it one hundred years ago. So the whole picture gets much more complex. This too is a challenge to the Church.

Q. *You have touched on the conflicts in Africa. We know that there are forty armed conflicts in the world today, sixteen of them in Africa. How do you view these conflicts? How do you read them?*

A. There are economic interests, political interests, local people who think only of their pockets and their bank accounts, some of these in banks overseas; then multinational corporations that see the opportunity to get rich—but at what cost in lives of peoples who may not even be primarily concerned, and frustration too for many people. Then there are governments elsewhere that want influence in the area, commercial interest. It all becomes very complicated.

Then there are those who produce arms and are just interested in selling them. And there is a little group of mercenaries too who take part in fighting and organizing for the conflict, but they know when to pull out and not die in the fight. During the civil war in Nigeria, one Catholic chaplain priest told me that there was a mercenary fighting for their group, and he told the soldiers where there would be a war the following year in another part of the world. He knew already there would be a war there, and he would be there, too!

This means there are all kinds of influences at work, beyond the immediate national ones. It's a pity.

Nevertheless, we must not despair. This is a world in which one country influences another, and one person influences another. Instead of sitting down and lamenting from morning till evening, we should use that time in organizing how the world could go better. And it can go better.

Q. *This is where the role of religion comes in.*

A. Yes, religion and good leadership. And religion should also influence the leaders, because the political decisions should also be influenced
by religious considerations in terms of justice, peace, development, and
fairness.

Q. *You've been here in the Vatican for sixteen years as head of the
Pontifical Council for Inter-Religious Dialogue, and you have watched the
changing religious scene in the world. What is your overall impression: Is there
greater harmony among religions now than when you first came here? Sometimes one gets the impression that there is a growing polarization in the
religious field, a rising fundamentalism in many religions.*

A. Some, a few, of the bigger religions have groups that take exaggerated positions, and they attract the attention of the media. But it is
also true, if we look back over the last twenty years, there really is
development in the positive sense of willingness to meet. There are a
high number of encounters today between people of two or three
religions, and the number of inter-religious groups or associations set up
is very many, though not all of them of the same quality or with the same
degree of success. This fact is already impressive. Whether it is between
Catholics and Muslims, even on the official level—as official as you can
call it—or whether it is simply local informal meetings.

As I mentioned earlier, there was one of the largest gatherings of
people at the United Nations in New York at the end of August 2000 for
the Millennium World Peace Summit of Religious and Spiritual Leaders.
Some inter-religious organizations and individuals in the United States
invited a thousand people of many religions mainly to discuss peace.
That is a sign of our times. I do not say that it has solved all the problems;
nevertheless, the fact in itself is already eloquent.

Within the Catholic Church too, for example, next week[7] we are
going to have, here in the Vatican, a meeting between our office for
dialogue and the representatives of four Islamic organizations on the
world level: the World Muslim League, the Muslim World Congress,
the Organization for Islamic Dawah and Relief—that means Islamic
mission work and social assistance—and the Organization of Islamic
Conference. We hold a meeting with them every year, generally the top
officials, so that we are in contact, and so that present-day problems in

---

[7] The meeting was in mid-February 2001.

Christian–Muslim relations can be examined. This is normal, and it is something significant.

At the end of next week, we will have our annual meeting with the leadership of Al-Azhar in Cairo, for two days. As I mentioned earlier, it was they in the Al-Azhar who suggested February 24 as the annual day for our meeting, because the Pope was received in Al-Azhar on February 24, 2000. That too is a sign of what we have reached in our times. Such meetings no are longer a surprise.

In many countries and universities they invite one another. We hear this more and more. For example, the Pontifical Gregorian University in Rome has an academic association with the University of Ankara; the Zaitouna University in Tunis has a link with the Pontifical Institute for Arabic and Islamic Studies and the Pontifical Gregorian University. And I just read this morning[8] that the Catholic University of the Holy Spirit in Beirut, Lebanon, has just signed a document of association with the University of Damascus in Syria. This sort of thing does encourage us.

The fundamentalists who take exaggerated right-wing stands, and some of them occasionally provoke violence, do not discourage people who are more middle-of-the-road.

My general assessment would be positive, because the efforts being made today are better than the efforts being made forty years ago, at the level of interaction between the religions.

Q. *Would it be true then to say that there is less polarization among religions today than forty years ago?*

A. Yes. You will notice that the United Nations has adopted the year 2001 as the year of Dialogue between Civilizations, and civilizations are heavily influenced by religions too.

The different religions should make and are making efforts to contribute to prevent the clash of civilizations, because it is realized more and more that if religions are not in good relationship, the clash-of-civilizations prophecy may get fulfilled, to the sorrow of all mankind.

---

[8] February 16, 2001.

Chapter 18

With the Pope in Greece, Syria, and Malta

Two significant events in the life of the Church took place in May 2001, as I was working on this book. Pope John Paul II visited Greece, Syria, and Malta, May 5–9,[1] and he called all the cardinals to Rome, May 21–24, to consult with them for the sixth time in his pontificate.[2] Cardinal Arinze participated in both events and on June 9, 2001, despite a busy schedule, kindly gave me a brief interview, in which he shared some reflections on those events.

I began with the Consistory of Cardinals in May, but focused only on the question of inter-religious dialogue. In his report to the cardinals on the Jubilee Year, Roger Cardinal Etchegaray singled out the international meeting of representatives of the world's religions in the Vatican in October 1999, as one event that had not been given adequate attention.[3] Many considered it a second Assisi-type meeting, after the historic one called by Pope John Paul II in October 1986, which we discussed earlier in this book. I asked the cardinal about this event and Cardinal Etchegaray's comment.

---

[1] The Pope considered his visit to Greece, Syria, and Malta a continuation of his Jubilee pilgrimage, following in the footsteps of Saint Paul. But the visit to Greece had a major ecumenical dimension, while the visit to Syria had both ecumenical and inter-religious ones, as well as a concern for peace in the Middle East.

[2] The agenda for that meeting was based on the main issues raised in the apostolic letter *Tertio Millenio Ineunte* (At the Beginning of the New Millennium), issued by the Pope on January 6, 2001.

[3] Cardinal Etchegaray's report was published in *L'Osservatore Romano*, May 21, 2001.

Q. *What is your memory of that inter-religious meeting from October 25 to 28, 1999, which, according to Cardinal Etchegaray, was not given adequate attention?*

A. It was an event in preparation for the Great Jubilee. It was an event that was examined and approved by the Council of the Presidency of the Central Committee for the Great Jubilee—a council of five cardinals. That council entrusted the Pontifical Council for Inter-Religious Dialogue with the task of organizing this assembly of people of many religions in view of the Great Jubilee, and it gave it the theme "Towards the Third Millennium: Collaboration between the Religions". Our pontifical council organized the meeting.[4] We invited a total of two hundred people from twenty religions. About half of the participants were Christian; the other half were from the other religions.

It wasn't exactly along the lines of the big Assisi event of October 1986. For the Assisi event, as I mentioned earlier, the Holy Father invited people of many religions to come and pray and fast for peace, in the International Year for Peace. There wasn't really any discussion at Assisi in 1986, but there was prayer and there was fasting, and then there was a general address by the Holy Father.

This time the two hundred participants met for four days in the synod hall in Vatican City. It is true that the third day was given to a pilgrimage to Assisi, because Saint Francis of Assisi is loved by people of many religions—Muslims, Buddhists, Shintoists, Hindus, and so on, not to mention Christians. So we went there, and it was beautiful. People really prayed over the tomb of Saint Francis, and there were reactions, reflections by a Hindu and a Muslim. And obviously Christians spoke, too.

---

[4] In preparation for this event, the Pontifical Council for Inter-Religious Dialogue published a book in several languages, *Journeying Together—The Catholic Church in Dialogue with the Religious Traditions of the World* (Vatican City: Libreria Editrice Vaticana, 1999). It presents the main features of the various religious traditions and the essential points of Christian doctrine.

The main assembly evolved in this way. There was an opening ceremony and welcoming speeches by Cardinal Etchegaray and myself. A woman, Mrs. Theresa EE-Chooi, from Kuala Lumpur, Malaysia, gave the keynote address; she was then president of the International Union of the Catholic Press. After that, one person from each of the major religions spoke briefly. Then there was discussion in a plenary session, and after that there were discussions in the workshops, which were divided according to languages. Each workshop gave a report back to the assembly.

On the very first day, our pontifical council made it clear to the assembly that we had no draft prepared for them to examine and correct, and that they would have to work out themselves the text of any final message they wanted to make public. So the message that was issued on the final day and also the general report that the plenary approved were drawn up by a special committee set up on the spot by the coordinating committee. Our pontifical council did not write a single line for them. It was the assembly that worked it all out.

We had quite a problem on the third day, because it was the day for the drafting committee to work on the results of what came out of the workshops, but most people wanted to go to Assisi. And those people who had to work and draft the text had to sacrifice the pilgrimage to Assisi. But finally we got enough people to make the sacrifice.

When the members returned from Assisi, they received the draft text, and they had the night to reflect on it. The following morning there was discussion in the plenary assembly on both the message and the general report. And when they finally agreed on the text, it was then polished by the drafting committee and made public.

In the afternoon of that final day, every religion had a separate place in which to pray. There was no common prayer. The Christians—Catholics, Orthodox, Anglicans, and Protestants—prayed in the church of Santa Maria in Traspontina, that big Carmelite church in the Via della Conciliazione. All the others—Muslims, Jews, Hindus, Buddhists, and so on—had separate places.

Then, at four o'clock in the afternoon, the final act took place in Saint Peter's Square. The Gen Rosso of the Focolare movement animated the gathering with their usual lively singing, but also with very meaningful words; some pieces were composed just for the occasion. There was also a Jewish choir, and there was a mixed choir of Christians and Muslims. It was really *suggestivo*, as the Italians would say; it was really something that conveyed a message.

Obviously, the Holy Father addressed the assembly. There were moments of silence. But there were also moments of testimony; a Jew, a Muslim, a Hindu, and a Buddhist spoke and gave their witness. A Catholic from each continent spoke too. Then there was the lighting of torches. And there was a symbol of peace—shaking hands. After the meeting there was supper, because it had been a day of fasting too.

The whole idea in this assembly was for the religions of the world to ask themselves what they are prepared to do in this millennium, and this century just beginning. What do they see as their duty? What do they see as their contribution to the world of today, and tomorrow? That's why we called it "The Religions of the World on the Eve of the Third Millennium: Collaboration between the Different Religions".

Our office has issued a book containing most of the major talks, the final report, and the message. It is called *Towards a Culture of Dialogue* and is in English, Italian, and French.[5] The Focolare movement has also produced a video of the event and the surroundings. So you could say that it was not, from a calendar point of view, in the actual Jubilee Year, but it was obviously in view of that year, and you could say it was the contribution of religions to the Jubilee 2000.

Q. *I was struck by the fact that Cardinal Etchegaray had selected this as a Jubilee event that had not been given its proper place. And I understand that a number of cardinals felt this should have been given great emphasis because it is such an important topic: this coming together of religions to work for peace and to contribute to a better human situation for everybody.*

A. When he said it had not been given its proper place, I think the cardinal meant it had not received sufficient attention; it had not received all the attention it deserved.

As regards the timing of this event, we in the pontifical council were happy with that. And the council of five cardinals was happy with it, and in any case it was we who made the calendar, so I cannot say I was not there. We saw that the actual year 2000 was rather crowded with events all over the place, and we also wanted a time where we would have the synod hall free. In short, there were many things to be considered in relation to the date.

Looking back now, I think the time we chose was excellent. It was

---

[5] *Towards a Culture of Dialogue* (Vatican City: Pontifical Council for Inter-Religious Dialogue, 2000).

excellent because it prepared people for the contribution of the religions, not just in the year 2000, but even after.

Q. *So how, then, would you summarize the central element of that event?*

A. I would put it this way. Here were people of various religious convictions, sitting together for four days, and working together. The word *harmony* is not an exaggeration here. I did not notice any major crisis or friction in their working together. I was really pleasantly surprised by the message the assembly issued, especially as no draft had been prepared before the meeting. I was really pleasantly surprised. I was happy because it was the genuine work of the four-day assembly. I have taken part in many meetings, world meetings, and sometimes the organizers prepare a draft even before the participants arrive. Not so in this case. We absolutely insisted in our pontifical council that we would do no such thing. It was a risk, but it worked out very well. So I think that was really something very good.

You know, on this last day of the meeting, many of the people said, "Look, Cardinal Arinze, we must not let this stop here. We must set up a permanent secretariat; we must continue." And I said to them, "We didn't invite you in order to set up one more bureaucracy." They said, "But we can't let this stop!" It was not easy to put that aside. Indeed, since then, our pontifical council has been reflecting on the message of that assembly, and what can be done. And we have not yet said the last word on it.

Q. *How has the Holy Father reacted?*

A. He encouraged us. He was there, and he gave a speech, which was greatly appreciated. We knew we had his support "from the word go", because obviously the council of five cardinals had to bring this idea to the Holy Father, and he approved it. We could not ask him to have done more.

Q. *Throughout these twenty-three years of his pontificate, he has been a very strong supporter of inter-religious dialogue. No one can see this better than you, since you have worked side by side with him for most of his pontificate.*

A. No doubt. Everyone knows the Holy Father's first encyclical is *Redemptor Hominis—The Redeemer of Man*. Everyone knows that Jesus

Christ is at the center of the Holy Father's apostolate and prayer. You notice even the titles of the encyclicals, *The Redeemer of Man* (1979), *The Mother of the Redeemer* (1987), *The Mission of the Redeemer* (1990), and his apostolic letter *The Guardian of the Redeemer* (Saint Joseph; 1989). You can see that the Redeemer is at the center of his thought. It's very clear, even from the titles of the encyclicals. For the same reasons, the Pope sees Jesus Christ as the Redeemer of man. So man, the Pope says, is "the way of the Church": the human person, no matter where, no matter who.

At Assisi, October 1986, he said, "Human nature is the same in all; Christ took on this human nature, thereby making himself a brother, almost identifying himself with everyone." This is said, too, in paragraph 22 of *Gaudium et Spes*, Vatican II's constitution on the Church in the modern world.

Attention to people of other religions is not something additional to the Holy Father's vision of the apostolate of the Church, the mission of the Church. The mandate of the Church, that which Christ sent the Church for, is to meet man, the human person, wherever he is. Whether that person is in Saint Peter's Basilica or in Bangkok, in Tokyo or in Canberra, in Singapore or Delhi, in Caracas or Lima, in Washington, D.C., London, or Paris, in Abuja or Cairo. Man is the way of the Church.

For the same reason we can say the Pope was following in the footsteps of Saint Paul in Athens, in Damascus, and in Malta. So it is for the same reason. I don't think, in fact I am sure, that it is not something additional, but it is something that is part and parcel of how the Holy Father sees the mission of the Church, what Christ sent the Church to do.

Q. *And, of course, it is how he sees the significance of Christ for all people.*

A. Definitely, because it is Christ who sends the Church. So the Holy Father says that Christ, as the Redeemer of man sent by the eternal Father, instituted the Church and sent the Church with a clear message to bring the good news of salvation to every person. That is done in many ways, as we have said before.

And so we notice how the Pope, in chapter 5 of *Redemptoris Missio*, lists the various ways in which the Church carries out this mandate and calls them "the paths of mission, the ways of mission". These ways are: by silence, by testimony, witness to Christ—like Charles de Foucauld, without a word; or by catechesis, announcing and proclaiming Christ, and baptizing; nourishing the Christian community; enculturation of the Gospel; but also by inter-religious dialogue; by human promotion, social work, assistance.

Mother Teresa of Calcutta, when she meets—she and her sisters—and all the other congregations of sisters and brothers along the corridors of Church history, when they meet the sick, the poor, the hungry, the homeless, they do not give them a lecture in dogmatic theology; they pick them up, bring them to a house, clean them, give them a bed to sleep on (and some of them, for some time, haven't had a decent bed); they give them something to eat, and give them medicine. If that is not evangelization, can you tell me what the spirit of Christ is? Of course it is, because Christ said, "What you do to the least of these my brethren, you do to me." So I think the Pope sees it the same way. Therefore, the Pope's moving to meet Muslims, Buddhists, Jews, Hindus, and others is not doing something extra.

Q. *From what you have said, I understand that since the October 1999 inter-religious meeting, you have been reflecting on how to move forward from there. I see you yourself are convinced that further action is desirable. I also heard that several cardinals at the Consistory of Cardinals in May 2001 appeared to be supportive of this.*

A. No doubt. I am convinced that further action is necessary. That assembly of October 25–28, 1999, gave a message, and an indication. It would be a pity if everything rested there and no further action was taken. That would be a pity. We think that further action should be taken. We are reflecting. We are not yet ready to share with the public possible ways in which further action can be continued, but we are working on it.

Q. *I presume you talked about this with the Pope after the October 1999 meeting?*

A. Yes. Though not specifically on what we will do now, because we should be ready with our project before we submit it to the Holy Father. But we have been discussing, with a wide circle of people, what can be done.

As you said, at the Consistory of Cardinals in May 2001, quite a number spoke on inter-religious relations, and not necessarily only those from Asia and Africa. That should encourage us.

Q. *So you found strong endorsement among the cardinals at the May consistory, for this line of action.*

A. There was no doubt. As I said, it was cardinals from various areas of the world, which shows that it is an objective need of the Church of our times.

Q. *Before that Consistory of Cardinals, you accompanied the Pope on his pilgrimage, in the footsteps of Saint Paul, to Greece, Syria, and Malta.*

A. Yes, thanks to God. I was happy for this.

Q. *I too was there, and I saw that it was a most extraordinary trip. What are your reflections on that journey?*

A. Of course, I was happy in the entire trip; three places, three countries, three steps of Saint Paul's life, each showing another dimension of the same apostolate of the Church.

The accent in Greece was on ecumenism, particularly the relations with the Greek Orthodox. But Saint Paul, speaking on the Areopagus, was speaking to the entire world, especially to the philosophical and cultural world of what could be considered Europe in those days. So it wasn't just ecumenism, but, nevertheless, the stress was ecumenism.

In Malta the emphasis was on rejoicing in our Catholic faith, with three people beatified. In Malta, which is a Catholic island, most of the people are Catholic, and they go to Mass; they are not just nominal Catholics. Some people said that between one-third and a half of the population of Malta were at the Pope's Mass. It was just a day to thank and adore God for our Catholic faith. And, why not? Our faith is good news. It's not a contraband good to be hidden away. It's a joy.

Q. *But in Athens it was different. What were your feelings when you were with the Greek Orthodox leaders?*

A. I felt that a historic step was being taken. It was the first time a pope was there in a thousand years. And considering also the load of history on both sides, perhaps we would not be able to size up all the repercussions now. But we beg God, in his providence, to use all this in history. As someone said, the Holy Father had his walking stick; he walked slowly, but those steps were historic.

Q. *You spoke with the Greek Orthodox bishops there. What impression did you get?*

A. I spoke with many of them. And in the evening, one of the Orthodox archbishops was very happy, and he told me so privately. He said he was happy that the Church of Rome took such a decision. That is something. I am not sure that I am ready to speak of all the other things we discussed, but he was transparently happy. So it was encouraging. We were not sure how the whole thing would work out, but I think Divine Providence uses all that.

Q. *So you really see the value of taking a risk in this field.*
A. Yes. The Holy Father is not afraid. He himself, on the day he inaugurated his pontificate, and since then, has often said, "Do not be afraid!" And he is not afraid. He gives us the example of apostolic courage. I would call it more "trust in Providence, trust in the Holy Spirit", rather than "courage" as such. It is God who works out the events, but we should not be afraid. Of course, it is easy to say, not so easy to do.

Q. *I understand that. But before the visit I heard many people saying he should not be going to Greece; even some in the Vatican were of this mind.*
A. I would not be surprised, because it is a situation in which people can have different ideas; and it is not easy to know, a priori, who is more to the point than the other. But everything considered, I think I'd prefer to follow the Holy Father. You have the Holy Spirit, I have the Holy Spirit, but I think the Holy Father has the Holy Spirit more than we. And he decides. He has obviously weighed it. Who am I to think I am wiser?

Looking back, I think the Holy Father made the correct decision. But again it is not something that is mathematical, in the sense that you could tell for certain how it would work out. Not even the Holy Father could tell that.

Q. *These are courageous decisions by any standards.*
A. Yes.

Q. *Because it's like going to visit people who were your friends a long time ago, but you had a bad argument with them, and now you go and visit their house to see if they are willing to talk to you.*
A. Yes. Courageous. Even though I appreciate this word, and while I don't reject the word "courageous", I prefer to call it trust in Divine

Providence, trust in the power of the Holy Spirit. It may eventually come to the same thing. It isn't just that a person takes a risk, like a soccer player who has a shot at a goal; it's more than that. It is trust in the Holy Spirit and in Jesus Christ that makes the Pope take a decision that in human terms is courageous.

Q. *I remember, when we spoke about Vatican II, you said the same thing; you said the thing that most impressed you was the courage of the bishops at the Council who had the courage to take certain steps and decisions then.*

A. Yes, and because of their trust in the guidance of the Holy Spirit. The Holy Spirit will not abandon the Church: it's not just because we are clever and intelligent, and we have calculated it, and we see we will take the risk—it's much more than that. It's more a question of faith, trust, and abandonment to God, but still not being afraid to do what we think God wants of us, so we are open to divine action.

Q. *And the same was evident when the Pope went to Syria and went into the mosque in Damascus.*

A. I think so. In Syria, of course, everybody spoke of the mosque. The Holy Father went in the mosque, and it was a major step; it had never happened before. But the Holy Father was also aware that it was the first time. There the message was very clear. Even if a person didn't read any of the speeches, the simple fact that the Holy Father was there was in itself eloquent. The Muslims were there in big numbers—outside. And they controlled how many got in at that particular time. Then, after the Holy Father went into the mosque and prayed where it is believed that Saint John the Baptist is buried, he came out to the courtyard, and there were speeches.

But even without those speeches, the whole event was eloquent. Even if a Muslim was in Indonesia or in Egypt or in Saudi Arabia and saw it on TV, it meant, "Oh, the Holy Father has respect for Muslims; he sits with their leaders; he has respect for their sacred place."

Nobody is going to think that the Holy Father thinks one religion is as good as another. Anybody who knows the Holy Father will see that he cannot say that. But by his visit he was saying that the human person deserves respect, and the religion of other people deserves respect. That, yes. He was also saying that people of many religions, and particularly Christians and Muslims—who together count for more than half of mankind—should cooperate together, and that we have a duty to cooperate together. That, yes! The event said all that.

The visit to the Mosque said that we are willing—we Christians, we Catholics—we are willing to meet the Muslims and also, implicitly, people of other religions. That was also implicit in the act. So the message of the visit was very clear.

Since the Holy Father went there, I have not heard any negative comment. I have not even heard right-wing Christians disagreeing with the idea. If there are some who disagree, I am not aware of them. There was no common prayer, so I do not know what people could object to.

Q. *But the Pope obviously was praying when he was there in the mosque, by the tomb of Saint John the Baptist.*

A. How can a person not pray in such a circumstance? I am sure that even the journalists prayed. I prayed. When the Holy Father was going around slowly, and one of the Syrians was explaining to him the wonderful building that has been there for many centuries, I was praying for greater mutual understanding between Christians and Muslims, for greater love of one another, for justice, for peace. I was praying for peace in the Holy Land, and an end to all the violence in Jerusalem and the area all around. I was praying for peace there. I was praying to John the Baptist to help us prepare the way for Christ. How could I not pray?

I think therefore it is a day not to be forgotten. And it should encourage our efforts that when we say Christian–Muslim dialogue we don't mean necessarily discussion, but we mean talking to one another as co-pilgrims on the journey of life.

Q. *And as brothers.*

A. Yes, as brothers in the journey of life. We are not threats to one another. We are not menaces to one another. We can cooperate together, and we should.

Q. *Had you ever been to a mosque before?*

A. Oh, many. Oh, yes, many in very many countries, including the big one in Jerusalem—the Al Asqa Mosque. And this one here in Damascus, I had already visited it on other another occasion, when I went to Syria many, many years ago. So, yes, I have been to several mosques in many countries. But that has stopped being news from the days of Cardinal Pignedoli.

Q. *But it was the first time that the Holy Father had been in a mosque.*
A. Yes.

Q. *Had he ever been in a mosque as a cardinal?*
A. I doubt it. I am not aware of it.

Q. *What was his reaction afterward?*
A. You journalists want to know everything! [*Laughs.*] I'm afraid that I didn't try to analyze the Holy Father's mind. I did not.

Q. *But what were your own feelings as you visited the mosque with him?*
A. My feelings were those of gratitude to God that we live in times like this. And prayer to God that tomorrow may be happier than yesterday in Christian–Muslim relations, and that better understanding might prevail. Also prayer that some of the extremists on one side or the other would be inspired by such events. Those were my prayers. That's how my thoughts were going. Such an event didn't take place fifty years ago. We must thank God that we live at this time. And we must ask ourselves what does God want of us today and tomorrow, because the event also gives us an assignment.

Q. *Before we conclude, is there any final reflection that you would like to add?*
A. Not much, just to say that Divine Providence directs history. God is the Director-General of history. We are only instruments. We come and go. God is the constant factor. Our task is to ask ourselves; Are we answering God's call? Are we doing what Divine Providence expects of us at this time? Because what God has assigned to you, he has not assigned to me. If any of us falls short, mankind will be the poorer for that. But if every one of us responds, then God's plan will be better responded to by all of us, to the benefit of all.

Chapter 19

From Oxford and Cardiff Universities to the World Economic Forum and Ground Zero

(2002)

The terrorist attack on the Twin Towers in New York, on September 11, 2001, was a major turning point in world history and led to great upheaval in the economic, social, cultural, and political fields, and to the war on terrorism.

It had a major impact on the religious world too, particularly on the relations between Christianity and Islam, and the Catholic Church worked hard to prevent damage being done here and to consolidate the relations with Islam worldwide.

Pope John Paul II and his collaborators did all in their power to prevent the subsequent U.S.-led war against terrorism being turned into a religious crusade and "the clash of civilizations" or "the clash of religions". For this reason, in Kazakhstan, less than two weeks after that attack on New York, he called on Christians and Muslims to reject violence as a means to political ends and appealed to them to cooperate together for peace and harmony in the world. To that end too, he invited representatives of all the major world religions to join him in Assisi on January 24, 2002, and to pray for peace in the world. Not surprisingly, he called on the Pontifical Council for Inter-Religious Dialogue, headed by Cardinal Arinze, to spearhead the effort to get the religions of the world, and particularly Christianity and Islam, to work together for peace.

On the eve of the Assisi meeting, the cardinal's office hosted an afternoon's dialogue in the Vatican with the representatives of the other world religions that had accepted the Pope's invitation to participate in the Assisi meeting, and the cardinal presided at that event. The following day, he accompanied the Pope on the "Peace Train" to Assisi, together with the representatives of the world religions and cardinals and bishops from different continents.

The day after the Assisi gathering, the cardinal flew to Oxford to participate in a conference on "Inter-Faith Dialogue as a Means to World Peace", organized by the Oxford University Catholic Chaplaincy, and the following day he traveled to Cardiff University to speak at another forum.

He went from there to New York to take part in the World Economic Forum (January 31 to February 4, 2002), to which he had been invited. The forum brings together some two thousand of the leading global political, business, academic, and religious leaders. Since it was founded, thirty-one years earlier, this event had always been held in Davos, Switzerland, but it was moved to New York that year, as a sign of solidarity with the U.S.A. following the September 11 terrorist attacks. During that forum, participants went to Ground Zero in New York to pray for those who had died there, and the cardinal, on behalf of the Catholic community, read a prayer that he composed for the occasion.

On his return to Rome, I interviewed him on all these visits,[1] and we naturally spoke a little about the Assisi meeting and the world situation in light of the war in Afghanistan.[2]

Cardinal Arinze began by saying that the Catholic chaplains to Oxford University, Father Peter Newby, and to Cardiff University, Father John Owen, had invited him to give lectures at these academic institutions (January 25–27), so as "to strengthen Catholic life and presence and contribution there".

---

[1] The interview took place on February 12 at the Pontifical Council for Inter-Religious Dialogue.

[2] The war on Afghanistan started on October 7, 2001.

Q. *That was immediately after the Assisi meeting.*

A. Yes, the day after Assisi. I went to Oxford first and paid a visit to the Oxford Centre for Islamic Studies. It was just a good-will gesture and lasted one hour.

Then the major event, the university lecture, took place at the Catholic chaplaincy at six thirty in the evening. I spoke on "The University as a Promoter of Inter-religious Dialogue". There were questions and answers after I had spoken. That was followed by a supper for many students and invited guests, at which we continued the discussion.

The following day there was a symposium on "Inter-faith Dialogue as a Means for World Peace". Altogether, six people spoke. Indeed, we continued our discussion after lunch, so, really, it lasted from ten A.M. to three P.M.

Then we went for evensong in the Oxford College chapel—vespers. On Sunday, there was Solemn Mass in the chaplaincy with the students; it was beautiful, beautiful.

Q. *What was your central message to the Oxford students?*

A. The central message was that the university has to take into account the pluralistic nature of the world today from the religious point of view. That means there are de facto many religions in the world. A university cannot afford to ignore that, because a university by definition is a place where many currents, cross-currents, and ideas are brought forward and discussed, where fresh thinking is allowed—not only allowed, but encouraged.

Most students come to the university already with a religious identity. There will be students, of course, who have no religious identity. It is not the primary duty of a university to give a religious identity to a student; that is for parishes, for the parochial catechism class, that is for the Catholic or Anglican or other religious communities at the university. Nevertheless, a university has no choice but to inform its students about the major religions in the area where they live and where they are likely to work. Then, a university also has to help the students to accept people of other religious convictions different from their own; to respect them, which does not mean to accept whatever they believe.

Respect for people of other religions should not be interpreted to mean religious or theological relativism or religious indifferentism. In other words, the fact that we Catholics respect not only other Christians but also Muslims, Jews, Hindus, Buddhists, people of Traditional Religion, and so on must not be interpreted to mean that we are saying that one religion is as good as another. We are not saying that it does not matter to which religion you belong, that religions are all basically the same thing. We are not saying that, because that would be to ignore the objectivity of truth, especially religious truth. That is, while some things are debatable, there are other things that are actually certain, objectively so. For example, that God exists: it's not a question of our opinion. There are in moral areas too, questions of right and wrong; there are some things that are objectively so: for example, to tell a lie is objectively sinful, is objectively wrong; to steal, to commit adultery, these are actually objectively wrong, independent of people's opinion.

When we say inter-religious courtesy, we are not saying theological indifferentism. We are not indifferent to what people believe, we are not ignoring the importance of searching for religious truth. But what we are saying is that we respect another person. That we will never impose our religion on anyone; that we will respect the man who is looking for religious truth; that human dignity requires that everybody be allowed the minimum freedom in matters of conscience or religion. That means that we respect the religious freedom of other people, so that even if we do not agree with what they believe, because they are men created by God, we respect them.

Q. *So you see that as the first contribution of the university to peace and to religious freedom?*

A. It's a very important contribution. If every individual really respected others in this matter, and also accepted that others can be different from him and accepted that he will not impose his religious convictions on others, then we would have condition number one for harmony in society, because refusal to accept differences is the mother of all fundamentalisms and extremisms.

Those who are harsh to others, those who will not allow anyone to think differently from themselves, those who do not realize, as Vatican II said in its declaration on religious freedom, *Dignitatis Humanae*,[3] that truth will impose itself by virtue of its own truth, not by physical force or political pressure, not by *cuius regio, eius religio*, as they did some times after the Protestant Reformation, which means the prince imposes his religion on everybody in his area. It is recognized now that that is not correct.

Q. This then was the first point that you sought to get across in Oxford: respect for the differences and acceptance of the differences.

A. Yes, that was the first point. I then made a second point, that, while we respect everyone, each of us also has the obligation to look for religious truth. So that in religious freedom, horizontal—with reference to my fellow men—I should be left completely free, and no one should use force on me. But the vertical dimension—with reference to God—I am not free whether to look for God or not. I am actually bound to look for God, because God created me; I am his creature. So it is a matter of honesty—I nearly said justice—on my part that I recognize my Creator. If I recognize my Creator, I adore him, I love him, I ask pardon for my offenses against him, and I ask him for what I need. If I do all that, I have a religion. That's what religion is all about. That means that with reference to God religion is not free. It is obligatory.

Many people are surprised when they hear this, because they have always thought that religion is free; I answer—with reference to my fellow men, yes! With reference to God, no! Because every man is bound to look for truth as regards God and our duties toward him, and, having found it, we are bound to embrace it. Which means we think that religion is necessary.

When I was pushed during the discussion, and someone said—it was in Cardiff—"I am not bound; religions are causing trouble and it is better without [a religion]." I said, "No. Genuine religion will not be the cause of trouble. If anybody is promoting violence or injustice, to that extent the person is not faithful to any religion worthy of the name." When the person pursued his argument, pushed back, and said, "I have no religion myself", I said, "Please, could I come back to that point. With reference to God, since we are his creatures, we are bound to recognize him. A

---

[3] The text was published by the Second Vatican Council on December 7, 1965.

baby must recognize the parents; a child who refuses to recognize *Papa* and *Mama* and refuses to thank them is not honest. Indeed," I said, "a person without religion is not normal. A normal human being recognizes God, his Creator. A normal child recognizes his parents. It's not a favor that the child does to his parents. It is a duty that the child performs."

Q. *In your lectures, both in Oxford and in Cardiff, you began by saying that one premise for harmony between people is to respect differences, that harmony is strengthened by the person's recognizing God, believing in God, and trying to live according to that belief.*

A. It is strengthened by that, in the sense that love of God includes love of neighbor. As Saint John says, "If anyone says, I love God, but does not love his neighbor, that person is a liar. Because if a person does not love the neighbor whom he sees, how can he say he loves God, whom he does not see?" which is another way of saying that the vertical dimension of religion—which means attention to God and is the primary push of religion—necessarily includes the horizontal dimension.

In other words, my neighbor is my way to God, so, that love of neighbor immediately shows that I love God. So, from the point of view of religious freedom, with reference to my neighbor, nobody should use force on me . . . although we must lament that there are parts of the world today where religious freedom—the exercise of that right—is not freely allowed to all the citizens, but only to some. That is a cause of a lot of tension, suffering, and even martyrdom.

But I also moved further to say that, in universities, religious indifferentism must not be regarded as a sign of liberalism, as a sign of free thinking, as a sign of an individual who has been emancipated. I said that great minds such as John Henry Newman and G. K. Chesterton, not to mention Thomas Aquinas or Augustine or Don Scotus—who will say that these are not great luminaries and a credit to mankind? For them religion wasn't something peripheral, additional, marginal, something you do if there is time. For them religion was so much of what gives sense and meaning and synthesis to life, a sense of direction.

I also mentioned the necessity of the chaplaincy for a particular religion in a university, so that while we would not expect a state university to be the one to educate and form the students in their religious communities specifically . . . although there would be some universities that from their origins were identified with one religious family, and then they would obviously have a faculty of theology of that religion. If there is the University of Ankara, and the Muslims saw it as a scientific articulation of what they believe, we would not be surprised if they would have a faculty of Islamic theology. If there is a pontifical university—Gregorian, Angelicum, Lateran, Urbanianum, and Antonianum—nobody is surprised that they have a faculty of Catholic theology. But there were also universities that were not set up by a specific religious community, but they are there—people of any religion can come there. Although in the universities of Oxford and Cambridge the monks figured very much in the earlier days, nevertheless, these universities are open to people of any religion, but a particular religion can have a chaplain there, and that chaplain has an important role, such as the two chaplains who invited me.

Their role would be to ensure, not only for the students of their religious communities, but also for the professors, the lecturers, the other staff—administrative and so on of the universities, because a university is really a town—to ensure for them a center of reflection, a center of prayer, a center in which they strive to make a synthesis of the various areas of learning with the light of their faith poured on all that.

A Catholic chaplain, for example, has to help the students to have a Catholic faith view of their entire university effort—studies, subjects—a philosophy of life inspired by their religion, which acts as a unifying spiritual view. In that way the student grows not only in mathematics, literature, science, physics, but also in the faith, so that the university graduate, when formed and now working outside, is not caught in an imbalance between growth in the faith and growth in his university speciality. That's very important. The university chaplaincy therefore will act practically as a parish, whether it is called that or not; the people pray there, they get their children baptized, they have Mass, but also they have lectures—not only from Catholics, but also from others, and they strive to make a synthesis so that their view on the whole field of learning has a type of unified assessment.

Q. *What particularly struck you at Oxford University and in Cardiff University?*

A. I was very interested in being taken around to see the various colleges, and not only the Catholic chaplains. It was not possible to meet all the officials, but I met many, including those who came for the lectures or for the Mass, or through the students.

What struck me most is the devotion, almost affection, that the students have for their college in Oxford. Even when they have left it five years ago, or twenty years ago, that affection remains. So that, for example, Prince Hassan El Talal of Jordan was in Assisi on January 24, and when he heard I was going to Oxford the following day, he asked me, "Are you going to speak in my college?" *My* college. So he has that affection, maybe he was there thirty or forty years ago. This sense of belonging is very strong.

And they explained to me that the colleges are not the university; they are units, and from the various colleges they go to the central place for lectures, and the exams are central. And the colleges have tutors and those who help you, but they are not the central lecturers—they could also be that, but they are not primarily that—but they are the place into which you are inserted. Everybody must be a member of a college, and from the college you are oriented to the bigger university. It's very fascinating. The Benedictine Fathers run one of the colleges, and I was staying there.

Q. *What impressed you most about the students?*
A. They work hard, and they also—in the college, Saint Bennett's Hall—they shared in the prayer with the monks, as far as was possible for the students, and they attended Mass, of course. But there was no pressure. The students' life is a very busy one, and they have to go up and down for this, for that.

But they did come for the talks, and they took the papers, and they were discussing it all. One of the interesting things was that, after the talk, when they should be gone, they stayed in little groups discussing it. That is a sign of interest.

Q. *Did you focus on belief in God as the central element of your lectures?*
A. Not really belief in God as the central element, but the fact that there are many religions, and what should the university do about it? I put the emphasis on why the university person should take religion seriously: that he should have a clear religious identity, and then he would be in a position to relate to people of other religions.

I also dwelt on the importance of one's religious identity and said that you cannot be an ambassador of your religious community if you are not a member in good standing in that community. A country does not send as an ambassador a citizen who has forgotten the name of the minister for foreign affairs and cannot distinguish the flag of his country among three other flags. There would be something wrong with that citizen; he would not be the ideal person to be sent as an ambassador.

It was important to stress that, because there is so much relativist thinking today. That is, people think that the fact that there are many religions is a sign that we should not emphasize any; that we should just wish everybody well, and that down, down, deep down the religions are saying the same thing, and that there's not much difference between them, and that therefore it does not really matter to which religion a person belongs. All these are very dangerous and erroneous opinions, and they would damage a Christian definitely, if a Christian held those views.

Obviously, also, people asked me about the Assisi celebration, and it was important to explain it so that no Catholic would be thinking that it meant that the Holy Father is saying that there is no difference between the religions. Most people would know that.

Q. *After Oxford, you went on to Cardiff University in Wales. What did you do there?*

A. In Cardiff the central event was also a lecture in the university. They showed great interest; the vice chancellor of the university was also there. The topic, however, was a bit different from that in Oxford. It read: "In a World of Growing Religious and Cultural Diversity, the Role of the University." Not only religious diversity, but cultural.

I was also very impressed by the minister of state for Wales, coming all the way from London to chair the lecture. He showed great interest. Then most of the important university people were there, with the vice chancellor leading. So that was already very encouraging. Then the student body attendance was also high, and the discussion was beautiful. So even though it was a long day for me, I liked it.

And because also there is a strong Muslim community there, the Muslims came to meet me in the chaplaincy, separately, and gave me a gift. And for a long time we discussed Christian–Muslim relations around the world.

Then, there could not but be a word on fundamentalism. Everybody thinks of September 11. We discussed it; that obviously it is not religion. There are other reasons. If a person is a good Muslim, he will not kill another person. The Qur'an itself says, "Your religion for you, my religion for me. There is no compulsion in religion." Many Christians do not know that the Qur'an says that, so that if a person promotes violence, killing other people, to that extent he is not a good Muslim. I think it's either in the Qur'an, or it is one of their traditions—Hadith—which tells the Muslims, "If you kill one person, you kill all of mankind." So that's very important. No serious Muslim leader approves of violence. Those who promote violence are actually an embarrassment for the more moderate members of their religion. This is so in every religion.

There was great interest shown by the people. That was one event in Cardiff.

There was another event in Cardiff that I should not forget to mention. It lasted for about two hours; it was an ecumenical meeting of the Christian leaders from all parts of Wales. It was an existing association—they didn't come together because of me. They are an existing association of Catholics, Church of Wales members, Methodists, and all the other Christian religious bodies there. They came, and I spoke, for a short time, on what inter-religious dialogue is all about and why the Catholic Church is interested in it. Then for more than one hour there was very fruitful discussion.

One of the questions they asked me was this: they said that they as Christian religious leaders are thinking of inaugurating an Inter-religious Council for Wales, meaning a group that people of other religions could join, especially the Muslims. They asked me what advice had I to give them. I encouraged them to do that. I said, ecumenical cooperation is already a positive move; because the more Christians can speak with one voice the better will be our approach to people of other religions. Also when there is an inter-religious council, they should not think that it is to play down our religious identity, for the reasons I already gave, because it is only when we know who we are that we can, without risk, meet other people.

Therefore inter-religious courtesy does not ask us to hide our religious identity, or even to put it in parentheses for the moment. No, no. We will not be aggressive, but we will not deny who we are. For example, I have noticed that some Catholic priests, some religious sisters, think that in meeting people of other religions they should not dress in a way that will identify them as Catholic priests or religious sisters. That is a mistake, theological and psychological. It's a mistake. Theological, because we are witnesses of Christ, and when we do inter-religious dialogue we are actually doing it as witnesses of Christ. So we don't hide who we are. We are not aggressive, but we are not secretive. Psychological error, because we are sort of telling the other person, don't bother about my being a Catholic; it's not very important. So we should just meet the other person as we are.

I will never forget when I visited a Buddhist monastery in Taiwan. The monastery was on a hill. It was a very hot day, and it took us two hours to get there, and when I reached there I asked for a room to change in. I put on my white cassock, cross, and zucchetto, and everything else. When I came out the monks and nuns beamed with joy. You could see them joyful, and I was with them for the better part of two or three hours. We had lunch together too. Then when I was going away—we were going to a railway station to take a train—I asked for a room, and I changed back to my clericals. They were sad, and they asked me, "Why are you changing?" And when two of the monks came to Rome, I invited them for supper, and they came, all down the Via Della Conciliazione right to my house, in their flowing yellow robes. Normal. This is really normal. We should meet people as we are.

But the meeting with the other [Christian] religious leaders, I thought was very fruitful.

Another dimension of my visit was the meeting with the students because, after all, they were the main reason for the visit. It was especially at Mass, both in Oxford and Cardiff, at the chaplaincies, that I met the students; and afterward, informal communication—which is sometimes better than formal communication. I thought that was good. The fact that they were in no hurry to go away was good; it was a sign of their interest.

Q. *What did you deduce from the level of the questions you got from the students?*

A. It showed their interest, and it showed their commitment. They were committed to our Catholic faith; they were also anxious to see what it is to believe in the world of today. They asked about the Assisi event and what it means. They asked about religion and extremism in the world today.

They also asked what can be done in the realm of prayer when people of many religions come together. Can they have an inter-religious prayer? I explained that to the extent that prayer is based on faith, to the extent that we believe in the same thing, we can have the same prayer. That is why the Christians in Assisi had ecumenical prayer, since as Christians we believe in God—Father, Son, and Holy Spirit; Jesus, Son of God, Redeemer of all mankind, who has spoken through the prophets, so the Old Testament books, the New Testament books. Therefore to that extent we can pray together.

It is interesting—many Christians don't think of it—but with the Jews also we can pray together because, you see, the Book of Psalms is Jewish Scripture. There are so many beautiful prayers the Jews formulate, and I can just say "Amen" to the whole of it.

When you go then to Muslims, you see you are widening now, and so it is becoming more difficult. Therefore, on major occasions it is better to allow each religion to pray separately, according to its own authentic way.

Q. *But the question is this: Can Christians pray with Muslims, since they both believe in the One God?*

A. The answer is not so simple. When it is a formal occasion like Assisi, we prefer that you pray on your own, and we pray on our own. If it is an informal occasion, say like a meeting, and the chairman of the meeting asks somebody to say a prayer in the beginning and asks another person to say a prayer to conclude, it's not a formal one. The person asked could formulate a prayer that would respect what the two parties believe. That would be all right. But when it is a formal occasion, like Assisi, or if it is a national day of thanksgiving or something similar, then if you have a common prayer you could be suggesting that the two religions believe the same thing. It can lead many people into error; it would be better then to have separate prayers.

There are other ways. Sometimes people ask a Muslim, please formulate a prayer from your religious community; they ask a Christian, please formulate a prayer: that is how we did ten days ago, when we went to New York for the World Economic Forum, and the religious leaders—the forty of us invited—we went to Ground Zero to pray. And there, there was no inter-religious prayer, but one representative from each major religious family was asked to pray for about two minutes—a prayer written out before. So a Catholic, an Orthodox, and an Anglican—the archbishop of Canterbury—were there.

Q. *Did one of you say the prayer for all the Christians?*

A. No. The Archbishop of Canterbury said the prayer for the Anglicans. I was asked to say the prayer for the Catholics, and there was another leader for the Orthodox too—so the three Christian religious families.

Then there was a Jew, of course, and a Muslim, a Hindu. Was there a Buddhist? I don't think so. Each of them made a prayer, and the others stood in reverent attention, without trying to offer that same prayer. There was also a moment of silence at Ground Zero, when each one prayed.

A similar thing happened when we had the forum here in the Vatican, on January 23, 2002, on the eve of the Assisi meeting. Then, our pontifical council invited people of other religions to the synod hall for three hours, to speak, to say what their religion teaches about peace, justice and peace. As for prayer, what I did was this: in the beginning, I said, "Please, could we have silent prayer for a few minutes?" The same thing at the end, without trying to formulate a prayer for everyone.[4]

Q. *Surely, that was something good.*
A. What we should not do is to act as if all the religions believe the same thing and can have the same prayer. Well, that's not theologically exact.

Q. *I interviewed Cardinal Paul Shan Kuo-hsi, of Taiwan, after the Assisi meeting, and we spoke about the fact that there was no formal prayer at that event. His response was interesting; he said: "Well, our first prayer was a common prayer. We were there together. The deepest desire is the deepest prayer, and we shared the common desire for peace, and since that is in conformity with the will of God, and inspired by the Spirit, that was our unspoken common prayer."*
A. Yes. God must bless the gathering of people standing before him; the human soul seeking contact with God, according to the religious equipment that that person is accustomed to. We must respect everyone who in that way strives to make contact with God.

For those Christians who are scandalized, and say, "Why did the Pope invite people of other religions to Assisi?" they have to consider it carefully. The Holy Father wants to respect every human soul who is looking for contact with God. That is not the same as saying that one

---

[4] In 2002, the Pontifical Council for Inter-Religious Dialogue published the book *Peace: A Single Goal and A Shared Intention*, which gives a full report on this inter-religious meeting held in the Vatican, January 23, 2002, and on the major inter-religious event in Assisi, January 24, 2002.

religion is as good as another. No. But it is saying that for every man who is seeking contact with God, we want to show respect. And then the Holy Father has written that every genuine prayer has somehow the hand of the Holy Spirit in it.

Saint Paul tells us, we do not know how to pray; it is the Holy Spirit who teaches us how to pray, every genuine prayer. There are some elements of some prayers we cannot agree with, so care is needed. But, what is certain is that we must rejoice that so many people want to pray. We should thank God for that.

Q. *Before I move on to other questions, is there something else you want to say about your visit to Oxford and Cardiff?*

A. Yes, I want to praise the bishops of Wales. All three bishops were present at all the events when I was there for the two days, the archbishop of Cardiff and the two other bishops. They were present at all the events: the supper at the student chaplaincy, the lecture at the university, the meeting with the religious leaders. They were there. The only event at which they were not present was my meeting with the Muslims.

This was very good, because the bishops not only showed interest but also involvement. After all, I was visiting for only two days, and it was to encourage and contribute to the effort of the local Church. By the bishops taking part in everything, it was the best thing that could be said. And to make it better still, the archbishop arranged a Mass in his cathedral. All of us went there on the last day, at midday. We celebrated Mass in the cathedral. There were very many people and a beautiful choir. So all those are reasons to thank God. Sometimes, the newspapers write only when there is something negative. There are so many happy things that happen that never get reported.

Q. *I understand the bishop did not come to the meeting in Oxford, as he was in the hospital, undergoing surgery.*

A. The bishop was not in good health—Archbishop Nichols of Birmingham. I know that. But he wrote to me earlier to say that he was in full support. I knew he was not well. Then many of his priests were there. Oh, yes, many. Indeed there was one supper where I met many of the priests, purposely invited by the chaplain. So it was good.

Q. *I get the overall impression that you felt it was really worthwhile going to Oxford and Cardiff for these events.*

A. Yes, and I thanked the two chaplains, because they had arranged all this.

Q. *Is there anything else you would like to say before we move on to another issue?*

A. There is one little point, about Oxford and Cardiff. I was discussing privately with the chaplains in both places, and I was saying that I can see that in Britain the word "inter-faith" has caught on and has become very popular. In continental Europe the usual term is *inter-religious*.

For us, in the Pontifical Council for Inter-Religious Dialogue, we prefer *inter-religious*; our reason is that in the Catholic tradition the word "faith" has a specific meaning, and we are not sure that you could call every religion a faith. But I realize that in popular English "inter-faith" has caught on, but if a person wanted to use a more exact word, I would advise "inter-religious" rather than "inter-faith".

Q. *As a writer on the subject, I notice that the word "inter-faith" seems to be more in vogue in the English-speaking world.*

A. Yes, but neither French nor Italian nor German would say that. It's a word people use without thinking; in the last ten years this word has caught on, and I don't think it would be easy to change it. But, as I see it, the more exact word is "inter-religious". Suppose I meet the Buddhists; well, we just prefer to say "inter-religious". But this is not a point I would like to fight about.

Q. *If you have time, Your Eminence, perhaps you could tell me something about your participation in the World Economic Forum in New York?*

A. The Economic Forum is really a meeting of businessmen and business women initiated by Professor Klaus Schawb. It has been going now for more than thirty years. These people meet; they contact one another. They have plenary sessions; they have workshops galore, so that each individual can choose which one he wants. But it isn't only people in business; they also invite people in government—some heads of government, some presidents, some kings, such as the king of Jordan. It seems that so far they had been inviting few religious leaders, but last year, 2001, in Davos, they invited more religious leaders than usual, maybe up to ten or fifteen.

Q. *Were you among those invited to the Davos meeting in 2001?*

A. No, not last year. I was not there in 2001, but I was invited and attended in the year 2000. At that time, we were the only two religious leaders who were invited.

Q. *Who was the other religious leader?*

A. One from Cairo, from Al-Azhar, a professor. They invited the Sheik Al-Azhar, who is the highest authority in Sunni Islam, but he could not come, so he sent one of their professors. Then we met principally with heads of state—with the president of Germany, Doctor Rau, at the head. He invited heads of countries around the Mediterranean, mainly to discuss Christian–Muslim relations. That was in February 2000. But in 2002, February again—the first four days—this time they invited up to forty representatives of the various religions; not only Christian, but also Jewish, Muslim, and Hindu.

The idea behind involving religious leaders, I think, is to hear from them about the ethical and religious dimensions of the responsibilities of businessmen. It was not easy to reject their invitation, because here are people in business appreciating that ethics and religion do have something to say to them. The people of various religions felt a type of obligation to attend.

Not everybody who was invited could come, but from the Catholic side there were the archbishop of Washington, Theodore Cardinal McCarrick, and Archbishop Diarmuid Martin, representative of the Holy See in Geneva, and myself. There were some priests too, but I would not know all of them, though I remember one priest who is a professor in Chicago and another from a country in Latin America.

The religious leaders did not take part in all the events the businessmen took part in, because obviously the interests would be different. There were some sessions for the religious leaders only. There were some plenary sessions where the religious leaders were encouraged to attend and speak. And there was one plenary session where the religious leaders met the whole assembly, and it was in the form of—you could call it—a symposium; Professor Schwab posed questions to each of the seven religious leaders invited, moving back and forth, and the assembly asked questions too.

Q. *Were you one of those seven religious leaders?*

A. I was.

Q. *What was your impression?*

A. My impression was that we must thank those who originated the idea; both the idea of business people meeting and the idea of involving people of religion in some form. It is not clear to me in what form it should continue, but that it should continue in some form to involve people of religion I have no doubt. In what form, I am not sure whether it is ideal that it be a Catholic bishop or cardinal, or whether perhaps it may not be better that it is a Catholic layman who is, perhaps, a professor in theology or economics or sociology. It can be debated. I am not sure which is better, but I am sure that someone who is not only a Catholic by name but lives our religion and is willing to share with business people reflections on religious and ethical dimensions of business life should be present to fulfill that role, and so for other religions.

Q. *Was it the ethical question or was it the peace question that was at the heart of the presentation of the religious leaders?*

A. The program was very rich, and therefore many, many such concerns figured. Peace, of course, could not but figure, because after all the forum was held each year in Davos, a place high up in the mountains in Switzerland, where in February it snows. And the only difference is more snow; you would see nothing except white, including the rooftops; everything was covered in snow. I was there once, in the year 2000. They moved it to New York in 2002 because of September 11. That's clear, and so peace could not but figure; justice and peace, and terrorism. Why terrorism? What can be done? You see, their business touches sociology and touches ethics and touches religion because life is of one piece.

Then they could not ignore the fact that another meeting was taking place at the same time in Pôrto Alegre, Brazil. That would be like a meeting of those who are poor, while the one in New York was of those who are rich. And they were not disconnected: a person like Mary Robinson—the former Irish president and now U.N. High Commissioner for Human Rights—she had attended the meeting in Pôrto Alegre and moved on to that in New York. The witness of such a person is precious. Then many bishops and other religious people said their hearts were in both; they could not condemn either, because the people at both of them were created by God. The rich people, the businessmen, are also God's children, and we must not abandon them.

There were also protesters outside the Waldorf-Astoria Hotel, but they were kept at a certain distance, but they too are human beings and they also have something to say. One bishop said to me that his heart was with the protesters. All that is healthy. I also walked outside, not that I joined the protesters, but I looked at them and at what they were carrying. And I went to the nearby church, Saint Patrick's Cathedral, so I could not but see them.

There were also heads of governments who spoke; I would not know all of them. Nor did I take part in many of the plenary events because the program was very full, from morning to ten or eleven at night.

Q. *Yes, I have seen the program; it was really full.*

A. There were plenty of choices for the workshops. Indeed, where I wanted to join, they told me the room was full—it was where Samuel Huntington was speaking.[5] He was there but I could not get in because I didn't register in time; it was full. So I went to another one. But there were many choices like that, excellent workshops, and you would like to attend four of them at the same time, but you can't. And there were meetings on regions, the Middle East, Northern Ireland, Latin America, parts of Africa, and so on. The program was very rich.

Q. *Did you feel that some of the real issues were touched on, such as the questions of justice, resolving conflicts, the clash of civilizations, and so forth?*

A. Well, it was not a seminar on moral theology or pastoral theology, and you could not expect that they would put in all the things that I would like for them to put in. They could not put in all of them; after all, they were really business people who came primarily to see how best to promote their business.

For instance, I met one person, I will not tell you who; we were sitting together in the bus as we went to Ground Zero, and I asked him, "Who are you?" He said he was the president or chief executive officer of one of these international corporations. I asked him, "What do you get from these five days?" He said, "Well, you see, I can meet many of my colleagues in a very short time here. I can also meet heads of govern-

---

[5] The U.S. scholar Samuel P. Huntington published a seminal article, in the summer of 1993, in the journal *Foreign Affairs*, entitled "The Clash of Civilizations?", which he developed into a book in 1996, *The Clash of Civilizations and The Remaking of World Order*, published in the U.K. by Simon & Schuster. In the article and the book, he speaks of the likelihood of such a clash in the coming years; his thinking gained new adherents following the attacks in the U.S.A. on September 11, 2001.

ments and presidents of countries who visit here, whereas if I had to ask for an interview and go to their countries it would take much more time. I would attract the journalists' interest and so on, it would not be so easy, but here it is quick, effective, and not too expensive." That's what he came for. How can you blame him? He has to promote his company. But then, while he was there he would meet people like me, too, who have a different angle of interest, and that's the healthy part of it. They would choose then what item they want or don't want.

Q. *What question did they put to you in the plenary session?*
A. I was asked the question of religious freedom. And I had no difficulty in speaking on that, much as what we were discussing earlier—respect for other religions also must mean leaving each one free to practice the religion he wants. I answered also that religious freedom must mean reciprocity, so that the right to religious freedom is not valid only in Europe and in North America, but also in the Arabic countries and other places all round the world. That it also means that a person who is an extremist is unjust to other people because he is not allowing them freedom. And that person is also unjust to the moderate members of his own religious community, because the extremists are an embarrassment not only to people of other religions but also to people of their own religion who are moderate.

But they also asked questions on religion and life, and on business ethics. They didn't ask me in particular; they asked the panel. I remember one question on business affairs: the archbishop of Canterbury, Doctor George Carey, took it up because that company is being investigated in the United States.

Q. *You mean Enron?*
A. Yes. It was the news on the front page of the papers at that time, and still is. So he said that's an example of where ethical and religious considerations have to come into business life, otherwise we all suffer.

Q. *During the economic forum you went to Ground Zero. What were your feelings as you stood there?*
A. My feelings . . . well, I had visited it at Christmastime, because I was in Newark, New Jersey, for Christmas, and I had asked to go there, so a second visit was very welcome to me. I felt, "How can people devise such evil?", because the number of people who died was just

unbelievable. They told me it wasn't only people in the upper floors who died—because those very tall buildings had many floors underground, and there was also a railway station underground and shops and people below. So the amount of damage was unbelievable.

To pray there was not too difficult. Indeed, I can give you a copy of the prayer that I offered there. The disaster brought people together in Ground Zero. One person in his prayer called it Ground Hero; the amount of bravery people showed; that Catholic chaplain who died administering the sacraments to another is just a model of one.

Indeed, I visited the New York Police Department office when I visited there at Christmas, and they gave me one of their caps and a miniature of the Twin Towers. They also gave me a miniature of the Twin Towers to give to the Holy Father, which I did. And they got back a letter of thanks.

Suffering does bring people together, and in a big country like the United States, where there is material well-being, I do not say there are not poor people there, but there is material well-being. The Twin Towers were a symbol of prosperity. And the United States is a country where it is known that in public places they wouldn't allow prayers in school and so on. I asked someone, "Do people after September 11 take another look at that stand?" September 11 shows us how weak we can be, even in the strongest country in the world, and that we actually need God perhaps even more than we realize. The person told me, "Yes, many are thinking in that light, even though nothing major has changed; but people are paying more attention to God."

As for the disaster of September 11, we don't want anything like that to happen again, but if it has helped many more people to think of God, that's good.

Suffering, however, remains very difficult to explain. We must not pretend that we can explain it all, because there are also people—we do not forget—who because of suffering tend to ask, Where is God? Where was God on September 11? Not that there is no answer.

I have read that people said: God was there because if it had happened three hours later the number of people in the Twin Towers—the number of visitors alone—would have been much higher. God was there, because there are many who could have been killed, but they were not killed. God was there because many people showed wonderful heroism. God was there because many people gave their lives for other people and showed great love. God was there because many of the people in the two aircraft that crashed there, their last words with their loved ones were words their loved ones will never forget. There are some values in life that are more than material things. Therefore it is not right to ask, Where was God on that day? He was right there.

Q. *I was struck some time back by a comment made by Juan Cardinal Sandoval Iñiguez, archbishop of Guadalajara, Mexico, when I interviewed him.*[6] *He told me he saw September 11 as "the first big protest" from the injustice in the world.*

A. That's an anger that we cannot forget. It doesn't justify the terrible deed, but it can help to understand it. A hungry person easily becomes an angry person, and even if the person who organized it—whoever that may be—may not have been a poor person, it could well be that he was angry because of seeing so many people suffering.

Indeed, soon after September 11, many people, not only I, many people said, "When will the Palestinians get their own state?" and "When will the relations between the Palestinians and Israelis be normalized?" Would normalcy between two of them, with the Palestinian state set up, would that not bring down the temperature in the international arena? If, however, the Palestinian question is not settled and this spiral of violence continues, do we think there will be peace in the world? Do we think we shall be more secure?

Could you tell me how many bombs we will drop, and then there will be peace? Remember that President Bush told the world last year that terrorists were identified in sixty countries. Will bombs be dropped on sixty countries? Also it seems that some terrorists are inside the United States. You see the complications?

This means that all of us cannot avoid asking ourselves the deeper questions: What could be the combination of events that drives people to extreme solutions? What could explain how young men who are engineers, who are not even very poor themselves, who can pilot an airplane, would be ready to die, provided they kill many others? Is that not really a reason to make us stop and begin to think? Shall we solve it by dropping bombs?

I am not denying what is called self-defense, but we cannot avoid asking ourselves deeper questions. After all, when all is said and done, there is also the question of original sin, evil. There are some people

---

[6] I interviewed him during the Synod of Bishops, held in Rome, October 2001.

who, even if they have enough money and they have a good job and a house, they will still steal and kill people.

But what is not to be doubted is that if there is oppression, repression, if there is imperialism, if there are unjust economic systems, if there is violence between states and between peoples, then we are all insecure, all of us. It gives all of us something to think about.

Q. *Was that kind of thinking floating around in the World Economic Forum?*

A. I do not know to what extent. I must not pretend that in four days everybody got converted or that the religious leaders were preaching every day. Not really! However, our very presence there delivered some minimal message, and who knows what ways it can be continued in future.

It also brought people of the religions together, many of them had met one another before, but it encouraged even more action, more so since many initiatives have been taken in inter-religious collaboration to promote justice and peace since September 11, 2001.

I think immediately of three major initiatives by Christian leaders in this direction: the ecumenical patriarch of Constantinople, Bartholomew I, called a major meeting in Brussels in December 2001, which I attended, and which brought together Christians, Jews, and Muslims; then the archbishop of Canterbury, Doctor George Carey, also called a major Christian–Muslim meeting, in Lambeth Palace, London, in January 2002; and he called another one in Alexandria, the same month, which brought together Christians, Muslims, and Jews.

Then, of course, there was the initiative of Pope John Paul II at Assisi on January 24, 2002, not three religions now, but most of the major religions in the world. All of these are more or less in the same direction—justice and peace, or, as the Pope summarized in his January 1 Message for the World Day of Peace 2002, "There is no peace without justice, there is no justice without forgiveness."

Q. *You have written a new book,* Religions for Peace: A Call for Solidarity to the Religions of the World,[7] *that is highly relevant for the present moment in the wake of these events and the subsequent discussion. Was that book distributed at the World Economic Forum?*

---

[7] Francis Cardinal Arinze, *Religions for Peace: A Call for Solidarity to the Religions of the World* (New York: Doubleday, January 2002). It has already been translated into Italian.

A. I made no effort at selling it, but since it was Doubleday who published it and that publisher is resident there, I left it to them. I do not know whether they distributed it. I have no idea.

Q. *You have spoken about a number of significant events in the religious field that have taken place since, and mainly as a result of, September 11, 2001. As you analyze these initiatives, do you perceive a real awakening among religious leaders today, a growing awareness among them, that they have a greater contribution to make, a bigger role to play, than perhaps they had been conscious of before September 11, 2001?*

A. Not that the religious leaders did not know they have a role— they knew. But the events encouraged the religious leaders to do more, and also the events enabled other people, such as business people, to listen just a little more to the religious leaders. That is, the events of September 11 made business people and government leaders appreciate a little more the role of religion as a contributor to justice and peace in the world. It is not a new doctrine, but it is an awareness encouraged by the events.

Chapter 20

The Only African Cardinal
in the Vatican

The year 2002 opened at a hectic pace for Cardinal Arinze, as we have seen in the previous chapter, and the pace did not slacken throughout the following months, but as the year entered its last quarter it brought a new and unexpected change in the cardinal's role and life in the Vatican.

From February to September, his mission to promote dialogue and harmonious relations between the Catholic Church and the major world religions had taken him to countries in Africa, Asia, Europe, North America, and the Middle East. But as he traveled, he always found time to speak to Catholic audiences, to explain to them the importance of inter-religious dialogue, particularly at this turbulent moment in human history.

At the end of July, he traveled to Toronto, Canada, to participate in the seventeenth World Youth Day, presided over by Pope John Paul II. The event attracted more than one hundred thousand young people from seventy-five countries, while a quarter of a million people attended the closing ceremonies. He had been invited as one of the keynote speakers at the English language catechetical sessions.

I was present for his conference on the third and final day of the World Youth Day catechesis, and I listened to him speak as a pastor, with passion and simplicity, to ten thousand young people, from all continents, on the theme of "Conversion, Reconciliation and Peace".[1] There, I witnessed his extraordinary ability to communicate and inspire the young, not only through his prepared talk, but especially by the profound, down-to-earth, and humorous way in which he responded to their many questions. They responded enthusiastically and, at the end, gave him a prolonged standing ovation.

---

[1] This was on July 26, 2002, when the cardinal gave his talk, took questions, and celebrated Mass for the young people.

A few weeks later, in August, he published a small book in which he developed the theme that has run through all these interviews—Divine Providence or, as he likes to put it, the Invisible Hand of God at work in the lives of individuals and in the history of the world.[2]

In September, this tireless traveler was visiting countries in Asia, on what proved to be his last official mission as president of the Pontifical Council for Inter-Religious Dialogue. He was actually in Suwon, South Korea, attending a meeting (September 24–27) of the Pontifical Council's Asian consultors and the secretaries of the National Episcopal Commissions for Inter-Religious Dialogue in Asia, when he received an unexpected telephone call from the Vatican, informing him that Pope John Paul II wished to appoint him head of one of the major Vatican offices and asking him to return to Rome immediately.[3]

On October 1, 2002, two days after his return to Rome, the Vatican announced that the Pope had appointed him prefect of the Congregation for Divine Worship and the Discipline of the Sacraments. It was yet another significant, unsought-for change in his life. The Pope was calling him from the mission of dialogue with the followers of the major world religions to a post that required a great ability to dialogue with those inside the Catholic Church. As we shall see later in this chapter, he accepted all this with great inner peace, reading it as yet another instance of the invisible hand of God at work in his own life.

The staff of the Pontifical Council for Inter-Religious Dialogue had long planned a celebration for him on his seventieth birthday, with the presentation of a book in his honor.[4] *The celebration, however, did not take place on his birthday, November 1; it was held instead on December 17, 2002, at the Pontifical Urban University, where he had once studied, and actually ended up as a farewell party, chaired by his long-time friend, Roger Cardinal Etchegaray.*[5]

At the beginning of 2002, there were two African cardinals in the Vatican, Bernardin Cardinal Gantin, dean of the College of Cardinals, and Francis Cardinal Arinze, but by the year's end there was only one. Having reached the age

---

[2] Francis Cardinal Arinze, *Divine Providence* (All Hallows Seminary, Onitsha, Nigeria: Saint Stephen's Press Inc., August 2002).

[3] A report on his visit to South Korea was later published by the Pontifical Council for Inter-Religious Dialogue, *Bulletin* 112, 2003/1, pp. 96–102.

[4] *Milestones in Inter-Religious Dialogue: Essays in Honour of Francis Cardinal Arinze, A Seventieth Birthday Bouquet,* edited by Chidi Denis Isizoh, with a preface by Bernardin Cardinal Gantin (Rome and Lagos: Ceedee Publications, 2002). It includes a bibliography of the cardinal's writings.

[5] The Pontifical Council for Inter-Religious Dialogue subsequently published all the talks given at the celebration in its review *Pro Dialogo, Bulletin* 112, 2003/1. My report on the celebration was published in *L'Osservatore Romano,* January 19, 2003.

of eighty, the much-loved Cardinal Gantin requested the Holy Father to accept his resignation and allow him to return to his native Benin, to spend the remainder of his life preaching the Gospel there. John Paul II reluctantly agreed, and the cardinal returned home in October. His departure meant that Cardinal Arinze was now the only African cardinal in the Roman Curia and the only African to head a Vatican office.

On December 11, 2002, two months after he had taken up his new post as prefect of the Congregation for Divine Worship and the Discipline of the Sacraments, I interviewed the cardinal one last time for this book. As on all previous interviews, he was very open and friendly and never once refused to answer a question, while his answers were often filled with good humor and laughter.

I began by asking him about his new appointment.

Q. *You were traveling in Asia, leading a delegation from the Pontifical Council for Inter-Religious Dialogue in September 2002, and you were actually in South Korea, when you were informed that the Holy Father had appointed you prefect for the Congregation for Divine Worship and the Discipline of the Sacraments, one of the main Vatican offices. When did you actually learn of this appointment? Did the news come as a surprise to you, or had you already some hint that this was in the wind?*

A. Well, the Holy Father, through one of his assistants, had asked me earlier, in April of this year, if I were assigned to the Congregation for Divine Worship and the Discipline of the Sacraments (CDW), whether I would accept? I said, "Yes, I would accept, just as I would accept any other appointment that the Holy Father would give me, any at all. So there is no need to ask whether I like or don't like, whether I accept or don't accept. I accept." They just raised the question in April, and after that I heard no more about it.

Then, in September, I was at a meeting in Suwon, South Korea, and intended to go from there to Japan, where very many events were scheduled, when I received a telephone call from the Secretariat of State. I was told that the Holy Father was going to transfer me and assign me to this congregation, and I was asked whether I would accept. I said yes, as I had said before. "In that case," I was told, "the Holy Father would suggest that you come back to Rome soon and cut short the Asian travel, so that you can be in Rome by the beginning of October."

I accepted that, rearranged my program and travel plans, and had to cut out the entire visit to Japan. The Japanese were not amused, as you might imagine, but I had no other choice. However, three other persons from the Council for Dialogue were traveling with me: Archbishop Michael L. Fitzgerald—my successor; Monsignor Felix Machado; and Father Linus Lee. These three members went on to Japan, as scheduled, and so the program was respected.

I returned to Rome and arrived here two days before the Vatican made the announcement on October 1, 2002. I had been informed that they would announce it on that day.

Q. *Were you surprised when they first raised the possibility of your transfer and assignment to this office?*

A. Well, my thoughts had not gone in that direction, because I was happy where I was working, in the office for inter-religious dialogue. I was making no speculation whatsoever. Yes, I was surprised in the sense that I had not even thought of it. Nevertheless, it did not disturb my sleep. I was calm in the sense that I saw it as God's will.

Q. *You have spent almost eighteen years of your life working to promote dialogue and harmony between the Catholic Church and the great religions of the world, seeking to cooperate with them and encourage them in the promotion of peace in the world. This new posting in the Congregation for Divine Worship is a very different task and provides you with a very different set of challenges. How do you understand, how do you reconcile, this transfer from the field of inter-religious dialogue to a vastly different area? It's a real change.*

A. Yes, that is true. I was named to the office of Inter-Religious Dialogue in 1984, and I actually began working there in September of that same year, so I was exactly eighteen years in that office. Obviously, there is a difference between the apostolate of the Church in Inter-Religious Dialogue and the apostolate of the Church in Divine Worship and the Discipline of the Sacraments. There is a big difference!

The work at inter-religious dialogue can be compared to that of an ambassador, meeting people of other countries; those working in the field of dialogue are ambassadors of the Church. They meet people of other religions, they try to understand those other believers, and they try to understand us, and we study what we can do together. So it's a work on the periphery—if I may use that word—on the boundaries, on the frontiers of the Church and, if I may say so, beyond the frontiers of the Church.

Inter-religious dialogue is beyond the frontiers of the Church; it is inter-religious work, whereas the work in the field of the office of Divine Worship is at the heart of Church life, because it is what the Church prays, it is what the Church lives.

The work in Divine Worship is at the heart of the Church's life, because the Church could not live without the sacraments, the Church could not live without divine worship. The Church exists in order to honor God the Father, the Son, and the Holy Spirit. The sacraments, therefore, are at the very heart of the Church, with the Holy Eucharist as the apex, the high point of Christian worship, and the center around which rotate all the other sacraments, the ministries of the Church, the apostolate of the lay faithful, and the life of the men and women religious; all rotate around the Holy Eucharist. The Holy Eucharist is central to the life of every Christian, not to mention the life of the bishop and priest.

Q. *And the Eucharist, of course, was the subject of your doctoral thesis here in Rome.*

A. You are right! In 1960, I wrote my thesis on sacrifice in the Traditional Religion of the Igbo people as a help toward catechesis of the Christian sacrifice in the Mass. Little did I know that I would finish up in this office!

Also, three years ago, the archabbot of Latrobe Benedictine Archabbey, in Pennsylvania, invited me to come and conduct some retreat conferences there, primarily for the friends of the monastery, but also for the monks, and he wanted it all focused on the Eucharist.

Q. *Is that the origin of your recent book on the subject?*

A. Yes. The archabbot, Douglas Nowicki, wanted the talks published as a book, and he told me that plainly before I wrote the talks. That is why he also wrote the introduction to the booklet, which was eventually published by Our Sunday Visitor, around Christmas 2000.[6]

But to return to your original question, yes, there is a big difference between the work here in the Congregation for Divine Worship and the work in the office for inter-religious dialogue. But we must nevertheless note that the same Church that worships God also meets other believers.

It's the same Church, and it's the same Second Vatican Council, which issued, in 1963, the document on the Liturgy, *Sacrosanctum Concilium,*[7] as its first document and, in 1965 during its last session, the document on dialogue, *Nostra Aetate.*[8] As you can see, the work of the

---

[6] Cardinal Francis Arinze, *The Holy Eucharist* (Huntington, Ind.: Our Sunday Visitor, 2000).

[7] The Constitution on the Sacred Liturgy, December 4, 1963.

[8] Declaration on the Relation of the Church to Non-Christian Religions, October 28, 1965.

Church is not just one single act, but it is still the same Church that acts in different ways; but there is no doubt that the perspectives are different.

Q. *In other words, you see your work as moving from that of a mission on the frontiers of the Church to a mission at the heart of the Church.*

A. Put in secular terms, yes!

Q. *But where is your heart? I ask this because I have watched you work in the field of inter-religious relations for many years; and you seemed so much at home there, I really felt your heart was in that work.*

A. Yes, my heart was in that work for dialogue, but now it is in this work of liturgy. It is the same Church, and I feel at home in both.

It is true that, after my appointment to this new office, some people in Nigeria, with whom I had worked as archbishop in that country for seventeen years, wrote to me and said, "You are in your element now; we know it." [*Laughs.*] That is, they noticed that I loved the liturgy when I was a priest and bishop in Nigeria, and it is true. And therefore, without asking me, they guessed that I might be happy in this particular work.

That is not an indication that this assignment is easy, but it is very much at the center of the Church's life and, therefore, at the center of everything I have loved in the Church.

Q. *Many people, when they saw your appointment to this congregation, said, "He's been engaged in dialogue outside the Church up to now, but now he'll have to promote dialogue within the Church, and there's a great need for such dialogue." Is that how you read it?*

A. You are right. People have written to me and said that they are confident that my experience of dialogue with other believers would be of great help to me in this office, because the work of this congregation very much includes contact with bishops throughout the world and with episcopal conferences, because the promotion of the sacred liturgy is crucial to the life of the Church. In the dioceses, the bishop is the moderator of the sacred liturgy by divine appointment. The bishop is the vicar of Christ for his diocese, therefore the organization of the worship of God is very much at the heart of what the bishop is there for in that place. The bishops of a given country, all together in the episcopal conference, have a very important role, too, in this matter. This is especially the case since the vernacular has been introduced in the liturgy. You can just imagine what it means in languages such as English, French,

German or Spanish, which are spoken in many countries, particularly English.

Now it matters very much how Holy Mother Church speaks English in Washington, D.C., in Toronto, in Dublin, in Edinburgh, and in London, but also in other places, such as Tokyo, New Delhi, Islamabad, Abuja, Canberra, Wellington, not to mention Dacca, Manila, and Jakarta. Here we are dealing with very different English usage, and it matters very much how the Church speaks in these places. Therefore, our office has to dialogue a lot on this matter.

It is true that our office also has to issue decisions in the name of the Holy Father, whereas in the office for dialogue with other religions we did not issue any decree at all: we had no authority over anybody; we only dialogued. But in this Congregation for Divine Worship, there comes a time when we have to make a decision, and this is decreed in the name of the Holy Father. For instance, we issue what is technically called a *recognitio*, that is, when a translation is to be used in the sacred liturgy in the name of Holy Mother Church, then this office has the duty to give it final approval.

It is not the duty of this congregation to translate the text; the bishops see to that, maybe through commissions they set up. And if the language is spoken in many countries, obviously it is in the interest of the whole Church that the bishops of all those countries join hands, have a mixed commission, which helps them arrive at a translation that would be acceptable on the lips of Holy Mother Church. Then, this congregation has to say finally, "Yes, we have looked at this in the name of the Holy Father", and we say, "Yes, that is liturgy; go on"—that is what is technically called *recognitio*. Or we might have to say, "We're sorry, you have to modify this or that word."

Q. *But it's basically a work of dialogue, trying to reach a consensus, even though the congregation has the final say.*

A. That is true. We're not here to act as commanding officers, ordering people around the place. Not at all! We are here to encourage the episcopate to produce the best translation when it comes to the vernacular, to look at the finished product and give the final approval to it.

You can just imagine if priests celebrate Mass in all those cities I mentioned around the world, and suppose they used different English in every one of them, how confusing it would be in a world where a person can be in Sydney yesterday and in London today. That's number one.

Number two. It isn't only a question of translation. The liturgy is primarily about the worship of God, but what the Church believes is also shown by how the Church worships. According to the directives of the Second Vatican Council, all the books that are used in the liturgy are to be reviewed, to make it easier for the people to participate and to make clear the various roles in the liturgy, that of the priest, the deacon, the choir, the faithful, and so on.

Then again, think of the various rites of the liturgy: baptism, confirmation, Holy Eucharist, forgiveness of sins. The discipline of the forgiveness of sins has to do with questions such as these: How do we confess our sins? How do we get forgiveness? Is it just one by one, as in individual confession, or can we absolve people all together in one gathering? This is a very delicate matter; it's something very serious from a theological point of view. Then our congregation has to consider the rites relating to the ordination of deacons, priests, and bishops; the actual rites themselves and the making of those rites, as well as the making of the rites for the blessing of an abbot, an abbess. Then it has to look at the rite for marriage: Will it vary according to the different countries?

Then there is the whole area of culture and worship. The Church today appreciates more and more the various cultures of the world, as Vatican II said in its Constitution on the Church, *Lumen Gentium*, no. 13,[9] where it says the Church does not destroy whatever the various peoples have that is true, noble, good, and beautiful, but assumes these. The Gospel story of the three wise men bringing their gifts to Christ is a symbol of the whole of mankind bringing the best of what they have to the Child Jesus. So, you see, the whole area of inculturation and liturgy also comes within our competence. It is not just a matter of translation; it is the actual text from the word "go" and the incorporation of the various cultures from all around the world. As you can see, it's a rather immense brief to oversee the proposals from the bishops' conferences.

Then the congregation has to watch out to ensure there are no abuses, because as long as you have human beings on earth, so long will you have people who fall short, people who will not follow the books, those who have their own funny ideas. For instance, there can be a priest who develops a funny idea on Saturday night, and on Sunday morning he

---

[9] The Dogmatic Constitution on the Church, November 21, 1964.

uses the people as guinea pigs to test his latest idiosyncratic concoctions: you can imagine the difficulties.

Q. In your work in the office for inter-religious dialogue, you told me you felt you were there to help and encourage the local bishops engage in dialogue with the other religions but not to substitute for them; you said you were there to work together with them and assist them to develop the best approach in dialogue with the different religions. Is this how you see your work here?

A. Yes. But there is also a difference. The difference is that in Divine Worship it isn't primarily the local Church that makes the fundamental texts, it is the universal Church, and this office has the major responsibility here. Think of the sacraments and the various rites I mentioned earlier, especially the Eucharistic celebration, the Mass. Now, it is not the local Church all around the world that will make its own rites, otherwise we would end up not recognizing the Latin Rite.

The texts will be made here, which does not mean just by our congregation; rather, our congregation has to take responsibility. But when the books for the rites are finally made and approved by the Holy Father, then it is up to the bishops around the world to ensure that the sacred rites are celebrated in each country according to the texts authorized by the Holy See. The bishops have the additional responsibility in matters touching culture, where the books foresee that the local Church could make a cultural adaptation under the usual Church laws; that is, these would have to be approved by Rome eventually.

There is therefore that difference between the work in this congregation and the work in the office for relations with other religions. But it is important to state here that there is no substituting for the local Church.

Q. I remember some years back, in an interview, you emphasized the importance of understanding the local cultures and the urgent need to do serious studies in this field so as to ensure that the whole process of inculturation of the Gospel be well thought-out, and that the riches of the local cultures be properly integrated into the liturgy at national and local levels. Is that how you still see it?

A. Yes, definitely.

Q. If I may return to another matter that we only touched on earlier, it is the whole question of the sacrament of reconciliation, or penance, as it was once called. It's no secret that some bishops and some episcopal conferences have requested that the Holy See give them the possibility for group absolution. This has been a thorny issue.

A. Yes.

Q. *Is the solution to this question to be worked out step-by-step with the episcopal conferences in the various countries, or how is it to be resolved?*

A. I'll try to answer your question in a few words, but anyone who wishes to have a broader understanding of the whole question should read the Holy Father's document of this year, *Misericordia Dei.*[10] One would have to read the relevant sections of the Code of Canon Law on this matter, as well as *Misericordia Dei*, but the long and the short of it is this.

Christ gave his Church the power to forgive sins, and the Church specifies in practice how the bishops and priests do this. Nobody except an ordained priest, or bishop, can forgive sins. The Church understands that the form in which this is done has changed through the centuries.

There are three forms known today: the first is the individual confession of sins—the individual confesses, and the priest gives him absolution—that is the ordinary, normal way. The second form consists in a general preparation of the people to repent of their sins, to resolve to do better, and, after a general rite of prayer and repentance, they go to the priest, one by one, for confession. There is also a third form known as "general absolution" or, to be more specific, absolution for a group, or collective absolution. The Church has very stringent conditions for that. The Church says when there is an emergency—such as the bombing of a city, or when a boat is sinking, or an aircraft is going to crash—and it is impossible for the people to go to confession one by one, then they can confess and the priest forgives them all together.

There is also another situation in a parish or diocese, where this third form can be used, but here the bishop of the diocese has to come in. It is the case where, in a parish or diocese, the gathering of the faithful is so great, the number of the faithful wanting to go to confession is so high, but there are so few priests present to hear their confessions that it would be impossible to hear them one by one, and the people would be left without forgiveness for a protracted length of time. This is not the

---

[10] Pope John Paul II's twelve-page document on the sacrament of reconciliation, *Misericordia Dei*, was published by the Vatican on May 2, 2002, and sets out norms for the celebration of this sacrament.

same situation as when a priest refuses to fix times for confessions, then Christmas or Easter comes and all the people want to go to confession, and he declares there is no opportunity for them to do so because he had not arranged times for confession during the previous four weeks when they could have come. That is an artificially created situation.

Obviously we cannot go into all the possible situations here; it is just sufficient to say that this third form is available, but there are stringent conditions for its use, and abuses can easily creep in. Some people think they will have it easier by being forgiven in a group, and so they don't go to confession individually. They should, however, reckon with one major condition; it is this: before their sins can be forgiven, even if there is an emergency, the individual must be prepared at the next available opportunity to confess personally every mortal sin, even those already forgiven. A person who is not really ready to confess his sins to the Church is, therefore, not forgiven. As you can see, this sort of thing entails both theology and canon law, and also watchfulness by the priests, bishops, and this congregation.

Q. *As I listen to you, it seems to me that, in terms of the internal life of the Church, your new assignment in Divine Worship is much more of a minefield than was your previous work in the area of inter-religious relations.*

A. To some extent, yes! You can see that this work touches many areas: doctrine, culture, liturgy, canon law, and the whole theology of religion and culture.

Q. *As you start this new work in the Congregation for Divine Worship, are there some goals you would like to realize? Are there some things in your heart that you feel you would like to be able to bring to the fore?*

A. Well, there are a few that I can mention.

First, to do whatever is possible to encourage love for divine worship in the Church. Fidelity to the approved rites by all those concerned, primarily it will be bishops, priests, but also the whole people of God, seeking to ensure that the rites approved by Holy Mother Church be faithfully followed. Many Catholics are upset, not because there is anything wrong in the rites but because the celebrant does not follow the book properly approved. That is the beginning of many sorrows.

Then, to encourage those who have to work hard to ensure that the Church also takes the cultures of various peoples seriously. This can be long-term, but it has to begin. To ensure that those who have to do this actually do it. It is very demanding; it will take time; but it has to be done.

Then that people also love the sacrament they have received. This office also has the unpleasant task of handling the situation, for example, of priests and deacons who are not living faithfully the life they have vowed and that they were consecrated to live. One of my prayers and hopes is that everyone may live much more fully this life to which we are consecrated, to the glory of God the Father, Son, and Holy Spirit. That is what this office is for!

Q. Some days ago, Her Majesty's ambassador to the Holy See gave a reception at the British Embassy in honor of Archbishop Michael L. Fitzgerald, your successor at the Pontifical Council for Inter-Religious Dialogue. Replying to Ambassador Colvin's toast, Archbishop Fitzgerald mentioned the fact that in the fifteen years he had worked with you, he had learned that the work of dialogue is not always about nice talking: sometimes it involves saying difficult things. But, he added, "Cardinal Arinze had the gift of being able to say even the most difficult things with a smile on his face; he always managed to say these things without ever offending other people."

A. [*Laughs.*] Well, nobody can be a judge in his own case! But I am convinced that this is the approach to adopt, because it is so easy to offend people because of the way we say things.

Q. Am I right in saying that you are the first African, not to mention Nigerian, ever to head this congregation?

A. Well, how many Africans have headed any office in the Vatican?

Q. I can only recall two, Bernardin Cardinal Gantin and you.

A. That's right. So it isn't a surprise in that sense, because we are so few. I am the only African now heading any office at the center.

Q. As you look over the past eighteen years, what abiding memories do you take with you from your work in the office for Inter-Religious Dialogue?

A. That it is worth it all. The Second Vatican Council made no mistake in its document on dialogue, *Nostra Aetate*; the Council's idea was right; it read history correctly. No matter what the difficulties, the Church does not regret her open-arms approach to other believers.

Something that could be said to summarize this approach was the gathering on January 24, 2002, when the Holy Father invited peoples of many religions to Assisi. It was a symbolic gesture, and it showed to people of goodwill that the followers of many religions can reflect together and can undertake together to make this world a better place in which to live.

Q. *So your experience over these past eighteen years has convinced you that the Second Vatican Council interpreted accurately this sign of the times?*

A. It did. It interpreted the signs accurately. The Council was not naïve; it was realistic, and it was courageous. It was optimistic in the sense of being courageous, because it made the decision knowing that some Catholics would find the idea of inter-religious dialogue difficult to digest and difficult to reconcile with the duty of the Church to preach Christ to the world. But the Council was also courageous and hopeful that, with time, people would see that the two activities are activities of the Church of Christ.

Q. *Now, thirty-seven years after Vatican II, would you agree that there is an even greater need for this dialogue between the religions than at the time of the Council? Would you say that it is even a greater priority now in the year 2002 than in 1965?*

A. It is a greater priority because, if anything, society today is more pluralistic than it was some forty years ago, when the Council first opened. Much has changed in the world today, compared to forty years ago. Intercontinental travel had started then, but there is far more now; there are more reasons for people to move from their home area today than at that time—work, the search for economic well-being, cultural and educational reasons too, as students seek out universities around the world, particularly in Europe and North America. People now study the various religions of the world much more than they did forty years ago, and serious studies are undertaken on this subject in such prestigious universities as Harvard, London, the Gregorian, and many more. Not long ago, a theologian and professor at one of the pontifical universities said, "You cannot do Catholic theology today without taking into serious account the religions of the world."

Q. *You would agree therefore that in this sense the Second Vatican Council was prophetic?*

A. It was prophetic, and in a sense courageous too.

Q. *As you reflect back on your work, over the past eighteen years, in the office for relations with the other religions, what would you identify as the biggest obstacles that you encountered?*

A. Sometimes prejudice on the part of those who are not Christians, and fear too. They think the Catholic Church has a hidden agenda, and so they are afraid. They are afraid of us; they think that we actually want to make all of them Catholics. Not that we don't want that, but we don't have it as a hidden agenda in our pocket. When we engage in dialogue, we mean what we say: we meet other believers, we seek to understand them, we listen to them, we try to work with them.

Then, there is foot-dragging on the part of some within the Church. Some Catholics think the Church has gone too far in meeting other believers, and they see in this the danger of being unfaithful to Christ. That is an obstacle too, but I think the number of such Christians is decreasing with the passing of time; they are coming to understand what the Congregation for the Evangelization of Peoples and the Pontifical Council for Inter-Religious Dialogue tried to say in their joint booklet, *Dialogue and Proclamation,*[11] namely, that it is not a question of either/or, because the Church wants both dialogue and proclamation. The same Council that issued *Ad Gentes*, the document on missionary work, also issued *Nostra Aetate*, the document on dialogue, and the other documents on the Church, *Lumen Gentium* and the Church in the Modern World (*Gaudium et Spes*). There is no contradiction.

A third obstacle can be the political situations in different countries around the world. Sometimes the difficulty in dialogue is not really the fault of the followers of one religion or another, but it can be due to political situations that prevent people from doing what they want to do.

Then again, there is religious extremism, which some call fundamentalism. We cannot forget this. There are those who exaggerate; they want in their country only their own religion, to the exclusion of every other religion. This means that they do not really accept the principle of religious freedom, the principle that the human person has the right to be free in matters religious.

Q. *I take it you are referring to article 18 of "The Universal Declaration of Human Rights", which was approved by the United Nations General Assembly on December 10, 1948?*

---

[11] Published in 1991.

A. Yes. That's fundamental. It also envisages the right to change one's religion. That right is coming from God, and the individual has to answer before God for his own decision in this matter. Without religious freedom, the individual is deprived of that minimum freedom without which the human person cannot be held answerable for his personal decisions in matters religious. That right to religious freedom leaves intact the duty of everyone to look for the truth, religious truth, and, having found it, the duty to follow it.

To say that every individual should be free in religious matters is not to say that religion is free, in the sense that you may have a religion or you may not or, if you wish, that religion is just a hobby. Ah, no! With reference to God, we are bound to worship God. But with reference to our fellow men, they should not use any force on us in matters of religion or conscience.

Q. *How do you understand this tendency to use force in religious matters? We've seen many examples of it throughout history, and much intolerance in the process. How do you explain all this?*

A. Men are tempted to be intolerant, but they must make an effort to resist this temptation.

Religious intolerance is not a virtue, and if Christians were intolerant at any time in history, as has happened, then we recognize it as a fault. The Holy Father was not equivocating at the ceremony of March 12, 2000, in Saint Peter's Basilica; he was very clear and said that all the times that any servant of the Church used force on other people in religious matters, even with the best of intentions, the Church regrets that and asks pardon from God. If every religion of the world did likewise today, I think the relations between religions would be better.

Q. *Speaking of the use of force, particularly in war, I was quite struck by what former U.S. President Jimmy Carter said in Oslo yesterday, when he received the Nobel Prize for Peace. Referring to the question of war, in the context of the long-announced war against Iraq, Carter said, "In order for us human beings to commit ourselves to the inhumanity of war, we find it necessary first to dehumanize our opponents, which is in itself a violation of the beliefs of all religions. Once we characterize our adversaries as beyond the scope of God's mercy and grace, then life loses all value." How do you react to this statement?*

A. I agree with what President Carter said. While being sincere in our religious beliefs, we must allow our fellow men that same freedom which we want for ourselves, that is, to be allowed to believe what we sincerely think in our conscience that we should believe.

It is not right to use force on another in that inner sanctuary of conscience—that's where the error lies. We can propose our religion to others, because if we think our religion is a good thing, then it is expected that we would propose it to others. But if we try to impose it, then that is not right; that's where the fault lies. Even if I think the religion of the other person is erroneous, I still should not impose mine, though I may propose it. Respect for the other person demands that I do not impose.

Q. *So the demonizing of the other, as happens in war, is in fact a breach of all religions?*

A. Of what most religions hold dear, yes! For Christians especially, it's based on the dignity God gave each person, so that disrespect for man is actually disrespect for God, because our dignity comes from God, not from ourselves.

Q. *So the demonization process is an anti-God process?*

A. It is, because it is against God, even though the person who does it may not realize in full what he is doing. But I prefer to use the word *disrespect* for that to make sure nobody will contradict it; demonize is a much stronger word. Even if we do not say the other person is a devil, but if we disagree with the other person, we should not declare that person to be outside the bounds of God's mercy, because although that person may not agree with my own idea of how to worship God, only God can finally judge that person. That is not the same as saying that religious truth is relative; but, as for the subjective state of the other person, finally, finally only God can judge that.

Q. *So one is in fact setting oneself up as God when one demonizes the other?*

A. That is if we want to judge the other as if we knew everything about that person. That means to condemn the other. I prefer the word *condemn* rather than *demonize*, even though the term "demonize" is popular and much used. But if we presume we know everything about the other, we set ourselves up as judges. That is probably why our Lord said to us, "Judge not, and you shall not be judged."

We may know that objectively today is Sunday, and that this person did not come to Mass, but it is quite another matter to say that this person has committed a mortal sin because he did not come to Mass on Sunday. There may be many other things we do not know about that person. For example, we don't know whether he realized it was Sunday; or we don't know whether his mother was dying, or his child or his sister was sick or dying. Then again, we don't know whether he went to Mass on Saturday evening, or will go to Mass on Sunday evening.

You see, we too easily make judgments about other people, and, of course, we are very often wrong. Somebody once said, "Of the one hundred times that I spoke, I think I made a mistake seventy times; as for the other thirty times, I regret that I spoke." Does that mean that we are not to talk anymore? Well, it may mean that we have to watch every word, and we should be very wary of setting ourselves up as judges over others, especially in matters of conscience. Whenever I hear someone say, "I know the reason why he did this or that . . .", I very strongly want to ask him, "How do you know why the person did that? How is it that you know his inner motivations? Do you even know all your own inner motivations? You may be totally wrong, or you may be only 5 percent correct or 20 percent correct! Have you judged yourself enough so that you have still time enough to judge the other?"

Q. *Am I right in saying that making rapid judgments about others or demonizing others is therefore against the Christian culture?*

A. It's not only against Christian culture, it's against the respect that is due to man, everyone, Christian or otherwise. Man deserves respect, because God created him.

Q. *Today we see an increase in violence in the world. We see the ongoing violence in the Middle East, the violent repression of the Palestinians there, and the suicide bombers against Israel; we see the attempt to impose the Sharia law in your own country, Nigeria; and we see the seemingly unstoppable push in the U.S.A. to war against Iraq. You have spent so many years of your life promoting harmony among religions, and most recently you have written a book,* Religions for Peace. *How do you read all this violence; how do you understand these events?*

A. They are sad developments, and the various religions of the world have a duty in this matter.

On the question of suicide bombings, religion has to come in:

human life is sacred. My own life: it is not even mine; it is God's gift. I don't even have a right to kill myself; much less have I a right to kill another person. So that answers it. But this is not to deny that there are situations of great injustice, oppression, and repression. There are these situations, but another solution has to be looked for. Violence is actually a surrender; it is a capitulation; it is not worthy of man. Other solutions have to be found. I repeat, this does not mean ignoring the sufferings of those who are oppressed, repressed, such as the Palestinians. But it does not justify suicide murders. There must be another solution. If any religion wants to justify suicide bombing, that religion condemns itself, because religion should be fundamentally adoration of God, worship of God, love of God, and it must include the horizontal dimension—love of my neighbor. If it does not, then that religion is flawed; there's something really wrong.

As for Sharia, let me say this. Everybody is free to live the values of his religion, but not free to impose that religion on others, nor to ignore the pluralistic nature of society today. So whether in Nigeria or elsewhere, it's difficult to see a society in which there is only one religion—except the Vatican City State! You know well the Vatican City is a very small area: you can walk around it in forty-five minutes, if you greet no one on the way. I have done it once! So obviously we don't expect Hindus to be working in the Pope's office for doctrine. That's obvious. But how many countries are like that? As regards Nigeria, my own country, you might like to know that I was told clearly by a Nigerian Muslim leader that it is not the Muslim leaders who are pushing the Sharia in Nigeria, it is the politicians. And they are pushing it for political reasons, not religious motives. So that gives you the whole answer.

Q. *Why then don't the Muslim religious leaders speak out in Nigeria?*
A. I do not know whether I will go into all that today! I think they themselves have to calculate what are likely to be the consequences when they speak, but I would not like to go into all that. I only want to say that there is a Christian–Muslim Association at the national level, where all the religious leaders come together. And my prayer and hope is that they will take the matter in hand, because good Muslims know that they can live the values of the Sharia without insisting that the Sharia be inserted in state law, in a religiously pluralistic state. That is all I would like to say on this matter.

Religion is really about love of God and love of my neighbor, not about violence. To the extent that someone is promoting violence, to that extent he is not a good member of any religion, including his own religion.

As for the war in Iraq, I do not see religion entering into it at all. I would only like to say that those who want to justify the war in Iraq, the onus is on them to prove that there is no other solution to the crisis there. I just want to know that there is really no other solution.

Q. *Many people say this is a war for oil, and a war to remake the political landscape of the Middle East, and that the question of the weapons of mass destruction is not the main issue.*

A. That is not for me to say. It is for those who are in favor of the war to tell us why that war should be, because we must presume that the war should not be. War is a sign of the failure of mankind.

You know that I come from Nigeria; we are a Third World country, while we regard most of Europe, and also the U.S.A. and Canada, as the "first world", as it is called. Well, I ask the developed countries, is the promotion of modern war, with all its destructive weapons of modern technology and science, a sign of development? Is it not rather a sign of surrender by mankind? At the beginning of the third millennium, can mankind not find any other solution except war with the most destructive weapons? Is that a sign of progress? Is that a sign of development? Is it not rather a defeat for mankind? Is that really a sign of spiritual development, or is it not rather a sign of spiritual underdevelopment? That is what I want to ask.

Q. *Many people are asking these same questions. When the Arab world sees the president of the U.S.A. on TV saying, "God bless America" and "God bless our troops", it raises many questions for them.*

A. Unfortunately, many Arabs consider America as Christian, and they consider the war as made by Christians. Well! Well! Well! Can't you see all the complications? Not to mention the children. Are we not sad enough that so many children have died in the last twelve years (as a result of the sanctions on Iraq)? How many more must die before we realize that this was not a good solution? These are my questions.

Q. *In recent months and weeks, I've heard many Vatican cardinals speak out strongly against the war. They, like you and very many other people, are asking if there is not another way to resolve the crisis in Iraq. But those who are advocating war seem almost unstoppable. So the question arises, and I put it to you who have lived through war in your own country, how does one stop war?*

A. People's hearts must be converted. The message of Jesus Christ is relevant for us today, as much as it ever was. The Sermon on the Mount is as valid today as it was when Christ stood near the Lake of Galilee.

The Holy Father has often said, "War is an adventure without return." The Holy Father preaches in favor of justice, reconciliation, and negotiation, but not in favor of war. We would not expect the Holy Father to be a chaplain to the army; we expect him to be the spokesman for the Prince of Peace. His words are not pious talk; they are actual reality. They are the formula for harmony and peace on earth. Peace on earth for men, who are the objects of God's love. That is God's will.

Q. *From your eighteen years working with the representatives and followers of other religions, seeking to understand them and to find ways to work together for peace and the good of mankind, has your understanding of God's plan for mankind changed? Have you come to see it in a different light?*

A. Obviously, all of us should grow in our understanding of God's plan for us. God's plan, of course, does not change, but our understanding of it, our living it, and our loving it should grow.

In that sense, I've tried to see God's hand in the events of life, God's providence, as we call it. I've tried to see it more than before. Not that I have any special illumination, but I beg God in prayer that I will see his will more and more, and that also means that I realize more and more that there is a mystery surrounding God's plan for all creation, and that we are only trying to understand a little of this. We must not imagine that we have understood much of God's plan. There are very many areas that would still remain beyond us, but maybe we can always have a little more light. The great saints trusted Divine Providence much more than we kindergarten Christians, and, therefore, those great saints were more at peace, more reconciled to God's will.

God's will, it is clearer and clearer to me, can be what God directly wants and what God permits. Often we do not understand why earthquakes happen, why a crash occurs at the roadside, or why little children die in a car accident, or in a bus accident on the day they have a school trip. Why that earthquake at San Giuliano, where little children died in the classroom? We cannot really explain it all, but we know that God's providence is there. Some things God wants directly, other things God permits. Why does he permit at all? Who are we to ask God why?

It is enough for us to do what we can to avoid earthquakes, if we are able, if science can help us; or likewise to avoid car accidents, or airplane crashes, or to avoid countries going to war. We must do what we can to avoid them, but when we have done all we can, there will still be suffering on this earth, there will be disappointment, there will be sickness, and there will be death. There will be rain on the day we planned a picnic, and there will be traffic on the way to the airport, causing us to miss our flight.

But it is important that we learn to see God's hand in all of these events. Maybe God wants them directly; maybe he only permits them. Who on Good Friday, seeing Christ on the Cross, would have understood God's whole plan? See all the events, see Judas, the minister for finance, selling his master for thirty coins! And yet God writes straight with crooked lines, and God's salvation comes to mankind through those events. The apostles—do we really blame them?—how could they have seen through the whole thing on that day?

We learn, and we strive and pray to understand more and more of God's plan; and more than understanding it, to love it and to live it, especially when we don't understand it. And to realize that even when we think we understand, what we understand is only the surface of the deeper mystery. But to sense that God loves us, and never to doubt this, that is important.

Q. *It's important to grasp this, because we are living in a world where we cannot fathom the final reality, a world that so often forces us down on our knees. It is as if God were teaching us in his own way.*

A. This is true. We cannot control everything; some things we can control, but so much we cannot, even when we do our best. But we must always realize that Divine Providence is over all.

Postscript

As I reread the final draft of this book, I realized there are many other questions I could have put to the cardinal. I am convinced, however, that the responses he gave to the ones I posed do, in fact, reveal the kind of person he is, how he thinks, feels, and makes decisions.

The cardinal has read the entire transcript for the original interviews and, with two minor exceptions—and those for personal reasons, which he explained to me—he has approved the original text without making any substantial change. The interviews presented in this book are his spontaneous responses to my various questions over sixteen years.

His long-time friend, Roger Cardinal Etchegaray, speaking in mid-December 2002 at the celebration for the cardinal's seventieth birthday, described him as a man known in the Roman Curia "for the good sense of his ideas" and "the fairness of his views", a man appreciated for the "almost legendary wisdom of his counsels" and "impartiality", a man known for his "great precision, readiness to listen, discretion" and "good humor".

That too is the man I know.

GERARD O'CONNELL

Rome, June 29, 2003

Photographs

CHRISTMAS 1954: The Arinze family.
SEATED: (*left to right*) Father, Mother, Cecilia, and Victoria.
STANDING: Catherine, Francis, Christopher, Linus, and Justin.

Francis.
SEPTEMBER 18, 1952

362

All Hallows Junior Seminary, Onitsha, Nigeria (opened June 29, 1952).

1949: Junior seminarians with Father Moses Orakwudo,
who preached their retreat.
Francis is seated on the left.

1953–1954: Bigard staff and Onitsha archdiocesan seminarians.
Francis is in back row, second from the right.

At Propaganda Fide, Rome: (*from left*) Father Maduka,
Francis Arinze, P. Umeh, and Father Ezeanya.

ROME, 1958:
Francis as a seminarian
at Propaganda Fide.

1955–1960: The Pontifical Urban University of Propaganda Fide,
where Francis lived as a seminarian and priest.

1957: Some African seminarians of Propaganda Fide
with Ambassador T. O. C. Orjiakor.
Francis is on the left of the ambassador.

Francis *(front row, left)* with other African students
at Propaganda Fide, Rome.

NOVEMBER 11, 1956:
Francis at the altar for the feast of
Saint Charles Borromeo.

SEPTEMBER 29, 1958:
Francis when he was ordained
a deacon.

AUGUST 29, 1965: Bishop Francis Arinze with some members of his family
on the day of his consecration as coadjutor bishop of Onitsha.
FRONT: (*from left*): Paul and Theresa (children of Victoria).
MIDDLE: Catherine, Father, Bishop Francis, Mother, and Victoria.
BACK: Justin, Angelina, and her husband, Christopher.

AUGUST 29, 1965: Bishop Francis Arinze with his father and mother
on the day of his consecration as coadjutor bishop of Onitsha.

Archbishop Charles Heerey, C.S.Sp., who sent Francis to study in Rome. Francis later became his auxiliary (1965) and succeeded him as archbishop of Onitsha on June 26, 1967, on the eve of the Nigerian civil war.

1969: Archbishop Arinze meets Pope Paul VI during the Nigerian civil war.

1987: Archbishop Arinze meets Pope John Paul II.

Francis Cardinal Arinze.

PHOTO: © L'OSSERVATORE ROMANO

Cardinal Arinze with Jerry Coniker,
founder of the Apostolate for Family Consecration.

OCTOBER 1988: Cardinal Arinze with Bishop John Joseph (*left*) and a Muslim leader at Faisalabad, Pakistan.

OCTOBER 1988: Cardinal Arinze with a Muslim holy man named Ali, at his hermitage near Faisalabad, Pakistan.

OCTOBER 1988: Cardinal Arinze speaking with a Pakistani woman,
in Faisalabad, Pakistan.

Cardinals Daneels (*Belgium*), Lope Trujillo (*Colombia and the Vatican*),
Arinze, and Schwery (*Switzerland*) at a synod meeting.

1990: Cardinal Arinze greeting President Daniel Arap Moi
in Mombasa at the celebration for the centenary of
the evangelization of Kenya.

SEPTEMBER 14–20, 1995: Cardinal Arinze accompanied Pope John Paul II on
the papal visit to Cameroon, South Africa, and Kenya.

PHOTO: © L'OSSERVATORE ROMANO

MARCH 1998: Cardinal Arinze with Pope John Paul II, during the latter's second visit to Nigeria, for the ceremony of beatification of Father Tansi.

MARCH 1988: Archbishop John Olorunfemi, of Abuja, Nigeria, and Cardinal Arinze in procession to the altar for the Mass on the occasion of the beatification of Father Tansi, in Onitsha. The vestments bear the image of the new Blessed.

MARCH 1998: In Abuja, Nigeria, Cardinal Arinze, Pope John Paul II,
President Sani Abacha of Nigeria, a presidential aide (background),
and Cardinal Tomko.

AUGUST 1998: Cardinal Arinze with the Cistercian monks
at Mount Saint Bernard Abbey, England,
praying at the site where Father Tansi
had been buried.